MEGAREGIONS
AND AMERICA'S FUTURE

MEGAREGIONS
AND AMERICA'S FUTURE

ROBERT D. YARO
MING ZHANG
FREDERICK R. STEINER

75 YEARS
LINCOLN INSTITUTE
OF LAND POLICY

© 2022 by the Lincoln Institute of Land Policy

First printing
All rights reserved.

Library of Congress Cataloging-in-Publishing Data

Names: Yaro, Robert D., author. | Zhang, Ming, 1963 April 22- author. | Steiner, Frederick R., author.
Title: Megaregions and America's future / Robert D. Yaro, Ming Zhang, Frederick R. Steiner.
Description: Cambridge, Mass. : Lincoln Institute of Land Policy, 2022 | Includes bibliographical references and index. | Summary: "Examines the socioeconomic, demographic, and climate challenges U.S. megaregions face in the 21st century and proposes new planning and policy strategies to tackle them"—Provided by publisher.
Identifiers: LCCN 2021035568 (print) | LCCN 2021035569 (ebook) |
  ISBN 9781558444287 (paperback) | ISBN 9781558444294 (adobe pdf) |
  ISBN 9781558444317 (epub)
Subjects: LCSH: Regional planning—United States. | Cities and towns—United States—Growth.
Classification: LCC HT392 .Y37 2022 (print) | LCC HT392 (ebook) | DDC 307.1/20973—dc23
LC record available at https://lccn.loc.gov/2021035568
LC ebook record available at https://lccn.loc.gov/2021035569

Cover designed by Studio Rainwater.
Composed in Arno Pro by Westchester Publishing Services in Danbury, Connecticut.
Printed and bound by Books International in Dulles, Virginia.

♻ The paper is FSC certified, acid-free, 30% post-consumer content.

MANUFACTURED IN THE UNITED STATES OF AMERICA

CONTENTS

List of Illustrations vii
Foreword xiii

PART I · SETTING THE CONTEXT
1. Introduction 3
2. U.S. Megaregions 21

PART II · U.S. MEGAREGIONAL TRENDS AND THREATS
3. Rising Inequality and Declining Affordability 67
4. Competitiveness of U.S. Megaregions 103
5. Building Environmental Resilience and Ecosystem Services 127
6. Changing Work and Travel Patterns in U.S. Megaregions 146

PART III · UNLOCKING THE ECONOMIC POTENTIAL OF MEGAREGIONS
7. The Green Mega Deal 171
8. A Strategic Plan for the Northeast Megaregion 206
9. High-Speed and High-Performance Rail 242
10. Governing U.S. Megaregions 267

PART IV · RETROSPECT AND PROSPECT
11. Reflections 285
12. Megaregions and the Next "American Century" 303

Acknowledgments 307
References 309
Index 327
About the Authors 349
About the Lincoln Institute of Land Policy 351

ILLUSTRATIONS

Figures

1.1 European Blue Banana   9
1.2 The 11 U.S. megaregions initially identified by the Regional Plan Association   12
1.3 French high-speed train traversing a bridge over the River Saône, near Macon, France   19
2.1 Three versions of U.S. megaregions as identified by Lang and Dhavale, Ross and Woo, and the Federal Highway Administration   25
2.2 U.S. megaregions by night   26
2.3 U.S. Census Bureau core-based statistical metropolitan areas and metropolitan planning organizations   30
2.4 Flows of workers in and between metropolitan planning organizations and counties in 2015   32
2.5 Megaregions and EPA Level III ecoregions in the United States   33
2.6 McSherry and Holmes's drainage basin commonwealths   34
2.7 Megaregions in the United States   35
2.8 Arizona Sun Corridor megaregion   37
2.9 Basin and Range megaregion   39
2.10 View of Salt Lake Valley at the foothills of the Oquirrh Mountains and the adjacent Great Salt Lake in the distance   40
2.11 Northern California megaregion   41
2.12 Southern California megaregion   43
2.13 Aerial view of Southern California   43
2.14 Aerial view of Cascadia megaregion   45
2.15 Cascadia megaregion   46
2.16 Central Plains megaregion   48
2.17 Rush hour on a highway leading into Miami   49
2.18 Florida megaregion   50

2.19 Front Range megaregion   52
2.20 Great Lakes megaregion   54
2.21 Aerial view of Chicago and Lake Michigan as dramatic fall weather rolls through   55
2.22 Railroad network in the United States   56
2.23 Gulf Coast megaregion   57
2.24 Piedmont Atlantic megaregion   58
2.25 Northeast megaregion   61
2.26 Texas Triangle megaregion   63
3.1a U.S. megaregion population growth, 1990–2020   70
3.1b U.S. megaregion population growth, 2020–2050   70
3.2 Aerial view of Route 441 through Paynes Prairie Preserve State Park, Florida   78
3.3 Snow-covered Longs Peak, part of the Rocky Mountains, towers over the Denver skyline   81
3.4 Aerial view of Barton Springs, Austin, Texas   81
3.5 Portland, Oregon, and Mount Hood in autumn   82
3.6a Spatial distribution of the older population in U.S. megaregions, 2020   84
3.6b Spatial distribution of the older population in U.S. megaregions, 2050 projection   85
3.7 Traffic jam on Route 91 in Southern California   86
3.8 Average daily trips per person by travel modes in U.S. megaregions   88
3.9 Average daily vehicle miles traveled per person by generation in U.S. megaregions   90
3.10 High-traffic corridors in the United States   93
3.11 Gini index of household income inequality in U.S. megaregions, 1990–2016   97
3.12a Household income inequality in the United States, 1990   99
3.12b Household income inequality in the United States, 2016   99
3.13 Poverty rates in U.S. megaregions, 1990–2018   101
4.1 Sunset over Oakland and San Francisco   106
4.2 Interstate 5 bridge over Lake Union leading into downtown Seattle   107
4.3 Phoenix metropolitan area at night, viewed from South Mountain   111
4.4 Aerial view of downtown Kansas City, Missouri, and Kansas   114
4.5 Percentage change in employment by community size, 2008–2017   124
5.1 Ecosystem services   128

5.2	Staten Island plans and the Hurricane Sandy evacuation map	130
5.3	London's Thames Barrier	133
5.4	Sea level rise projections for New York City	135
5.5	Sea level rise projections for New York City neighborhoods by 2100 assuming 2.7°F and 7.2°F	135
5.6	Depiction of the impacts of conventional development patterns on the characteristics of rural landscapes	143
7.1	Submerged freeways and widespread flooding in Houston after Hurricane Harvey	174
7.2	Apple fire as seen from Route 243 in Southern California	175
7.3	Depiction of a wildlife crossing to connect bifurcated landscapes	177
7.4	Student landscape design proposals to restore offshore and shoreline habitats of the Mississippi delta	178
8.1	North Atlantic Rail's early action projects	215
8.2	North Atlantic Rail's full system map	215
8.3	Proposed modernized commuter rail system for Boston	222
8.4	Proposed Regional Express Service map	223
8.5	Hartford400 vision for a new River Road capping Interstate 91 through downtown Hartford, Connecticut, and reconnecting the city to its waterfront	223
8.6	Map of New York City region flooding after Hurricane Sandy	238
8.7	Sandy Sea Gate system map	239
8.8	Storm surge barrier near Massdijk, Netherlands, showing design similar to that proposed for the Outer Harbor Sea Gate in New York	240
9.1	High Speed 1 train in the United Kingdom	254
9.2	Javelin high-speed commuter route in southeast England	254
9.3	Proposed trans-America passenger network in the United States	259
9.4	Comparison of international high-speed rail corridors with California's proposed rail system and Amtrak's Northeast Corridor	260
10.1	Texas Triangle at night	268
10.2	Aerial view of a flooded solar power station with dirty river water in rainy season	277

Tables

2.1	Commuting Flows, 2015	32
2.2	Summary Statistics of U.S. Megaregions, 2018	36

2.3   Metropolitan Areas Ranked by GDP in the Arizona Megaregion, 2018   37

2.4   Top 10 Metropolitan Areas Ranked by GDP in the Basin and Range Megaregion, 2018   39

2.5   Top 10 Metropolitan Areas Ranked by GDP in the Northern California Megaregion, 2018   42

2.6   Top 10 Metropolitan Areas Ranked by GDP in the Southern California Megaregion, 2018   44

2.7   Top 10 Metropolitan Areas Ranked by GDP in the Cascadia Megaregion, 2018   47

2.8   Top 10 Metropolitan Areas Ranked by GDP in the Central Plains Megaregion, 2018   49

2.9   Top 10 Metropolitan Areas Ranked by GDP in the Florida Megaregion, 2018   51

2.10   Top 10 Metropolitan Areas Ranked by GDP in the Front Range Megaregion, 2018   53

2.11   Top 10 Metropolitan Areas Ranked by GDP in the Great Lakes Megaregion, 2018   55

2.12   Top 10 Metropolitan Areas Ranked by GDP in the Gulf Coast Megaregion, 2018   57

2.13   Top 10 Metropolitan Areas Ranked by GDP in the Piedmont Atlantic Megaregion, 2018   59

2.14   Top 10 Metropolitan Areas by GDP in the Northeast Megaregion, 2018   62

2.15   Top 10 Metropolitan Areas by GDP in the Texas Triangle Megaregion, 2018   64

3.1   U.S. Megaregion Population Trends, 1990–2050   69

3.2a   Population Counts (millions) of Four Generations in U.S. Megaregions and Nonmegaregions   76

3.2b   Population Percentages of Four Generations in U.S. Megaregions and Nonmegaregions   77

3.3   U.S. Megaregion Older Population Counts and Changes, 1990–2050   79

3.4   Aging Population Trends in U.S. Megaregions   80

3.5   Average Daily Trips per Person by Travel Mode in U.S. Megaregions   87

3.6   Average Daily Vehicle Miles Traveled per Person by Generation in U.S. Megaregions   89

3.7   High-Priority Routes for High-Performance Transit   94–95

3.8   Gini Index of Household Income Inequality in U.S. Megaregions, 1990–2016   98

3.9	Poverty Rates in U.S. Megaregions, 1990–2018	100
4.1	Largest Export-Oriented Industry Groups in Manufacturing Megas U.S. Megaregions, by Number of Employees	105
4.2	Largest Export-Oriented Industry Groups in Successfully Transformed U.S. Megaregions, by Number of Employees	108
4.3	Largest Export-Oriented Industry Groups in Strengthening Specialized Services U.S. Megaregions, by Number of Employees (Subgroup 1)	109
4.4	Largest Export-Oriented Industry Groups in Strengthening Specialized Services U.S. Megaregions, by Number of Employees (Subgroup 2)	110
4.5	Largest Export-Oriented Industry Groups in Resource Dependent, Gradually Transforming U.S. Megaregions, by Number of Employees	113
4.6	Change in GDP per Capita in U.S. Megaregions	115
4.7	Change in GDP per Worker in U.S. Megaregions	116
4.8	Change in GDP per Square Mile of Developed Land in U.S. Megaregions	117
4.9	Employment in Seven Advanced Producer Services in U.S. Megaregions, 2002	119
4.10	Employment in Seven Advanced Producer Services in U.S. Megaregions, 2018	120
4.11	Location Quotients Displaying Relative Strengths in APS Industries in U.S. Megaregions	121
4.12	Utility Patents in U.S. Megaregions	122

FOREWORD

AS A LONGTIME COLLABORATOR AND FRIEND OF Bob, Ming, and Fritz, I congratulate them on the publication of *Megaregions and America's Future* and briefly locate this volume in the body of the Lincoln Institute of Land Policy's earlier contributions on megaregions, spatial planning, and regional governance published during my tenure at the Institute. The urban planning studio at the University of Pennsylvania I cotaught with Bob and Jonathan Barnett in 2004, described in the book, is an inflection point in a long engagement with the authors that began some years before and has continued to the present day.

The authors give due recognition to the role of Andreas Faludi with his *European Spatial Planning*. The European model Andreas helped propagate was seminal to our thinking about megaregions in the United States. In addition to that title, published by the Institute in 2002, we published two other volumes by Faludi, *Territorial Cohesion and the European Model of Society* (2007) and *European Spatial Research and Planning* (2008). These provide further insights into transnational regional strategies and policy applicable to working across state boundaries in the United States.

Of evergreen relevance given the governance concerns raised in *Megaregions*, the Institute published a Policy Focus Report by Kate Foster in 2001, *Regionalism on Purpose*, which offered case studies from a decade of transboundary innovation. In a graphic diagram, "A Region's Regions," in that report, Kate presciently shows the nesting of scales from the metropolitan up to the bioregional, including ad hoc regions. The ad hoc theme, which arguably will become increasingly important in the world of megaregions, was the subject of a forum at Lincoln House in 2001, followed by the publication of the Policy Focus Report *Exploring Ad Hoc Regionalism* by Doug Porter and Allan Wallis in 2002.

The imperative to embrace natural systems evident in *Megaregions* follows from the Institute's long-standing interest in integrating nature with urban planning, perhaps reflected most centrally in the book *Nature and Cities* (2016), edited by Fritz, George Thompson, and me. Some years earlier, Matt McKinney and Shawn Johnson authored a book on regional collaboration, *Working Across Boundaries: People, Nature, and Regions*, published by the Institute in 2009. Soon after, in 2010, we brought out a Policy Focus Report by Matt, Lynn Scarlett, and Dan Kemmis, *Large Landscape Conservation*, which had an immediate impact on national policy. I end with a compendium that addresses the state of the art for the broad field: *Regional Planning in America: Practice and Prospect* (2011), which I coedited with Ethan Seltzer, includes chapters by both Fritz and Bob.

Beyond serving as a grace note to *Megaregions*, I hope the preceding proves a useful guide to some of the relevant Lincoln Institute works.

Armando Carbonell
Vice President, Programs
Lincoln Institute of Land Policy

PART I
SETTING THE CONTEXT

1
INTRODUCTION

The circuited city of the future will not be the huge hunk of concentrated real estate created by the railway. It will take on a totally new meaning under conditions of very rapid movement. It will be an information megalopolis.

—MARSHALL McLUHAN

MEGAREGIONS ARE EMERGING AS THE PREDOMINANT URBAN form in much of the industrialized world. Scholars in the United States, Europe, and Asia have identified more than 40 megaregions in the world, such as the U.S. Northeast, Europe's Pentagon, Japan's Tokaido, and China's Pearl River Delta (Faludi 2002; Groff and Rau 2019; Hall and Pain 2006; Scott 2001; Segbers 2007; Sorensen 2018; Xu and Yeh 2011).

In this book, we review megaregions' economic, ecological, demographic, and political features that can be harnessed to improve the prosperity, health, and quality of life for their millions or, in some cases, tens of millions of residents. Megaregions are an essential part of national and global strategies for sustaining large ecological systems, minimizing carbon production, and preparing for the impacts of climate change. We consider how megaregions can adapt to the ever-changing communications technology landscape. Finally, we outline transportation, governance, natural resource preservation, and other measures required to fully realize the megaregion potential. This book focuses on megaregions in the United States, but we draw on concrete examples from around the world for how infrastructure investments, economic development, governance systems, and other plans and policies have improved the functionality of diverse megaregions.

The megaregion concept is more than half a century old, and its relevance came to the fore in 2020. Recognizing that the COVID-19 pandemic could not be successfully addressed by city or even state governance alone, governors in several U.S. megaregions—Northeast, Great Lakes, Front Range, Texas Triangle, Southern and Northern California, and Cascadia—mobilized at the megaregion scale to first address public health in the midst of the virus and then reopen and rebuild their economies in its aftermath. Furthermore, the concept is now being used by officials at the U.S. Department of Transportation to determine transportation needs as well as national policies and investments.

ORIGINS OF THE MEGAREGION CONCEPT

In 2004, researchers at the Weitzman School of Design at the University of Pennsylvania (Penn), in collaboration with the Regional Plan Association (RPA) and the Lincoln Institute of Land Policy, first identified and defined megaregions as metropolitan regions networked by their shared economies, natural resource systems, infrastructure, history, and culture. Then teams from Penn, the University of Texas at Austin (UT Austin), the University of Michigan, and other schools held a series of workshops where they applied this understanding of megaregions to create frameworks for the Northeast, Texas Triangle, Great Lakes, and other megaregions. The workshops were held at Fundación Metrópoli in Madrid, Spain, and the frameworks were informed by plans for European megaregions. Since then, other researchers have embellished the megaregion definition, with perhaps the most important insight being that megaregions are greater than the sum of their parts. Megaregions have the potential to become the most powerful and quite possibly the most resilient urban and economic structures of our time.

There are approximately 40 recognized megaregions in the world, with several more rapidly forming in China, India, and Southeast Asia. Perhaps the world's best-known megaregion is the U.S. Northeast, stretching from Boston to Washington, DC, and home to 55 million people closely networked in economic and cultural relationships.

More recent analysis suggests that the Northeast functions as two separate megaregions with New York City as their hinge. One of these is the North Atlantic megaregion, encompassing downstate New York and the six New England states, and the other, the Mid-Atlantic megaregion, stretching from New York City to northern Virginia. In this book, we keep them together for historical and practical reasons. Another of the 13 U.S. megaregions is the Texas Triangle, with a population of 18 million, fully three-quarters of the total Texas population.

Research at Penn, UT Austin, and other universities in the last decade has continued to examine the Northeast and Texas Triangle megaregions; their analogues in Europe, Asia, and North Africa; and the investments in high-speed rail, landscape restoration, and preservation initiatives needed to unlock their economic and ecological potential. Among the findings of this work has been that the economic synergies between cities and metropolitan places within a megaregion can be unlocked only with infrastructure investments designed to shorten travel times, reduce congestion, and expand mobility between these places. Analysis of commuting patterns by Nelson and Rae (2016) determined that in some places, like the U.S. Northeast, the majority of daily commutes occur within a single metropolitan area, and intermetropolitan commutes are limited by increasingly congested interstate highways and airports and by the absence of reliable and frequent rail services with affordable fares.

To fully realize the economic potential of the Northeast and other U.S. megaregions, those regions need the kind of high-speed rail service that is already available or being planned in almost every other existing or emerging industrial economy. Improving the reliability of intercity legs of the interstate highway system and major airports could also provide these essential links; however, it must be noted that distances between cities in megaregions are often too great to be quickly traversed by road or conventional rail and too small to be efficiently traversed by air.

Research at Penn and other institutions has also determined that advanced technology, service industries, and research universities are major beneficiaries of improved links between cities and regions within a megaregion. By linking key industry clusters of a megaregion, larger economic agglomerations are created, providing access to more resources across the whole megaregion. The highly skilled workers and researchers necessary to these industries can gain access to a broader set of employment and collaborative research opportunities across the megaregion.

It is also widely recognized that the pioneers and entrepreneurs who drive innovation and investment in advanced technology and service industries go where the quality of life is best and the pool of skilled labor is largest. For this reason, provision or strengthening of major research universities and teaching hospitals, urban amenities, clean air and water, efficient mobility systems, and access to recreational resources are key elements of success for any megaregion.

The larger consequence of these steps is that if megaregions' future growth and development is well planned, they can be the new form of urbanization that best offers solutions to the existential threats now facing early 21st-century metropolitan regions and their residents, including the following:

- *Climate change*—rising sea levels, storm surges, more and hotter urban heat islands, more frequent severe rain events and drought.
- *Traffic congestion*—paralyzing numbers of vehicles on city streets and highways.
- *Escalating housing costs*—rapidly increasing rents that cause metro residents to dedicate 40 percent or more of their income to housing.
- *Growing social and economic inequality*—widening economic disparities and spatial segregation that leave many communities behind in metro prosperity.

By addressing these threats, well-planned and well-governed megaregions can provide all their residents with opportunities to live a better life, with greater opportunities for employment, more affordable housing and services, and improved environmental quality. If the growth of megaregions remains poorly planned and unmanaged, however, these places might represent a new form of 21st-century megasprawl.

Planning at the megaregion scale also presents the opportunity to protect and restore large-scale natural resource systems, including surface water and groundwater resources critical to public water supply watersheds, major forest and estuarine ecosystems, and significant tracts of prime soils for close-to-home agricultural production. The scale is large enough that the natural resource systems of a megaregion contribute to broader climate mitigation and adaptation strategies. The systems can also contribute to the quality of life for human settlements bordering these places.

Urban centers can also take steps to rebuild their resilience by, for example, re-creating forest canopies to reduce urban heat island effects. New York City's Million Trees initiative and related widespread efforts to paint dark roofs white are early examples. Greenway systems can be built to preserve or re-create migratory systems within and between metropolitan areas, while they provide urban residents with access to countryside and natural areas. The RPA initiative to create a network of large protected regional reserves around watersheds of the New York–New Jersey–Connecticut region is an excellent example of this strategy.

In another example, protection of the vast forest resources of the Appalachian Highlands in the U.S. Northeast megaregion creates the opportunity for large-scale carbon capture and sequestration as well as what might become the first in a national or even international network of climate reserves. The Appalachians can also function as a "geneway," in which species can migrate northward as climate change unfolds. At the same time, these resource systems can provide assured public water supplies, clean air, food, and recreational opportunities for the 55 million residents of nearby Northeast cities.

Parallel research on the Texas Hill Country adjoining the Texas Triangle (Bock et al. 2016) concurred that large rural landscapes provide the basic life-support systems needed to make urban living possible and desirable in the megaregion, including public water supplies, clean air, wildlife sanctuaries, and recreational resources. This research also determined that, in the Hill Country and similar landscapes, planning for landscape conservation at the megaregion scale can enable these systems to be more resilient in the face of climate change.

As a result of these attributes, megaregions and their constituent natural resource systems can become building blocks for more resilient human settlements in an era of rapid climate change.

HOW MEGAREGIONS WERE REDISCOVERED AND DEFINED

The modern term *megalopolis* traces back to the Scottish polymath Patrick Geddes. In his 1915 book *Cities in Evolution*, Geddes describes the network of urban assemblages stretching from New York to Boston as a conurbation, much of what we now call the Northeast megaregion. Geddes recognized that urban development through planning was the means for people to participate in their own evolution. A similar megaregion concept, but still not the precise word, was also popularized by the French geographer Jean Gottmann in his 1961 book *Megalopolis*. Gottmann lived for long periods in the United States and was a keen observer of its urbanization and regional growth dynamics. He forecast that the continued growth of the northeastern United States would result in a continuous band of urbanization from Boston to Washington, DC, which he called a "megalopolis."

In 1966, Rhode Island senator Claiborne Pell published *Megalopolis Unbound: The Supercity and the Transportation of Tomorrow*, which proposed building a high-speed rail route between Boston and Washington, DC. Unfortunately, this concept advanced only modestly because the Northeast's private railroad companies at the time were all in financial crisis and lacked the means to fulfill the high-speed rail proposal.

Then, in 1968, the RPA's Second Regional Plan included a section on what it called the "Atlantic Urban Region." This provided an in-depth analysis of the infrastructure and urban development patterns of the Northeast between Boston and Washington, DC. The RPA also offered proposals for improved intercity rail and large-landscape conservation across the Northeast.

The megaregion concept languished until the 1980s, when a group of European geographers and planners began to map linked metropolitan regions in western and central Europe. Development of these networks was being advanced by Europe's Regional Development Fund and the Trans-Europe Express high-speed rail and motorway networks. One of the first conceived of these linked metropolitan regions was the so-called Dorsale européenne (European backbone), also known as the Blue Banana, stretching from Manchester, England, to Milan, Italy, and credited to the French geographer Roger Brunet in 1989 (Faludi 2015). Brunet and his colleagues argued that the Dorsale and its linked network of large metropolitan areas was the economic engine for all of Europe.

This and other conceptualizations of networks among European metropolitan regions were examined by a team of European geographers and planners in the late 1990s, convened by the Dutch geographer Andreas Faludi. In *ESDP: European Spatial Development Perspective*, published in 1999 by the European Commission, the team proposed aiding the integration of European cities into networks as part of a broader strategy to promote "territorial cohesion" for the European Union (EU), which was then in the process of adding 12 eastern and southern European countries to its membership (European Commission 1999, 13).

FROM MEGALOPOLIS TO MEGAREGION

In 1996, one of us, Bob Yaro, completed work on the RPA's Third Regional Plan for the largest U.S. urban area, the New York metropolitan region (Yaro and Hiss 1996). The plan outlined how to reverse the decades-long decline of New York City and other urban centers in its metropolitan region. By the proposed investment of $150 billion in the region's rail networks and other transportation infrastructure, for instance, the plan supported broader efforts to reduce congestion and promote urban mobility. The vision to create a metropolitan greensward system of large regional reserves, areas of 100,000 to 3 million acres, also protected large public water supply watersheds and ecological and estuarine reserves.

Over the succeeding quarter century, in part as a result of the RPA's advocacy efforts, most of these objectives were realized, with the following outcomes:

- New York City and other urban centers reversed decades of decline, gaining more than 1.5 million residents and 1 million jobs in the two decades following 1996.
- The regional transit system reversed decades of disinvestment and gained its first expansion in six decades.
- Major new urban districts were developed in places like Manhattan's Hudson Yards and Long Island City.
- A network of large regional reserves was created to protect the region's public water supply watersheds in such places as the 100,000-acre Long Island Pine Barrens, the 1-million-acre New York City watersheds, and the 3-million-acre New Jersey Highlands.

In 1997, Yaro was invited by the Organisation for Economic Co-operation and Development to present the Third Regional Plan at a forum in Paris on metropolitan planning. Another participant in this event was Andreas Faludi, from the Technical University of Delft in the Netherlands, who presented his research on an EU initiative to prepare a spatial development strategy for an expanding EU. Impressed by the ambition of this project, Yaro raised with Faludi the possibility of replicating it for the United States.

This was the work Faludi's team summarized in the 1999 *ESDP*, a document approved by the Informal Council of EU Ministers for Spatial Planning in Potsdam, Germany (European Commission 1999). Key elements in the document were the Blue Banana, Pentagon, and other linked metropolitan regions at the heart of western Europe's economy (Faludi 2002; see figure 1.1). Offended that Paris was left out of

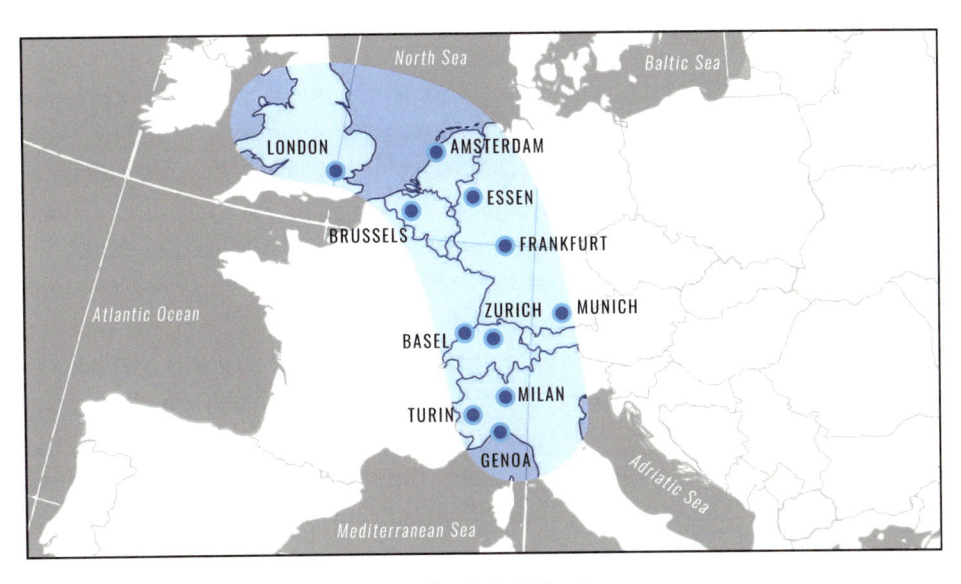

FIGURE 1.1 European Blue Banana. *Source: Charles E. Weber II.*

the Blue Banana, French planners and geographers prepared their own map, which put the French capital at the center of a pentagon of European cities.

In *European Spatial Development Perspective*, the authors also discussed expanding the economic centers of Europe into other regions as the EU grew. They highlighted the role that Europe's high-speed rail network could play in furthering integration of the economies and mobility systems of these large metropolitan networks. These proposals and investments became policy because they were essential elements of the EU's strategy of territorial cohesion, or measures to promote the integration of nations into the EU.

In the late 1990s, Yaro also participated in the Salzburg Congress on Urban Planning and Development, where European participants discussed how to plan for declining populations across Europe, particularly in Italy and the new eastern members of the EU, including Hungary and Romania.

At the same time, the U.S. Census Bureau published forecasts for rapid population growth in the first decades of the 21st century, which predicted that the United States would add 50 percent or more to its population by midcentury. However, unlike the EU, the United States had no planning process or institutions to manage this growth.

A TRADITION OF NATIONAL PLANNING IN THE UNITED STATES

In 1999, Robert Fishman's book *The American Planning Tradition* outlined the long history of national planning in the United States. At several America 2050 and Rockefeller Foundation events Yaro organized, Fishman remarked that most Americans think that "national planning is an activity best left to the French.... But au contraire!" Contrary to conventional wisdom, Fishman wrote, the United States had a rich tradition of over two centuries of national-scale planning for territorial cohesion with infrastructure, urban, and natural resource development. Key milestones in this history were President Thomas Jefferson's 1808 Gallatin Plan, so called because its key author was Treasury Secretary Albert Gallatin, which outlined a nationwide network of national roads and canals to strengthen ties between the East Coast and the newly acquired Louisiana Purchase lands in the west. In addition, the Gallatin Plan proposed making federal land grants to private or state developers of these improvements. These grants paved the way for the creation of the western rail and national road systems throughout the 19th century.

A second milestone was President Theodore Roosevelt's Pinchot Plan, completed in 1908. The plan was named after its prime author, Gifford Pinchot, director of the newly established U.S. Forest Service and from a wealthy Pennsylvania family. He was a pioneering forester who had studied at the French National School of Forestry in Nancy after his graduation from Yale. Pinchot adhered to the idea of multiple uses for a sustained yield, a precursor of sustainable development in which land could be used for several purposes, such as forestry and recreation, with long-lasting benefits for future generations. Pinchot's 1908 plan called for harnessing the nation's rivers and other resources to promote development of underdeveloped areas of the West and formerly developed areas of the South. To achieve this goal, Pinchot's plan outlined multistate irrigation, flood control, and hydropower systems in such places as the Tennessee, Colorado, and Columbia River Basins, proposals realized in the 1930s and 1940s by the New Deal's Tennessee Valley Authority, Colorado River Project, and Bonneville Power Administration.

Fishman's book was a revelation to Yaro, leading him to consider the need for a third national plan to shape U.S. growth in the 21st century, including new urban development patterns and infrastructure systems for accommodating the next 100 million citizens expected to be in the country by 2050, along with emerging concerns about climate change. When Yaro first read Fishman's book after its release two decades ago, he thought that the third national plan should shoot for a completion date of 2008, to commemorate the centennial of the Pinchot Plan and the bicentennial of the Gallatin Plan. Inspired by Fishman's account of U.S. national planning, Yaro began to outline the components of a third century plan for the country.

Progress on this effort was delayed when the World Trade Center attacks occurred on September 11, 2001. For the next three years, Yaro and the RPA focused almost exclusively on creating and leading the Civic Alliance to Rebuild Downtown New York, which led efforts to gain public support for plans to rebuild the World Trade Center and revitalize the surrounding Lower Manhattan district. In addition, Yaro left his teaching position at Harvard's Graduate School of Design in December 2001 when he accepted an appointment as professor of practice at Penn in January 2002.

2004 PLAN FOR AMERICA STUDIO

In 2004, in partnership with Professor of Practice Jonathan Barnett and Visting Professor Armando Carbonell from the Lincoln Institute of Land Policy, Yaro led Penn's Plan for America graduate planning studio, which had the ambitious goal of outlining a national growth strategy for the United States. One of the key elements of the studio was an effort led by Barnett to map future urban development patterns across the country (Barnett 2020).

In March of that year, with support from the Ford Foundation, the Penn faculty took the studio to London for a weeklong charrette to discuss preliminary findings with a distinguished group of European and American planners. This gathering was hosted by Sir Peter Hall, a professor at University College London, at his studio in East London's Bethnal Green neighborhood. Other participants in the charrette included Faludi; Alfonso Vegara, director of Fundación Metrópoli in Madrid; Vincent Goodstadt, president of the Royal Town Planning Institute; and Mark Pisano, executive director of the Southern California Association of Governments.

Rediscovering Megaregions—by Accident!

During this charrette, when the studio projected its maps forecasting future urban and regional development patterns on the screen, what became plain was that across the country the suburbs of adjoining metropolitan regions were merging—precisely the pattern that Jean Gottmann had predicted would happen in the Northeast megalopolis four decades earlier. But this trend was occurring in almost a dozen different places across the United States. Yaro recalls, "I attribute this discovery not to any deep insight but, instead, to my poor close-up eyesight, which left these images blurred. When I squinted at these images, I realized that what we were witnessing was a new form of urban development that I began to call supercities."

During the week in London, the Penn team and their European and American colleagues identified and named 10 supercities across the United States. (Later, Robert Lang identified an 11th, the Arizona Sun Corridor. Two more, the Basin and Range and the Central Plains megaregions, have recently been identified by us, and we also note the possible future splitting of the Northeast into two.) One of the Penn students, Lee Farmer, created an iconic map of the country's megaregions, which was later refined by RPA researchers (figure 1.2).

Yaro coauthored a report over the summer of 2004 summarizing the studio's findings with studio participant Kyle Gradinger, now division chief of the California

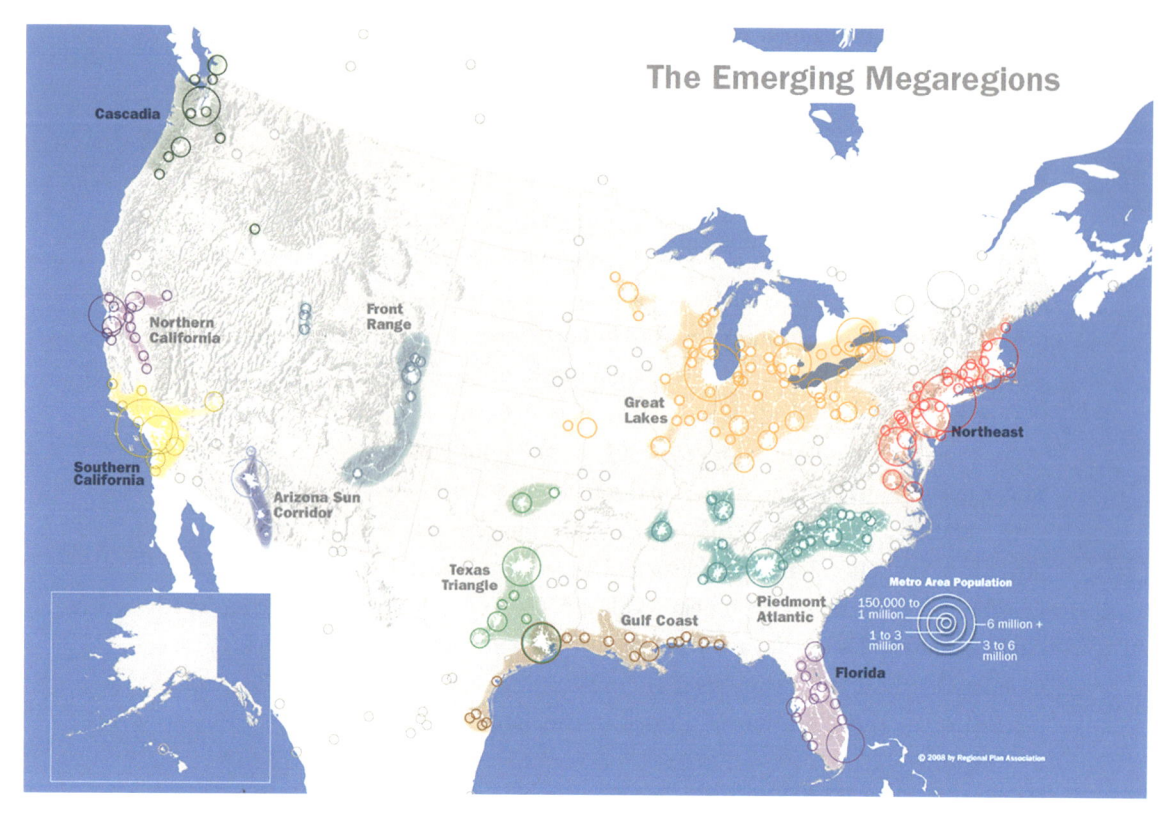

FIGURE 1.2 The 11 U.S. megaregions initially identified by the Regional Plan Association.
Source: Regional Plan Association.

Department of Transportation's Rail and Mass Transit. Titled *Toward an American Spatial Development Perspective* (Yaro and Gradinger 2004), the report emulated the approach taken in 1999 by our European counterparts in *European Spatial Development Perspective*. As is done in European reports, Yaro and Gradinger did not use the word *plan* because of its potential to become a lightning rod for opposition to the idea of a national plan. In the fall of 2004, this report became the focal point for a roundtable discussion hosted by the RPA and Penn at the Rockefeller Brothers Fund's Pocantico Conference Center in Tarrytown, New York. In addition to the Europeans at the London charrette, prominent American planners and geographers participated, including Catherine Ross from Georgia Tech, Robert Lang from the Fannie Mae Foundation, Frederick Steiner from UT Austin, Ethan Seltzer from Portland State University, and Margaret Dewar from the University of Michigan.

This group strongly endorsed the supercity concept; however, Armando Carbonell recommended that these new places be called "megaregions" because of the strong anti-urban prejudice in much of the country. Hence, we applied this name.

At the meeting's conclusion, several of the participants resolved to create development strategies for their own megaregions, a process that continued for several years. Action strategies resulted from this process for the Northeast (Penn and RPA), Piedmont Atlantic (Ross), Great Lakes (Dewar), Texas Triangle (Steiner plus Kent Butler and Ming Zhang, also from UT Austin), Arizona Sun Corridor (Lang, who moved from Fannie Mae to the University of Nevada at Las Vegas), Cascadia (Ethan Seltzer, Portland State University), Northern California (Gabriel Metcalf, San Francisco Planning and Urban Renewal Association), and Southern California (Mark Pisano, University of Southern California).

America 2050

Following the Pocantico conference, the RPA and the Lincoln Institute initiated America 2050, a multiyear collaborative project to shape plans and policies for megaregions and the nation as a whole (Carbonell and Yaro 2005). The America 2050 team conducted research on the economies, travel patterns, infrastructure, and natural resource protection needs for 11 U.S. megaregions. They also collaborated with local planners, scholars, elected officials, and planning advocacy groups on megaregion-scale strategies for high-speed rail and natural resource protection. Congressman Earl Blumenauer (D-OR) participated in many of these efforts and convened the project's participants for annual forums at the Library of Congress. The America 2050 team also collaborated with the U.S. Chamber of Commerce and the American Federation of Labor and Congress of Industrial Organizations (AFL-CIO) to gain their support for a national infrastructure investment program.

The RPA and its partners at the Lincoln Institute, Penn, the University of Southern California, and UT Austin also conducted in-depth research on national transportation systems and prepared plans for a national high-speed rail network serving all 11 megaregions and for national freight rail networks and global gateways, such as airports, seaports, and international border crossings.

The America 2050 high-speed rail proposal and the research on its economic benefits (later summarized in *High Speed Rail in America* [Todorovich and Hagler 2011]) helped shape the Barack Obama administration's inclusion of $10 billion for development of high-speed rail routes as a part of the 2009 stimulus program (the American Recovery and Reinvestment Act). The program received an additional $1 billion from Congress in 2010; however, when Republicans took control of Congress that year, they shut this down as well as any further appropriations for the program. Republican governors in Florida, Ohio, and Wisconsin also killed high-speed rail projects in their states.

Beginning in 2010, several Penn megaregion and high-speed rail studios made their final presentations to top-level executive staff at the U.S. Department of

Transportation. Two Transportation officials, Assistant Secretary Polly Trottenberg and Deputy Federal Railroad Administrator Karen Rae, accompanied Penn studios on field visits to London. Subsequently, the Department of Transportation began to use the megaregion concept to frame transportation needs and investments—a process that continued through the Donald J. Trump administration. However, despite repeated meetings with domestic policy staff in the George W. Bush and Barack Obama administrations to discuss proposals for a 21st-century national transportation plan and federal support for investments, proponents of America 2050 failed to gain support from any administration for these efforts. Perhaps it may be reborn as part of a Green New Deal–like initiative, the nonbinding resolution introduced in the House on February 7, 2019 (*Recognizing the Duty* 2019), which we address later in this book.

Two other America 2050 research projects broadened the program to include preserving large landscapes and reducing the inequality between regions across the country:

- In partnership with the Doris Duke Foundation, the RPA mapped and profiled all the local and regional landscape conservation efforts across the Northeast megaregion. And then in 2012, the RPA convened leaders of more than 50 major conservation groups across the Northeast to discuss ways to preserve large landscapes and adapt them to anticipated climate change (RPA and America 2050 2012).
- A project studied the growing economic inequality across the country. Through an analysis of economic indicators, America 2050 researchers identified large areas of the country—most, but not all, outside the megaregions—that had been left behind as the country prospered over the previous three decades (RPA, Lincoln Institute of Land Policy, and America 2050 2009).

These places voted overwhelmingly for Donald Trump in 2016 and again in 2020, motivated in part by anger over the nation's neglect of their economic and infrastructure needs. Steiner and Yaro presented a national landscape strategy in 2009 that would significantly benefit such places through tourism and recreation (Steiner and Yaro 2009).

Megaregion Research at the University of Pennsylvania

The 2004 Plan for America studio initiated research that continues today on issues confronting megaregions in the United States and around the world.

The Penn School of Design (now the Stuart Weitzman School of Design) convened from 2005 to 2008 a series of graduate planning studios and research seminars focused on the Northeast megaregion and its European counterparts. Through these research projects, we gained a deep understanding of the economic and urban dynamics of these places and their infrastructure needs. In partnership with Spain's

Fundación Metrópoli, we held studios on megaregions in the Mediterranean area stretching from Lisbon to Milan (the so-called European Diagonal), the Mediterranean Diamond (the megaregion encompassing Madrid, Barcelona, and Valencia), and the Tangier-Casablanca megaregion in Morocco. Each of these studios included charrettes held at Fundación Metrópoli's headquarters in Madrid (or in the case of the Morocco project, in Casablanca), where studio teams from other U.S. universities (UT Austin, the University of Michigan, and Portland State University) conducted comparative analyses on U.S. and European megaregions.

In 2010, a Weitzman studio proposed transformation of the Northeast rail corridor into a high-speed rail route, realizing Senator Pell's vision of half a century earlier. This studio's final presentation was held at the White House. In attendance were Joe Biden, then vice president; the president of Amtrak; the Federal Railroad administrator; and other high-level officials. This led to Amtrak developing its own high-speed rail plan for the Northeast Corridor and to a tier 1 environmental impact statement for the project from the Federal Railroad Administration (2017). However, many of the corridor planning recommendations from this study were controversial, and no action has yet been taken by the Federal Railroad Administration or the White House to implement its recommendations.

In 2011–2015, Weitzman studios, led by Yaro and the former dean (and now professor) Marilyn Taylor, investigated phasing, financing, and delivering this $100 billion project, including an intensive look at how to gain support for the proposed Gateway rail tunnel under the Hudson River. These studios also investigated using the Gateway project to catalyze a modern regional rail network around the New York metropolitan region and a circumferential, surface rapid network for the city, similar to the new London Overground system, formed from abandoned and underused rail rights-of-way. In each case, studio charrettes in London introduced United Kingdom and European innovations in project planning and delivery to Penn's students, who incorporated these insights into their studio recommendations.

In 2016 and 2017, Weitzman studios traveled to Asia to explore the effect of high-speed rail and regional rail networks on megaregion-scale mobility and economic development in China and Southeast Asia. The first of these studios, led by Taylor, Yaro, and Richard Weller, chair of the Department of Landscape Architecture and Regional Planning, produced a plan to transform the economy and mobility system of the Jing-Jin-Ji megaregion around Beijing and Tianjin. The studio proposed building a regional rail network to complement existing high-speed rail and mass transit networks and thereby promote a network of new and expanded regional centers across the megaregion. The Jing-Jin-Ji studio also proposed ambitious strategies to restore the ecology of the entire megaregion and Bohai Bay.

The 2017 Singapore studio at Weitzman, led by Taylor and Yaro, developed a plan for a new central business district adjoining the proposed high-speed rail station at the western end of the island. This new station would serve as the terminus of the planned Kuala Lumpur, Malaysia–Singapore high-speed rail line. Plans for the station and surrounding district explored how the next generation of mobility technologies—including automated vehicles, electric vehicles, and shared mobility systems such as Uber and Lyft—could support more diverse types of energy sources and additional climate change strategies, and they could further improve the quality of life in Singapore while also expanding the island's central business district.

In 2016 and 2018, Weitzman studios investigated the potential of a high-speed rail and high-performance rail network between New York and Boston to revitalize a score of older industrial cities across New England. From this studio emerged the Reboot New England plan, now called the North Atlantic Rail initiative. In addition, the 2018 studio, led by Yaro and Weitzman dean Steiner, examined whether a new inland portion of the Northeast rail corridor between eastern Connecticut and western Rhode Island could balance the needs of the railroad with preservation of the Last Green Valley National Heritage Corridor and other important natural and historic resources in northeastern Connecticut and western Rhode Island.

As part of these projects, studio teams traveled to the north of England to meet with proponents of the U.K. Northern Powerhouse initiative. This project is using investments in two new high-speed rail lines as the foundation for a broader revitalization of the left-behind cities in northern England, as part of the U.K. national leveling-up agenda.

Finally, Penn's Weitzman School has partnered with UT Austin, Texas Southern University, and Louisiana State University in CM^2 (Cooperative Mobility for Competitive Megaregions), a U.S. Department of Transportation–sponsored University Transportation Center. CM^2 conducts research on the transportation needs of U.S. megaregions and identifies technologies that improve mobility, economic development, quality of life, public health, and climate for the 13 U.S. megaregions.

BOOK OVERVIEW

In the chapters that follow, we describe current thinking about the role that U.S. megaregions can play in shaping the nation's economic, social, environmental, and climate future. We analyze the current demographic, economic, and geographic conditions of the nation's 13 megaregions. Finally, we provide a road map for how national and megaregion-scale policies and investments can address the urgent issues facing these places and can help them become more resilient, equitable, and prosperous in the decades to come.

The book contains 12 chapters organized in four parts: Part 1 sets the context and includes two chapters, this introduction and chapter 2, which describes the rationale and process of our working definition of the megaregion concept. Our work led to the delineation of 13 megaregions in the contiguous United States. We then present geographic and socioeconomic profiles for each megaregion.

The four chapters of part 2 highlight the trends and threats facing U.S. megaregions. Chapter 3 examines their demographic trends over a time frame of 60 years—from 1990 to 2050. The chapter summarizes generational demographic characteristics (for baby boomers; Generation X; millennials, or Generation Y; and Generation Z) and looks at issues pertaining to the aging U.S. population. Chapter 4 profiles the economic characteristics of U.S. megaregions and examines their industrial specializations 30 years ago and today. On the basis of the analyses, the chapter characterizes the features and conditions of economic transformations experienced by the megaregions. Chapter 5 applies a 5R framework—resilience, resistance, restoration, retention, and retreat—to address the effects of climate change in U.S. megaregions. We use the ecosystem services concept to help explain the potentials for megaregions in environmental and climate planning. Chapter 6 explores the influence that innovations in information and communications technologies, in computing, and in new mobilities could have on how people work and travel, transforming the economic geography of U.S. megaregions.

In part 3, we propose action strategies gleaned from domestic and international practice to tackle the striking challenges facing the United States. Chapter 7 presents ideas for a Green Mega Deal, demonstrating that megaregions can help advance the Green New Deal in four areas: infrastructure, climate, social justice, and energy and the environment. The chapter discusses governance, finance, and implementation for achieving goals in those four areas and illustrates the contributions of megaregional frameworks to these goals. This section recommends that each megaregion should develop short- and long-term plans to address its unique conditions. There should not be a one-size-fits-all framework for all U.S. megaregions. Chapter 8 presents an example, outlining the key components of a plan for the Northeast megaregion and the kinds of institutional and governance systems that would be needed to prepare and implement these plans. Chapter 9 focuses on the critical role that high-speed and high-performance rail can play in unlocking the economic potential of U.S. megaregions. The discussions on high-speed and high-performance rail for megaregions are important and timely because the Joe Biden administration proposes them (along with electric vehicles) as the future of U.S. transportation. We also explore the unique potential of these rail networks for mobility, social equity, public health and safety, and climate resilience. Chapter 10 discusses the governance reforms and innovations that U.S. megaregions will need before they can realize their potential in the 21st century. We argue that effective megaregion governance will require a reinvention of the federal system and an adoption of a nationwide program of innovation and experimentation.

The two chapters of part 4 look to the past and to the future. In chapter 11, we each recall our path to becoming an urban and regional planner, reflect on what we learned, and connect those lessons with successful planning. The short coda of chapter 12 reprises the most important takeaways from the book and urges Americans to seize the moment.

CONCLUSION

Successful megaregions have several key characteristics: they are economic powerhouses offering a wide range of employment opportunities; they are well connected in terms of transportation and communication systems; they present a range of housing and lifestyle options from dense inner-city zones to open peri-urban and rural landscapes; and they are political and cultural hubs serving, ideally, as incubators of innovation. But none of these are possible unless the megaregion is embedded in a healthy natural environment.

—RICHARD WELLER, "CONSTRUCTING AN ECOLOGICAL CIVILIZATION," BEAUTIFUL CHINA

Over the last decade and a half, books, scholarly articles, and forums at Penn, the RPA, and the Lincoln Institute of Land Policy have stimulated a global interest in megaregions and the adoption of national strategies to improve these places. Interestingly, whereas U.S. attention to the needs of its megaregions has been limited, China has made extensive improvements. The Chinese government has invested several hundred billion dollars to create the world's largest high-speed rail network. This network has been designed to strengthen existing megaregions in the Pearl River Delta that encompass Hong Kong and Guangzhou; in the Yangtze River Delta that include Shanghai, Nanjing, Hangzhou, Suzhou, Ningbo, Wuxi, and Changzhou; and in the Jing-Jin-Ji region around Beijing and Tianjin. This national high-speed rail system connects major cities within these megaregions and links them with incipient megaregions in coastal and inland areas of the country.

Further, as part of its ambitious Belt and Road project, China is also extending high-speed rail routes into Southeast Asia that will eventually support creation of road, rail, and waterborne links stretching from Indonesia to southern China. Another component of the Belt and Road high-speed rail network will connect western China with central Asian countries and eventually Europe.

Altogether, Australia and dozens of countries in Europe and Asia have built or are planning to build high-speed rail systems, which are often part of broader megaregion-scale economic development and mobility initiatives (see figure 1.3). In many ways, the United States is being left behind in this global enterprise.

FIGURE 1.3 French high-speed train traversing a bridge over the River Saône, near Macon, France. *Source: istock.com/ollo.*

The United States has daunting economic, demographic, climatic, environmental, and spatial development challenges. Many of these ignore existing jurisdictional boundaries and spread over large regions. The recent near collapse of the Texas power grid because of a climate-induced cold snap and poor planning, for example, underscores the urgent need to design and manage this and other infrastructure systems at a scale beyond even that of our largest states. The complexities of coming decades are likely to evolve in dynamic spatial processes that our current fragmented political geographies and rigid institutional systems will not be able to adequately address.

The U.S. population will grow by 67 million in the next 30 years, with fully 88 percent of that growth occurring in the nation's 13 megaregions. At the same time, the population profile will be dramatically different from that of 30 years ago or even today. By 2050, the country's share of the population 65 years and older is projected to reach 22 percent, compared with 13 percent in 1990. And according to the U.S. Census Bureau, by 2045 the U.S. population will be predominantly nonwhite, requiring attention now to the nation's growing racial and economic inequality.

Whereas younger generations and new immigrants will largely concentrate in metropolitan areas, counties outside metropolitan cores and in rural areas will become much grayer, and mobility and health care needs of older Americans will increase. Many cities and regions, especially the large ones, have prospered from economic globalization and technological innovations. At the same time, many medium- and small-sized communities have been left behind because of production outsourcing and public disinvestment, contributing to the nation's growing racial, economic, and spatial inequities.

In the post-COVID era, congestion will once again take over streets, highways, and airports throughout the country. Yet there have not been major breakthroughs that curb the rising demands for driving or improve mobility access in general. Discussions of infrastructure upgrades have been too often limited to the interests of local jurisdictions and mode-specific agencies. High-performance and high-speed regional and intercity rail networks could provide alternatives to overcrowded highways and airports. However, to be effective, these systems must be planned and operated at the megaregion scale. Properly designed systems could benefit future work and travel patterns and transform the nation's economic geography in positive ways.

Climate change has been made real to Americans in recent years by hurricanes, wildfires, exceptional heat and cold waves, coastal and Great Lakes flooding, and other extreme-weather-related events that have caused billions of dollars of property damage, hundreds of deaths, and thousands of households to be displaced. Building resilience against these trends cannot be accomplished by individual cities or metros alone. The devastating COVID-19 pandemic and the ensuing loss of more than 750,000 lives and economic dislocation taught another costly lesson on the criticality of effective coordination across local and state lines, which is largely lacking in the existing U.S. governance system.

The megaregion framework proposed in this book does not provide detailed solutions to these pressing difficulties. Rather, it offers a specific lens to examine the trends and presents a means to find solutions. To be clear, we strongly believe that not every problem should be addressed at the scale of the megaregion. Indeed, as we point out in the following chapters, most can be successfully addressed at the local, metropolitan, or state level by existing institutions. But for many of our greatest challenges—including racial and economic equity, climate change and habitat preservation, economic competitiveness, and intercity travel—the megaregion best fits the size of the problem and potential solutions.

2

U.S. MEGAREGIONS

Our ability to reach unity in diversity will be the beauty and the test of civilization.

—MAHATMA GANDHI

IN THIS CHAPTER, WE BRIEFLY REVIEW RESEARCH conducted on U.S. megaregions over the last two decades, beginning with a working definition and delineation of 13 U.S. megaregions. We present demographic and economic profiles on each of these megaregions. The 13 megaregions possess different population, economic, settlement, and environmental characteristics. In addition, there is considerable diversity within megaregions.

DEFINITION AND DELINEATION

The first wave of megaregion research since the early 2000s generated considerable output in academic and professional journals, books, public workshops, and scholarly seminars. These efforts have a shared interest in big urban and regional issues that go beyond the existing jurisdictions, which may refer to cities or counties, metropolitan areas, or the service areas of public agencies. The area of least consensus is where the beyondness ends. The megaregions identified and delineated by many scholars and agencies have varied quite significantly.

Researchers at the Lincoln Institute of Land Policy, Penn, and the RPA initially identified eight supercities in the continental United States (Lincoln Institute of Land Policy and RPA 2004; University of Pennsylvania School of Design 2004) and then revised this to 10 places defined as megaregions (RPA 2006). These initial megaregion identifications accorded with the agglomerating trends of people, jobs, and wealth shown in the U.S. Census Bureau's 2000–2050 projections, coupled with the researchers' qualitative knowledge about the history, culture, and environment of these large geographies. The precise boundaries of the megaregions, however, were intentionally left "fuzzy," encouraging later studies to delineate boundaries when additional data become available and further refined analysis methods are applied. These early studies on the existing and emerging megaregions in the United States echoed a practical principle in regional planning, that of creating a case for "shared interests" rather than determining exactly where the megaregion boundaries are situated (Seltzer and Carbonell 2011, 5). This megaregion concept has attracted attention from many scholars, planners, and policy makers.

Early delineations of several megaregions—Great Lakes, Cascadia, Southern California, and the Texas Triangle—cross over international boundaries into Canada or Mexico. This was consistent with the delineation of Europe's Pentagon and Blue Banana megaregions, whose boundaries extend over several countries. The geological, ecological, historical, and cultural connections between Cascadia and British Columbia, Southern California and Baja, and Ontario and the Great Lakes states are strong and deep.

The economic, mobility, and environmental benefits of megaregional policies and investments could extend into vast rural areas across the country. The early RPA America 2050 maps depict megaregions adjoining rural hinterlands. For example, the rural hinterlands of the Great Lakes megaregion extend into North and South Dakota and eastern Nebraska. Similarly, the Front Range's hinterlands extend into western Nebraska and eastern Montana. This extended scope would incorporate the four lower 48 states that have not been formally included within the boundaries of the nation's 13 megaregions to date, leaving only Hawaii and Alaska beyond these areas, although clear economic and cultural ties exist between Cascadia and Alaska and between the West Coast states and Hawaii. In this sense, all states would benefit from policies and investments focused on the needs of the nation's megaregions.

In 2009, the RPA updated its 2006 study (Hagler 2009) and demarcated 11 megaregions by applying a scoring system to rank and cluster counties on the basis of five equally weighted criteria: (1) being part of the U.S. Census Bureau–defined core-based statistical area; (2) population density exceeding 200 people per square mile in the 2000 census; (3) population growth rate greater than 15 percent and growth amount exceeding 1,000 people by 2025; (4) population density increasing by 50 or more people per square mile between 2000 and 2025; and (5) employment growth rate greater than 15 percent and growth amount exceeding 20,000 people by 2025. These 11 megaregions account for 26 percent of the nation's total land area, 74 percent of population (year 2000), and are expected to grow 28 percent by 2025 compared with 24 percent in the rest of the country (see figure 1.2 in chapter 1).

To maintain consistency with the Census Bureau's criteria and naming convention for identifying and characterizing mega agglomerations, Lang and Dhavale (2005) propose "megapolitan," a term conveying a conceptual and spatial extension from the existing census geographies of micropolitan and metropolitan areas. A megapolitan area consists of counties as the basic geographic unit and combines two or more existing metropolitan areas along with their contiguous micropolitan areas. These constituent geographies of a megapolitan area have similar cultural and historical characteristics as well as physical environmental ones. Major transportation infrastructure (largely highways) provides strong connections between the multiple urban centers in the megapolitan area. The U.S. Census Bureau (or more precisely, the U.S. Office of Management and Budget) designates metropolitan areas by population thresholds (minimum of 50,000 people for the urbanized core) and micropolitan areas (at least one urban cluster with a population between 10,000 and 50,000). Following this threshold-setting practice, Lang and Dhavale (2005) specify that a megapolitan area should have a projected minimum of 10 million people by 2040.

Nelson and Lang (2011) define a megapolitan area as a territory traversable in a day by car (about 200 miles) with a projected population of 4 million or more. In addition, a megapolitan area must have at least one core metropolitan area of more than 4 million people and two or more secondary metropolitan areas of more than 250,000 people each. The secondary metropolitan areas should each have a strong economic tie with the core metropolitan area, measured by 15 percent or higher employment interchange rate between them. This revised definition of a megapolitan area, as the authors acknowledge, is equivalent to the combined statistical area of the U.S. census, except that megapolitan areas refer to the largest combined statistical areas anticipated to emerge in the future (by 2040). Nelson and Lang (2011) also introduce the concept of "megapolitan cluster," which denotes groups of megapolitan areas. A megapolitan cluster includes all metropolitan areas within 500 miles of the identified megapolitan areas and having close historical and cultural connections. The megapolitan cluster proposed by Nelson and Lang (2011) is conceptually analogous to the megaregion from the Lincoln Institute, Penn, and the RPA.

The work on defining and delineating megaregions by Ross and Woo (2009) involved extensive statistical analysis. They adopted a core-periphery model to structure a megaregion consisting of two elements, the core area and the area of influence, which were identified separately. The core area holds the highly agglomerated centers, and the area of influence supports the functions of the core area and presents historical, cultural, and environmental characteristics similar to those of the core. A megaregion may have multiple cores with corresponding areas of influence, which are all interconnected. To identify the core area, they used spatial cluster analysis techniques (e.g., the Moran's I index, which is often used to find nonrandom clusters) for detecting the concentration patterns of people and employment. They used graph theory and Markov chain modeling to determine the hierarchy of core areas of different sizes and identified the area of influence by applying density profiling (which measures the density gradient as a function of distance to the center point) and geographically weighted regression that took into consideration multiple demographic, economic, and environmental factors. The resulting megaregions identified by Ross and Woo (2009) differ quite significantly from those of the RPA (2006), Hagler (2009), and Lang and Dhavale (2005). Not only do the exact boundaries of each megaregion differ but so does the specific designation of megaregions. For instance, the Texas Triangle and the Gulf Coast, which are two different megaregions in the RPA's designation, merge into one in Ross and Woo's work. In addition, Ross and Woo (2009) propose a new megaregion, Central Plains, which comprises multiple metropolitan areas and their surrounding counties in Oklahoma, Kansas, and Missouri (figure 2.1).

The planning office of the U.S. Federal Highway Administration (FHWA) lists 13 megaregions (FHWA 2018). Although no detailed information is available on the rationale and the method used to define these 13 megaregions, the FHWA's megaregions appear most like those of Ross and Woo (2009), with one distinction. The FHWA identified one additional megaregion, the Mid-South. This new megaregion starts in New Orleans, Louisiana; crosses the entire state of Mississippi through its middle; and ends in Memphis, Tennessee, and Little Rock, Arkansas, to the north.

Florida et al. (2008) dismiss the population-based approach taken by most researchers for megaregion delineation. Instead, they emphasize the economic mass presented by polycentric agglomerations of cities and their hinterlands. Their study aims to discern what they call "mega-regions" at the global level. Subnational data on economic activities for all countries in the world are not readily accessible, if they even exist. Florida et al. (2008) used nighttime light data published by the Earth Observation Program of the National Geophysical Data Center at the National Oceanic and Atmospheric Administration. The data report light intensity for each grid cell of 30 arc-seconds between 65 degrees south and 65 degrees north latitudes from satellite images of the world at night (figure 2.2). Florida et al. (2008) calibrated the relationships between light intensity and population and between light intensity and economic output from the established areas in the United States. Applying this calibrated rate of light to economic activities, they estimate economic products for the rest of the world per unit area at the spatial resolution provided by the satellite data. Florida et al.'s work identifies the top 40 megaregions around the world, 11 of which come from the continental United States. These megaregions not only produce "mega" economic output but also manifest as agglomerating places of innovation, measured by number of patents and scientific publications.

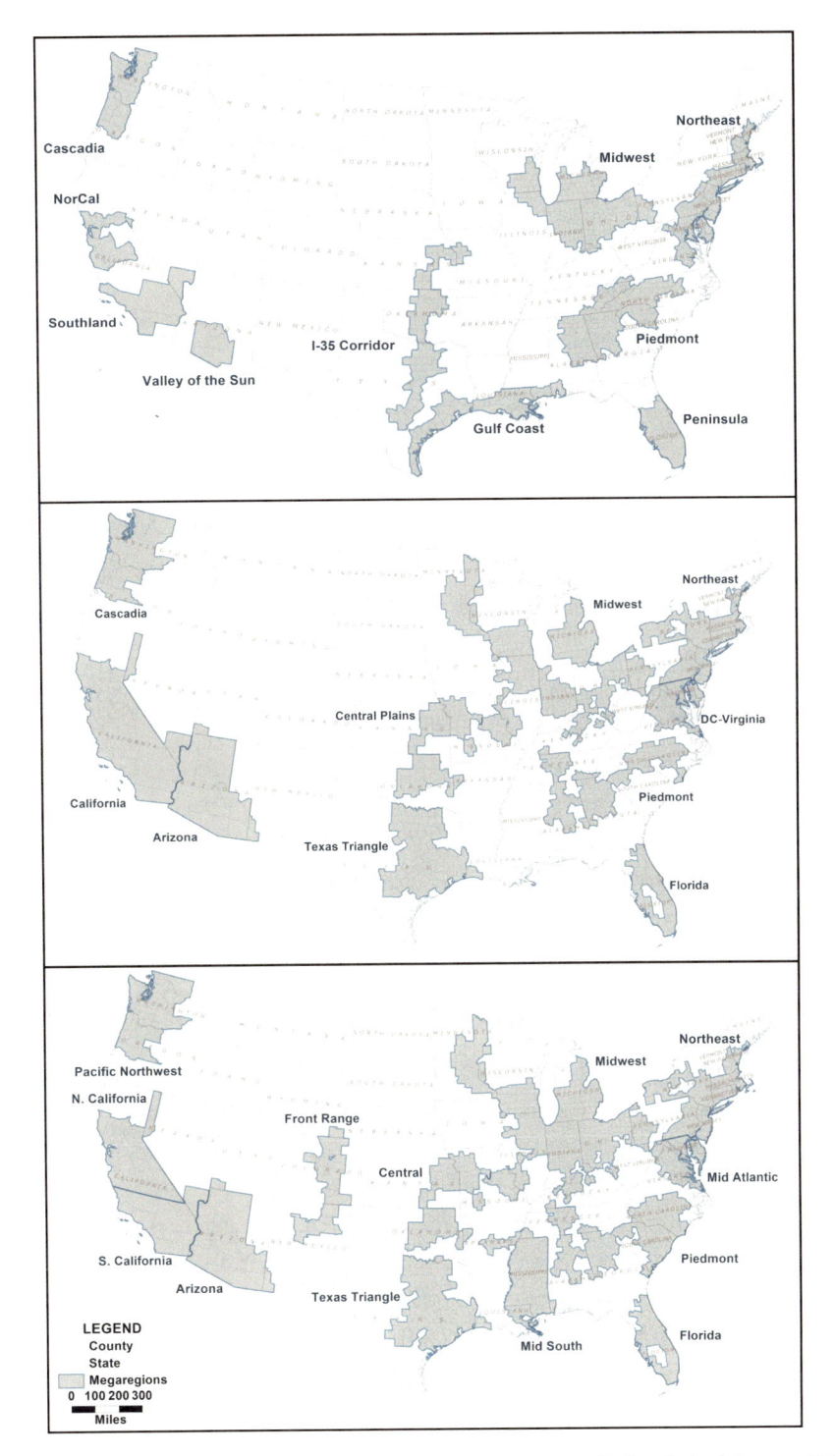

FIGURE 2.1 Three versions of U.S. megaregions as identified by Lang and Dhavale (*top*), Ross and Woo (*middle*), and the Federal Highway Administration (*bottom*). Source: *Adapted by Ming Zhang from Federal Highway Administration (2018); Lang and Dhavale (2005); Ross and Woo (2009).*

FIGURE 2.2 U.S. megaregions by night (Earth Observation Program of NOAA's National Geophysical Data Center). *Source: NASA.*

OUR PROCESS

The diversity of methods for and differences in outcomes when identifying megaregions as shown in the preceding section are not surprising, however. They just offer additional evidence demonstrating the two fundamental, recurring challenges facing all studies of regions: what a region is and where the region's boundaries go. These challenges persist partly because of the ambiguity associated with the term *region* (Kelbaugh 1997). A region may refer to spaces formed by ecological or biophysical processes. It may also refer to territories shaped by economic, political, or cultural activities and traditions. These many defining and shaping factors of regions can be measured at several spatial scales (e.g., subnational, continental), and they likely change over time. In the United States, many regional agencies—for example, metropolitan planning organizations (MPOs) and water authorities—have explicit jurisdictional designation. In most cases, however, regions do not appear with formal demarcations, leaving the definition and delineation of a region as a research question in itself. The lack of a formal designation also often results in the lack of institutional authorization, tendering another unique difficulty to planning and plan implementation for regions compared with other jurisdiction-based planning and policymaking. The megaregion, which may be interpreted as a region of regions, inherits these problems. Five of the 13 megaregions we define (Arizona Sun Corridor, Southern California, Cascadia, Great Lakes, and Gulf Coast) are binational megaregions. We discuss only the U.S. parts of the megaregions.

For regional planning and policy-making, defining a region often takes a purpose-driven approach, exploring and combining overlapping, interconnected characteristics essential to the specific planning or policy interest, then defining and delineating the area of interest accordingly (Seltzer and Carbonell 2011). We adopt this practical approach in this study.

Megaregional thinking promotes and facilitates collaborative efforts by a megaregion's constituencies to address their common big-picture, long-term strategic challenges. By crossing boundaries of existing jurisdictions or administrations and natural or human-made borders, formerly disparate groups and causes can act as a collective whole. With this thinking in mind, we take the following three steps to develop our working definition and the geographic scope of megaregions in the United States: (1) identify building blocks; (2) analyze spatial relationship and functional linkage; and (3) qualitatively assess historical, cultural, and ecological and environmental factors.

Identify Building Blocks

We select the building blocks of a megaregion, considering specifically those that have their boundaries already defined formally by legal, authoritative, or generally accepted sources. Initial building blocks are counties, metropolitan statistical areas, and areas of MPOs and councils of government. Starting from these building blocks with explicit governance functions minimizes the ambiguity effects of regions and megaregions, enables the use of multisourced data with a relatively high consistency for subsequent analyses, and increases the ability to implement future megaregional planning and policy initiatives.

Counties and county equivalents are largely the legal divisions of states and are relatively stable in their legal boundaries and names (U.S. Census Bureau 2020b). This stability makes counties a suitable choice as the basic spatial unit of analysis for many applications. The U.S. Census Bureau uses counties and county equivalents as the building blocks for defining metropolitan and micropolitan statistical areas. This boundary stability also provides county-level demographic and economic accounts with a high level of spatial consistency over time, which is particularly desirable for studying regional or megaregional trends and dynamics with multiyear, multidecade information.

Metropolitan statistical areas (MSAs) are defined by the U.S. Census Bureau, which updates their designation on the basis of information from decennial censuses. Standards and criteria published by the Office of Management and Budget (OMB 2000) designate two types of statistical areas: metropolitan and micropolitan, together termed core-based statistical areas (CBSAs). A metropolitan statistical area consists of an urbanized area of 50,000 or more people plus the contiguous

Councils of Government

Councils of government (COGs), also known as regional councils or commissions, are a type of regional planning and coordinating organization existing in all 50 U.S. states. Geographically, a typical COG serves multiple counties, and its governing body is composed of elected officials from county, city, and other local governments in the region. COGs' main mission is to "promote collaboration among local governments, working across the jurisdictional silos of states, counties, and municipalities" (NARC 2020; Vlassis 2007).

COGs develop solutions for matters extending beyond individual jurisdictions; coordinate regional plans in matters including economic development, pollution control, transit administration, human services, hazard mitigation, and emergency responses; and provide technical assistance and service delivery to their members.

COGs initially, in the 1940s, were voluntary, nonprofit organizations. They grew rapidly in the 1960s and 1970s as a result of federal and state funding. The number and functions of COGs decreased significantly during and after the Ronald Reagan administration when federal aid to local governments was extensively reduced. As of 2020, the National Association of Regional Councils reports more than 500 COGs, whose populations range from fewer than 50,000 to more than 19 million.

MPOs are a particular type of COG specializing in regional transportation planning and project funding involving federal funds. In some regions—for example, the Dallas–Fort Worth, Texas, area—the MPO and COG function as a single entity. In other places—for example, the Austin, Texas, area—the regional MPO and COG operate as separate agencies.

outlying counties that have a 25 percent or higher employment interchange rate with the central county. A micropolitan statistical area includes urban clusters of at least 10,000 but fewer than 50,000 people plus contiguous outlying counties that have a minimum of 15 percent employment interchange rate with the central county. The CBSAs provide relatively unambiguous and consistent characterization of agglomeration patterns across the country. Most megaregion researchers agree in principle that megaregions consist of two or more metropolitan areas and their integrated hinterland. Analogous to the urbanized nuclei of an MSA, MSAs themselves are the nuclei of megaregions. CBSAs, however, are defined solely for statistical purposes. The OMB and the U.S. Census Bureau do not endorse using CBSAs as a geographic framework for nonstatistical activities or formula funding programs, except for those specifically approved by Congress (OMB 2000). Accordingly, we consider two additional building blocks for defining megaregions.

MPO jurisdictions are the first additional building block. The rationale of explicitly including MPO jurisdictions in megaregion delineation lies in the criticality of transportation infrastructure to megaregions (and vice versa). Early discussions on tying transportation infrastructure with megaregions go back to the mid-1960s, not long after Jean Gottmann (1961) published his megalopolis study. Pell (1966), in *Megalopolis Unbound: The Supercity and the Transportation of Tomorrow*, advocated megaregional transportation planning and proposed intercity passenger rail services in the Northeast megaregion.

MPOs were first authorized in 1962 by the Federal-Aid Highway Act. The act required all urbanized areas with populations greater than 50,000 to establish MPOs to coordinate regional transportation planning and federally supported transportation improvements under a continuing, cooperative, and comprehensive process. As population continues to grow and urbanize in the country, MPOs have increased in numbers and expanded in boundaries from their initial jurisdictions in fast-growing metropolitan regions. As of 2020, there are over 400 MPOs in the United States.

Although the requirement for any region meeting the population threshold to establish an MPO comes from federal law, the actual designation of individual MPOs is made by agreement between state governors and sufficient units of local governments that together represent at least 75 percent of the region's population. MPOs receive the most resources from federal planning funds that are channeled to and managed by state departments of transportation. In their first three decades of operation, MPOs mainly had an advisory or consulting role in supporting state DOTs and local governments with their highway-centered transportation planning and project implementation. The Intermodal Surface Transportation Efficiency (ISTEA) of 1991 and subsequent federal transportation acts boosted MPOs' authority over

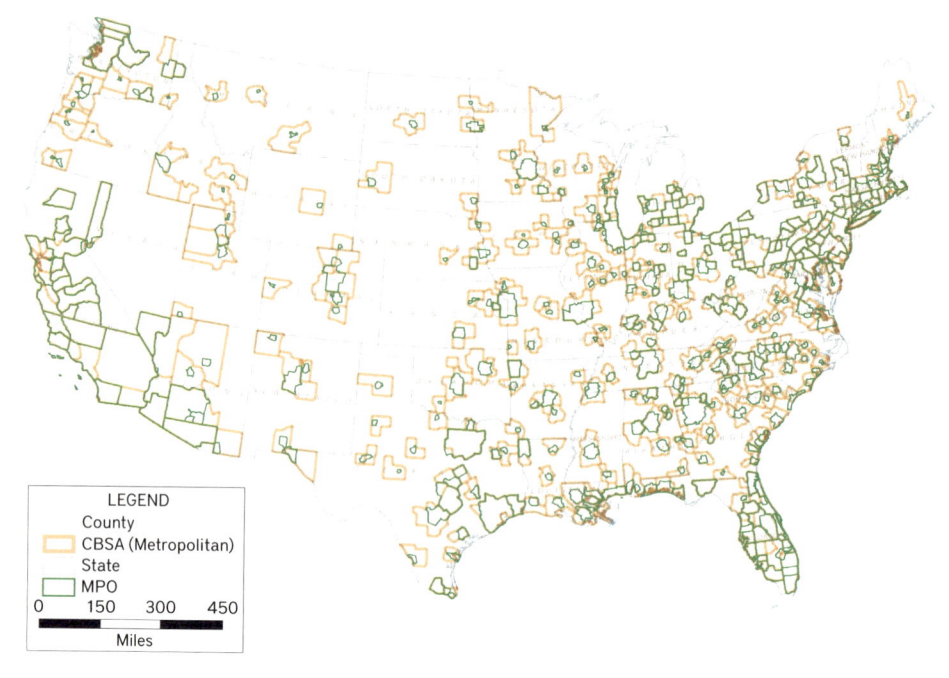

FIGURE 2.3 U.S. Census Bureau core-based statistical metropolitan areas (CBSAs) and metropolitan planning organizations (MPOs). *Source: Ming Zhang.*

project selection and funding. These acts allowed the use of highway trust funds for transit, pedestrian, bike, and other nonhighway transportation projects. At the same time, MPOs' responsibilities have also increased, extending from a rather narrow focus of building and preserving the transportation infrastructure to including air quality, environmental preservation, access equity, and social justice (FHWA 2014). These broader issues often span MPO boundaries, beyond the jurisdictional and financial provisions given to MPOs (Oden and Sciara 2020).

Nevertheless, MPOs remain one of the most prevalent regional transportation agencies authorized and funded by federal legislation in the United States. Despite constraints and limitations on MPOs, they can be an effective force for regional transformation (Sciara 2017).

MSAs and MPOs may share urbanized areas in their cores. However, as illustrated in figure 2.3, they do not always share boundaries.

Analyze Spatial Relationship and Functional Linkage

We examine the spatial relationships (contiguity, overlap, or containment) among the building blocks and identify clusters of blocks as the candidate subareas of a megaregion. Neighboring building blocks likely have shared interests and concerns. Further, some are partially or fully contained geographically within neighboring building blocks. For this reason, cross-border collaboration and coordination on planning and policy-making would be naturally desired.

We analyze flows between the building blocks. Commuting, freight shipping, and information exchanges reveal the functional and social ties between the flow origin and destination places. Flow traffic also has important implications for the places along the origin and destination routes. OMB has long applied commuting criteria to define metropolitan areas, and commuting thresholds change when new standards and criteria are published. In this study, we explore data on freight, air passenger, and information flows when data are available, in addition to the data on commuting flows readily available from the census. Strongly linked building blocks form the core elements of a megaregion.

Adjacent MSAs and contiguous MPOs become candidate components of a megaregion. Adjacent MPOs coordinate planning for cross-MPO freight and passenger movement and other transportation-related issues. Two examples in Texas are the Capital Area MPO in the Austin region and the Alamo Area MPO in the San Antonio region. The two MPOs have separate long-range plans, but they have engaged in a joint planning study coordinated by the Texas Department of Transportation.

MPOs not contiguous but having a strong linkage also become candidate components of a megaregion. Intercounty, inter-MPO commuting indicates the strength of a linkage. The specific threshold, however, requires a judgment call. The absence of intercity and regional rail networks in most megaregions precludes much inter-MPO travel. The U.S. Census Bureau applies commuting thresholds when defining different types of metropolitan areas. For MSAs, surrounding counties with 25 percent of their labor force commuting to the core county will qualify as part of the MSA. For combined statistical areas, a threshold of 15 percent applies for two or more adjacent micro- and metropolitan areas.

Table 2.1 and figure 2.4 display the commuting patterns between and within MPOs with data from the American Community Survey (U.S. Census Bureau 2019a). Commuting occurs largely within MPO counties. In 2015, intra-MPO commutes accounted for about 80 percent of the total worker commuting flows. Another 10 percent of worker flows are MPO related, having either travel origins or destinations outside individual MPOs. The remaining 10 percent or more of worker flows happened within or between non-MPO counties.

The intercounty commuting pattern looks quite different when measured by person miles of travel. Intra-MPO commuting contributed 58 percent of total person miles of travel. The remaining 42 percent came from the work commute involving non-MPO counties. Given that personal travel is predominantly by car, inter-MPO commutes are a factor in investment and policy solutions when delineating megaregion boundaries for issues such as transportation emissions and environmental justice.

Table 2.1. Commuting Flows, 2015

OD Commuting Type	OD Pairs	Worker Flow (millions)	Share (%)	PMT (millions)	Share (%)	PMT/w
Intra-MPO Counties[a]	4,082	112.42	78.9	2,084.35	58.3	18.54
Inter-MPO Counties[b]	47,723	8.19	5.8	856.16	24.0	104.48
MPO Counties to Non-MPO Counties[c]	19,288	1.64	1.2	122.59	3.4	74.72
Non-MPO Counties to MPO Counties[d]	30,678	3.54	2.5	202.82	5.7	57.32
Inter-Non-MPO Counties[e]	30,521	2.83	2.0	108.88	3.0	38.52
Intra-Non-MPO Counties[f]	2,207	13.85	9.7	199.87	5.6	14.43
Total		142.47	100.0	3,574.67	100.0	25.09

Source: U.S. Census Bureau (2019a).

Note: OD = origin to destination; PMT/w = person miles of travel per worker.

[a] Commutes to work between cities or counties within the same metropolitan planning organization (MPO) area.

[b] Commutes between two or more MPO areas.

[c] Commutes starting from a county belonging to an MPO and ending in a rural county.

[d] Commutes starting from a rural county and ending in an MPO.

[e] Commutes between places that neither end of which was located in an MPO.

[f] Commutes within a county not located in an MPO.

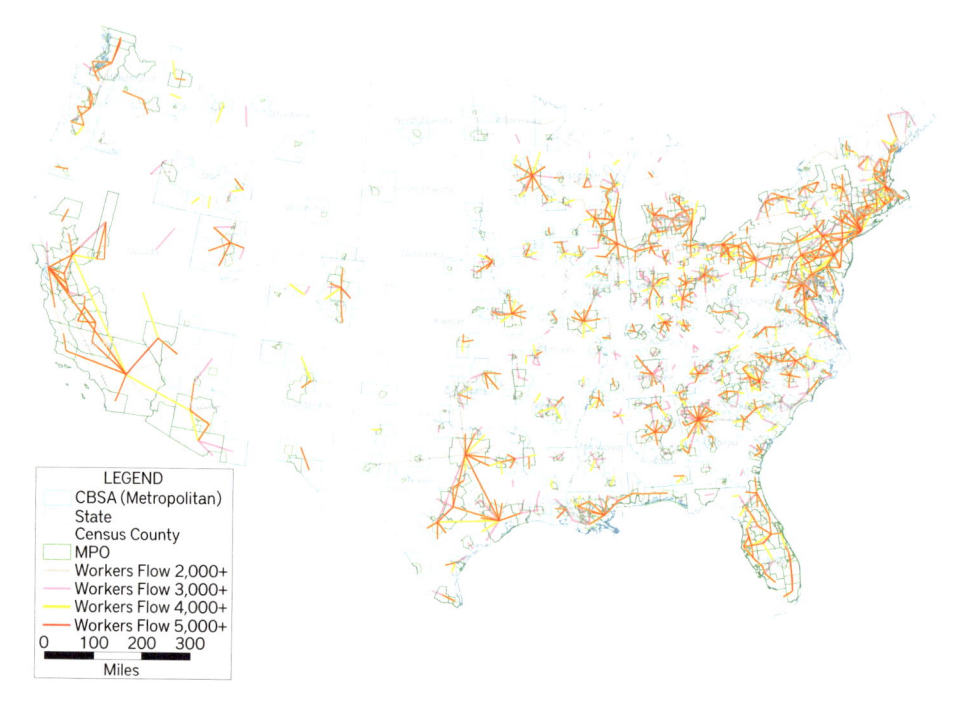

FIGURE 2.4 Flows of workers in and between metropolitan planning organizations (MPOs) and counties (residence-work locations in different MPOs and counties) in 2015. *Source: Ming Zhang.*

Qualitatively Assess Historical, Cultural, and Ecological and Environmental Factors

We apply qualitative knowledge to fine-tune the border areas of individual candidate megaregions. Delineating explicit edges of a megaregion is necessary for analytic tasks, especially quantitative data analysis. However, we do not apply rigid, singular criteria to draw the border lines. For different megaregions or for different analytic purposes, we consider weighted historical, cultural, and ecological and environmental factors, exercising flexibility.

Figure 2.5 shows the U.S. Environmental Protection Agency Level III ecoregions on the U.S. continent (EPA 2020). When delineating megaregions, we consider the contextual ecoregion characters, a common practice in previous megaregion research. Many megaregions derive their names from their ecoregional background, for instance, Cascadia, Great Lakes, Piedmont Atlantic, Central Plains, and Basin and Range (see further details in the later "Megaregion Profile" section). The EPA based its ecoregion model on the lifework of Robert Bailey (1983), a geographer with the U.S. Forest Service.

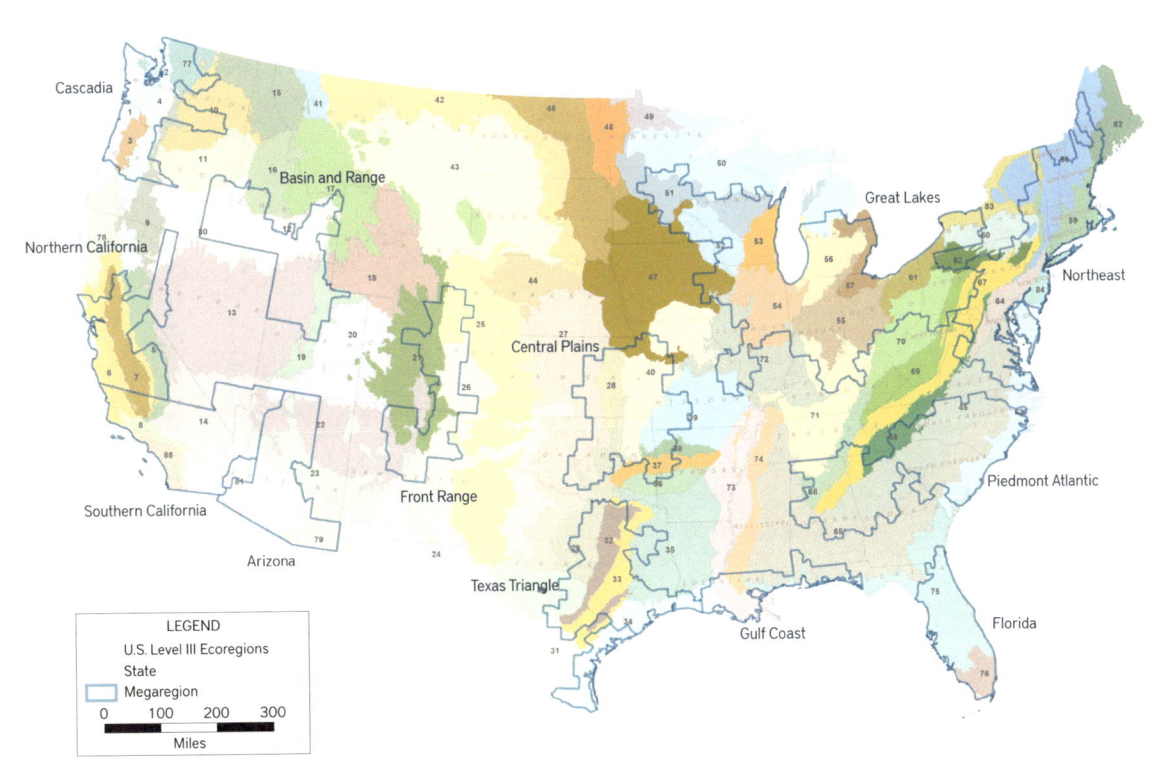

FIGURE 2.5 Megaregions and EPA Level III ecoregions (different areas shown in different colors) in the United States. *Source: Ming Zhang.*

Biology is but one of many environmental methods for designating regions and megaregions. Physiography and hydrology are two other common references. Drainage basins are especially useful for planning, as in New Deal programs such as the Tennessee Valley Authority and watershed soil conservation programs. In the late 19th century, John Wesley Powell suggested settling the arid lands of the American West on the basis of drainage basins. Powell was a keen observer of the connections between where Indigenous people and Mormons settled and the locations' hydrology. He based his arid lands proposal—an alternative to Thomas Jefferson's geometric grid approach to settlement—on his observations (Powell et al. 1879).

In 2012, Laurel McSherry and Robert Holmes updated and expanded Powell's idea (Holmes 2012) (figure 2.6). They proposed reorganizing the United States in drainage-basin-based commonwealths. Much like megaregions, these commonwealths would provide more effective environmental management, especially in terms of water resources. Their work suggests a parallel system of natural resource–based megaregions.

By taking these three steps, we defined 13 megaregions in the United States. Figure 2.7 shows them, and summary statistics are reported in table 2.2.

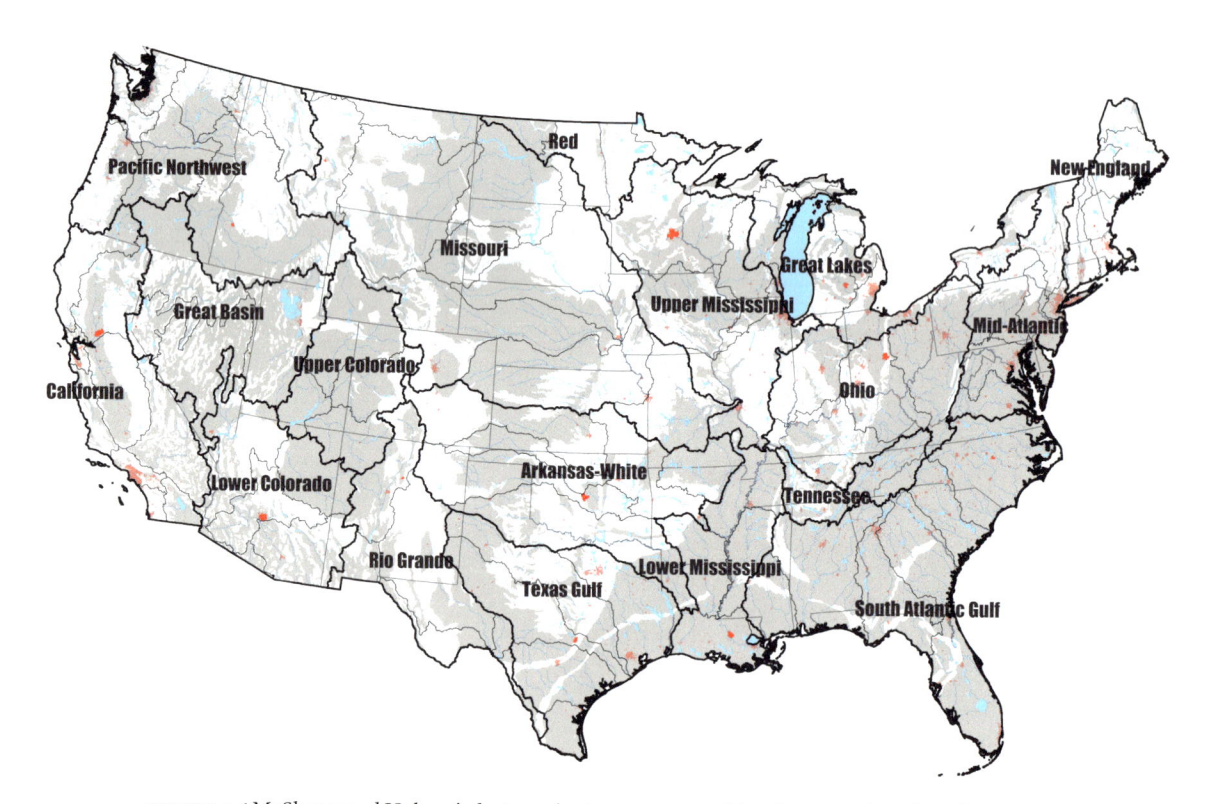

FIGURE 2.6 McSherry and Holmes's drainage basin commonwealths. *Source: Holmes (2012).*

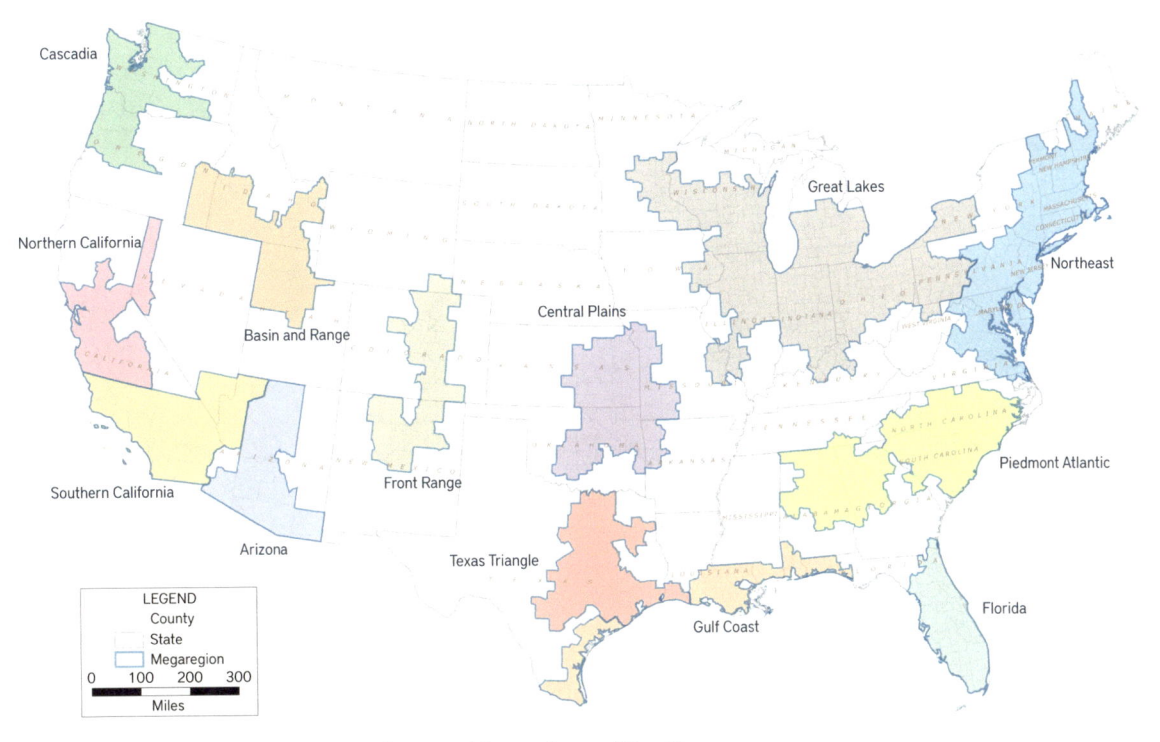

FIGURE 2.7 Megaregions in the United States. *Source: Ming Zhang.*

MEGAREGION PROFILES
Arizona Sun Corridor

The Arizona Sun Corridor megaregion on its U.S. side comprises eight counties and seven MSAs, all within Arizona (figure 2.8). The megaregion covers 63,570 square miles. In 2018, the megaregion had 3.67 million jobs and an economy of $330.19 billion, about the same as Denmark and slightly lower than Singapore, the two countries that megaregion thinkers frequently cite as the international benchmark. The entire state's population is predominantly urban, concentrating mostly in the megaregion; 9 of 10 Arizonans live in the Arizona Sun Corridor megaregion, which holds 6.66 million people (table 2.3). The megaregion's name reflects the morphological characteristics of the MSA cluster in the region: except for the Yuma metropolitan area bordered by the Southern California megaregion to the west, these MSAs align in a north–south corridor over about 350 miles through central Arizona. The Phoenix-Mesa-Chandler metropolitan area, also called the Valley of the Sun or simply the Valley by most Arizonans, dominates the megaregion, with its population, jobs, and gross domestic product (GDP) accounting for around 75 percent of the Sun Corridor's total.

Table 2.2. Summary Statistics of U.S. Megaregions, 2018

	Number of Counties	Area (thousands of sq. miles)	Population (millions)	Jobs (millions)	GDP (billions)
Arizona	8	63.57	6.66	3.67	330.19
Basin and Range	34	71.87	4.10	2.62	220.15
Northern California	33	51.08	15.34	9.52	1,341.80
Southern California	12	78.67	26.36	16.06	1,774.33
Cascadia	36	57.59	9.59	6.01	707.45
Central Plains	118	84.27	8.90	5.45	469.49
Florida	44	41.03	19.66	11.57	969.34
Front Range	31	61.40	6.18	4.08	385.19
Great Lakes	422	229.50	60.11	37.40	3,635.23
Gulf Coast*	55	42.02	7.20	4.02	342.60
Northeast	242	111.36	61.36	38.50	4,540.03
Piedmont Atlantic	221	116.07	26.81	15.90	1,468.38
Texas Triangle	80	69.82	22.35	14.15	1,438.23
Subtotal	1336	1,078.25	274.62	168.94	17,622.40
Rest of USA	1,905	2,516.23	52.44	29.38	2,598.57
Total	3,241	3,594.49	327.06	198.32	20,220.97
Megaregion Share	41.2%	30.0%	84.0%	85.2%	87.1%

Sources: U.S. Bureau of Economic Analysis (2019); U.S. Census Bureau (2020a).

* The Gulf Coast and Texas Triangle megaregions overlap in the Houston area. The Gulf Coast numbers exclude the overlapped areas to avoid double counting.

Two key features present both problems and potential to the Sun Corridor megaregion.

- *Desert environment.* Many of the Sun Corridor settlements have developed in the Sonoran Desert. Scarce water and urban heat islands add to the natural desert heat and pose lasting challenges to cities and metros in the megaregion, which continue to grow and agglomerate. At the same time, the wild desert landscape offers precious geological value and tourist attractions. The spectacular Painted Desert in the northern part of the megaregion and Grand Canyon in northwestern Arizona attract millions of recreational and educational visitors every year from the rest of the United States and around the world.

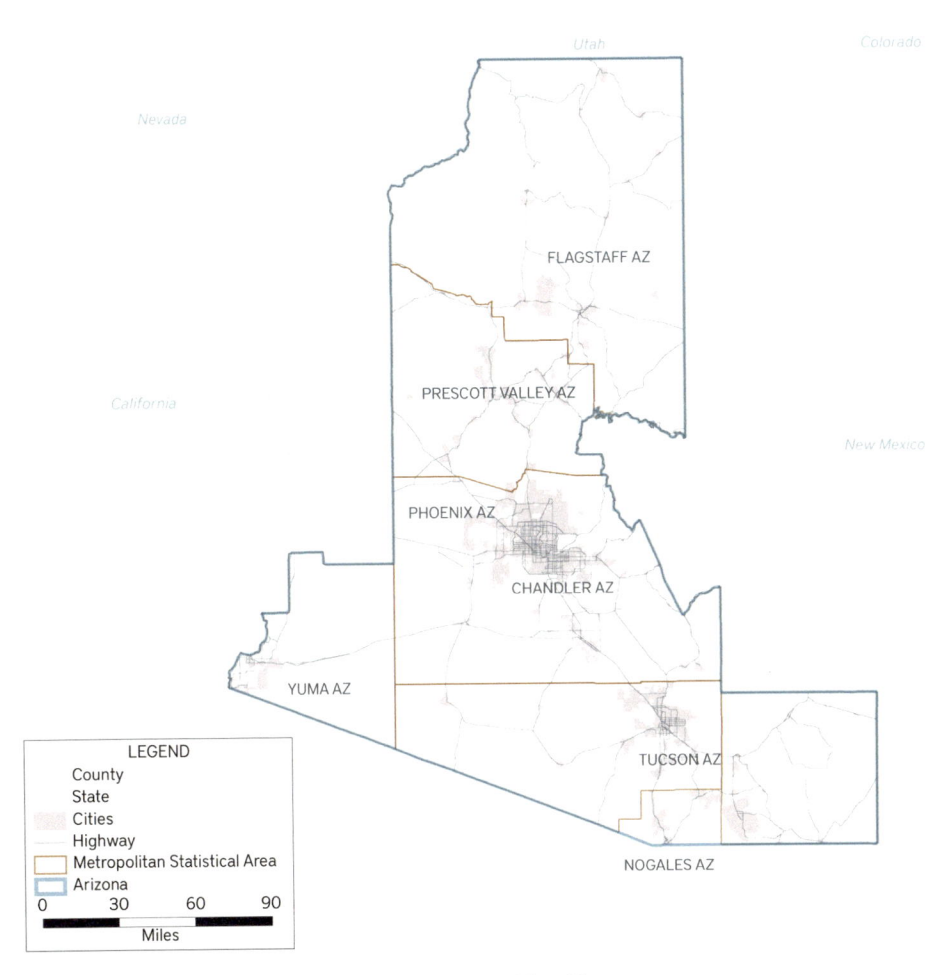

FIGURE 2.8 Arizona Sun Corridor megaregion. *Source: Ming Zhang.*

Table 2.3. Metropolitan Areas Ranked by GDP in the Arizona Megaregion, 2018

	Area (sq. miles)	Population (millions)	Jobs (millions)	GDP (billions)
Phoenix-Mesa-Chandler	14,605.29	4.858	2.792	255.212
Tucson	9,195.29	1.039	0.527	44.876
Yuma	5,522.06	0.212	0.090	8.331
Flagstaff	18,659.08	0.143	0.088	7.718
Prescott Valley–Prescott	8,129.10	0.232	0.102	7.222
Sierra Vista–Douglas	6,223.49	0.127	0.052	4.910
Nogales	1,239.11	0.047	0.021	1.917
Total	63,573.42	6.657	3.671	330.186

Source: U.S. Bureau of Economic Analysis (2019).

- *Transnational ports.* There are six land-based border ports of entry between Arizona and the Mexican state of Sonora. Among them, the port in Nogales, Arizona, has the highest transborder connectivity, provided by transnational highway and railroad links. Every day, thousands of personal vehicles, commercial trucks, and freight trains cross these ports. A twin-city type of community has developed on both sides of the border around each of the ports. High border-crossing traffic and cogrowth of border communities demonstrate the strong economic and cultural ties between the Sun Corridor and Sonora, making them a functionally and culturally integrated transnational megaregion. The megaregion statistics reported here show only those from the U.S. portion, but planning and policy discussions on the Sun Corridor must recognize the importance of the transnational ports and binational coordination.

Arizona's pioneering Groundwater Management Act of 1980 provides a model for ensuring that this megaregion's vital natural resources are passed on to future generations. In addition, the U.S. Environmental Protection Agency encouraged international cooperation to manage water on both sides of the Mexico-U.S. border in the 1990s, and the U.S. Fish and Wildlife Service promoted borderlands habitat conservation through the Malpai Borderlands Habitat Conservation Plan in 2008 (Steiner et al. 2019). New biodiversity and habitat challenges, however, have been created by the border wall.

Basin and Range

Previous efforts have not defined the Basin and Range as a megaregion, although that has been discussed. We consider it a megaregion despite its small population compared with other megaregions. We delineate the Basin and Range megaregion by three anchor cities that form a triangle: Salt Lake City, Utah, to the south; Idaho Falls, Idaho, to the northeast; and Boise, Idaho, to the northwest (figure 2.9; table 2.4). The three anchor cities and their respective counties and metros form a region on the joint of three EPA Level III ecoregions: North Basin and Range, Central Basin and Range, and Snake River Basin. The Wasatch and Uinta Mountains and the middle Rockies to the east of the plains create a natural barrier, forcing, in a sense, the people and business in the Salt Lake area to go north and west. Boise and Salt Lake City interact closely, evidenced by a long-distance bus service, Salt Lake Express, that offers scheduled economy and executive services between Boise Airport and Salt Lake City and many other destinations throughout Utah and beyond. Southern Idaho and Utah share many historical and cultural roots. Early immigrants came to Idaho from the south through Utah. In addition, the bistate region has the highest percentage of Mormons in the world. Latter Day Saints temples and churches and the Mormon culture are predominant in the region. Major challenges facing Basin and Range

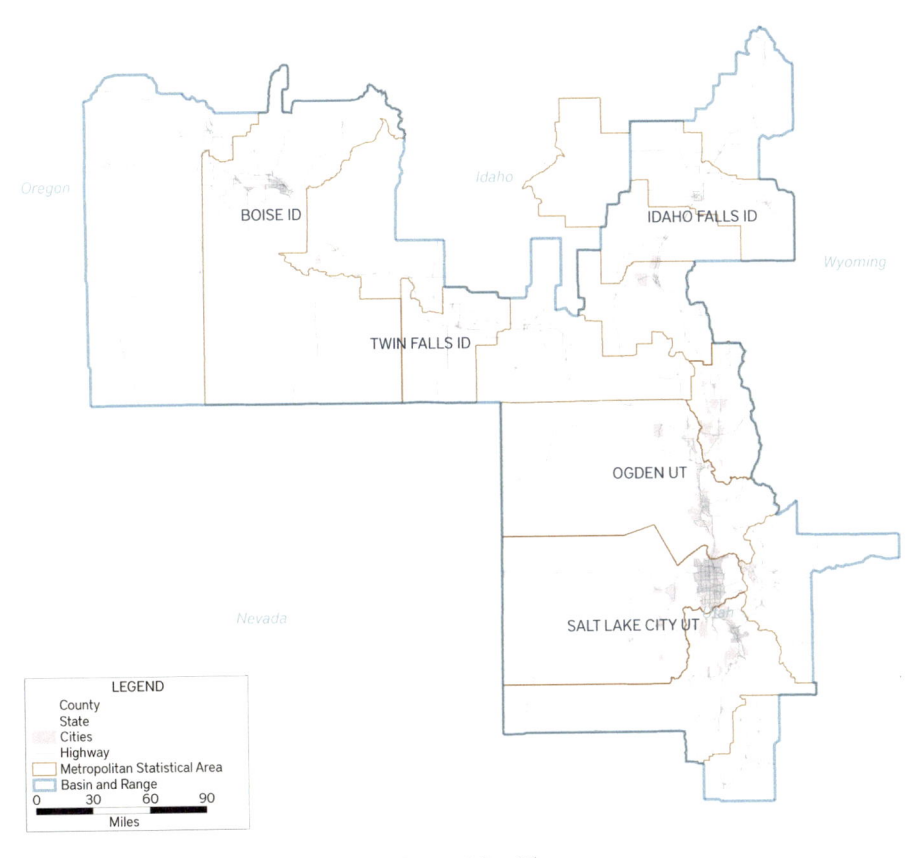

FIGURE 2.9 Basin and Range megaregion. *Source: Ming Zhang.*

Table 2.4. Top 10 Metropolitan Areas Ranked by GDP in the Basin and Range Megaregion, 2018

	Area (sq. miles)	Population (millions)	Jobs (millions)	GDP (billions)
Salt Lake City, UT	8,084.14	1.223	0.946	94.307
Boise, ID	11,812.28	0.730	0.446	34.392
Ogden-Clearfield, UT	8,621.28	0.675	0.369	28.900
Provo-Orem, UT	5,544.61	0.634	0.367	27.244
Logan, UT-ID	1,838.62	0.141	0.085	5.700
Twin Falls, ID	2,526.41	0.110	0.065	4.884
Heber, UT	3,084.26	0.075	0.060	4.287
Pocatello, ID	2,585.74	0.095	0.053	3.530
Burley, ID	3,337.72	0.045	0.027	2.311
Ontario, OR-ID	10,321.08	0.054	0.028	2.117
Total	57,756.13	3.78	2.45	207.67

Source: U.S. Bureau of Economic Analysis (2019).

FIGURE 2.10 View of Salt Lake Valley at the foothills of the Oquirrh Mountains and the adjacent Great Salt Lake in the distance. *Source: istock.com/© Salil Bhatt.*

result from the rapid recent growth in the Salt Lake City (figure 2.10) and Boise areas. The Envision Utah (2000) initiative provides a model for smart, regional growth management in this megaregion.

Northern California

Researchers have identified consistently, with only minor variations in the edge delineations, the Northern California and the Southern California megaregions as two distinct areas despite both being largely situated in the same state. The state as a whole has been at the forefront of environmental protection, from coastal zone management to greenhouse gas reduction, but sufficient dissimilarities in culture and development characteristics between the north and south justify this distinction.

The Northern California megaregion defined in this study is formed of 33 counties and 21 MSAs (figure 2.11). All but four MSAs are inside California. Reno and three other MSAs from neighboring Nevada join the Northern California's MSA cluster because of their high degree of economic ties as revealed by inter-MSA commuting. The megaregion covers 51,080 square miles and in 2018 had 15.34 million people and 9.52 million jobs. In 2018, the Northern California megaregion's GDP

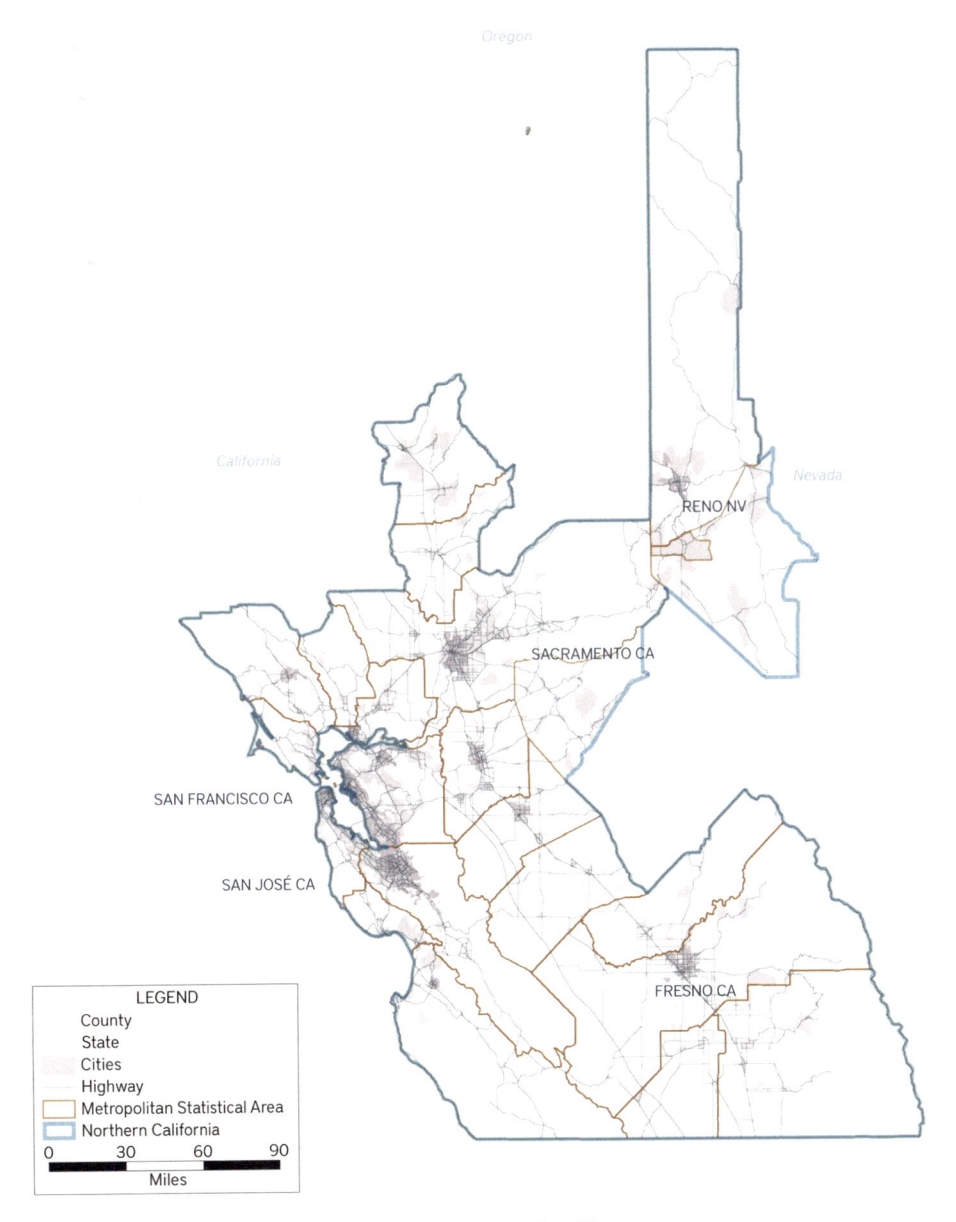

FIGURE 2.11 Northern California megaregion. *Source: Ming Zhang.*

was $1,341.8 billion, the highest among all megaregions on a per capita or per job basis. Table 2.5 ranks the megaregion's top 10 MSAs by GDP. Principal cities in the megaregion are San Francisco, Oakland, San Jose, Sacramento, and Reno.

Northern California offers rich natural amenities and cultural heritage, a vibrant business environment, and several highly rated educational and research institutions. These attractions make Northern California a favorite destination for many firms and for domestic and international migrants. High demand for office space,

Table 2.5. Top 10 Metropolitan Areas Ranked by GDP in the Northern California Megaregion, 2018

	Area (sq. miles)	Population (millions)	Jobs (millions)	GDP (billions)
San Francisco–Oakland–Berkeley, CA	2,517.63	4.729	3.437	548.613
San Jose–Sunnyvale–Santa Clara, CA	2,688.60	1.999	1.474	331.020
Sacramento-Roseville-Folsom, CA	5,303.81	2.345	1.385	145.480
Fresno, CA	6,015.72	0.994	0.510	47.409
Stockton, CA	1,425.41	0.753	0.340	32.328
Santa Rosa–Petaluma, CA	1,587.86	0.500	0.312	31.960
Reno, NV	6,805.47	0.470	0.316	28.156
Salinas, CA	3,314.18	0.436	0.257	27.423
Vallejo, CA	846.37	0.447	0.205	26.441
Modesto, CA	1,513.77	0.550	0.254	25.134
Total	32,018.82	13.22	8.49	1,243.96

Source: U.S. Bureau of Economic Analysis (2019).

housing, and other services has driven up the cost of living in the region to an extraordinary level. Lack of affordability has long been a major problem in Northern California communities and the whole megaregion.

Southern California

The Southern California megaregion consists of 12 counties and 10 MSAs from three adjacent states. Las Vegas, Henderson, and Paradise of Nevada and Lake Havasu City and Kingman of Arizona are functionally integrated parts of the megaregion in addition to the seven MSAs in California (figures 2.12 and 2.13). Southern California covers 78,670 square miles, about 50 percent larger than Northern California, and it hosts about 70 percent more people (26.36 million) and jobs (16.06 million) than the north. In 2018, the Southern California megaregion produced a total GDP of $1,774.3 billion. This represents about 20 percent lower per capita and per job GDP in the south than in the north. Table 2.6 lists the Southern California megaregion's top 10 metropolitan areas ranked by GDP (in 2018).

This megaregion is a global hub for the arts, film, television, and internet production. Los Angeles, in particular, has also become an important fashion and music center.

Transportation and logistics industries also play a vital role in Southern California's economy. The region operates seaports, land ports, and airports, all ranked among the largest in the United States. In 2018, the Port of Los Angeles and the Port of Long Beach handled 5.04 million and 4.36 million shipping containers (20-foot

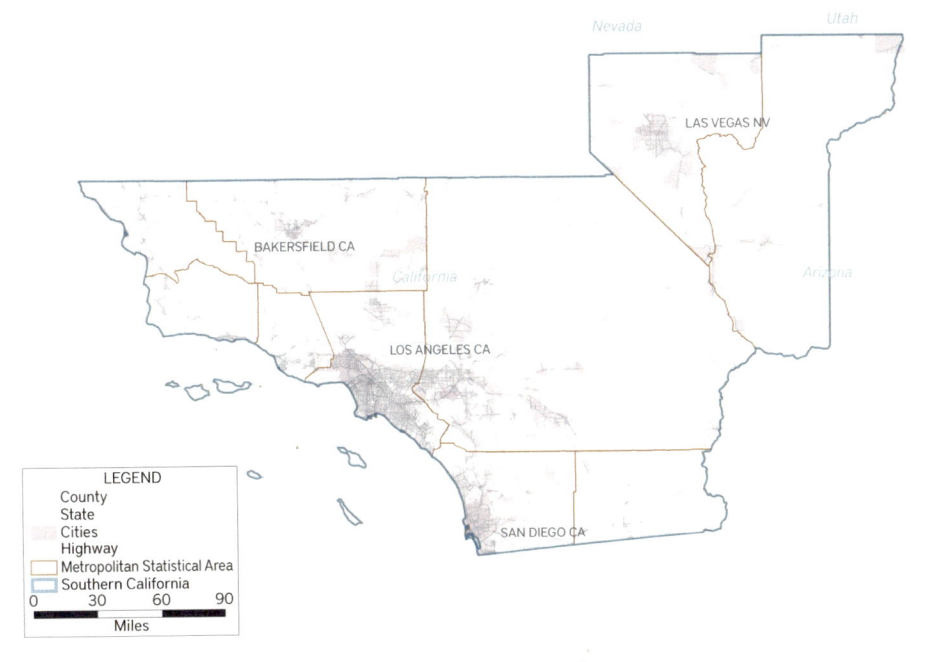

FIGURE 2.12 Southern California megaregion. *Source: Ming Zhang.*

FIGURE 2.13 Aerial view of Southern California. *Source: NASA, with notations by Aaron O'Neill.*

Table 2.6. Top 10 Metropolitan Areas Ranked by GDP in the Southern California Megaregion, 2018

	Area (sq. miles)	Population (millions)	Jobs (millions)	GDP (billions)
Los Angeles–Long Beach–Anaheim, CA	4,888.15	13.291	8.890	1,047.661
San Diego–Chula Vista–Carlsbad, CA	4,239.66	3.343	2.177	245.139
Riverside–San Bernardino–Ontario, CA	27,412.53	4.622	2.128	187.109
Las Vegas–Henderson–Paradise, NV	8,095.00	2.232	1.351	122.424
Oxnard–Thousand Oaks–Ventura, CA	1,857.32	0.851	0.476	59.631
Bakersfield, CA	8,161.27	0.897	0.425	49.514
Santa Maria–Santa Barbara, CA	2,749.79	0.447	0.282	30.192
San Luis Obispo–Paso Robles, CA	3,319.43	0.284	0.176	18.521
El Centro, CA	4,483.93	0.182	0.081	8.445
Lake Havasu City–Kingman, AZ	13,459.61	0.210	0.072	5.689
Total	78,666.69	26.36	16.06	1,774.33

Source: U.S. Bureau of Economic Analysis (2019).

equivalent units), respectively, ranking them as the two busiest ports in the United States (Burnson 2019). The San Ysidro port of entry between San Diego, California, and Tijuana, Mexico, is also the busiest land-border crossing point between the United States and Mexico. Northbound traffic (from Mexico to California) through this port averages 70,000 vehicle passengers and 20,000 pedestrians daily (Snibbe 2019). Los Angeles International Airport is the second-busiest airport in the United States, handling 84.5 million passengers in 2019. These ports serve as gateways to Southern California and the rest of the country. Maintaining efficient operations of these ports and the region's infrastructure systems is critical to not only travelers and shippers but also the economic activities in Southern California and beyond.

Cascadia

Cascadia generally denotes a bioregion that, most broadly defined, stretches from Northern California to coastal Alaska. The Cascadia megaregion comprises the northwestern corner of the United States, including portions of Oregon, Washington, and the adjacent Canadian province of British Columbia (figure 2.14). The megaregion on the U.S. side consists of 36 counties and 21 MSAs, with a total area of 58,590 square miles (figure 2.15). In 2018, the Cascadia megaregion was home to 9.59 million people and 6.01 million jobs. The region generated a GDP of $707.45 billion, comparable to Switzerland, whose GDP ranked 20th worldwide by national economic output. Table 2.7 lists the 10 largest MSAs. Principal cities in the region are Seattle, Portland, and Vancouver.

FIGURE 2.14 Aerial view of Cascadia megaregion. *Source: NASA, with notations by Aaron O'Neill.*

U.S. MEGAREGIONS | 45

FIGURE 2.15 Cascadia megaregion. *Source: Ming Zhang.*

The major cities and metros in Cascadia have not continuously urbanized spatially as have those in the Northeast megaregion. The Cascadia megaregion is dotted with urban areas separated by rural areas and wildlands. Researchers and planners refer to Cascadia as an *ecolopolis* or *ecotopia* because of these morphological and ecological assets. They propose strengthening its unique character by improving connectivity between metros and cities (ideally by high-speed rail) and maintaining

Table 2.7. Top 10 Metropolitan Areas Ranked by GDP in the Cascadia Megaregion, 2018

	Area (sq. miles)	Population (millions)	Jobs (millions)	GDP (billions)
Seattle-Tacoma-Bellevue, WA	5,935.55	3.939	2.683	392.037
Portland-Vancouver-Hillsboro, OR-WA	6,801.59	2.479	1.613	164.420
Salem, OR	1,934.00	0.432	0.228	18.258
Eugene-Springfield, OR	4,607.23	0.380	0.212	17.205
Kennewick-Richland, WA	3,017.73	0.296	0.156	15.345
Bellingham, WA	2,156.26	0.226	0.129	14.640
Olympia-Lacey-Tumwater, WA	733.88	0.286	0.155	14.065
Yakima, WA	4,301.41	0.251	0.136	10.517
Bend, OR	3,048.75	0.192	0.131	9.327
Mount Vernon–Anacortes, WA	1,749.61	0.128	0.071	8.114
Total	34,286.00	8.61	5.51	663.93

Source: U.S. Bureau of Economic Analysis (2019).

separation by preserving the functional and wild landscapes between them (PSU 2010).

Central Plains

The Central Plains megaregion combines 118 counties and 20 MSAs from the four states of Oklahoma, Kansas, Missouri, and Arkansas (figure 2.16). Together, these counties and MSAs occupy 84,270 square miles. In 2018, they had a population of 8.9 million and 5.45 million jobs and produced a GDP of $469.49 billion. Table 2.8 lists the megaregion's top 10 metropolitan areas ranked by GDP in 2018.

The westernmost portion of this megaregion in the U.S. heartland is within the EPA Level III ecoregions of Central Great Plains, Central Irregular Plains, and Western Corn Belt Plains; its eastern portion is within the ecoregions of Ouachita Mountains, Arkansas Valley, Boston Mountains, and Ozark Highlands. These plains and highlands support extensive dry farming and cattle ranching, and its contribution to U.S. food and agricultural supplies and securities makes the Central Plains an important megaregion.

Railroad development brought prosperity to the Central Plains' cities and counties in the 19th century. Today, the region still has an extensive railroad network, ranking it third among all megaregions (after the Great Lakes and Northeast) in railroad length per square mile of land area. The region's historical prosperity dwindled when agriculture production and railroads lost their relative significance to the nation's economy and transportation systems. Nevertheless, the region's agriculture and food production base and its rail infrastructure are strong assets in reinventing the Central Plains.

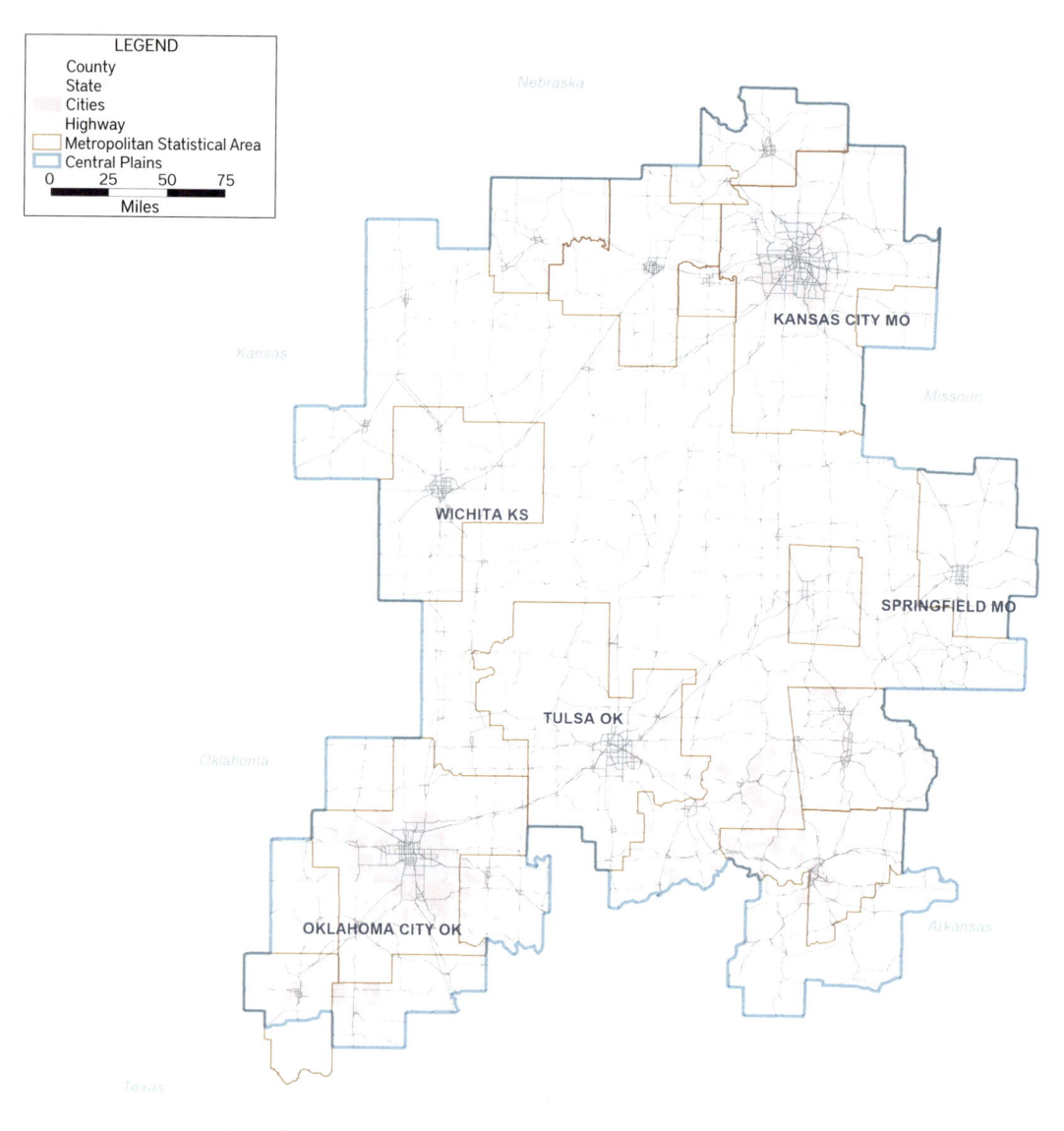

FIGURE 2.16 Central Plains megaregion. *Source: Ming Zhang.*

Florida

The Florida megaregion's morphological character derives from its peninsular geography: multiple chains of urbanized areas, mostly along the coast and some through the center, intertwined with many "green hearts" such as Three Lakes Wildlife Area, Ocala National Forest, and Okefenokee National Wildlife Refuge (figures 2.17 and 2.18). The Everglades National Park and the Everglades ecosystem, generally, have been the focus of conservation efforts since the 1930s. The future of south Florida largely rests on the health of this fragile ecosystem.

Table 2.8. Top 10 Metropolitan Areas Ranked by GDP in the Central Plains Megaregion, 2018

	Area (sq. miles)	Population (millions)	Jobs (millions)	GDP (billions)
Kansas City, MO-KS	7,367.21	2.144	1.408	132.704
Oklahoma City, OK	5,581.52	1.396	0.889	81.017
Tulsa, OK	6,458.77	0.994	0.614	57.233
Wichita, KS	4,179.17	0.638	0.399	36.699
Fayetteville-Springdale-Rogers, AR	2,672.89	0.526	0.322	25.718
Springfield, MO	3,019.35	0.467	0.288	20.296
Topeka, KS	3,287.15	0.233	0.146	11.322
Fort Smith, AR-OK	2,484.10	0.250	0.135	9.671
Joplin, MO	1,267.39	0.179	0.104	7.747
Manhattan, KS	1,886.65	0.131	0.091	7.079
Total	38,204.18	6.96	4.39	389.48

Source: U.S. Bureau of Economic Analysis (2019).

FIGURE 2.17 Rush hour on a highway leading into Miami. *Source: istock.com/CHUYN.*

The megaregion consists of 44 counties and 25 MSAs over an area of 41,030 square miles. In 2018, this rapidly growing megaregion had nearly 20 million people and 11.57 million jobs and produced a GDP of $969.34 billion. Table 2.9 lists the megaregion's top 10 metropolitan areas ranked by GDP in 2018.

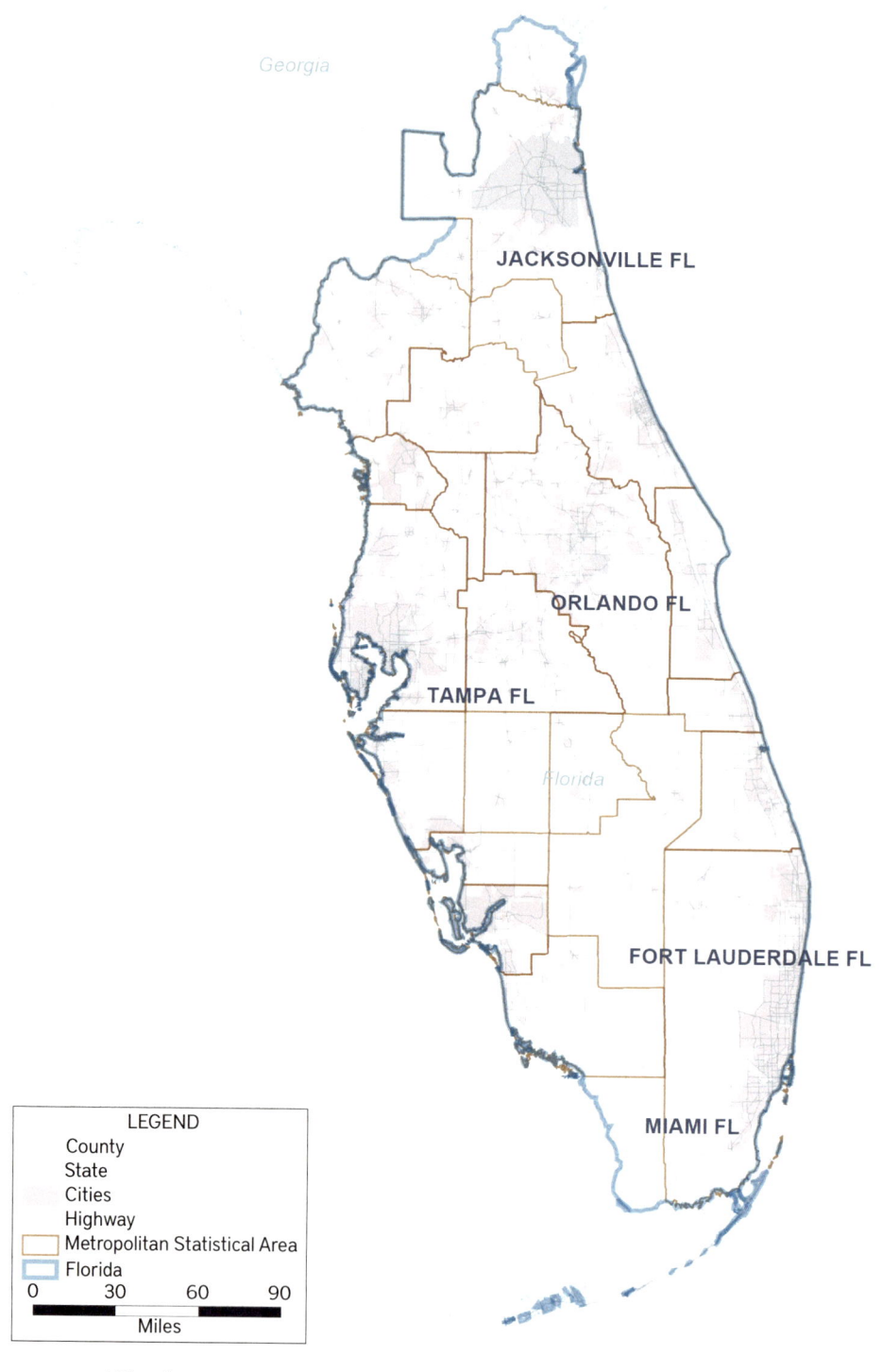

FIGURE 2.18 Florida megaregion. *Source: Ming Zhang.*

Table 2.9. Top 10 Metropolitan Areas Ranked by GDP in the Florida Megaregion, 2018

	Area (sq. miles)	Population (millions)	Jobs (millions)	GDP (billions)
Miami–Fort Lauderdale–Pompano Beach	5,438.60	6.199	4.069	354.740
Tampa–St. Petersburg–Clearwater	2,616.29	3.143	1.828	159.003
Orlando-Kissimmee-Sanford	4,016.98	2.573	1.712	138.948
Jacksonville	3,423.80	1.535	0.935	83.187
North Port–Sarasota–Bradenton	1,332.89	0.822	0.447	34.278
Cape Coral–Fort Myers	820.46	0.755	0.390	30.584
Palm Bay–Melbourne–Titusville	1,296.24	0.597	0.303	25.676
Lakeland–Winter Haven	2,013.61	0.708	0.310	25.268
Deltona–Daytona Beach–Ormond Beach	1,775.04	0.660	0.295	20.972
Naples–Marco Island	2,041.54	0.378	0.230	17.911
Total	24,775.47	17.37	10.52	890.56

Source: U.S. Bureau of Economic Analysis (2019).

The Sunshine State megaregion attracts more retirees than any other U.S. state. Renowned for its warm-water beaches, amusement parks, and other recreational destinations, it also attracts millions of visitors every year. Further, the region's location makes Miami and other Florida cities gateways to Latin America. The Florida megaregion features arguably the first and the only privately owned high-speed rail line in the United States. The Brightline intercity rail system began its first phase of operations, passenger services between Fort Lauderdale and West Palm Beach, in 2017. The full alignment of three phases will connect Miami, Fort Lauderdale, West Palm Beach, Tampa, and Orlando International Airport, for a total track length of more than 300 miles (the COVID-19 pandemic shutdowns in 2020 suspended rail services and may delay the construction of future phases).

Front Range

Geologically, the Front Range refers to the Rocky Mountains between the southern Rockies and the High Plains in the west-central United States (figure 2.19). The Front Range megaregion extends from Albuquerque, New Mexico, in the south to Cheyenne, Wyoming, in the north, aligning 31 counties and 15 MSAs in a corridor approximately 125 miles wide (east–west) and 500 miles long (north–south). Interstate 25 goes through the corridor, providing essential ground connectivity in the region. The 2018 census data reported 6.18 million people, 4.08 million jobs, and an economy of $385.19 billion in GDP for the Front Range, making it one of the three smallest megaregions in the United States. Despite its relatively small size, the Front

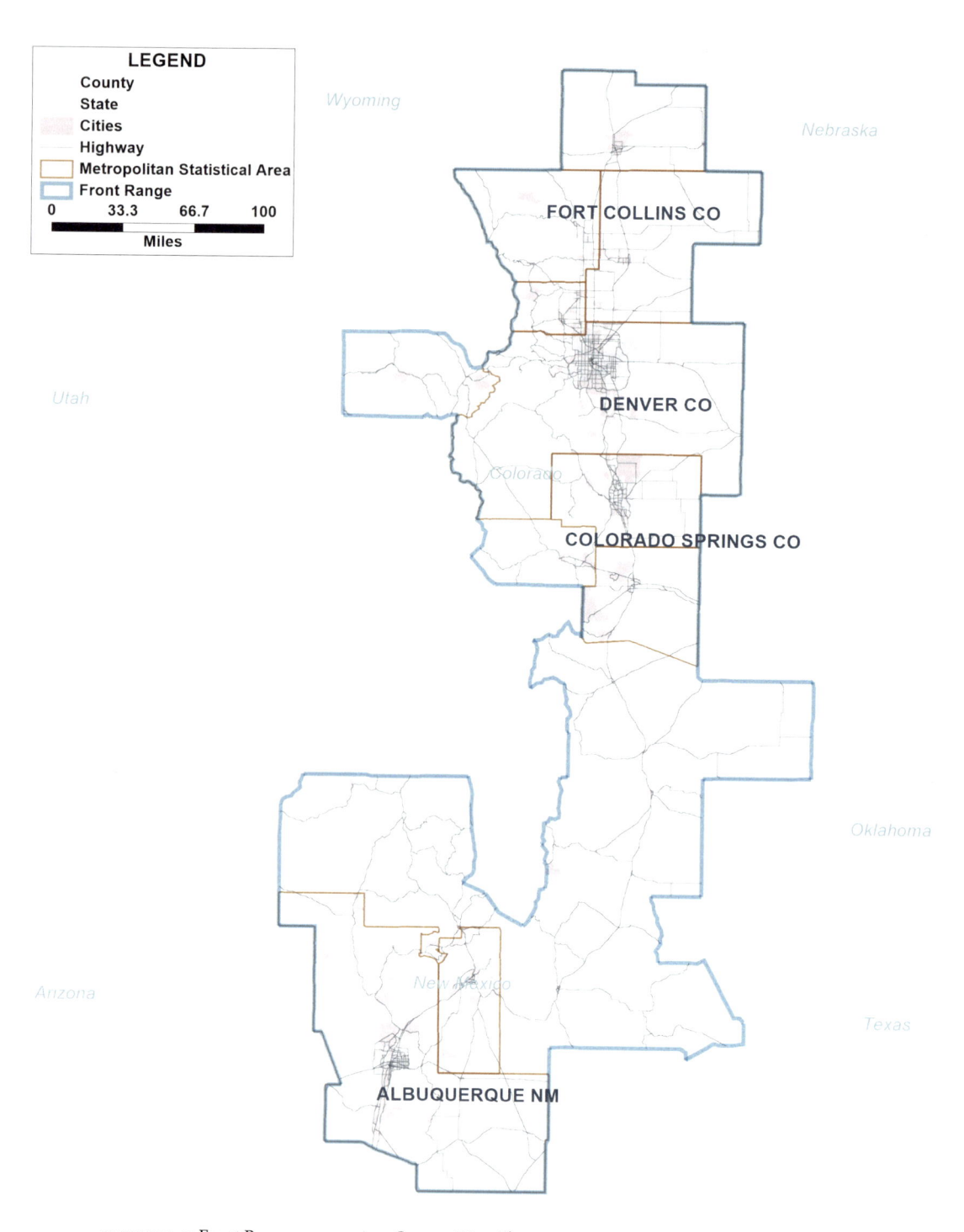

FIGURE 2.19 Front Range megaregion. *Source: Ming Zhang.*

Table 2.10. Top 10 Metropolitan Areas Ranked by GDP in the Front Range Megaregion, 2018

	Area (sq. miles)	Population (millions)	Jobs (millions)	GDP (billions)
Denver-Aurora-Lakewood, CO	8,379.63	2.863	2.041	205.383
Albuquerque, NM	9,297.51	0.916	0.510	42.896
Colorado Springs, CO	2,686.35	0.739	0.436	37.939
Boulder, CO	750.34	0.326	0.275	27.534
Greeley, CO	4,016.85	0.314	0.162	19.760
Fort Collins, CO	2,630.74	0.351	0.240	18.783
Pueblo, CO	2,396.23	0.168	0.081	6.888
Santa Fe, NM	1,910.75	0.150	0.095	6.685
Cheyenne, WY	2,683.86	0.099	0.070	5.743
Edwards, CO	1,690.07	0.055	0.049	3.903
Total	36,442.32	5.98	3.96	375.51

Source: U.S. Bureau of Economic Analysis (2019).

Range is one of the fastest-growing U.S. megaregions. Table 2.10 lists the megaregion's top 10 metropolitan areas ranked by GDP in 2018.

The megaregion offers popular recreational and tourist destinations, attracting mountain bikers, hikers, climbers, and campers in the summer and skiers and snowboarders in the winter. Colorado ranked fourth, following Massachusetts, Virginia, and Washington, in concentration of high-tech workers in the nation (Schwartz 2019).

Denver, the city and county, is a national front-runner in transit-oriented development. Partnering with transit operators, transportation planning agencies, and local communities, the Denver region has been planning and implementing ambitious transit-oriented development to achieve regional sustainable transportation and land development (COD 2014).

Great Lakes

Among the 13 U.S. megaregions identified in this study, the Great Lakes is the largest in area (229,500 square miles) and in number of constituent counties (422) and MSAs (179) (figures 2.20 and 2.21). Over this massive area, metros, cities, and towns spread and form an extensive system of agglomerations that is well characterized as a "network-galaxy" by Banerjee (2009, 93). Three defining factors tie these communities together to make one recognized megaregion: (1) the geoecological landscape of the five naturally interconnected freshwater lakes; (2) the sweeping impact of Thomas Jefferson's Northwest Ordinances of the 1780s; and (3) the communities' shared industrial past. Table 2.11 lists the megaregion's top 10 metropolitan areas ranked by GDP in 2018.

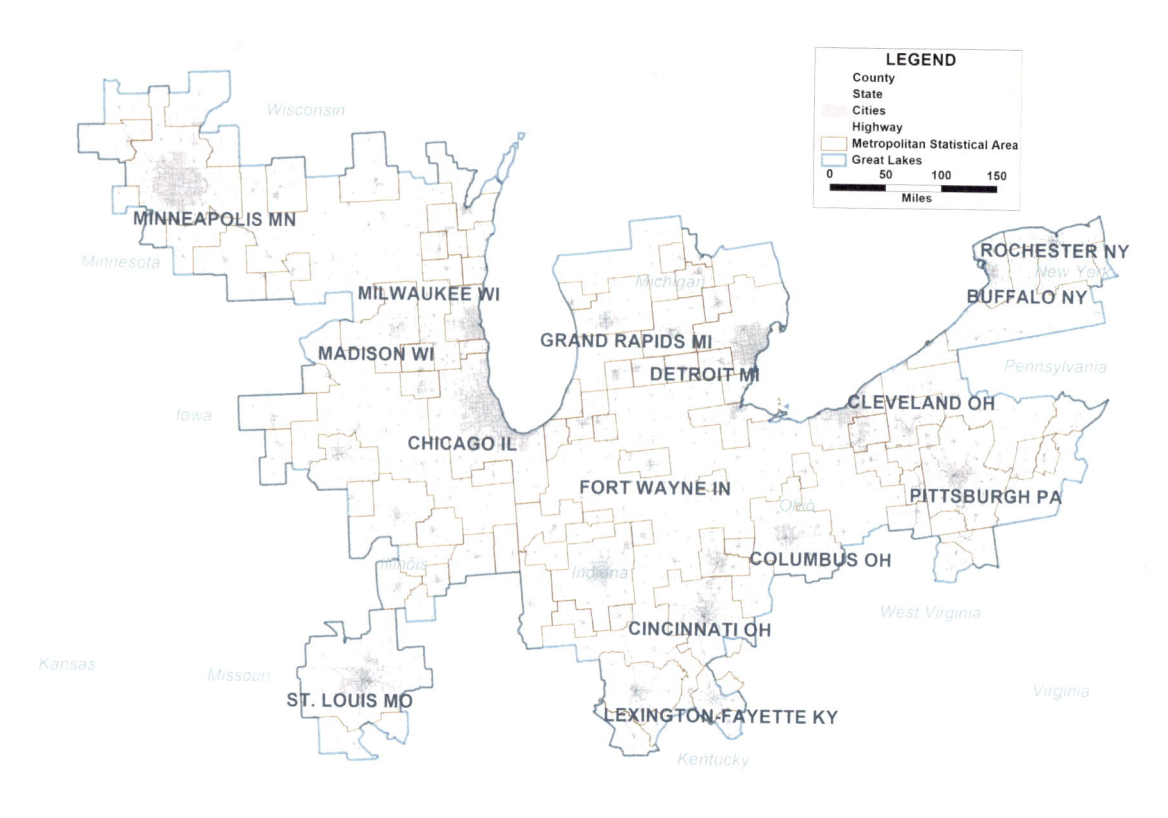

FIGURE 2.20 Great Lakes megaregion. *Source: Ming Zhang.*

Once the industrial heartland of the United States, the megaregion has been declining because of deindustrialization and the flight of manufacturing jobs. Some cities—Chicago, Indianapolis, and Columbus, for example—have successfully transformed their economies to specialize in service and high-tech industries. Other cities—Detroit, Dayton, and Toledo, for instance—continue to shrink and decline. Many medium or small cities and towns are also struggling, being bypassed by new investments and development opportunities in the late 20th and early 21st centuries. Regenerating these communities through megaregional coordination must be addressed collectively by public and private leaders from across the Great Lakes megaregion.

Yet, the Great Lakes has tremendous assets and potential. The megaregion has abundant freshwater resources for potable water, recreational, and energy industry uses and some of the richest soils on the planet. The region could also reinvent itself and regenerate by building on its industrial heritage (Germany's Rhine-Ruhr region offers an exemplar). Figure 2.22 illustrates the railroad network in the United States. The Great Lakes region has the highest railroad density, at 15.71 miles per 100 square miles of land area, of any U.S. megaregion. The region's industrialization legacy offers a strong footprint for high-performance rail services to expand passenger and freight movement.

FIGURE 2.21 Aerial view of Chicago and Lake Michigan as dramatic fall weather rolls through. Source: istock.com/Skyhobo.

Table 2.11. Top 10 Metropolitan Areas Ranked by GDP in the Great Lakes Megaregion, 2018

	Area (sq. miles)	Population (millions)	Jobs (millions)	GDP (billions)
Chicago-Naperville-Elgin, IL-IN-WI	7,291.81	9.499	6.187	689.465
Detroit-Warren-Dearborn, MI	3,975.91	4.326	2.629	267.731
Minneapolis–St. Paul–Bloomington, MN-WI	7,502.15	3.614	2.546	263.691
St. Louis, MO-IL	8,075.59	2.805	1.798	169.839
Pittsburgh, PA	5,336.29	2.325	1.504	152.841
Cincinnati, OH-KY-IN	4,626.59	2.213	1.398	141.053
Indianapolis-Carmel-Anderson, IN	4,336.25	2.049	1.355	140.762
Cleveland-Elyria, OH	2,014.40	2.057	1.351	134.370
Columbus, OH	4,846.02	2.107	1.401	129.328
Milwaukee-Waukesha, WI	1,490.21	1.576	1.068	103.732
Total	49,495.21	32.57	21.24	2192.81

Source: U.S. Bureau of Economic Analysis (2019).

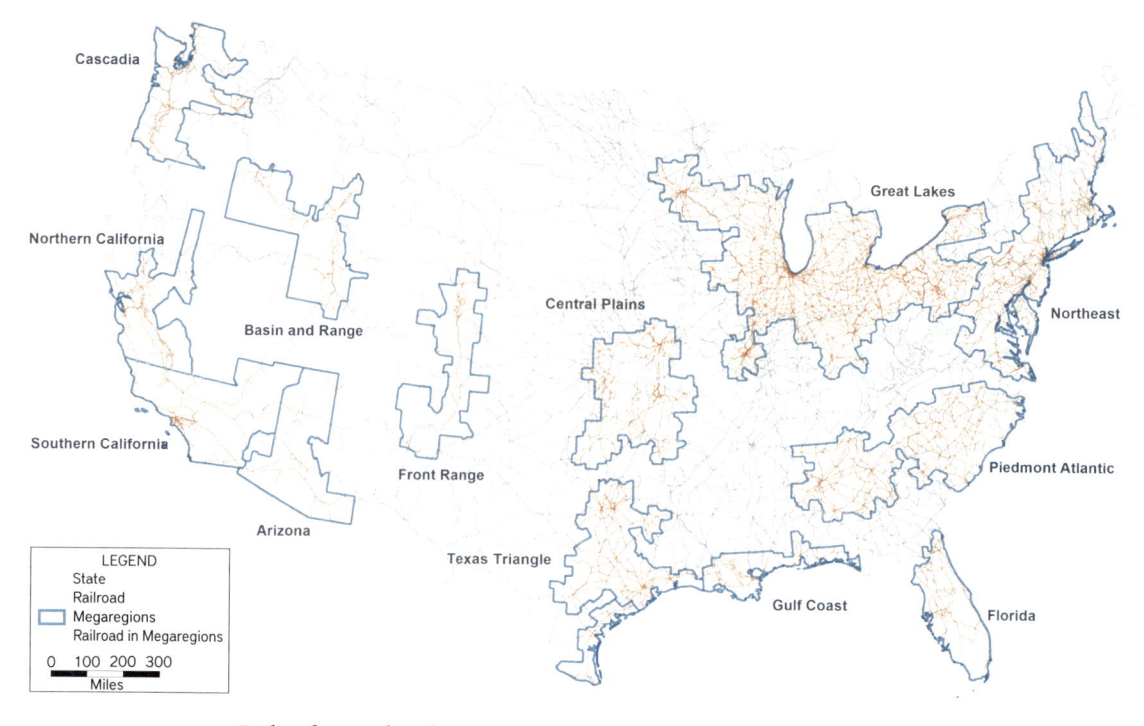

FIGURE 2.22 Railroad network in the United States. *Source: Ming Zhang.*

The binational Great Lakes megaregion borders Canada with multiple land-, water-, and air-based ports of entry. The crossing points in Detroit, Michigan, and Buffalo, New York, are among the top 20 busiest land ports of entry in the nation. Megaregional thinking for the Great Lakes should go beyond the boundaries delineated here and reach out to the other side of the U.S.-Canada border.

Gulf Coast

The Gulf Coast megaregion extends along 1,000 miles of the coastline of the Gulf of Mexico, stretching from Brownsville, Texas, on the southwest end to Panama City, Florida, at the east end (figure 2.23). The linear megaregion on its U.S. side consists of 69 counties and 27 MSAs, out of which 14 counties in 3 MSAs (Houston and Port Arthur in Texas and Lake Charles in Louisiana) overlap with the Texas Triangle and are omitted here. The Gulf Coast megaregion covers 55,500 square miles and had 14.8 million people and 8.66 million jobs in 2018. The megaregion's GDP totaled $869.86 billion, to which the Houston metro area contributed around 55 percent. Table 2.12 lists the top 10 metropolitan areas in the Gulf Coast (not counting the three MSAs overlapping the Texas Triangle).

What links this diverse group of counties and MSAs is their vulnerability to natural disasters, especially hurricanes, which have been threatening the coastal communities at a rate increasing every year since 1994. The most devastating ones at the time

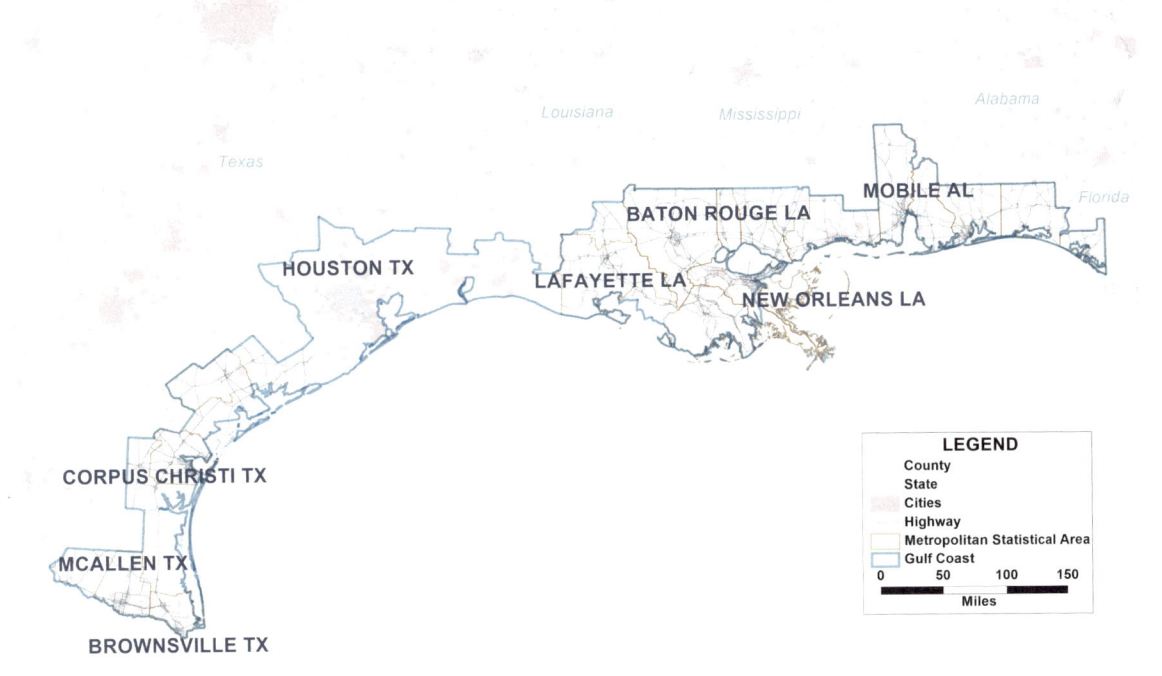

FIGURE 2.23 Gulf Coast megaregion. *Source: Ming Zhang.*

Table 2.12. Top 10 Metropolitan Areas Ranked by GDP in the Gulf Coast Megaregion, 2018

	Area (sq. miles)	Population (millions)	Jobs (millions)	GDP (billions)
New Orleans–Metairie, LA	3,807.17	1.270	0.812	80.287
Baton Rouge, LA	4,534.60	0.854	0.537	56.316
McAllen-Edinburg-Mission, TX	1,585.60	0.866	0.386	23.349
Corpus Christi, TX	1,553.90	0.429	0.255	23.169
Lafayette, LA	3,671.17	0.489	0.291	22.996
Mobile, AL	2,347.12	0.430	0.245	20.861
Pensacola–Ferry Pass–Brent, FL	1,694.13	0.495	0.254	20.389
Gulfport-Biloxi, MS	2,259.65	0.416	0.220	19.357
Crestview–Fort Walton Beach–Destin, FL	2,008.12	0.279	0.178	14.677
Brownsville-Harlingen, TX	946.14	0.424	0.196	11.339
Total	24,407.60	5.95	3.37	292.74

Source: U.S. Bureau of Economic Analysis (2019).

of writing, Hurricane Harvey in 2017 and Hurricane Katrina in 2005, caused more than $200 billion in damage and more than 1,000 deaths. Hurricanes displace households and businesses regularly, and across city, county, and state lines. Hurricanes are predicted to increase in number and severity with global climate change because the Gulf of Mexico is especially susceptible to warming. Building resilience cannot be achieved by the individual cities or metro areas alone. Megaregional coordination offers a solution.

Piedmont Atlantic

The Piedmont Atlantic megaregion gained its name from the Piedmont plateau, an EPA Level III ecoregion between the Atlantic coastal plain and the central Appalachian Mountains (figure 2.24). In this study, the Piedmont Atlantic extends east to include counties and MSAs in the next two ecoregions, Middle Atlantic Coastal Plain and Southeastern Plains. The newly identified Piedmont Atlantic megaregion consists of 221 counties, 80 MSAs, 26.81 million people, and 15.9 million jobs spread over 116,070 square miles. The region produced $1,468.38 billion GDP in 2018. Table 2.13 lists the megaregion's top 10 metropolitan areas ranked by GDP in 2018.

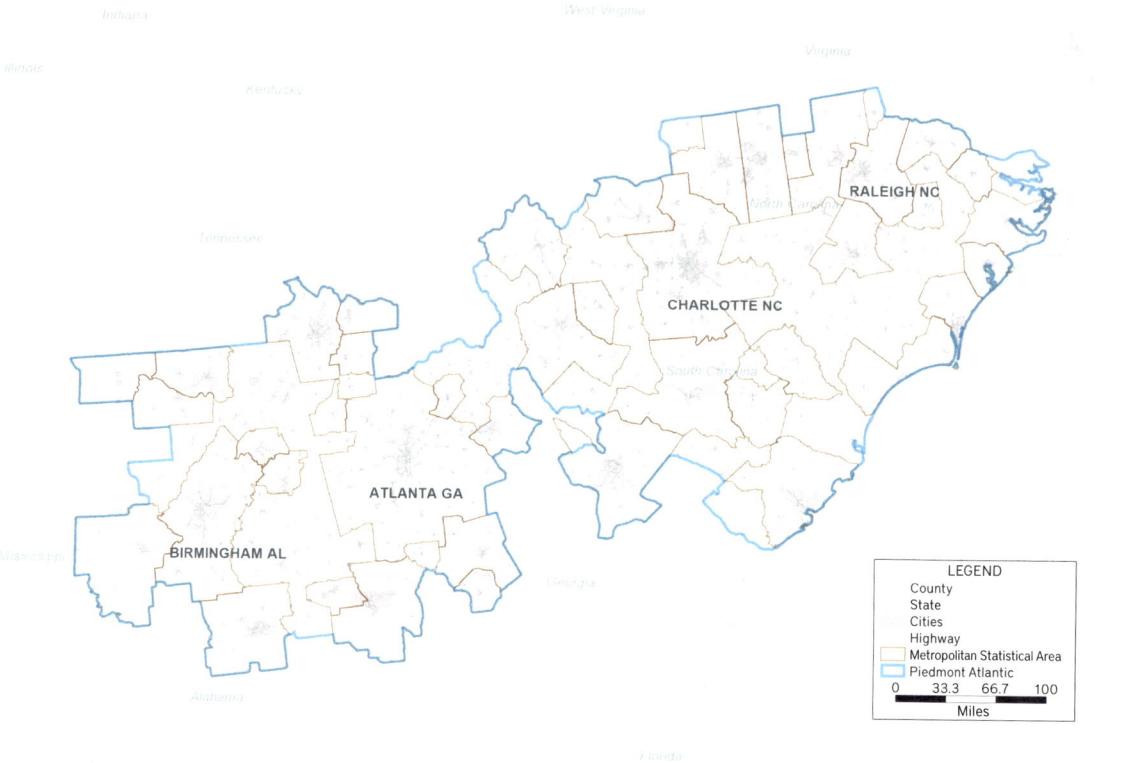

FIGURE 2.24 Piedmont Atlantic megaregion. *Source: Ming Zhang.*

Table 2.13. Top 10 Metropolitan Areas Ranked by GDP in the Piedmont Atlantic Megaregion, 2018

	Area (sq. miles)	Population (millions)	Jobs (millions)	GDP (billions)
Atlanta–Sandy Springs–Alpharetta, GA	8,838.66	5.950	3.875	397.261
Charlotte-Concord-Gastonia, NC-SC	5,716.13	2.594	1.639	169.863
Raleigh-Cary, NC	2,147.42	1.363	0.875	83.666
Birmingham-Hoover, AL	4,566.38	1.088	0.669	62.881
Durham–Chapel Hill, NC	2,349.48	0.636	0.446	54.687
Greenville-Anderson, SC	2,788.52	0.907	0.545	46.431
Greensboro–High Point, NC	2,019.18	0.768	0.478	43.155
Columbia, SC	3,834.78	0.833	0.512	43.119
Charleston–North Charleston, SC	2,817.95	0.788	0.500	42.709
Winston-Salem, NC	2,039.73	0.671	0.361	33.974
Total	37,118.22	15.60	9.90	977.75

Source: U.S. Bureau of Economic Analysis (2019).

Agglomerations in the Piedmont Atlantic megaregion exhibit a galaxy pattern, like that of the Great Lakes megaregion. This area has been experiencing rapid population growth, mainly due to the relatively low cost of living and high quality of life it offers. However, the region's transportation infrastructure has not kept pace with its rapid population and job growth, resulting in severe airport runway and highway congestion and associated air pollution.

Hartsfield-Jackson Atlanta International Airport was the busiest airport in the world before the COVID-19 pandemic, handling over 110 million passengers in 2019. Delta Airlines, which is headquartered in Atlanta, handles a high proportion of passenger traffic there. The Atlanta airport ranks 11th by area in the United States, covering 4,700 acres of land, less than one-seventh of the area for Denver International Airport. Because of this high volume-to-area ratio, Atlanta airport has earned a reputation for being the most efficient airport in the world. Yet, airport congestion has been worsening.

Cities in the Piedmont Atlantic megaregion also suffer from highway congestion. The 2019 Urban Mobility Report (Schrank, Eisele, and Lomax 2019) released by the Texas A&M Transportation Institute reports an average 77 hours spent each year in traffic delays, ranking as the eighth worst in the United States. Finding sustainable solutions to congestion calls for coordination among the member cities and metros in the megaregion.

Northeast

The Northeast megaregion is a linear conurbation along the northern Atlantic coast of the United States and is the inspiration for the megaregion concept (figure 2.25). Gottmann's (1961, 4) study on the U.S. megalopolis observes that it is an "almost continuous system of deeply interwoven urban and suburban areas" stretching more than 600 miles between Portland, Maine, and Norfolk, Virginia. The RPA in its 1967 study referred to the area as the "Atlantic Urban Region" (Shore 1967). Also in 1967, the American futurist Herman Kahn nicknamed the megalopolis "BosWash," a portmanteau word blending "Boston" and "Washington, DC," marking the northern and southern core metros of the corridor (Kahn and Wiener 1967, 719).

Early in this century, joint studies of the Northeast region by the Lincoln Institute of Land Policy and the Weitzman School of Design at Penn renewed interest in the megalopolis notion and instigated a new wave of megaregion study. Despite the common recognition of the Northeast as a mega-agglomeration, the exact delineation of the Northeast megaregion varies among different scholars and organizations. This study adapts the RPA–Lincoln Institute–Penn definition of the Northeast megaregion, with minor modifications when considering the border counties.

In this study, the Northeast megaregion comprises 242 counties, 272 cities, 551 towns or villages, and 696 boroughs across a geography of 14 states plus Washington, DC, making the most heavily and densely populated megaregion in the United States. Its land area of 111,360 square miles accounts for only 3.1 percent of the total U.S. land area but houses 61.36 million, or over 18.8 percent, of the U.S. population. Because it contributes more than 22.45 percent of U.S. GDP, the Northeast megaregion deserves the title of economic powerhouse for the United States. In 2018, the Northeast offered more than 38.5 million jobs and produced a GDP of $4.54 trillion, slightly larger than the GDP of Germany. Five major metro areas—Boston, New York, Philadelphia, Baltimore, and Washington, DC—are the engines for the region's economic power. Table 2.14 lists the Northeast megaregion's top 10 metropolitan areas ranked by GDP in 2018 and their land areas, populations, and jobs. The sum of GDP for these 10 major metros ($3.73 trillion) accounts for 80.6 percent of the Northeast's total.

Texas Triangle

Five major Texas cities—Dallas, Fort Worth, Houston, San Antonio, and Austin, all ranked among the 15 largest U.S. cities by population—shape the Texas Triangle (figure 2.26). The western edge, from Dallas–Fort Worth to San Antonio, measures 271 miles; the southern base, from San Antonio to Houston, is 197 miles; and the eastern edge, from Houston to Dallas–Fort Worth, is 241 miles. Austin is approximately one-third of the way north from San Antonio to Dallas–Fort Worth along the western edge.

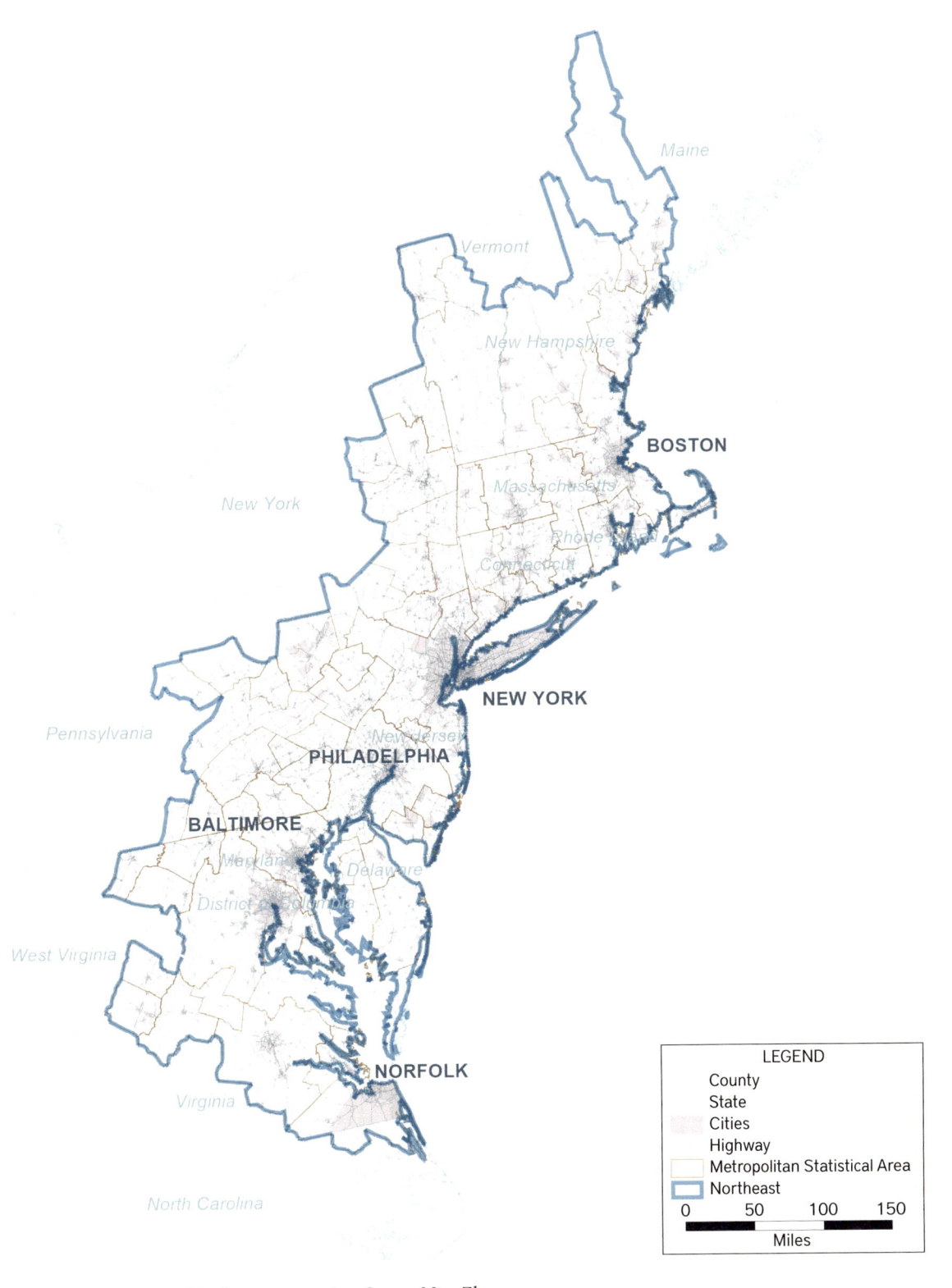

FIGURE 2.25 Northeast megaregion. *Source: Ming Zhang.*

Table 2.14. Top 10 Metropolitan Areas by GDP in the Northeast Megaregion, 2018

	Area (sq. miles)	Population (millions)	Jobs (millions)	GDP (billions)
New York–Newark–Jersey City, NY-NJ-PA	6,909.35	19.30	12.92	1,772.32
Boston-Cambridge-Newton, MA-NH	3,607.03	4.88	3.69	463.57
Philadelphia-Camden-Wilmington, PA-NJ-DE-MD	4,697.17	6.10	3.86	444.15
Washington-Arlington-Alexandria, DC-VA-MD-WV	6,642.82	6.26	3.18	400.01
Baltimore-Columbia-Towson, MD	2,634.29	2.80	1.87	205.31
Hartford–East Hartford–Middletown, CT	1,548.95	1.21	0.83	99.47
Virginia Beach–Norfolk–Newport News, VA-NC	3,612.79	1.77	0.99	92.85
Bridgeport-Stamford-Norwalk, CT	644.35	0.94	0.67	89.39
Providence-Warwick, RI-MA	1,645.66	1.62	0.95	87.41
Richmond, VA	4,454.03	1.28	0.78	78.50
Total	36,396.45	46.16	29.73	3,732.98

Source: U.S. Bureau of Economic Analysis (2019).

The name *Texas Triangle* has a long history. About 140 years ago, the region's first freight trains connected the triangle cities, boosting their initial growth. According to Barry Popik (2007), an etymologist, the term appeared as early as 1936 when the Missouri Pacific Railroad announced its new overnight services from Saint Louis and Memphis to link Dallas, Fort Worth, Houston, Austin, and San Antonio. The Missouri Pacific, one of the first railroads west of the Mississippi River, operated passenger train services in the Southwest in the early years of the 20th century. The Texas Triangle was one section of the Missouri Pacific's premier name services, the "Sunshine Special" service. Today, the Texas Triangle passenger train service no longer exists. Three interstate highways, Interstate 35, Interstate 45, and Interstate 10, provide intercity connections and delineate the Triangle, as shown in figure 2.26. To the general public, Texas Triangle more often means the National Basketball Association teams of the Dallas Mavericks, the Houston Rockets, and the San Antonio Spurs. Whether referring to the historical train services or the contemporary basketball games, Texas Triangle has gradually come to denote a place brand for the cluster of agglomerations in Texas.

Post–World War II economic and population growth have led to increased interaction between communities within the original triangle cities and their neighboring communities. In our delineation, the Texas Triangle megaregion extends east to include Tyler and Longview at the northern end because of their strong economic

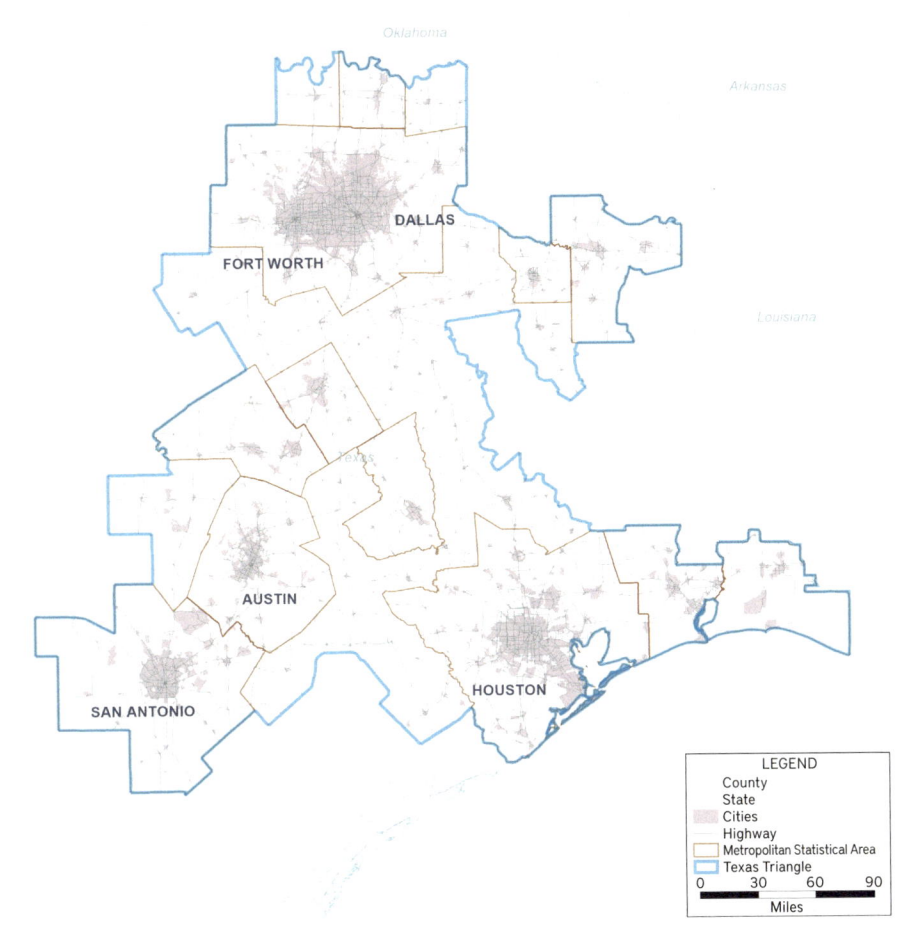

FIGURE 2.26 Texas Triangle megaregion. *Source: Ming Zhang.*

ties with the Dallas–Fort Worth area. The southeast vertex of the Triangle extends east from the Houston metropolitan area to Port Arthur, Texas, and Lake Charles, Louisiana. The Texas Triangle and Gulf Coast megaregions are the only overlapping pair of megaregions of the 13, sharing the three metropolitan areas of Houston, Port Arthur, and Lake Charles.

The Texas Triangle covers 69,820 square miles, slightly more than two-thirds of the total area of the United Kingdom. Within this geography are 80 counties, 544 cities, and 12 metropolitan areas. As part of the Sunbelt, the Texas Triangle has experienced continuing growth since the 1970s. In 2018, the megaregion was home to 22.35 million people, offered more than 14 million jobs, and produced a GDP of $1.438 trillion. Table 2.15 lists the Texas Triangle's top 10 metropolitan areas ranked by GDP in 2018 and their land areas, population, and jobs. The sum of GDP for the top four major metros ($1.272 trillion) accounts for more than 88 percent of the

Table 2.15. Top 10 Metropolitan Areas by GDP in the Texas Triangle Megaregion, 2018

	Area (sq. miles)	Population (millions)	Jobs (millions)	GDP (billions)
Dallas–Fort Worth–Arlington, TX	9,011.22	7.47	5.08	512.51
Houston–The Woodlands–Sugar Land, TX	8,557.12	7.00	4.28	478.78
Austin–Round Rock–Georgetown, TX	4,284.55	2.17	1.51	146.78
San Antonio–New Braunfels, TX	7,394.18	2.52	1.49	133.63
Beaumont–Port Arthur, TX	2,223.47	0.40	0.21	30.68
Killeen-Temple, TX	2,861.15	0.45	0.23	18.84
Lake Charles, LA	2,696.46	0.21	0.15	17.79
Longview, TX	2,724.18	0.29	0.17	16.64
Waco, TX	1,835.59	0.27	0.16	14.29
College Station–Bryan, TX	2,135.60	0.26	0.16	13.25
Total	43,723.51	21.03	13.45	1,383.20

Source: U.S. Bureau of Economic Analysis (2019).

Triangle megaregion's total. The five-county Envision Central Texas (2004) initiative provides an example of how to create growth options within this megaregion.

CONCLUSION

Delineating megaregion boundaries involves both quantitative analysis and qualitative assessment. This chapter describes our working definition of U.S. megaregions and presents their spatial and socioeconomic profiles. These profiles illustrate the baseline standards for identifying a megaregion and the varied forms and character among megaregions. Although all megaregions feature large, diverse urban expanses, each megaregion has unique physical, historical, transportation, and economic ties that result in distinct identities and opportunities. Areas within each megaregion also express differences, some benefiting more and some less from population and economic growth. We focus on some of the social consequences in the next chapter.

PART II
U.S. MEGAREGIONAL TRENDS AND THREATS

3

RISING INEQUALITY AND DECLINING AFFORDABILITY

The cost of liberty is less than the price of repression.
—W.E.B. DU BOIS

IN THIS CHAPTER, we highlight the threats of rising spatial and racial inequality alongside declining affordability. We summarize census data on population counts and aging trends; travel patterns of Generations X, Y, and Z; and megaregional geographies of inequality and poverty.

Any discussion of policy and investment for a sustainable future for U.S. megaregions should begin with an analysis of their long-term demographic and socioeconomic trends. The time frame for megaregional analysis may span years to decades. In this study, we take a time frame of 60 years—30 years back from 2020, to 1990, and 30 years into the future, to 2050. Furthermore, we adopt a generational analysis approach to understand the trending characteristics of megaregion demographics in the United States.

Generations denote cohorts of people of similar ages over a 15- to 20-year period. A person's age is one of the most important variables explaining and predicting their behavior, including travel. Age conveys two important pieces of information about the person: place in the life stage (e.g., youth, workforce, or retired) and membership in the cohort of people born in the same time period. By grouping individuals into age cohorts, researchers can explore what are known as cohort effects and period effects, aside from the individual effects, on the phenomenon in question (Ryder 1965). Cohort effects refer to the variations resulting from the experiences, attitudes, preferences, and values shared by the people in a cohort. Period effects refer to the variations resulting from external factors such as economic cycles, technological innovations, and natural disasters that affect all individuals and cohorts in the specific temporal context.

Historians, sociologists, and the popular press have named the age cohorts born after World War II as baby boomers, Generation X, Generation Y (millennials), and Generation Z. The exact age definitions for these generations vary slightly among scholars and agencies. Most have adopted the definitions suggested by the Pew Research Center (Dimock 2019): baby boomers were born between 1946 and 1964; Generation X, 1965 and 1980; millennials, 1981 and 1996; and Generation Z, 1997 and 2012 (or after).

GROWING POPULATION IN U.S. MEGAREGIONS

Megaregions dominate population growth in the United States. Table 3.1 (left panel) shows the population in the 13 megaregions in 1990 and 2020. In this time, megaregions grew at an average rate of 37.2 percent, nearly twice as high as that in the rest of the nation, at 19.1 percent. Megaregions added more than 75 million people in those three decades.

Among the megaregions, however, the growth trends vary quite significantly. The Florida, Piedmont Atlantic, and Texas Triangle megaregions had the largest population gains, over 10 million each. In percentage terms, Arizona Sun Corridor grew the fastest, with its total population more than doubling in the 30-year period.

Population projections indicate that megaregions will continue to grow 30 years into the future from 2020, although at a pace slower than in the prior three decades. Table 3.1 (right panel) reports two population growth scenarios for U.S. megaregions based on the county-level population projections created by the U.S. Environmental Protection Agency (EPA). Dot density maps shown in figures 3.1a and 3.1b illustrate the population growth in 1990–2020 and 2020–2050, respectively. Within each megaregion, the past population growth and the projected future growth occur largely in the metropolitan counties.

Population changes in each area result from the net changes of four components: birth, death, and in- and out-migration. Environmental and human factors (including public policy interventions) contribute to the components' dynamics, creating uncertainties in population projections, especially for the long-term future. The U.S. Census Bureau publishes population projections only at high levels of aggregation—for instance, nationwide or by state. Some states (Texas, for instance) provide long-term, county-level population projections. Nationwide projections by counties, however, remain largely the exercise of academic researchers (e.g., Hauer 2019; Striessnig et al. 2019) or agency-sponsored, project-based efforts without periodic updates.

The EPA (2017) released county-level population projections for the continental states covering up to 2100, as part of the agency's Integrated Climate and Land Use

Table 3.1. U.S. Megaregion Population Trends, 1990–2050

	1990	2020	Growth	%	S1 (2020)	Growth	%	S2 (2050)	Growth	%
Arizona Sun Corridor	3.34	6.89	3.55	106.1	7.57	0.68	9.8	8.48	1.59	23.0
Basin and Range	2.27	4.24	1.97	86.9	4.84	0.60	14.1	5.34	1.10	25.9
Northern California	11.04	15.44	4.40	39.9	19.62	4.18	27.1	21.94	6.50	42.1
Southern California	19.10	26.42	7.32	38.3	35.40	8.97	34.0	39.09	12.66	47.9
Cascadia	6.15	9.80	3.65	59.4	10.10	0.30	3.0	10.74	0.94	9.6
Central Plains	6.75	9.01	2.26	33.5	9.71	0.70	7.7	10.69	1.68	18.6
Florida	9.88	20.09	10.21	103.4	26.20	6.10	30.4	30.42	10.33	51.4
Front Range	3.68	6.33	2.65	72.0	9.26	2.93	46.3	10.92	4.59	72.5
Great Lakes	53.40	60.32	6.93	13.0	65.67	5.35	8.9	69.90	9.57	15.9
Gulf Coast	5.45	7.25	1.80	33.1	9.46	2.21	30.4	10.69	3.44	47.4
Northeast	51.76	61.50	9.74	18.8	78.19	16.69	27.1	86.55	25.05	40.7
Piedmont Atlantic	17.35	27.47	10.12	58.3	33.37	5.89	21.4	38.59	11.12	40.5
Texas Triangle	12.32	23.02	10.70	86.8	28.71	5.69	24.7	32.88	9.86	42.8
Subtotal	202.50	277.80	75.30	37.2	338.08	60.28	21.7	376.23	98.43	35.4
Nonmegaregion	44.27	52.72	8.45	19.1	45.71	−7.02	−13.3	45.37	−7.35	−13.9
Total	246.76	330.52	83.76	33.9	383.79	53.27	16.1	421.60	91.08	27.6

Sources: Population for (2020) was estimated by the authors using the (1990) and (2019) census counts. EPA (2007); U.S. Census Bureau (1991, 2020a).

Notes: Numbers show population counts in millions.

S1 and S2 refer to two of five projected scenarios by the Environmental Protection Agency that correspond to shared socioeconomic pathways (see text box, "Shared Socioeconomic Pathways"). We selected S1 for its projected population total in 2020 that is closest to the observed U.S. population and S2 because it assumes the fastest growth rate.

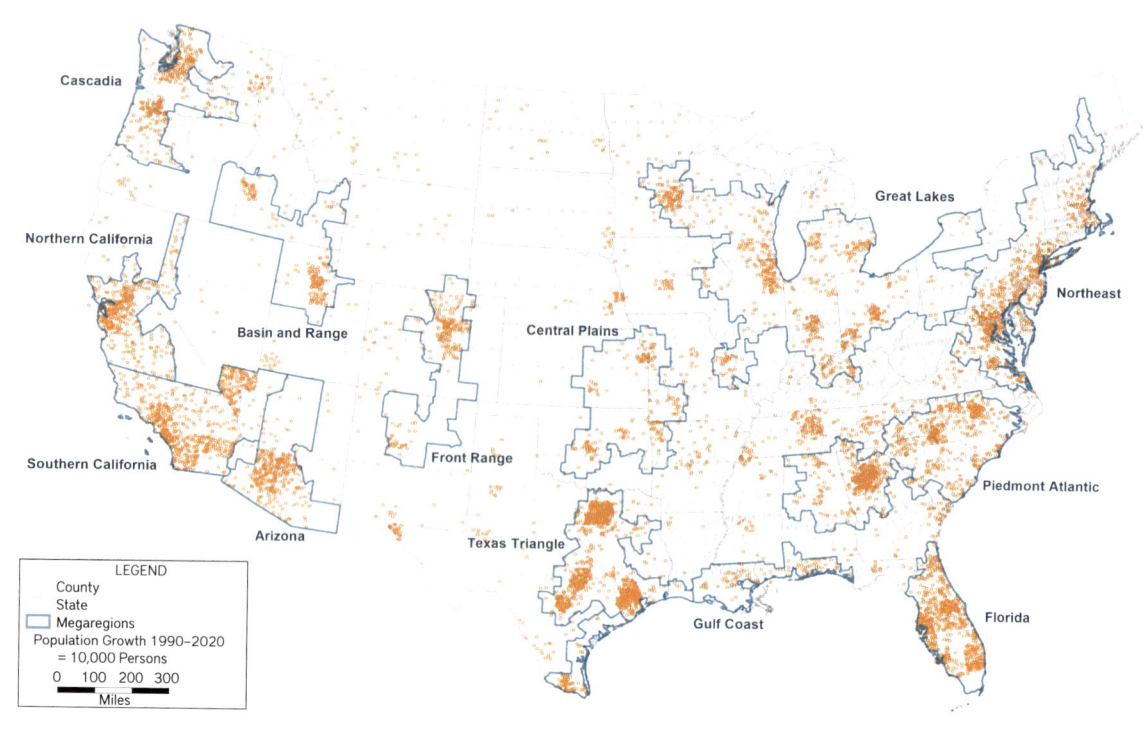

FIGURE 3.1A U.S. megaregion population growth, 1990–2020. *Source: Ming Zhang.*

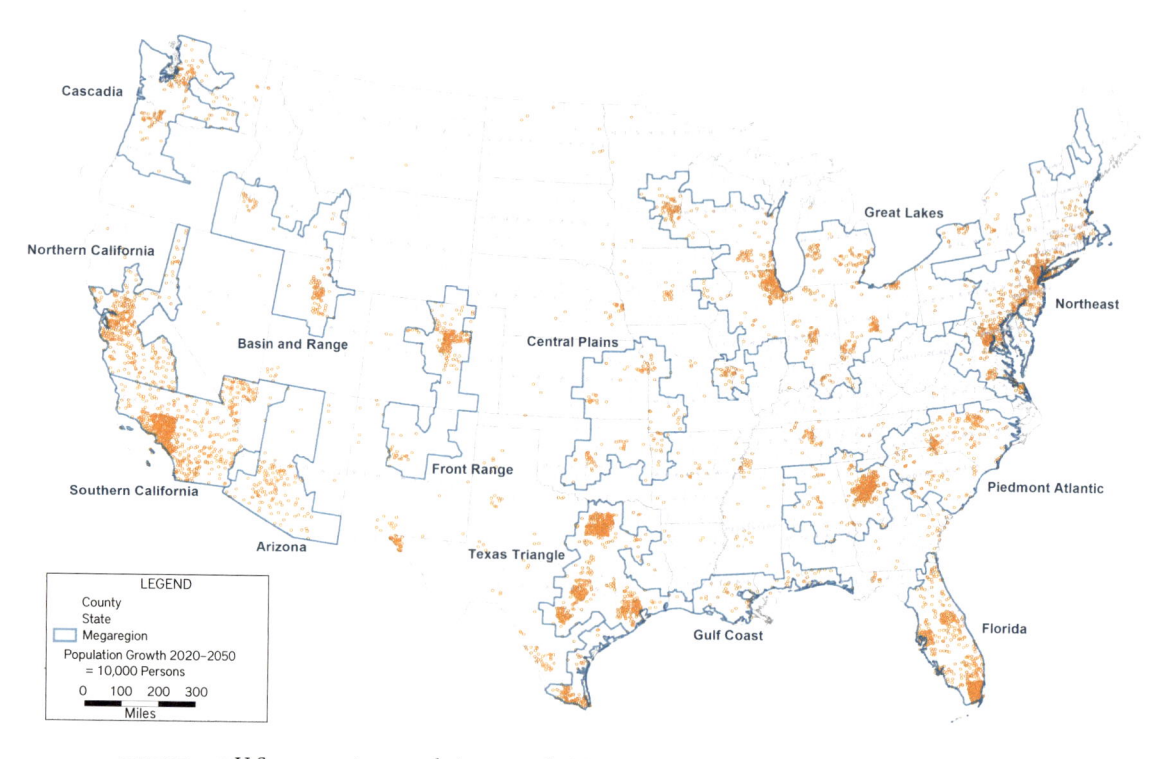

FIGURE 3.1B U.S. megaregion population growth, 2020–2050. *Source: Ming Zhang.*

Shared Socioeconomic Pathways

Shared socioeconomic pathways (SSPs) project global changes up to the year 2100. These scenarios by an international team of climate scientists, economists, and energy systems analysts update an analysis of the world's future scenarios for the 21st century from a similar effort during the 1990s. The Intergovernmental Panel on Climate Change, the United Nations body for assessing the science related to climate change, published four global environmental scenarios and related analyses concerning greenhouse gases and aerosol precursor emissions in a series of reports from 1990 to 2000. The final report, *Special Report on Emissions Scenarios*, described in detail the four scenarios (Nakicenovic et al. 2000). The report's scenarios examined the interplays between two sets of driving forces: strong economic values versus strong environmental values and increasing globalization versus increasing regionalization. In contrast, the SSP effort modeled how socioeconomic factors, including population, economic growth, education, urbanization, and technological innovations, may change over the 21st century. In addition, a parallel effort explored global greenhouse gas and radiative forcing scenarios, described as representative concentration pathways (Wayne 2013), which provide an environmental element to SSP development. O'Neill et al. (2017) developed qualitative descriptions for five versions of SSPs:

SSP1: Sustainability (Taking the Green Road)

>The world shifts gradually, but pervasively, toward a more sustainable path, emphasizing more inclusive development that respects perceived environmental boundaries.... Management of the global commons slowly improves.... Educational and health investments accelerate the demographic transition... [and] the emphasis on economic growth shifts toward a broader emphasis on human well-being.... Driven by an increasing commitment to achieving development goals, inequality is reduced both across and within countries.... Consumption is

oriented toward low material growth and lower resource and energy intensity. (172)

SSP2: Middle of the Road

The world follows a path in which social, economic, and technological trends do not shift markedly from historical patterns. Development and income growth proceeds unevenly, with some countries making relatively good progress while others fall short of expectations.... Global and national institutions work toward but make slow progress in achieving sustainable development goals.... Environmental systems experience degradation, although there are some improvements and overall the intensity of resource and energy use declines.... Global population growth is moderate and levels off in the second half of the century.... Income inequality ... persists or improves only slowly ... and challenges to reducing vulnerability to societal and environmental changes [remain]. (173)

SSP3: Regional Rivalry (a Rocky Road)

A resurgent nationalism, concerns about competitiveness and security, and regional conflicts push countries to increasingly focus on domestic or, at most, regional issues.... Policies shift over time to become increasingly oriented toward national and regional security issues.... Countries focus on achieving energy and food security goals within their own regions at the expense of broader-based development.... Investments in education and technological development decline. Economic development is slow, consumption is material-intensive, and inequalities persist or worsen over time.... A low international priority for addressing environmental concerns leads to strong environmental degradation in some regions.... Population growth is low in industrialized and high in developing countries. (173)

SSP4: Inequality (a Road Divided)

Highly unequal investments in human capital, combined with increasing disparities in economic opportunity and political power, lead to increasing inequalities and stratification both across and within countries. Over time, a gap widens between an internationally connected society that ... contributes to knowledge- and capital-intensive sectors of the global economy, and a fragmented collection of lower-income, poorly educated societies that work in a labor intensive, low-tech economy.... Social cohesion degrades and conflict and unrest become increasingly common. Technology development is high in the high-tech economy and sectors.... Energy companies hedge against price fluctuations partly through diversifying their energy sources, with investments in both carbon-intensive fuels like coal and unconventional oil, but also low-carbon energy sources. Environmental policies focus on local issues around middle- and high-income areas. (173–174)

SSP5: Fossil-Fueled Development (Taking the Highway)

This world places increasing faith in competitive markets, innovation and participatory societies to produce rapid technological progress and development of human capital as the path to sustainable development. Global markets are increasingly integrated.... There are also strong investments in health, education, and institutions to enhance human and social capital. At the same time, the push for economic and social development is coupled with the exploitation of abundant fossil fuel resources and the adoption of resource and energy intensive lifestyles around the world. All these factors lead to rapid growth of the global economy.... There is faith in the ability to effectively manage social and ecological systems, including by geo-engineering, if necessary. While local environmental impacts are addressed effectively by technological solutions, there is relatively little effort to avoid potential global environmental impacts due to a perceived tradeoff with progress on economic development. Global population peaks and declines in the 21st century. (174)

Scenarios (ICLUS) project. ICLUS echoed the efforts made by international communities to explore global development scenarios known as shared socioeconomic pathways and modeled future changes in population, housing density, and land uses for the United States. However, the ICLUS project does not provide detailed age composition for the projected county population. Striessnig et al. (2019) project U.S. county populations in five scenarios under the assumptions consistent with the five shared socioeconomic pathways. Their efforts produced population estimates by gender and by age structure with 10- to 25-year intervals. For this study, we combined the county population projections created by the EPA and Striessnig et al. (2019) and supplemented them with U.S. census data to create a database of county population by gender and by age cohorts of 5-year intervals for the years up to 2050. The 5-year age cohorts were derived from interpolating the 10- to 25-year cohorts in Striessnig et al. (2019) with the observed 5-year cohort data from the census for 1990–2019 (U.S. Census Bureau 2016b, 2017, 2020a).

GENERATIONAL TRENDS

By 2030, all baby boomers will be 65 years or older, and most will leave the workforce. Fifteen years later, in 2045, Generation X will turn 65 or older. Between 2020 and 2050, millennials (Generation Y), ages 24–69, will be the generation that stays in the labor force the longest among all generations. Generation Z will follow; its youngest members (born in 2012) will not turn 18 until 2030.

Millennials have attracted much attention from news media and in academia, partly because they have become the largest generation in the current U.S. population. Millennials reportedly differ from prior generations: they tend to travel less, drive less, and are more likely to choose urban locations to live and work (Chair of the Council of Economic Advisers 2014; Fry, Igielnik, and Patten 2018). If this is indeed the case, the public and the private sectors should respond accordingly—for example, adding capacity to urban transit services and supplying more live-work urban housing.

Empirical efforts to verify the reported differences in travel and lifestyle preferences among millennials, Generation X, baby boomers, and others are ongoing. Generation Z also deserves attention. This generation is growing up in a booming sharing economy, with shared mobility as a prime sector driven by autonomous and communications technologies and new social norms such as bike-sharing, car-sharing, and ride-sharing. Dramatic global events like the COVID-19 pandemic and international trade conflicts will also mark their childhoods. How the generation's education, career, and life choices will be affected and how these effects may reshape cities, regions, and megaregions warrant careful research. Additional research will also be needed to ascertain whether the changes in travel, work, and residential patterns for all cohorts begun during the pandemic will be sustained over time.

Tables 3.2a and 3.2b report population distribution by generation in population counts and percentages, respectively. In 1990, baby boomers were the largest generation in the country and among all megaregions combined. This was also the case for all individual megaregions, except Basin and Range, where Generation X (640,000) outnumbered the baby boomer generation (630,000) by a small margin. Numbers of millennials, who were then younger than 9, were between baby boomers and Generation X. By 2020, millennials overtook baby boomers as the largest generation. Thirty years later, in 2050, Generation Z will become the largest through attrition of older millennials.

Some generational trends across megaregions are more clearly expressed in the percentages of table 3.2b than by the raw numbers in table 3.2a. In 2020, millennials, who were mostly in their early career stages, had the highest population shares (above 24 percent) in Front Range and Cascadia, where high-tech and creative industries offered relatively rich opportunities. In contrast, the Florida megaregion had the lowest proportion of millennials in its total population (20.31 percent). By 2050, however, it becomes the one with the highest percentage of millennials (19.50 percent) among the 13 megaregions, suggesting intermegaregion migrations over time (figure 3.2).

Aging Megaregions

Historical records and future projections demonstrate a national trend of population aging in the United States (Mather, Jacobsen, and Pollard 2015). In this study, we observe that the aging population trends of megaregions are consistent with national trends, but variations exist among megaregions. Table 3.3 shows our analysis results, which exhibit three notable characteristics.

The first pertains to the size and the magnitude of growth in the older population. As shown in table 3.4, from 1990 to 2020, the population ages 65 and older increased from 25.13 million to 44.75 million in the 13 megaregions combined. The size of this group is expected to expand further to 71.04 million by 2050, in the modest projection scenario. Among the 13 megaregions, Great Lakes and Northeast had the largest net increase in people ages 65 and older, more than 1 million each in every decade from 1990 to 2020. In the next three decades, this population in these two megaregions is expected to continue to grow, by 5.05 million and 5.47 million in Great Lakes and Northeast, respectively.

In percentage terms, the Arizona Sun Corridor, Front Range (figure 3.3), and Texas Triangle megaregions experienced the fastest growth of this older population

Table 3.2a. Population Counts (millions) of Four Generations in U.S. Megaregions and Nonmegaregions

	1990				2020				2050			
	Baby Boomer	Gen X	Gen Y	Baby Boomer	Gen X	Gen Y	Gen Z	Baby Boomer	Gen X	Gen Y	Gen Z
Ages	26–44	10–25	0–9	56–74	40–55	24–39	8–23	86–104	70–85	54–69	38–53
Arizona Sun Corridor	1.02	0.80	0.52	1.44	1.32	1.52	1.48	0.23	1.20	1.45	1.49
Basin and Range	0.63	0.64	0.44	0.69	0.78	1.00	1.09	0.12	0.62	0.84	0.91
Northern California	3.64	2.52	1.67	3.10	3.14	3.68	3.16	0.57	2.47	3.34	3.67
Southern California	6.20	4.73	3.01	5.12	5.44	6.36	5.58	0.91	4.00	5.79	6.66
Cascadia	2.00	1.38	0.91	2.06	1.98	2.37	1.90	0.33	1.61	2.10	2.12
Central Plains	2.00	1.60	1.01	1.61	1.48	1.95	2.32	0.29	1.31	1.78	1.82
Florida	3.33	2.32	1.47	4.80	4.05	4.12	3.62	0.91	4.04	5.00	4.94
Front Range	1.26	0.86	0.57	1.30	1.27	1.56	1.30	0.23	1.21	1.56	1.64
Great Lakes	16.13	12.62	7.84	13.30	11.95	12.88	12.40	2.24	9.62	12.47	12.41
Gulf Coast	1.60	1.40	0.90	1.49	1.39	1.59	1.59	0.24	1.22	1.64	1.68
Northeast	16.05	11.55	6.92	13.18	12.48	13.45	11.95	2.37	9.70	13.56	14.19
Piedmont Atlantic	5.39	4.28	2.47	5.80	5.69	5.97	5.80	0.82	4.49	6.06	6.43
Texas Triangle	4.02	3.07	2.00	4.13	4.75	5.51	5.20	0.64	3.36	4.83	5.80
Subtotal	63.26	47.77	29.74	58.02	55.72	61.95	57.37	9.90	44.86	60.42	63.76
Nonmegaregion	12.16	10.43	6.41	11.69	9.65	10.47	10.81	1.74	8.24	10.56	9.65
Total	75.42	58.20	36.15	69.71	65.37	72.42	68.18	11.64	53.10	70.98	73.41

Table 3.2b. Population Percentages of Four Generations in U.S. Megaregions and Nonmegaregions

	1990				2020				2050			
	Baby Boomer	Gen X	Gen Y	Baby Boomer	Gen X	Gen Y	Gen Z	Baby Boomer	Gen X	Gen Y	Gen Z
Ages	26–44	10–25	0–9	56–74	40–55	24–39	8–23	86–104	70–85	54–69	38–53
Arizona Sun Corridor	30.32	23.72	15.43	20.74	18.99	21.91	21.25	2.84	14.67	17.64	18.12
Basin and Range	27.81	28.29	19.54	16.09	18.23	23.41	25.38	2.25	11.92	16.09	17.32
Northern California	33.02	22.87	15.10	19.87	20.14	23.60	20.29	2.99	13.01	17.59	19.29
Southern California	32.45	24.76	15.74	19.15	20.32	23.77	20.84	2.70	11.83	17.15	19.71
Cascadia	32.43	22.40	14.87	20.88	20.13	24.06	19.31	2.93	14.36	18.80	19.00
Central Plains	29.59	23.64	15.02	17.75	16.33	21.53	25.55	2.89	13.09	17.69	18.16
Florida	28.23	19.67	12.48	23.67	19.96	20.31	17.87	3.53	15.76	19.50	19.25
Front Range	33.92	23.12	15.51	20.33	19.92	24.41	20.33	2.75	14.17	18.28	19.23
Great Lakes	30.20	23.63	14.68	21.97	19.74	21.27	20.48	3.41	14.67	19.02	18.93
Gulf Coast	29.28	25.73	16.57	20.38	19.00	21.80	21.72	2.66	13.63	18.26	18.68
Northeast	31.44	22.63	13.56	21.60	20.45	22.04	19.58	3.27	13.38	18.71	19.59
Piedmont Atlantic	31.06	24.67	14.22	20.98	20.57	21.57	20.96	2.51	13.67	18.44	19.56
Texas Triangle	32.63	24.91	16.20	17.78	20.43	23.68	22.35	2.17	11.35	16.32	19.61
Subtotal	31.05	23.44	14.60	20.80	19.98	22.21	20.57	2.99	13.55	18.25	19.26
Nonmegaregion	28.08	24.09	14.81	22.66	18.70	20.29	20.95	3.30	15.62	20.02	18.31
Total	30.53	23.56	14.63	21.09	19.78	21.91	20.63	3.03	13.83	18.49	19.13

FIGURE 3.2 Aerial view of Route 441 through Paynes Prairie Preserve State Park, Florida. *Source: istock.com/Michael Warren.*

from 1990 to 2020, at 178.4 percent, 164.7 percent, and 153.1 percent, respectively. In the next 30 years, the Front Range, Basin and Range, and Texas Triangle will take the lead in the growth of the population ages 65 and older.

The second characteristic of an aging megaregion population lies in the structural change of the demographics. As the amount has increased, the proportion of the oldest cohort in the total population has also become larger, from 12.3 percent in 1990 to 16.0 percent in 2020 and then to 21.5 percent in 2050 (table 3.4). Among the 13 megaregions, Florida has the highest proportion of older-age population at 19.9 percent, 21.2 percent, and 25.0 percent in 1990, 2020, and 2050, respectively. Warm weather, low tax rates, and other amenities have made Florida one of the most attractive destinations for retirees (Wallace 2020). In contrast, Texas Triangle (figure 3.4) has the smallest proportion of its population in the older-age group (9.2 percent, 12.4 percent, and 17.7 percent in 1990, 2020, and 2050, respectively).

A growing population of older adults has many important implications. Budget allocations for Social Security and pensions must increase sufficiently for older people and retired workers to enjoy a reasonable standard of living. Health care costs go up as people age because of requirements for hospitals, doctors and nurses, and skilled labor trained to care for older patients. The financial and social burden on

Table 3.3. U.S. Megaregion Older Population Counts and Changes, 1990–2050

	Population Count (1990, millions)	Population Count (2020, millions)	Change (1990–2020, millions)	Growth (1990–2020) (%)	Population Count (2050, millions)	Change (2020–2050, millions)	Growth (2020–2050) (%)
Arizona Sun Corridor	0.44	1.21	0.78	178.4	1.86	0.64	52.8
Basin and Range	0.21	0.51	0.29	138.3	0.97	0.47	91.9
Northern California	1.22	2.38	1.17	96.0	3.95	1.56	65.6
Southern California	1.93	3.87	1.94	100.1	6.41	2.54	65.7
Cascadia	0.74	1.57	0.82	110.5	2.53	0.97	61.8
Central Plains	0.88	1.25	0.36	41.2	2.09	0.84	67.6
Florida	2.35	4.30	1.95	82.8	6.40	2.10	48.8
Front Range	0.36	0.95	0.59	164.7	1.87	0.93	97.6
Great Lakes	6.75	10.19	3.45	51.0	15.24	5.05	49.5
Gulf Coast	0.58	1.13	0.55	94.4	1.91	0.78	68.8
Northeast	6.58	10.15	3.57	54.2	15.62	5.47	53.9
Piedmont Atlantic	1.94	4.36	2.42	124.5	6.96	2.61	59.8
Texas Triangle	1.14	2.88	1.74	153.1	5.23	2.35	81.6
Subtotal	25.13	44.75	19.62	78.1	71.04	26.30	58.8
Nonmegaregion	6.08	9.42	3.34	55.0	13.01	3.59	38.1
Total	31.21	54.17	22.96	73.6	84.06	29.89	55.2

Sources: EPA (2007); U.S. Census Bureau (1990, 2019b).

Table 3.4. Aging Population Trends in U.S. Megaregions

	Population Ages 65 and Older (millions) and Share (%)						Dependency Ratio*					
	1990		2020		2050		1990		2020		2050	
	Amount	Share	Amount	Share	Amount	Share	Younger Age	Older Age	Younger Age	Older Age	Younger Age	Older Age
Arizona Sun Corridor	0.44	13.0	1.21	17.4	1.86	22.6	52	23	44	31	45	42
Basin and Range	0.21	9.3	0.51	11.8	0.97	18.5	72	18	55	21	56	35
Northern California	1.22	11.0	2.38	15.3	3.95	20.8	48	18	42	26	41	37
Southern California	1.93	10.1	3.87	14.5	6.41	19.0	51	17	42	24	42	33
Cascadia	0.74	12.1	1.57	15.9	2.53	22.7	48	20	39	26	36	40
Central Plains	0.88	13.1	1.25	13.7	2.09	20.8	51	23	60	26	45	38
Florida	2.35	19.9	4.30	21.2	6.40	25.0	43	36	38	37	39	46
Front Range	0.36	9.7	0.95	14.9	1.87	22.0	48	16	40	24	37	39
Great Lakes	6.75	12.6	10.19	16.8	15.24	23.2	50	22	42	29	42	43
Gulf Coast	0.58	10.7	1.13	15.5	1.91	21.3	58	19	48	27	43	39
Northeast	6.58	12.9	10.15	16.6	15.62	21.6	45	21	40	28	39	38
Piedmont Atlantic	1.94	11.2	4.36	15.8	6.96	21.2	49	19	43	27	49	40
Texas Triangle	1.14	9.2	2.88	12.4	5.23	17.7	52	16	47	21	48	32
Subtotal	25.13	12.3	44.75	16.0	71.04	21.5	49	21	43	27	42	39
Nonmegaregion	6.08	14.0	9.42	18.3	13.01	24.7	53	25	45	32	39	46
Total	31.21	12.6	54.17	16.4	84.06	21.9	49	22	43	28	42	40

*Youth dependency ratio = (population ages 19 and younger ÷ population ages 20–64) × 100; older-age dependency ratio = (population ages 65 and older ÷ population ages 20–64) × 100. Some studies use age 16 as the cutoff point to group the working adults. Accordingly, they define youth as those ages 15 and younger. Our study follows the U.S. Census Bureau's methods: ages 20–64 are defined as working adults for calculating dependency ratios (Vincent and Velkoff 2010).

FIGURE 3.3 Snow-covered Longs Peak, part of the Rocky Mountains, towers over the Denver skyline. *Source: istock.com/milehightraveler.*

FIGURE 3.4 Aerial view of Barton Springs, Austin, Texas. *Source: istock.com/RoschetzkyIstockPhoto.*

FIGURE 3.5 Portland, Oregon, and Mount Hood in autumn. *Source: istock.com/4nadia.*

working-age adults rises with the growing share of the older population. Dependency ratios provide a direct metric to indicate the level of burden facing a country or economy. Table 3.4 also reports the younger-age dependency ratios and the older-age ratios for U.S. megaregions and the rest of the country. From 1990 to 2020, the youth dependency ratios in all but one megaregion (Central Plains) decreased, whereas the older-age dependency ratios all increased. The shift from a younger population to an older one is expected to continue to 2050. Four megaregions in particular—Cascadia (figure 3.5), Florida, Front Range, and Great Lakes—and all counties not in any megaregion are projected to see older-age dependency ratios surpassing those of the younger group.

The third characteristic of an aging megaregion population concerns the spatial concentration of the older population in suburban or nonmetro counties within each megaregion. Figures 3.6a and 3.6b map the older population indexes for urban, suburban, and non-MSA counties in 2020 and in 2050, respectively. In this study, we define the older population index for a county in a megaregion as the ratio of the county's older population percentage to the county's total population percentage. An older population index value of 1.0 means that a county has a share of older population proportional to the megaregional level. An index of 1.5 indicates that the county has an older population that is 50 percent higher than the megaregional average. Figure 3.6a displays a pattern of older population largely concentrating in suburban counties and nonmetropolitan counties in 2020. Core counties in metropolitan statistical areas (MSAs; shown in light yellow) tend to have shares of older population below the megaregional average. A similar pattern can be observed for 2050 (figure 3.6b). The spatial concentration of older population in suburban and non-MSA counties attests to the importance of a megaregional approach to support the aging population.

Generational Travel Characteristics

Whether baby boomers, millennials, and Generation X differ in their travel behavior and preferences is a question of broad interest. Data from eight waves of national travel surveys (five Nationwide Personal Transportation Surveys before 2000 and three National Household Travel Surveys after 2000) reveal intergenerational variations and similarities in trip making. Initial findings from studies (e.g., Blumenberg et al. 2012; Choi, Jiao, and Zhang 2017; da Silva et al. 2019; McDonald 2015) suggest that younger generations traveled fewer miles and made fewer trips than previous generations at the same life stage. These studies, however, using survey data from two or three time points (the survey years), had data constraints. The temporal limitations of two to three surveys, which took place every six to eight years, did not provide sufficient cohort samples for time series analysis over the life course of the generations. A 2019 study by MIT researchers (Knittel and Murphy 2019) used five sets of survey data, from 1990 to 2017, to analyze millennials' car ownership and usage. After controlling for the confounding effects of demographic and macroeconomic factors, they found little intergenerational difference between millennials and their older cohorts (figure 3.7).

Scholars have also explored other data sources to study millennials' travel preferences and behavior compared with other generations. Garikapati et al. (2016), for example, performed a longitudinal analysis of the 2003–2013 American Time Use Survey data series. They identified intragenerational variations, reporting that younger millennials were less likely to do out-of-home activities, including travel, than older millennials. Older millennials, however, had activity patterns similar to those of Generation X. Millennials, compared with prior generations, delayed the milestone life-stage events, such as graduating, getting jobs, and forming families. Their activity-travel patterns, as observed by Garikapati et al. (2016), eventually converged with those of prior generations when they aged into their 30s and beyond. Other researchers have conducted surveys on specific project topics and regions pertaining to millennial travel (e.g., Circella et al. 2018). Efforts to understand millennials and intergenerational travel are also ongoing in other countries—for example, Canada (Newbold et al. 2005), Germany (Krueger, Rashidi, and Vij 2019), and the United Kingdom (Chatterjee et al. 2018).

In our study, we combined data from six national travel surveys, three from 1983, 1990, and 1995 and three from 2001, 2009, and 2017. Each of the surveys consists of

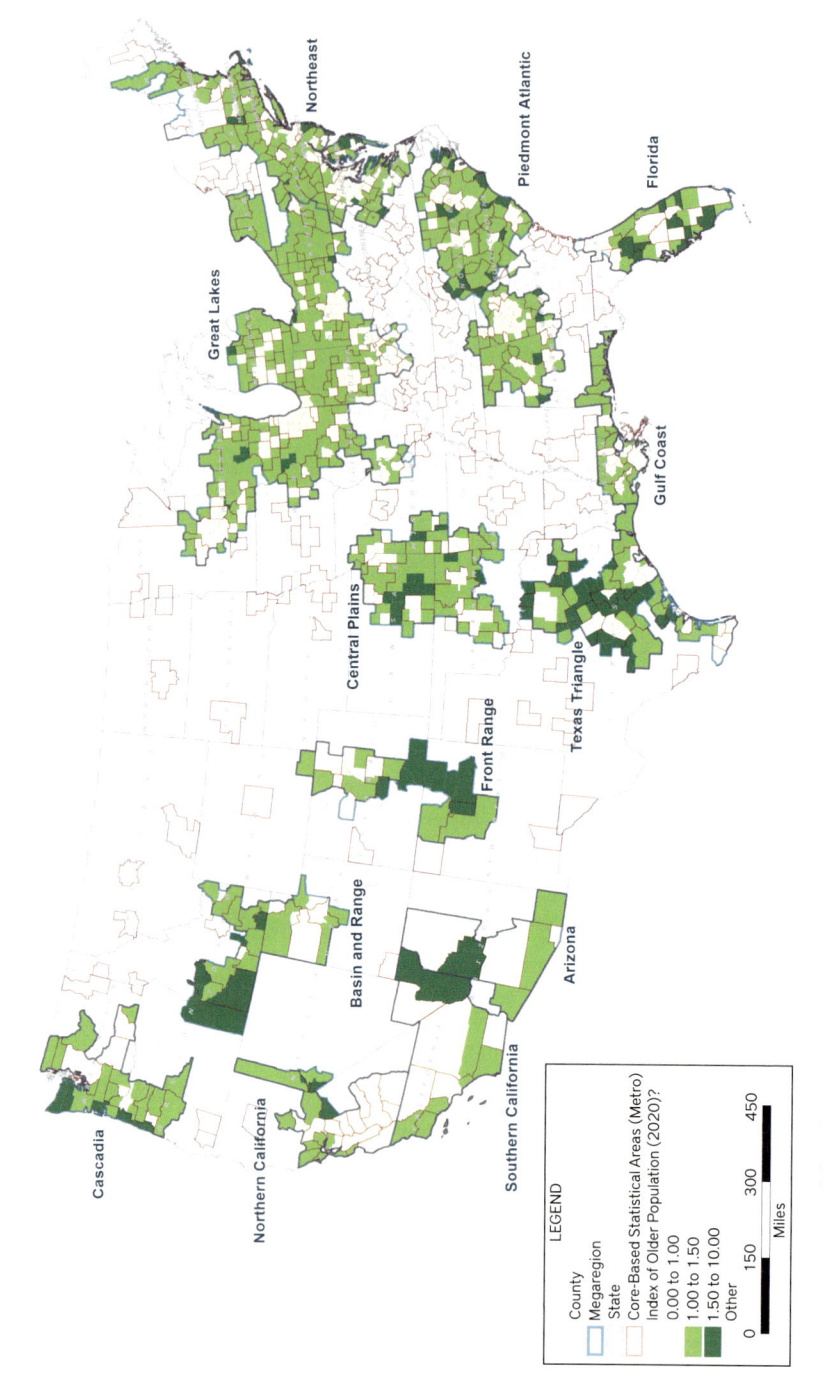

FIGURE 3.6A Spatial distribution of the older population in U.S. megaregions, 2020. *Source: Ming Zhang.*

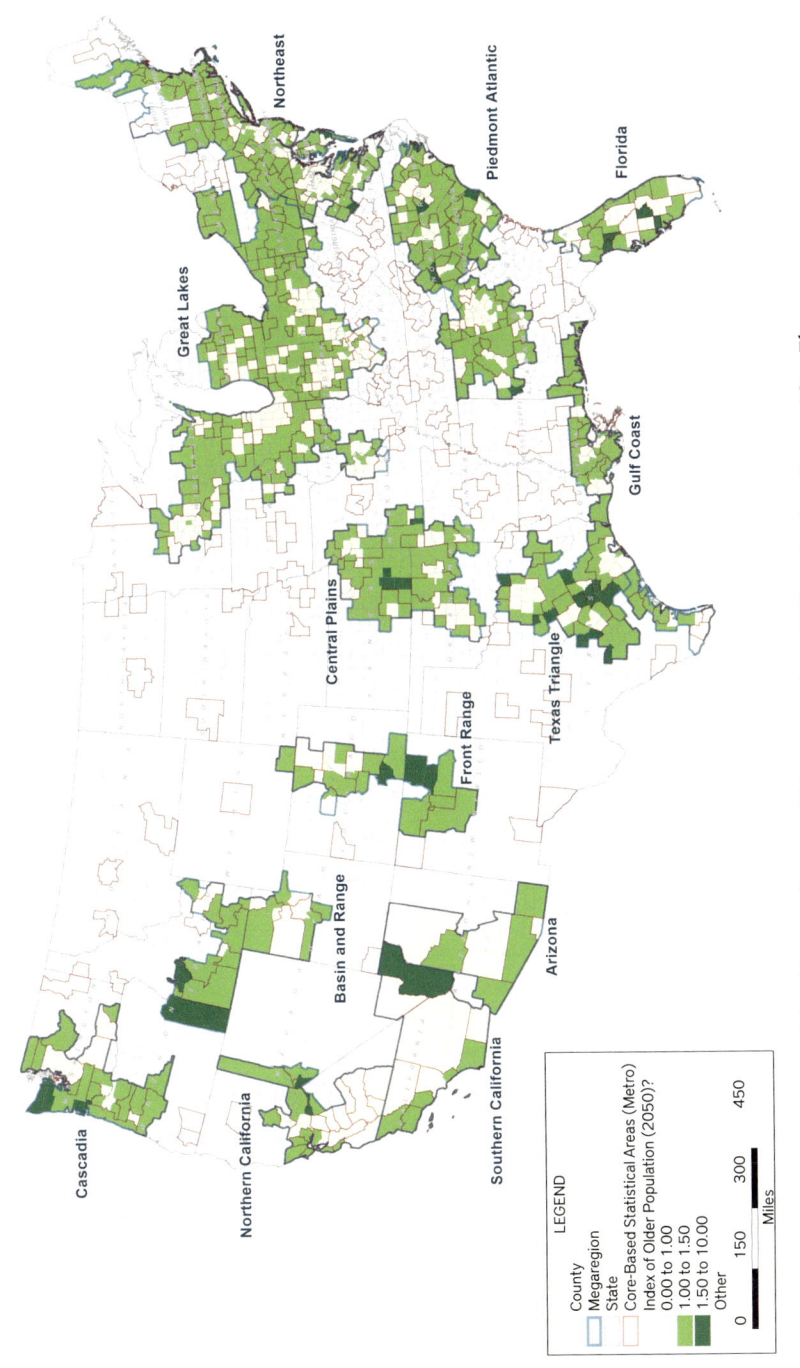

FIGURE 3.6B Spatial distribution of the older population in U.S. megaregions, 2050 projection. *Source: Ming Zhang.*

FIGURE 3.7 Traffic jam on Route 91 in Southern California. *Source: istock.com/MCCAIG.*

data on the attributes of the travelers, their households, and their vehicles and 24-hour travel logs. The surveys have spatial limitations, however. Because of privacy concerns, the survey records suppress the address information on survey respondents' homes, activities, and trip origins and destinations. We used the locational information available at the MSA level (for major MSAs only) and combined samples from the MSAs by their corresponding megaregions for megaregion-level analysis and reporting.

Table 3.5 reports the average daily trips per person by three types of travel modes—driving (alone and carpool), transit, and bike or walk—for baby boomers, Generation X, and Generation Y in 13 megaregions and the rest of the country. The modal trip rates are also illustrated in figure 3.8. The table and figure reveal trip-making characteristics across three generations:

- Millennials (Generation Y) drove less frequently than did baby boomers or Generation X in all megaregions and nonmegaregion areas. Northeastern millennials drove the least, at a daily rate of 2.27 trips per person. Between baby boomers and Generation X, variations existed among megaregions. For instance, Generation X drove more than baby boomers did in Arizona Sun Corridor, Basin and Range, and Front Range, whereas the two generations showed no difference in average daily driving in Southern California and Piedmont Atlantic. In the other eight megaregions and the rest of the country, baby boomers outpaced Generation X in driving.
- Millennials rode on transit more than other generations. Northeastern millennials stood out again by being the most frequent transit riders among all

Table 3.5. Average Daily Trips per Person by Travel Mode in U.S. Megaregions

	Baby Boomer			Generation X			Generation Y		
	Driving	Transit	Bike/Walk	Driving	Transit	Bike/Walk	Driving	Transit	Bike/Walk
Arizona Sun Corridor	3.97	0.06	0.39	4.03	0.07	0.04	3.21	0.25	0.55
Basin and Range	4.04	0.08	0.21	4.29	0.09	0.01	3.07	0.16	0.77
Northern California	3.69	0.13	0.61	3.41	0.20	0.10	3.03	0.21	0.67
Southern California	3.78	0.11	0.51	3.78	0.13	0.04	2.98	0.19	0.65
Cascadia	4.03	0.13	0.30	3.59	0.22	0.06	2.90	0.40	0.53
Central Plains	5.20	0.03	0.09	4.82	0.06	0.04	3.45	0.31	0.38
Florida	4.04	0.06	0.41	3.93	0.06	0.04	3.00	0.26	0.46
Front Range	4.12	0.10	0.30	4.32	0.06	0.05	3.26	0.25	0.61
Great Lakes	4.13	0.09	0.28	3.81	0.17	0.03	2.92	0.43	0.51
Gulf Coast	4.21	0.07	0.41	3.94	0.28	0.15	2.41	0.42	0.63
Northeast	3.61	0.26	0.49	3.19	0.37	0.03	2.27	0.57	0.74
Piedmont Atlantic	4.00	0.08	0.24	4.00	0.11	0.02	3.40	0.27	0.42
Texas Triangle	4.02	0.06	0.28	3.94	0.09	0.02	3.35	0.16	0.37
Nonmegaregion	4.02	0.07	0.27	3.94	0.12	0.03	3.22	0.29	0.43

Source: Author estimates based on data from Oak Ridge National Laboratory (2020).

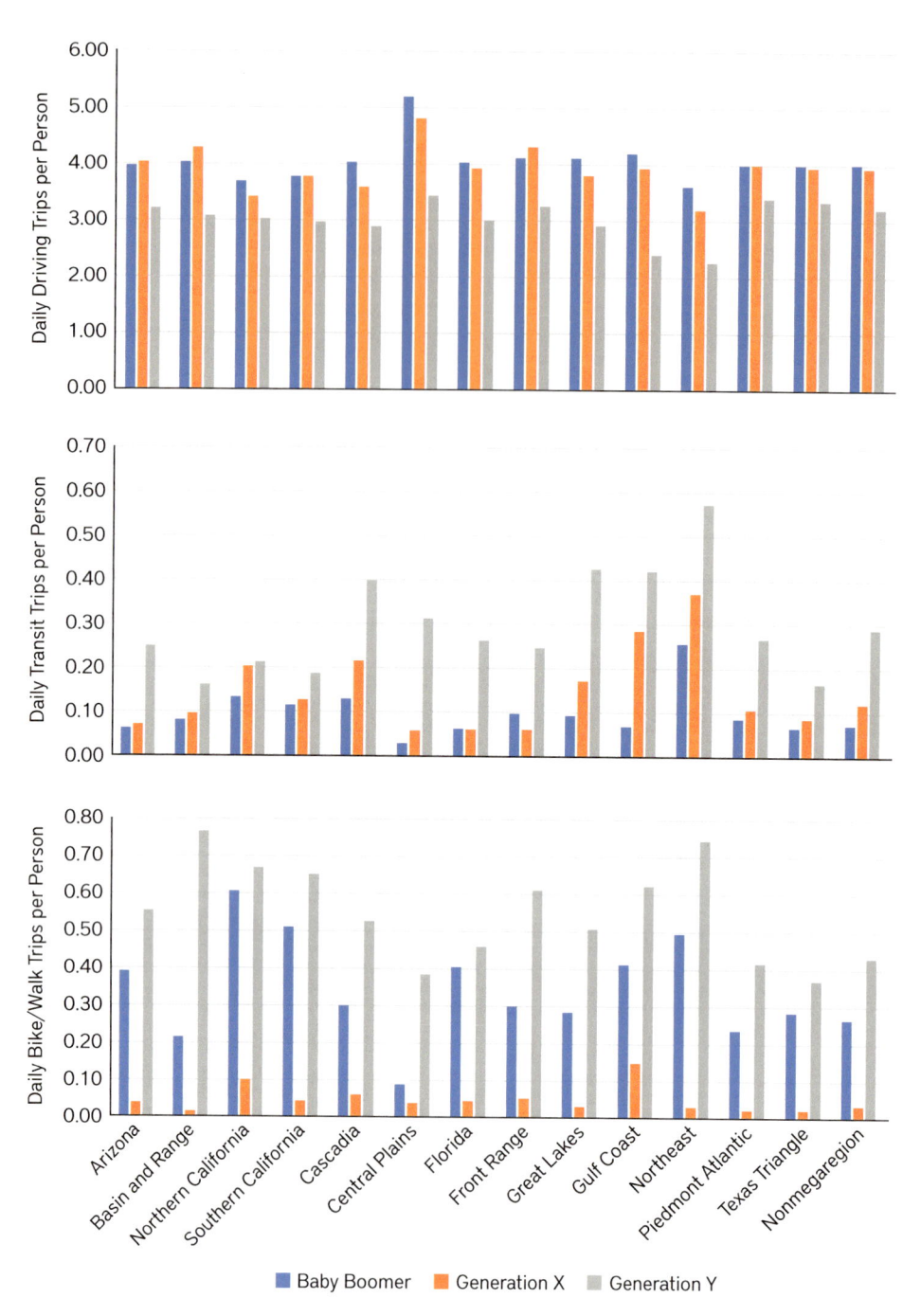

FIGURE 3.8 Average daily trips per person by travel modes in U.S. megaregions. *Source: Ming Zhang.*

Table 3.6. Average Daily Vehicle Miles Traveled per Person by Generation in U.S. Megaregions

	Baby Boomer	Generation X	Generation Y
Arizona Sun Corridor	33.55	34.18	26.03
Basin and Range	39.05	37.47	27.79
Northern California	31.93	29.75	30.17
Southern California	33.60	34.30	27.12
Cascadia	37.40	34.60	22.04
Central Plains	46.78	46.09	29.28
Florida	34.05	35.22	30.33
Front Range	37.29	42.15	23.60
Great Lakes	35.47	34.18	22.61
Gulf Coast	29.81	35.02	15.09
Northeast	32.90	30.21	17.95
Piedmont Atlantic	38.19	40.61	34.57
Texas Triangle	37.47	37.69	31.90
Nonmegaregion	38.29	38.61	29.28

Source: Author estimates based on data from Oak Ridge National Laboratory (2020).

generations. The frequent transit use by millennials in the Northeast megaregion can be attributed to the relatively high level of transit supply in metros like New York, Boston, and Washington, DC. Generations X and Y showed no difference between-megaregion variation in transit usage as they had in driving.

- For nonmotorized travel, millennials again outnumbered Generation X in daily biking or walking in all megaregions. In contrast to transit riding, baby boomers biked or walked daily more than Generation X did across all megaregions.

Another travel indicator of important policy interest concerns the total amount of travel made by motorized vehicles (measured as vehicle miles traveled, or VMT). From multiyear travel survey data sets, we calculated the average daily VMT per person for each of the three generations, reported in table 3.6 and illustrated in figure 3.9.

The average daily VMT per person of millennials was the lowest among the three generations for all megaregions. Intragenerational differences also existed. For instance, Gulf Coast millennials drove the lowest number of daily VMT, at 15.09, less than half the VMT driven by the millennials in Piedmont Atlantic (34.57). The significant difference in VMT by millennials suggests the influence of factors external to the generational lifestyle preferences affecting travel behavior.

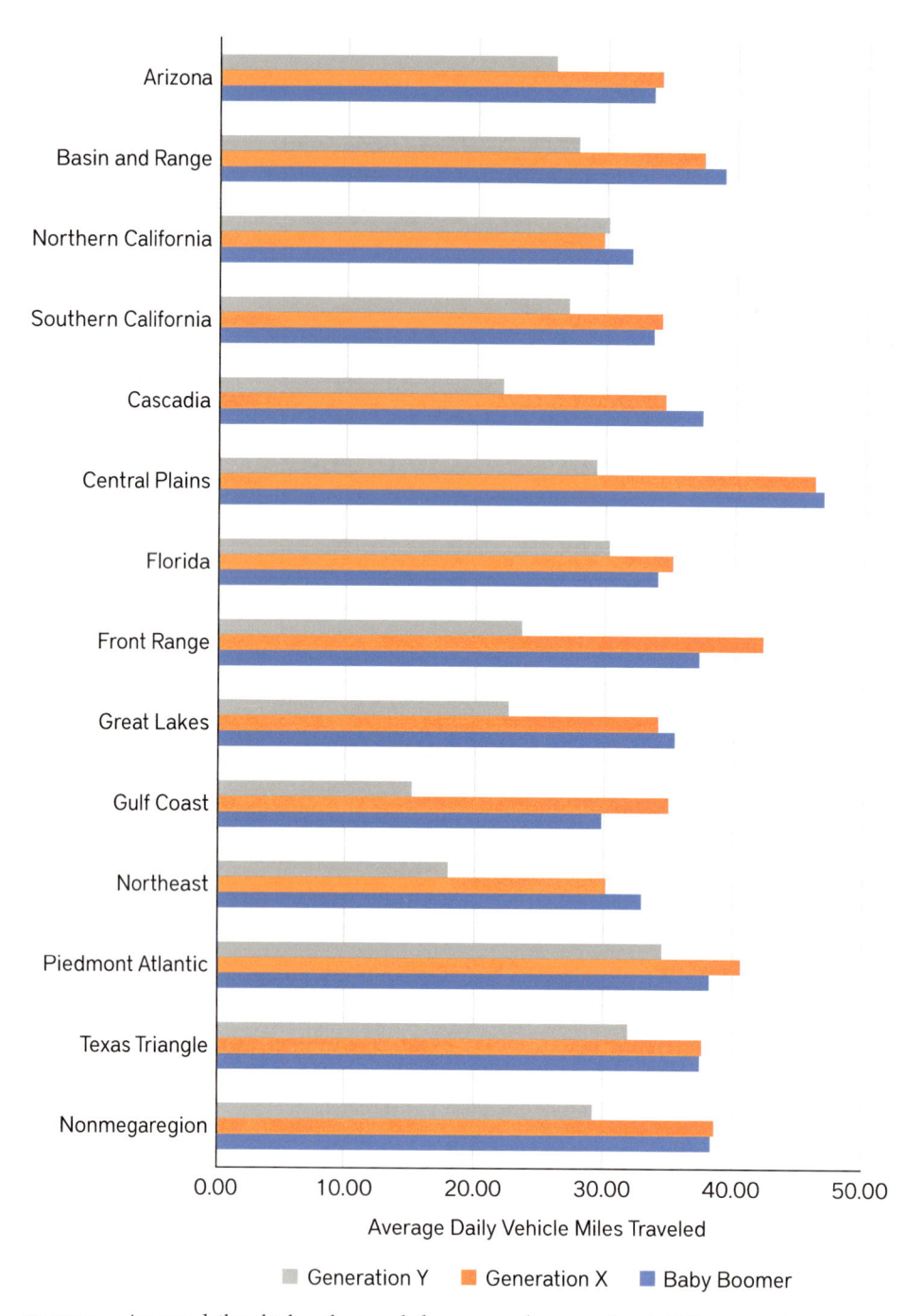

FIGURE 3.9 Average daily vehicle miles traveled per person by generation in U.S. megaregions. *Source: Ming Zhang.*

What factors could explain these differences? Studies have shown that information and communications technologies (ICT) usage for purposes such as telecommuting and online shopping plays a role in the change of physical travel (Cao 2009). To verify this possible explanation, we calculated the proportion of people having work-from-home options for 2017 (no similar data are available from the surveys completed between 1983 and 2001). The calculation showed the same level of ICT access for Generations X and Y, with the proportion of work-from-home being 10.98 percent and 10.97 percent, respectively. Choi, Jiao, and Zhang (2017) found that significantly more people among 27–44 and 45–63 age groups in 2009 had the option to work from home than did the same age groups in 2001. However, the availability of the option of working from home does not reflect the work location on the day the daily trip information is obtained. Choi, Jiao, and Zhang (2017) found that the option to work from home correlated positively with automobile usage. Having the work-from-home option does not necessarily mean that people will substitute teletravel for physical travel. Blumenberg et al. (2012) reported that having the work-from-home option was associated with increased personal miles traveled for all age groups. Increasing online shopping and entertainment would likely reduce shopping and social trips (Davis, Dutzik, and Baxandall 2012).

Our analysis suggests important implications. Intergenerational travel characteristics display a complex picture that demands careful, in-depth analysis of the impacts these trends will have on travel demand. It would be overly simplified to declare travel behavior of millennials and baby boomers or other generations converging. Generation X deserves further research attention. Most existing studies tend to center millennials because of their large proportion in the current U.S. population (and probably because of the extensive media coverage of them as well). Generation X, the emerging Generation Z, and others warrant further research and policy attention as well. Furthermore, aside from intergenerational comparative studies, specific cohorts (e.g., older and younger groups) require specific attention because their mobility conditions and needs are different from other adult cohorts. Finally, the COVID-19 pandemic has clearly and dramatically altered daily trips across all cohorts. A question for the future: Has the pandemic accelerated the tendencies already displayed among millennials to travel less into an even more widespread phenomenon?

A broader question is whether the dramatic increase in working from home during the COVID-19 pandemic will be sustained over time following the end of this public health emergency. Further, it is unknown whether the dramatic reduction in transit ridership that occurred during the pandemic will continue when it is safe to travel again. Continuation of these trends could have a profound impact on residential and business locations and traffic volumes. One possibility is that transit ridership will return to prepandemic levels when it is safe to travel again. Another possibility is that many people will choose to live farther from center-city offices if they are not required to be there more than once or twice a week. An additional possibility is that firms may decide to reduce their footprints in center-city offices because of the reduction in office populations. Research will be needed to monitor these changes and determine what impacts they will have on transportation networks and land use patterns.

TRAVEL MARKETS FOR HIGH-PERFORMANCE TRANSIT

Future travel demand in U.S. megaregions will increase along with the anticipated population growth. The questions of planning and policy interest are where the demand increase will occur the most and how the demand can be accommodated efficiently. High-speed rail, which offers competitive services for trip distances between 100 and 500 miles, is a high-performance mode widely recommended for megaregional travel. In their effort to identify the potential market with the highest demand for high-speed rail services in the United States, Hagler and Todorovich (2009) developed a scoring method considering six factors: city and metropolitan area population, distance between city pairs, existing transit systems in metropolitan areas, metropolitan GDP, level of highway congestion, and geographic location within megaregions. Their analysis found 50 city pairs that had potentially the highest high-speed rail ridership.

We extended Hagler and Todorovich's work and analyzed two additional sets of data. The first was the data on intercounty worker flows that we used for delineating megaregion boundaries (see chapter 2). The second was the annual reports of airline passenger volumes released by the U.S. Bureau of Transportation Statistics. With the two data sets we mapped potential high-speed rail corridors by their traffic densities (figure 3.10). We recommend these corridors—of 100–500 miles and mostly involving intramegaregion travel—as candidate routes for high-speed rail or similar high-performance mass rapid transportation such as hyperloop. Table 3.7 lists the high-priority metro pairs grouped by megaregion. For intramegaregion travel, high-speed rail or similar high-performance mass rapid transportation offers a mobility alternative that operates more efficiently for traffic throughput than private cars and emits less pollution than air travel.

Improved mobility could address wide and growing increases in inequality within megaregions. In Southern California, for example, the Inland Empire in Riverside and San Bernardino Counties has fallen behind the megaregion's coastal counties in household income, job creation, and wealth formation. Construction of high-performance regional rail networks, like those proposed for New York, Boston, and Chicago, could link inland areas to employment centers in Los Angeles, Orange, and San Diego Counties and could begin to close these disparities. This network could also open up more affordable housing opportunities to low- and moderate-income residents of these high-priced coastal regions. Finally, this transportation

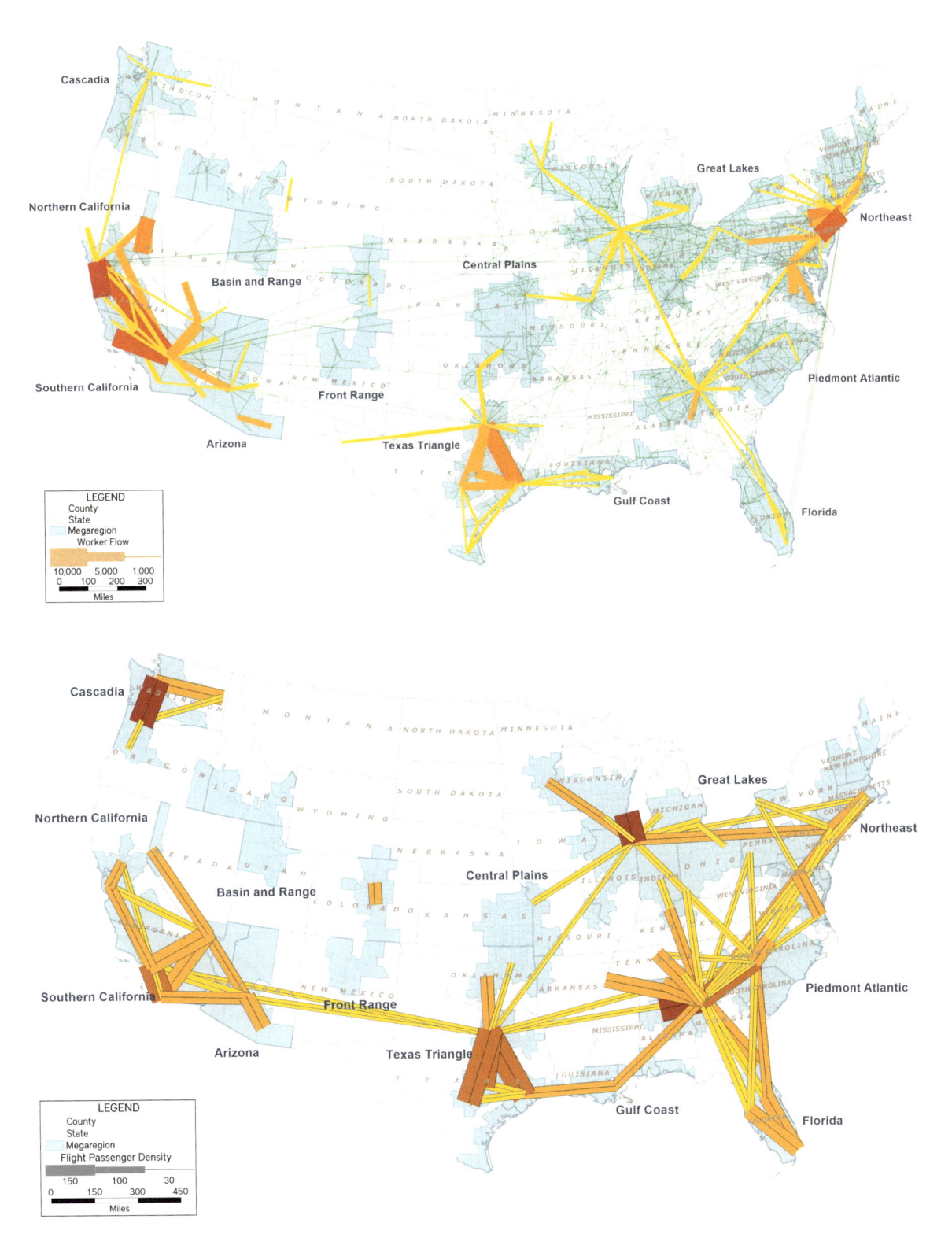

FIGURE 3.10 High-traffic corridors in the United States: intercounty worker flows (*top*) and air passengers (*bottom*). Source: Ming Zhang.

Table 3.7. High-Priority Routes for High-Performance Transit

Metropolitan Pairs		Length (miles)
Northeast Megaregion		
New York–Newark–Jersey City, NY-NJ	Philadelphia-Camden-Wilmington, PA-NJ-DE	114
New York–Newark–Jersey City, NY-NJ	Allentown-Bethlehem-Easton, PA	124
Washington-Arlington-Alexandria, DC-VA	Richmond, VA	104
Washington-Arlington-Alexandria, DC-VA	New York–Newark–Jersey City, NY-NJ	246
Boston-Cambridge-Newton, MA-NH	New York–Newark–Jersey City, NY-NJ	155
Washington-Arlington-Alexandria, DC-VA	Virginia Beach–Norfolk–Newport, VA	154
Washington-Arlington-Alexandria, DC-VA	Philadelphia-Camden-Wilmington, PA-NJ-DE	133
New York–Newark–Jersey City, NY-NJ	Allentown-Bethlehem-Easton, PA	115
Philadelphia-Camden-Wilmington, PA-NJ-DE	Harrisburg-Carlisle, PA	105
Albany-Schenectady-Troy, NY	New York–Newark–Jersey City, NY-NJ	143
Washington-Arlington-Alexandria, DC-VA	New York–Newark–Jersey City, NY-NJ	183
Washington-Arlington-Alexandria, DC-VA	Salisbury, MD-DE	104
Philadelphia-Camden-Wilmington, PA-NJ-DE	Pittsburgh, PA	247
Subtotal		1,928
Cascadia, Northern and Southern California Megaregions		
Portland-Vancouver-Hillsboro, OR-WA	Seattle-Tacoma-Bellevue, WA	156
San Francisco–Oakland–Berkeley, CA	Salinas, CA	122
Reno, NV	Gardnerville Ranchos, NV	118
Fernley, NV	Reno, NV	116
Sacramento-Roseville-Folsom, CA	Reno, NV	146
San Francisco–Oakland–Berkeley, CA	Riverside–San Bernardino–Ontario, CA	410
Sacramento-Roseville-Folsom, CA	Riverside–San Bernardino–Ontario, CA	405
San Francisco–Oakland–Berkeley, CA	San Diego–Chula Vista–Carlsbad, CA	461
Subtotal		1,936
Piedmont Atlantic, Florida Megaregions		
Columbus, GA-AL	Atlanta–Sandy Springs–Alpharetta, GA	106
Augusta–Richmond County, GA-SC	Atlanta–Sandy Springs–Alpharetta, GA	145
Atlanta–Sandy Springs–Alpharetta, GA	Orlando-Kissimmee-Sanford, FL	535
Miami–Fort Lauderdale–Pompano, FL	Orlando-Kissimmee-Sanford, FL	155
Orlando-Kissimmee-Sanford, FL	Jacksonville, FL	135
Subtotal		1,075

(table continues on next page)

Table 3.7. High-Priority Routes for High-Performance Transit *(continued)*

Metropolitan Pairs		Length (miles)
Arizona, Southern California, Front Range Megaregions		
Tucson, AZ	Sierra Vista–Douglas, AZ	121
Phoenix-Mesa-Chandler, AZ	Riverside–San Bernardino–Ontario, CA	237
Yuma, AZ	Riverside–San Bernardino–Ontario, CA	182
Bakersfield, CA	Riverside–San Bernardino–Ontario, CA	148
Santa Maria–Santa Barbara, CA	Riverside–San Bernardino–Ontario, CA	205
Riverside–San Bernardino–Ontario, CA	Las Vegas–Henderson–Paradise, NV	153
Lake Havasu City–Kingman, AZ	Riverside–San Bernardino–Ontario, CA	179
Fresno, CA	Riverside–San Bernardino–Ontario, CA	246
Denver-Aurora-Lakewood, CO	Pueblo, CO	108
Subtotal		1,578
Texas Triangle, Central Plains, and Gulf Coast Megaregions		
Dallas–Fort Worth–Arlington, TX	Midland, TX	296
Dallas–Fort Worth–Arlington, TX	Houston–The Woodlands–Sugar Land, TX	229
Austin–Round Rock–Georgetown, TX	Dallas–Fort Worth–Arlington, TX	164
Austin–Round Rock–Georgetown, TX	Houston–The Woodlands–Sugar Land, TX	151
Houston–The Woodlands–Sugar Land, TX	San Antonio–New Braunfels, TX	194
Dallas–Fort Worth–Arlington, TX	San Antonio–New Braunfels, TX	224
Houston–The Woodlands–Sugar Land, TX	McAllen-Edinburg-Mission, TX	291
Oklahoma City, OK	Tulsa, OK	106
Oklahoma City, OK	Dallas–Fort Worth–Arlington, TX	186
Dallas–Fort Worth–Arlington, TX	Tyler, TX	114
Corpus Christi, TX	McAllen-Edinburg-Mission, TX	107
Subtotal		2,063
Great Lakes Megaregion		
Columbus, OH	Cincinnati, OH-KY-IN	102
Detroit-Warren-Dearborn, MI	Grand Rapids–Kentwood, MI	125
Chicago-Naperville-Elgin, IL-IN	St. Louis, MO-IL	261
Chicago-Naperville-Elgin, IL-IN	Detroit-Warren-Dearborn, MI	247
Chicago-Naperville-Elgin, IL-IN	Champaign-Urbana, IL	120
Chicago-Naperville-Elgin, IL-IN	Indianapolis-Carmel-Anderson, IN	173
Chicago-Naperville-Elgin, IL-IN	Minneapolis–St. Paul–Bloomington, MN	342
Cleveland-Elyria, OH	Columbus, OH	112
Subtotal		1,482

network, and similar innovations in other megaregions, might provide a platform for broader economic development measures in left-behind areas of the nation's megaregions. Although transportation investment alone will not solve this problem, it could stimulate new opportunities and initiatives to address income and racial inequality in megaregions across the country.

INCOME INEQUALITY AND POVERTY TRENDS IN MEGAREGIONS

Growing economic and racial inequality has gained more awareness in the United States with the help of the Black Lives Matter demonstrations in cities across the country in 2020. Economic inequality is increasing in the nation's megaregions, and race, income, and geography are highly correlated.

Kuznets's (1955) hypothesis suggests that income inequality rises in the early stage of economic growth. As the economy develops further, income inequality reaches a peak and then descends. Empirical observations for the last decades of the 20th century from OECD countries, however, do not confirm Kuznets's trajectory. Alderson and Nielsen (2002) report that 10 of 16 OECD countries displayed an upward trend of income inequality over the period 1967–1992.

A 2020 study from the Pew Research Center also shows widening gaps in income between upper-, middle-, and lower-income groups of U.S. households from 1980 to 2018 (Horowitz, Igielnik, and Kochhar 2020). Furthermore, income inequality in the United States is greater than in peer countries. The counter-Kuznets trend, known as the "great U-turn" (Alderson and Nielsen 2002), has motivated many scholars to examine factors explaining income inequality rising with economic growth and the policy implications.

In this study, we calculated the Gini indexes of household income for all U.S. counties in 1990, 2000, 2010, and 2016 (the latest year with data available) and also aggregated the indexes up to the megaregional level. Figure 3.11 graphs the megaregion Gini indexes to illustrate the inequality trends. The higher the Gini index value, the higher the inequality.

Household income inequality in U.S. megaregions followed the national upswing trend, but some megaregions experienced slight variations in the intermediate years. The two California megaregions and the Northeast megaregion had inequality surges in the 1990–2000 decade. After 2000, inequality continued to rise in these three megaregions, although not as fast as in the prior decade. In contrast, income inequality in the Texas Triangle, Central Plains, Gulf Coast, and Great Lakes megaregions decreased during 1990–2000 but trended upward thereafter. The remaining six megaregions saw steady increases in income inequality since 1990. By Gini index

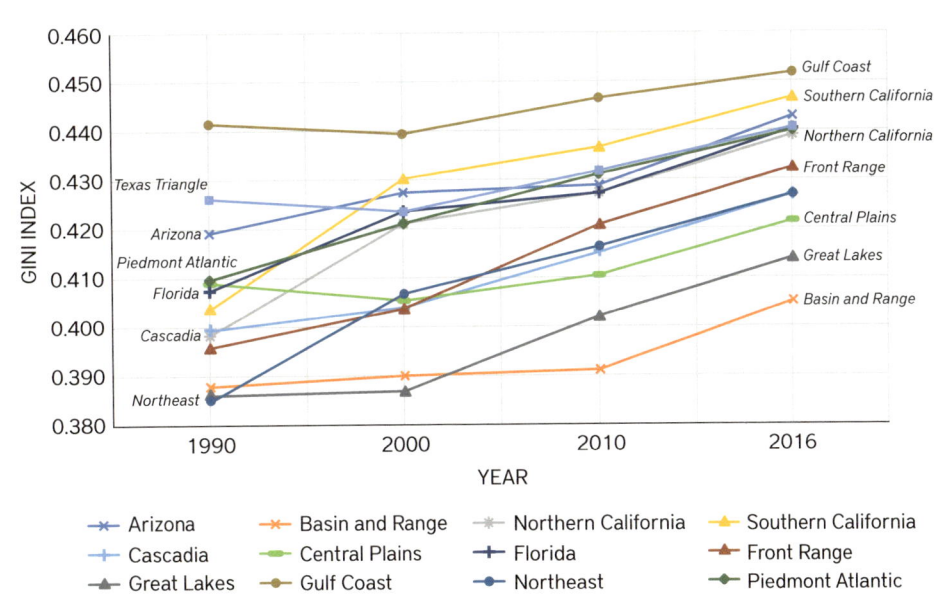

FIGURE 3.11 Gini index of household income inequality in U.S. megaregions, 1990–2016.
Source: Ming Zhang.

measures, income inequality in the Gulf Coast has been the highest among all 13 megaregions since 1990 (table 3.8). The Northeast once had the lowest income inequality, in 1990. By 2016, it had moved up and ranked close to the national average. Basin and Range has had the lowest income inequality since 2000. Income inequality of megaregion counties and nonmegaregion counties seemed to converge. In 1990, income inequality in megaregion counties (Gini index 0.405) was lower than that of nonmegaregions (Gini index 0.420). This gap narrowed in 2000 and again in 2010. By 2016, they both had an average Gini index of 0.433.

Figures 3.12a and 3.12b map the county-level geographic distribution of income inequality by Gini indexes in 1990 and 2016, respectively. The 1990 map (figure 3.12a) shows relatively low inequality in the Great Lakes, Northeast, and megaregions in the West and Midwest. The Piedmont Atlantic megaregion also presented relatively low inequality, except for a number of counties on the southern edge of the megaregion. High-inequality counties occurred largely in the Texas Triangle and Gulf Coast megaregions and particularly outside the megaregions. Figure 3.12b shows an overall geographic pattern of income inequality similar to that of 1990. The number of counties with high income inequality in 2016 is clearly higher than in 1990.

The growing literature on this issue reveals a range of factors contributing to the longitudinal trend and cross-sectional variations of income inequality in the United States (Moller, Alderson, and Nielsen 2009). One set of factors pertains to skill-based

Table 3.8. Gini Index of Household Income Inequality in U.S. Megaregions, 1990–2016

	1990	2000	2010	2016
Arizona Sun Corridor	0.419	0.427	0.429	0.443
Basin and Range	0.388	0.390	0.391	0.405
Northern California	0.398	0.421	0.427	0.439
Southern California	0.404	0.430	0.437	0.447
Cascadia	0.399	0.404	0.415	0.427
Central Plains	0.409	0.405	0.410	0.422
Florida	0.407	0.424	0.427	0.440
Front Range	0.396	0.404	0.421	0.432
Great Lakes	0.386	0.387	0.402	0.414
Gulf Coast	0.442	0.439	0.447	0.452
Northeast	0.385	0.407	0.416	0.427
Piedmont Atlantic	0.410	0.421	0.431	0.440
Texas Triangle	0.426	0.424	0.432	0.441
Megaregion Average	0.405	0.414	0.422	0.433
Nonmegaregion Average	0.420	0.423	0.423	0.433
U.S. Average	0.413	0.418	0.423	0.433

Source: Author estimates based on data from U.S. Census Bureau (1990, 2000, 2010, 2016a, 2020a).

technological change. Advances in computer technologies and their applications to manufacturing industries have led to the increased demand for highly educated and skilled workers. Growth in the tertiary sector—for instance, finance, insurance, and real estate—also explains the rising income inequality because these industries tend to pay high wages.

Institutional and policy context also matters. For instance, the minimum wage, which has declined in real value over time, is one of the key sources of rising inequality, especially at the bottom end of the income distribution. Sociodemographic factors associated with race, age, and family composition certainly play important roles. Black workers have a systematic income disadvantage relative to whites. Counties with a larger percentage of Hispanic population likely have a higher level of income inequality. Studies have shown a strong association between household income inequality and proportion of households headed by single women. Urbanization also affects income inequality, but studies have produced complex and mixed results on the direction and magnitude of the effects. Despite the many declarations that rapidly urbanizing counties have high inequality, rural counties often have higher inequality than urban

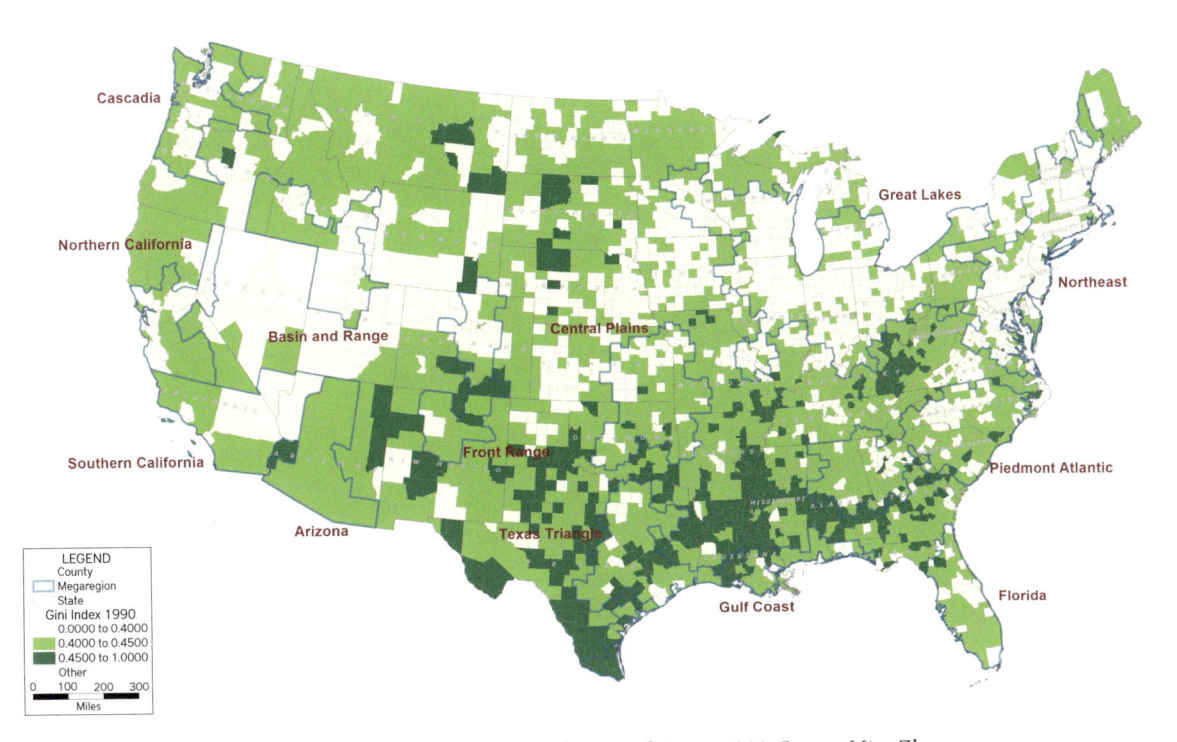

FIGURE 3.12A Household income inequality in the United States, 1990. *Source: Ming Zhang.*

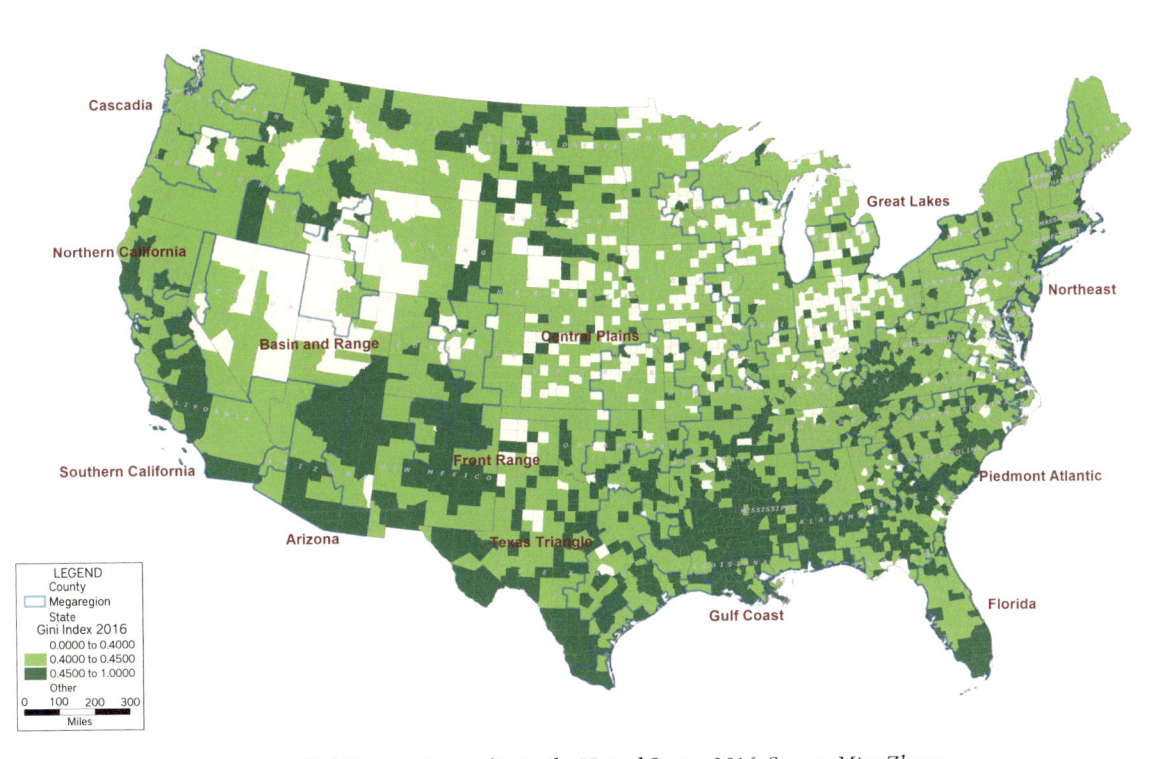

FIGURE 3.12B Household income inequality in the United States, 2016. *Source: Ming Zhang.*

RISING INEQUALITY AND DECLINING AFFORDABILITY | 99

Table 3.9. Poverty Rates in U.S. Megaregions, 1990–2018

	1990 (%)	2000 (%)	2010 (%)	2018 (%)
Arizona Sun Corridor	14.6	13.1	16.6	13.4
Basin and Range	11.5	9.7	13.0	9.7
Northern California	11.5	12.2	14.3	11.8
Southern California	12.9	15.0	15.7	13.4
Cascadia	10.7	10.4	13.3	10.5
Central Plains	13.5	11.9	15.2	13.4
Florida	11.1	11.2	14.8	13.0
Front Range	12.0	9.9	13.7	10.5
Great Lakes	11.6	10.1	14.1	12.5
Gulf Coast	23.8	20.3	20.8	19.3
Northeast	9.8	10.7	11.8	11.0
Piedmont Atlantic	13.6	12.5	16.6	14.1
Texas Triangle	15.2	12.9	15.6	13.3
Megaregion Rate	12.1	11.7	14.4	12.6
Nonmegaregion Rate	17.5	15.2	17.3	15.8
U.S. Rate	13.1	12.3	14.8	13.1

Source: Author estimates based on U.S. Census Bureau (1989–2019, 2020a).

counties. Many rural counties that have good connections with urbanized areas are doing better in income distribution than the more isolated rural counties.

Poverty in the overall population has trended downward since President Lyndon B. Johnson's War on Poverty, declared in 1964 (Chaudry and Wimer 2016). Poverty rates still fluctuated, largely following economic cycles. For instance, the percentage of the population living in poverty fell dramatically following the economic expansions in the 1960s and early 1970s. At the beginning of the new century, but especially in the years before and after the Great Recession, poverty rates rose quickly and then declined gradually during the ensuing economic recovery. Many safety net programs and federal expenditures helped reduce poverty and its impacts on low-income individuals and families.

For this study, we used the U.S. county-level poverty estimates to calculate poverty rates in the 13 megaregions in 1990–2018 (shown in table 3.9 and figure 3.13). Poverty rates in most of the 13 megaregions closely resemble national trend and fluctuation cycles. Exceptions occurred in the two California and the Northeast megaregions; in all three megaregions, poverty rates increased continuously from 1990 to 2010 and then fell in 2018. The Florida megaregion shows the same trend, but the

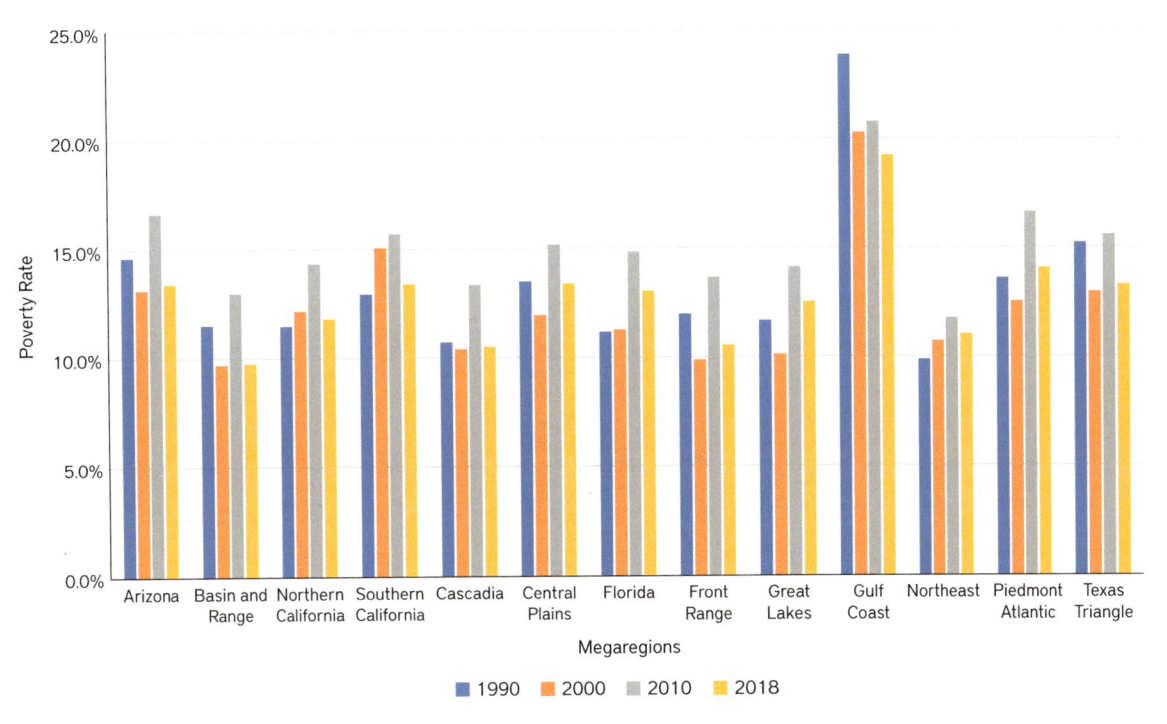

FIGURE 3.13 Poverty rates in U.S. megaregions, 1990–2018. *Source: Ming Zhang.*

change is more abrupt. Gulf Coast stood out as having the highest poverty among all megaregions throughout the years.

The COVID-19 pandemic and the corresponding economic crisis have changed the course of U.S. poverty, now trending upward. In the early months of the pandemic, initial shutdowns and unemployment were about to send many families and individuals into poverty. This did not happen because income tax credits for eligible families offset some losses. In addition, the federal economic relief package—the Coronavirus Aid, Relief, and Economic Security (CARES) Act—provided stimulus checks to qualified individuals. The federal relief package helped lift 18 million people out of poverty, dropping the U.S. poverty level to 13.9 percent in April 2020. After the unemployment benefit expired, the poverty rate soared to 17 percent in August. The pandemic has also widened the poverty disparities between white and Black and Hispanic people. The estimated poverty rate reached 12.3 percent for white individuals in August. At the same time, Black and Hispanic individuals saw new poverty rates of 26.3 percent and 26.9 percent, respectively. The child poverty rate reached 21.4 percent. On March 11, 2021, President Joe Biden signed a $1.9 trillion COVID-19 relief bill, the American Rescue Plan, into law, which sent $1,400 stimulus checks to those in need.

CONCLUSION

"Trend is not destiny," declared René Dubos (1971). The trend since World War II has been for people to move from the Rust Belt to the Sunbelt. The Sunbelt has become warmer and is likely to become even hotter as climate change accelerates. In addition, the Sunbelt megaregions are increasingly prone to both natural and human-induced disasters. Might this result in mass migrations of climate refugees? How might this exacerbate growing wealth disparities?

It has been over a half century since the Lyndon B. Johnson administration's War on Poverty set out to reduce poverty levels across the country. In the absence of any similar strategies in recent decades, the last 30 years has seen income inequality worsen and poverty nearly stagnate across the country. Housing has become less affordable and access to transportation, jobs, and food more problematic. The Black Lives Matter movement, especially in 2020, has shed light on these inequalities and the extent that they are perpetuated by systemic racism. The time has come again to address these issues with decisive actions. This time, we hope that poverty and income inequalities will be resolved. We believe megaregion-scale planning will be helpful in the creation of a more equitable future.

4
COMPETITIVENESS OF U.S. MEGAREGIONS

Productivity depends on many factors, including our workforce's knowledge and skills and the quality of the capital, technology, and infrastructure that they have to work with.

—JANET YELLEN

FOSTERING MEGAREGIONS HAS INTERESTED MANY COUNTRIES IN Europe and Asia as a spatial strategy to strengthen local and national competitiveness in the globalized world market. This chapter profiles the economic characteristics of U.S. megaregions to understand the relationship between industrial specializations and economic productivity. In addition, it identifies and quantifies the effects of factor input, such as labor, developed land, and innovations, on the economic success of counties in the megaregions.

INDUSTRIAL SPECIALIZATIONS OF U.S. MEGAREGIONS

A location quotient (LQ) analysis provides a snapshot of a region's industrial specializations relative to a larger economy—typically, a nation. An LQ is the ratio of an industry's share in the local economy (e.g., a metro area) to that industry's share in the national economy (or any reference economy in which the local economy resides). Industries with LQ values greater than 1 are export oriented because they produce more than the consumption demand of the local market. Larger LQ values indicate the local region's greater specializations and stronger competitiveness in those industries. The export-oriented industries bring in external dollars and contribute to the local and regional economies.

An LQ analysis can be carried out at any given level of geographic scale—for example, city, county, or metropolitan area—depending on study purposes. In this book, we calculate LQs at the megaregion level. This analysis focuses on the industries with LQ values greater than 1.5. A literal interpretation of these industries with LQs greater than 1.5 is that the shares of the industry employment in the megaregion are at least 50 percent greater than the shares of the respective industries in the total national employment. Because our LQ indexes are the ratio of megaregion to national total, we can compare megaregion LQ values, which allows for quick assessments of the competition or complementarity and the relative strength of industries across the megaregions.

We highlight each megaregion's industrial characteristics by examining its top five export-oriented industries (ranked by the number of employees). Discussion limited to the top five industries tells only part of the story of each megaregion's economy. Industries not making the top five list and those with LQs less than 1.5 are also essential to the local and megaregional economies. Another cautionary note concerns the level of industrial classification. The economic censuses of industries by the U.S. Census Bureau follow the North American Industry Classification System (NAICS), known before 1997 as the Standard Industrial Classification (SIC) system. In this study, we use data at the SIC three-digit level to match the NAICS four-digit level for industrial groups.

On the basis of industrial compositions observed for 1990 and 2018, we categorize the 13 U.S. megaregions into four types: manufacturing megas, successfully transformed, strengthening specialized services, and resource dependent but gradually transforming.

Manufacturing Megas

The Great Lakes and Piedmont Atlantic megaregions deserve the title of U.S. manufacturing megas. From 1990 to 2018, Great Lakes maintained its specialization in manufacturing production. In 1990, its five largest export-oriented industries specialized in miscellaneous manufactures, plastic products, metalworking machinery, metal forgings and stampings, and industrial machinery. Nearly 30 years later, the region's five largest export-oriented industries remain the same (and keep SIC industry titles under the new NAICS). In total, these five industries employed nearly 900,000 workers in 2018. In Piedmont Atlantic, four of its five largest industries came from manufacturing or construction in 1990. One service industry, telephone communications, was in the top five, largely owing to the presence of the BellSouth Corporation. By 2018, Piedmont Atlantic remained highly specialized in manufacturing, with four of its five largest industries from manufacturing. The region's telephone communications service remains important (LQ of 1.49 and thus not listed here) but declined in its relative significance to the megaregion's economy because of

Table 4.1. Largest Export-Oriented Industry Groups in Manufacturing Megas U.S. Megaregions, by Number of Employees

SIC/NAICS	Industry Group	Employees	LQ
	Great Lakes		
	1990		
399	Miscellaneous manufactures	452,837	1.59
308	Miscellaneous plastic products (not elsewhere classified)	269,394	1.69
354	Metalworking machinery	257,651	2.96
346	Metal forgings and stampings	199,786	3.19
359	Industrial machinery (not elsewhere classified)	145,579	1.66
	2018		
3363	Motor vehicle parts manufacturing	286,693	3.03
3261	Plastics product manufacturing	221,729	2.00
3327	Machine shops; turned product; and screw, nut, and bolt manufacturing	146,819	2.06
3231	Printing and related support activities	136,981	1.68
3339	Other general purpose machinery manufacturing	107,187	2.24
	Piedmont Atlantic		
	1990		
225	Knitting mills	107,430	10.79
251	Household furniture	98,475	5.97
151	General building contractors	83,684	1.54
228	Yarn and thread mills	57,896	14.43
481	Telephone communications	52,318	1.50
	2018		
3363	Motor vehicle parts manufacturing	67,682	1.89
3261	Plastics product manufacturing	65,126	1.56
2211	Electric power generation, transmission, and distribution	51,548	1.52
3116	Animal slaughtering and processing	50,039	2.12
3371	Household and institutional furniture and kitchen cabinet manufacturing	33,890	2.38

advances in telecommunications technologies worldwide and the rapid growth of competing service carriers since the 1990s in the United States.

Within these two megaregions, some cities, such as the state capitals Indianapolis and Columbus in the Great Lakes megaregion, are or are becoming successfully transformed, with strong service sectors differing from this manufacturing dominance (table 4.1). Columbus, for example, had for most of its history the third-largest population in the state, behind the industrial and manufacturing powerhouses of Cleveland and Cincinnati. Before the 1950s, it was more similar in size to Toledo, Akron, and Dayton. As other cities in Ohio have declined in population since the 1960s, Columbus has boomed, with its strong base in government and higher education. The city has also benefited from being at the intersection of two interstate highways and having strategic annexation policies.

Successfully Transformed

Northern California (figure 4.1) and Cascadia (figure 4.2) are successfully transformed megaregions, both of which experienced major economic transformation between 1990 and 2018. In 1990, Northern California's economic base, as indicated by its five largest export-oriented industries, was dominated by the manufacturing of electronic components and accessories, computer and office equipment, computer and data processing services, telephone communications, and measuring and controlling devices. By 2018, none of the manufacturing industrial groups even made it to the top 10 list. Four of the new top five industries came from the service sector; one came from health care and social assistance. Computer systems design and related services became the largest employer in Northern California, followed by software publishers, other information services, outpatient care centers, and scientific research and development services. Silicon Valley and San Francisco are significant high-tech hubs in the region. Napa Valley and other Northern California areas are famous for their wine production but sadly, increasingly also for wildfires, which threaten that industry.

Cascadia's industrial transformation was equally remarkable. In 1990, three of Cascadia's top five export-oriented industries came from lumber and wood products and related trade, including millwork, plywood and structural members, sawmills and planing mills, and lumber and construction materials (table 4.2). By 2018, in much the same way as for Northern California, none of them appeared on the top five list. Led by Microsoft Corporation's growth, software publishers replaced millwork

FIGURE 4.1 Sunset over Oakland and San Francisco. *Source: istock.com/yhelfman.*

FIGURE 4.2 Interstate 5 bridge over Lake Union leading into downtown Seattle.
Source: istock.com/MarkHatfield.

as the largest export-oriented employer in the region. The Boeing Company contributed to the growth of aerospace product and parts manufacturing, Cascadia's second-largest export-oriented industry in 2018. Cascadia's largest cities, Seattle and Portland, have become magnets for the "creative class" (Florida 2002). Amazon, Microsoft, Starbucks, and Nike are all retail companies grounded in innovation. As noted above, Cascadia is also known as an ectopia (Callenbach 1975) and has some of the most progressive environmental and planning laws in the nation.

Strengthening Specialized Services

The second half of the 20th century witnessed the rise of the service economy and the declining contribution to global manufacturing by the U.S. economy (Witt and Gross 2020). Data from 1990 to 2018 reveal particularly strong evidence of six of the 13 U.S. megaregions growing and strengthening in specialization of services. Four of them—Arizona Sun Corridor, Basin and Range, Front Range, and Northeast—have become increasingly specialized in what Sassen (1991) and Hall and Pain (2006) characterize as advanced producer services (APS), or industries serving businesses. The other two, Southern California and Florida, have strengthened their functions as international gateways and destinations for entertainment and recreation. Accordingly, we later introduce the six megaregions as two separate subgroups, shown in tables 4.3 and 4.4, respectively.

Table 4.2. Largest Export-Oriented Industry Groups in Successfully Transformed U.S. Megaregions, by Number of Employees

SIC/NAICS	Industry Group	Employees	LQ
	1990		
	Northern California		
367	Electronic components and accessories	152,724	4.66
357	Computer and office equipment	113,033	8.03
737	Computer and data processing services	110,797	1.58
481	Telephone communications	49,049	1.71
382	Measuring and controlling devices	43,500	3.04
	Cascadia		
243	Millwork, plywood, and structural members	28,800	5.21
242	Sawmills and planing mills	28,416	7.12
481	Telephone communications	26,323	1.81
503	Lumber and construction materials	21,354	2.01
802	Offices and clinics of dentists	20,101	1.51
	2018		
	Northern California		
5415	Computer systems design and related services	144,142	1.65
5112	Software publishers	117,358	3.82
5191	Other information services	103,389	7.13
6214	Outpatient care centers	90,543	1.75
5417	Scientific research and development services	82,091	2.34
	Cascadia		
5112	Software publishers	85,042	4.27
3364	Aerospace product and parts manufacturing	69,558	6.47
6233	Continuing care retirement communities and assisted living facilities for the elderly	48,043	1.70
2383	Building finishing contractors	42,226	1.75
2381	Foundation, structure, and building exterior contractors	40,643	1.53

The Arizona megaregion's export-oriented industries in 1990 concentrated in construction and manufacturing sectors. By 2018, three of its top five industries came from the finance and insurance sectors. Business support services became the largest employer in the region (table 4.3).

Counties in Arizona are huge. For instance, Maricopa County, the location of Phoenix, encompasses 9,224 square miles—nearly the size of Massachusetts. Phoenix has grown through aggressive annexation, including strip annexation, or annexation of narrow strips of land bordering Phoenix that bring prized developments into the city (figure 4.3). Phoenix and other Arizona cities also benefit from adjacent large tracts of state land. Arizona has given a preference to developers willing to buy these lands with the revenues generated mainly benefiting schools.

Table 4.3. Largest Export-Oriented Industry Groups in Strengthening Specialized Services U.S. Megaregions, by Number of Employees (Subgroup 1)

SIC/NAICS	Industry Group	Employees	LQ
	1990		
	Arizona		
367	Electronic components and accessories	49,439	5.51
701	Hotels and motels	33,118	1.77
174	Masonry, stonework, and plastering	22,815	1.87
481	Telephone communications	19,255	2.46
451	Air transportation, scheduled	17,868	3.10
	Basin and Range		
514	Groceries and related products	18,008	1.97
594	Miscellaneous shopping goods stores	15,810	1.57
421	Trucking and courier services, except air	15,713	1.72
554	Gasoline service stations	7,597	1.60
802	Offices and clinics of dentists	5,314	1.54
	Front Range		
871	Engineering and architectural services	36,164	1.51
737	Computer and data processing services	30,859	1.54
873	Research and testing services	17,449	2.05
481	Telephone communications	15,105	1.85
357	Computer and office equipment	10,209	2.55
	Northeast		
822	Colleges and universities	293,185	1.99
873	Research and testing services	206,018	1.53
513	Apparel, piece goods, and notions	175,052	2.30
233	Women's and misses' outerwear	168,020	1.93
621	Security brokers and dealers	146,631	2.24
	2018		
	Arizona		
5614	Business support services	33,145	2.23
2381	Foundation, structure, and building exterior contractors	27,316	1.65
5222	Nondepository credit intermediation	24,279	2.10
3364	Aerospace product and parts manufacturing	20,487	3.07
5223	Activities related to credit intermediation	19,254	3.46
	Basin and Range		
6113	Colleges, universities, and professional schools	31,951	1.64
5614	Business support services	23,977	2.46
2381	Foundation, structure, and building exterior contractors	19,934	1.84
5112	Software publishers	17,493	2.16
5419	Other professional, scientific, and technical services	15,975	1.95
	Front Range		
5413	Architectural, engineering, and related services	47,926	1.63
5173	Wired and wireless telecommunications carriers	42,382	2.08
5417	Scientific research and development services	37,945	2.61
5614	Business support services	34,251	2.24
2381	Foundation, structure, and building exterior contractors	26,651	1.57
	Northeast		
6113	Colleges, universities, and professional schools	616,434	1.92
5415	Computer systems design and related services	569,283	1.50
6232	Residential intellectual and developmental disability, mental health, and substance abuse facilities	236,328	1.52
5417	Scientific research and development services	233,255	1.53
5239	Other financial investment activities	229,092	2.03

Table 4.4. Largest Export-Oriented Industry Groups in Strengthening Specialized Services U.S. Megaregions, by Number of Employees (Subgroup 2)

SIC/NAICS	Industry Group	Employees	LQ
	1990		
	Southern California		
372	Aircraft and parts	247,362	6.32
781	Motion picture production and services	231,741	6.27
367	Electronic components and accessories	117,272	1.77
233	Women's and misses' outerwear	115,712	2.97
175	Carpentry and floor work	72,521	1.66
	Florida		
736	Personnel supply services	180,703	1.61
701	Hotels and motels	103,605	1.93
799	Miscellaneous amusement, recreation services	90,256	2.00
174	Masonry, stonework, and plastering	53,392	1.53
655	Subdividers and developers	25,512	2.67
	2018		
	Southern California		
7211	Traveler accommodation	323,576	2.04
5616	Investigation and security services	119,988	1.59
5121	Motion picture and video industries	102,368	4.49
7131	Amusement parks and arcades	54,899	3.35
3364	Aerospace product and parts manufacturing	51,212	1.85
	Florida		
7211	Traveler accommodation	173,282	1.55
5614	Business support services	69,807	1.61
7131	Amusement parks and arcades	65,348	5.64
5313	Activities related to real estate	57,958	1.50
5312	Offices of real estate agents and brokers	37,586	2.03

Surprisingly, even as Maricopa County development has sprawled across the Sonoran Desert, some short-term water benefits have been realized because suburban houses use less water than the cotton or citrus they replaced. The state has also benefited greatly from former governor Bruce Babbitt's prescient Groundwater Management Act of 1980. Still, most of Arizona is desert and thus especially vulnerable to climate change. "Between 2040 and 2060 extreme temperatures will become commonplace in the South and Southwest, with some counties in Arizona experiencing temperatures above 95 degrees [F] for half the year." In addition, "southwestern Arizona will see soaring wet bulb temperatures," which will make "it dangerous to work outdoors and for children to play school sports" (Shaw, Lustgarten, and Goldsmith 2020).

Basin and Range was consumer service oriented in 1990, as shown by its largest employers in groceries and related products, miscellaneous shopping goods stores,

FIGURE 4.3 Phoenix metropolitan area at night, viewed from South Mountain. *Source: istock.com/Gregory Clifford.*

gasoline service stations, offices and clinics of dentists, and to some extent trucking and courier services (excluding via air). By 2018, its top industries had shifted toward APS, including colleges, universities, and professional schools; business support services; software publishers; and other professional, scientific, and technical services. Similarly, Front Range's specialization in APS also strengthened from 1990 to 2018.

The Northeast megaregion is the cradle of U.S. higher education. Its colleges and universities have attracted thousands of students from around the world. It is thus not surprising to see that colleges, universities, and professional schools were the region's largest employers in both 1990 (professional schools were not part of the category in 1990) and 2018. Its specialization in APS also strengthened from 1990 to 2018, evidenced by its top industries in computer systems design and related services, scientific research and development services, and other financial investment activities.

Southern California's economic transition took place between the secondary and tertiary sectors. In 1990, three of its five largest industries specialized in manufacturing production: aircraft and parts, electronic components and accessories, women's and misses' outerwear, and carpentry and floor work. Motion picture production and services was the second-largest export-oriented employer in 1990 and remained one of the top five in 2018 (table 4.4). Carpentry and floor work in the construction division was the megaregion's fifth largest in 1990 but dropped off the top five list in 2018. Traveler accommodation stood out as the largest employer in Southern California due to the fast growth in air, maritime, and ground transportation. Amusement parks and arcades also made it to the top five because of Disneyland Parks and similar attractions.

The Florida megaregion augmented its Disney-related business and economic activities from 1990 to 2018. One of the five largest industries in 1990, miscellaneous amusement and recreation services, remained on the top five list in 2018, as amusement parks and arcades. Similar to Southern California, the Florida megaregion saw the traveler accommodation industry rise because of its function as the gateway to and from Latin American countries. Activities related to real estate and offices of real estate agents and brokers are among the largest export-oriented industries, which can be attributed to the vast demand for seasonal and retirement homes in Florida.

Resource Dependent but Gradually Transforming

Three megaregions—Texas Triangle, Gulf Coast, and Central Plains—are in this group (table 4.5). In 1990, the Texas Triangle's economic base depended heavily on mining and related activities, and three of its five largest export-oriented industries were heavy construction, except highway (mainly construction of oil and gas pipeline and related structures); oil and gas field services; and miscellaneous nonmetallic minerals. By 2018, this reliance on mining and related activities did not change much, because the construction of oil and gas pipelines and related structures contributed the most (by size of employment) to the Triangle's export-oriented economic activities, and support activities for mining remained on the top five list. During the same period, the Texas Triangle was transforming by having three of its top five industries in the service industries: nondepository credit intermediation, scheduled air transportation, and specialty hospitals.

In the Texas Triangle, scheduled air transportation became the third-largest industry in 2018, reflecting the fast business expansions by major airlines such as American Airlines and Southwest Airlines (both headquartered in Dallas–Fort Worth) and Continental Airlines (headquartered in Houston and merged with United Airlines in 2010). Furthermore, specialty hospitals joined the top five, resulting from the Texas health care boom. Houston is also home to the Texas Medical Center, the largest of its kind in the world.

Texas counties are weak, whereas Texas cities are powerful. The state's annexation laws empower its cities to expand spatially with few constraints. Texas even grants cities extraterritorial jurisdiction, allowing them to control development beyond their city limits. These annexation laws have facilitated the rapid growth of the state's big cities, as illustrated by the 2020 census (U.S. Census Bureau 2021). Texas

Table 4.5. Largest Export-Oriented Industry Groups in Resource-Dependent, Gradually Transforming U.S. Megaregions, by Number of Employees

SIC/NAICS	Industry Group	Employees	LQ
	1990		
	Central Plains		
421	Trucking and courier services, except air	49,259	1.62
805	Nursing and personal care facilities	47,161	1.61
372	Aircraft and parts	44,103	5.22
866	Religious organizations	41,102	1.70
481	Telephone communications	24,828	1.99
	Gulf Coast		
508	Machinery, equipment, and supplies	35,935	1.58
138	Oil and gas field services	35,182	10.58
514	Groceries and related products	32,787	1.51
449	Water transportation services	26,318	13.27
162	Heavy construction, except highway	19,793	3.37
	Texas Triangle		
481	Telephone communications	64,692	2.13
162	Heavy construction, except highway	59,068	2.94
138	Oil and gas field services	52,057	4.59
149	Miscellaneous nonmetallic minerals	50,202	11.87
344	Fabricated structural metal products	43,943	1.60
	2018		
	Central Plains		
8131	Religious organizations	66,743	1.55
4841	General freight trucking	47,342	1.84
3364	Aerospace product and parts manufacturing	30,969	3.41
3116	Animal slaughtering and processing	30,496	3.73
4842	Specialized freight trucking	21,495	1.76
	Gulf Coast		
6241	Individual and family services	64,999	1.91
4523	General merchandise stores, including warehouse clubs and supercenters	60,779	1.51
6216	Home health care services	53,210	2.03
2371	Utility system construction	52,253	4.88
6111	Elementary and secondary schools	34,303	1.83
	Texas Triangle		
2371	Utility system construction	107,583	2.73
5222	Nondepository credit intermediation	70,356	1.68
4811	Scheduled air transportation	61,772	2.15
2131	Support activities for mining	60,017	2.80
6223	Specialty (except psychiatric and substance abuse) hospitals	37,184	3.23

cities are also very different from each other. El Paso is physically closer to San Diego than to Houston and is sociodemographically more similar to Tucson and Albuquerque than to Dallas or Fort Worth. The state capital, Austin, is well known for its progressive politics, which often puts it at odds with its neighbors. Of course, the Texas Triangle and the Gulf Coast are especially vulnerable to climate change. In addition to extreme heat and humidity, these megaregions are especially susceptible to sea level rise and more frequent hurricanes. The Texas Triangle is also especially prone to drought, flash floods, and wildfires.

The Gulf Coast displayed an economic structure and gradual changes like those of the Texas Triangle. In 1990, two of its top five industries came from mining and related activities. By 2018, only one of these remained. Four of its top five industries came from service sectors, a large increase from 1990. These service industries were mainly consumer oriented, rather than APS oriented, as seen in the megaregions of the prior group (e.g., Arizona and Northeast).

Central Plains experienced the least compositional change among all megaregions in its top five export-oriented industries. Four of its top five remained unchanged from 1990 to 2018. No industries in mining and related activities made to the top five but did make it to its top 10 industry list. Therefore, we put the Central Plains in the same group as the Texas Triangle and Gulf Coast megaregions (figure 4.4).

FIGURE 4.4 Aerial view of Kansas City, Missouri, and Kansas. *Source: istock.com/Skyhobo.*

ECONOMIC PRODUCTIVITY

This section reports megaregion GDPs for 2001 and 2016 measured by three indicators: GDP per capita, GDP per worker, and GDP per square mile of developed land (or built-up area). Although these three measures relate to each other closely, they characterize different aspects of the megaregion economy. GDP per capita offers a good representation of the region's standard of living. Changes in GDP per capita indicate the average economic well-being in the study regions. GDP per worker (per employed person) measures labor productivity. Shifts in workforce participation may result in growth of GDP per capita, whereas GDP per worker may remain the same or even decline. GDP per square mile of built-up area measures land productivity and may also indicate land use efficiency.

GDP per Capita

From 2001 to 2016, per capita GDP grew in all megaregion and nonmegaregion counties (table 4.6). Their starting GDPs and growth paces, however, differed, leading to changes in relative levels of well-being. In 2001, per capita GDPs in the 13 megaregions were all higher, even in the Gulf Coast ($28,352), than the average of the rest of the United States ($27,387). Northeast, Northern California, and Front Range had the highest per capita GDPs at $45,355, $44,914, and $42,169, respectively. By 2016, their well-being relative to other megaregions shifted slightly. Northern

Table 4.6. Change in GDP per Capita in U.S. Megaregions

	2001 ($)	2016 ($)	Change (%)
Arizona	33,683	45,864	36.2
Basin and Range	31,439	49,591	57.7
Northern California	44,914	76,888	71.2
Southern California	37,664	61,373	62.9
Cascadia	40,598	66,419	63.6
Central Plains	31,927	48,448	51.7
Florida	32,044	46,043	43.7
Front Range	42,169	57,015	35.2
Great Lakes	36,736	56,324	53.3
Gulf Coast	28,352	43,217	52.4
Northeast	45,355	72,474	59.8
Piedmont Atlantic	35,706	51,198	43.4
Texas Triangle	39,520	59,498	50.5
Rest of USA	27,387	45,032	64.4

California championed per capita GDP growth, achieving a 71 percent increase from 2001 to 2016. Cascadia moved up to become the third-richest megaregion, following Northern California and Northeast.

In 2016, the Gulf Coast's per capita GDP level ($43,217) fell below the average of the nonmegaregion counties ($45,032) despite a 52 percent increase from its 2001 level. Hurricane Katrina certainly played a role. This Category 5 tropical storm struck the Gulf Coast area in August 2005 and caused over 1,800 deaths and $125 billion in damage, and it disrupted the business and life of the area in post-Katrina years.

GDP per Worker

Northern California, Northeast, and Cascadia took the top three positions in labor productivity, measured by GDP per worker in 2016 (table 4.7). These megaregions have concentrated high-tech firms and tertiary industries, which typically pay more than manufacturing industries. Among these three megaregions, Northeast slipped from its lead in 2001 to be surpassed by Northern California in 2016. Per worker GDP in nonmegaregions appeared to have grown remarkably, reaching $80,375 in 2016, higher than that of the Basin and Range, Central Plains, and Gulf Coast. Given the wide spread of the nonmegaregion counties across the country, identifying the reasons for growth in these counties requires further research. Our data set contains a few exceptional county observations that may partly

Table 4.7. Change in GDP per Worker in U.S. Megaregions

	2001 ($)	2016 ($)	Change (%)
Arizona	60,975	85,192	39.7
Basin and Range	51,497	79,479	54.3
Northern California	76,185	128,447	68.6
Southern California	68,361	104,172	52.4
Cascadia	66,694	108,905	63.3
Central Plains	51,843	80,078	54.5
Florida	58,401	80,846	38.4
Front Range	63,805	88,568	38.8
Great Lakes	61,501	92,421	50.3
Gulf Coast	54,448	78,948	45.0
Northeast	77,031	113,593	47.5
Piedmont Atlantic	60,712	88,379	45.6
Texas Triangle	65,341	96,282	47.4
Rest of USA	49,862	80,375	61.2

explain the high value of average per worker GDP. One nonmegaregion county, Loving County, Texas, for example, had 117 persons and 92 jobs in 2016. Its total GDP was recorded as $1,524 million, which gives a per worker GDP of $16.57 million, the highest among U.S. counties. An additional five nonmegaregion counties—Glasscock, McMullen, Upton, and Roberts of Texas and Eureka of Nevada—all had per worker GDP exceeding $500,000. A surging demand for shale drilling in the Permian Basin contributed to the exceptional increase in these counties' economic outputs.

GDP per Square Mile of Developed Land

When measured by GDP per unit of developed land, productivity was highest in Northern California, Southern California, and Northeast in both 2001 and 2016 (table 4.8). Cascadia's GDP per square mile of developed land ($77.30 million) lagged behind seven other megaregions in 2001. However, from 2001 to 2016, GDP per square mile of developed land in Cascadia grew by 94 percent, to $150.0 million. Still, it was lower than five other megaregions (Northern California, Southern California, Northeast, Front Range, and Texas Triangle). The figure reflects the morphological characteristics of Cascadia megaregion, described in chapter 2. The major cities and metros in Cascadia are ecologically tied but have not continuously urbanized.

Table 4.8. Change in GDP per Square Mile of Developed Land in U.S. Megaregions

	2001 ($ millions)	2016 ($ millions)	Change (%)
Arizona	90.60	137.00	51.2
Basin and Range	56.80	106.00	86.6
Northern California	163.00	303.00	85.9
Southern California	157.00	273.00	73.9
Cascadia	77.30	150.00	94.0
Central Plains	43.00	69.80	62.3
Florida	74.20	123.00	65.8
Front Range	105.00	155.00	47.6
Great Lakes	79.60	120.00	50.8
Gulf Coast	52.70	83.70	58.8
Northeast	160.00	257.00	60.6
Piedmont Atlantic	60.20	94.80	57.5
Texas Triangle	86.70	153.00	76.5
Rest of USA	22.30	37.60	68.6

KNOWLEDGE-INTENSIVE BUSINESS SERVICES IN MEGAREGION ECONOMY

European scholars have observed that the knowledge economy is key to driving the competitiveness of their megacity regions in the era of globalization, and an important component is APS industries. Recall, APS industries are those serving businesses, not individual and household consumers. Sassen (1991, 127) stresses the key role played by APS industries in her "global cities" thesis. Hall and Pain (2006) adopt APS as one of the four key concepts in their research on eight megacity regions in northwest Europe, which considered eight industries as core APS: accounting, advertising, banking and finance, design consultancy, insurance, law, logistic services, and management consultancy and information technology.

In our study, we compiled APS industry employment data for all U.S. megaregions for 2002 and 2018, as reported in the County Business Pattern data set. As we previously noted, the economic censuses, in 1997 and earlier, reported industrial statistics using SIC codes and implemented NAICS after 1997. Although the U.S. Census Bureau provides bridge files between SIC and NAICS, we found significant inconsistencies in the data reporting for the APS industries between the two systems. Hence, we decided to use data from 2002 and after.

Tables 4.9 and 4.10 report the census-recorded jobs in seven APS industries. Interestingly, the overall trend of employment in the APS industries seems not to support the thesis that seven APS industries are core. Nationwide, the share of APS industry employment in the country decreased from 11.4 percent in 2002 to 9.9 percent in 2018, although the absolute number of employees increased from 10.544 million to 12.203 million for the same period. All megaregions experienced declining shares of APS industries in their employment bases, with two exceptions, Arizona and Texas Triangle, each showing a slight increase.

To explore in further detail megaregional specialization in specific APS industries, we calculated the LQs of these industries (table 4.11). The Northeast megaregion demonstrates its relative strength over other megaregions in APS. Advertising and logistics and management in Northeast showed the highest concentration of APS and an increasing rate of concentration relative to anywhere else in the country between 2002 and 2018. Northeast was also the most specialized in banking and finance services in 2002 (LQ of 1.33). In 2018, Northeast dropped slightly in the ranking of banking and finance services, second only to Arizona (LQ of 1.43). Northeast had strength specializing in accounting, insurance, and law services, although it was not the strongest in these areas among all megaregions.

Other megaregions had their comparative advantages in different APS industries, as shown by the LQs in table 4.10. For example, Arizona was most specialized in banking and finance and insurance services in 2018. Front Range attracted designers

Table 4.9. Employment in Seven Advanced Producer Services in U.S. Megaregions, 2002*

	Acc.	Adv.	Ban./Fin.	Des.	Ins.	Law	Logi.	APS	APS (%)	Non-APS	Total
Arizona	21.9	4.2	70.0	28.8	34.5	15.1	11.9	186.4	11.0	1,515.7	1,702.1
Basin and Range	11.2	2.8	40.9	18.6	13.5	9.2	8.0	104.1	11.8	775.5	879.6
Northern California	65.3	19.5	152.1	87.8	89.9	58.4	38.8	511.8	11.3	4,016.7	4,528.6
Southern California	260.8	40.5	246.1	114.3	154.8	88.0	64.9	969.4	11.7	7,293.2	8,262.7
Cascadia	24.3	10.5	86.5	42.0	57.4	28.9	16.5	266.2	10.2	2,346.0	2,612.2
Central Plains	24.4	8.1	80.7	31.9	53.3	26.9	14.6	240.0	10.2	2,119.1	2,359.1
Florida	72.1	17.0	218.7	78.5	115.6	75.5	43.2	620.6	12.0	4,537.9	5,158.5
Front Range	19.0	5.1	63.2	38.7	39.0	20.8	16.3	202.1	11.5	1,553.9	1,756.0
Great Lakes	220.8	88.0	710.5	244.4	494.9	208.3	171.1	2,138.1	10.7	17,890.2	20,028.3
Gulf Coast	19.2	3.9	48.6	28.2	25.3	26.0	8.4	159.7	9.2	1,572.3	1,732.0
Northeast	229.6	125.3	1,035.9	308.7	567.3	292.8	220.3	2,780.0	13.8	17,405.3	20,185.2
Piedmont Atlantic	67.0	23.0	290.2	103.0	160.8	70.8	60.7	775.5	11.7	5,829.1	6,604.6
Texas Triangle	58.6	21.2	191.9	103.8	125.6	65.2	55.0	621.3	10.6	5,236.9	5,858.1
Megaregion Subtotal	1,094.4	369.0	3,235.4	1,228.7	1,931.9	986.0	729.8	9,575.3	11.7	72,091.7	81,667.0
Nonmegaregion	113.6	24.6	327.0	112.9	192.6	143.7	55.0	969.4	9.1	9,675.0	10,644.3
Total	1,208.0	393.6	3,562.4	1,341.6	2,124.5	1,129.7	784.8	10,544.6	11.4	81,766.7	92,311.3

* By thousands of people.

Acc. = accounting; Adv. = advertising; APS = advanced producer services; Ban./Fin. = banking/financing; Des. = design consultancy; Ins = insurance; Logi. = logistics and management.

Table 4.10. Employment in Seven Advanced Producer Services in U.S. Megaregions, 2018*

	Acc.	Adv.	Ban./Fin.	Des.	Ins.	Law	Logi.	APS	APS (%)	Non-APS	Total
Arizona	19.1	5.2	101.0	28.5	65.5	17.0	23.4	259.7	11.2%	2,049.7	2,309.5
Basin and Range	14.9	5.0	57.1	20.3	22.9	12.5	16.0	148.7	9.8%	1,364.2	1,512.9
Northern California	47.4	24.5	162.9	85.4	85.7	53.5	65.0	524.5	9.2%	5,204.0	5,728.5
Southern California	84.8	54.8	242.3	132.4	148.9	101.8	100.6	865.8	9.1%	8,683.8	9,549.6
Cascadia	26.3	13.7	90.1	53.0	56.4	30.3	37.7	307.5	8.3%	3,406.7	3,714.2
Central Plains	29.3	10.1	97.8	41.5	59.2	27.2	24.0	289.1	9.2%	2,850.3	3,139.4
Florida	63.7	23.7	173.5	81.9	156.8	89.0	79.0	667.7	9.9%	6,075.0	6,742.8
Front Range	20.0	7.6	70.5	51.1	49.5	21.7	31.0	251.4	10.6%	2,127.3	2,378.7
Great Lakes	204.8	97.3	722.4	302.9	636.2	197.3	228.2	2,389.2	9.9%	21,640.1	24,029.3
Gulf Coast	17.4	4.1	55.4	40.1	33.8	24.9	14.5	190.3	8.4%	2,072.2	2,262.5
Northeast	258.8	150.5	946.3	356.9	546.4	313.4	378.1	2,950.4	11.8%	21,998.2	24,948.6
Piedmont Atlantic	78.8	30.1	274.0	123.9	176.8	78.1	95.3	857.0	9.4%	8,221.7	9,078.7
Texas Triangle	72.7	27.8	294.8	149.0	173.2	75.1	106.8	899.4	10.8%	7,437.3	8,336.6
Megaregion subtotal	938.0	454.5	3,288.1	1,467.1	2,211.4	1,041.9	1,199.6	10,600.6	10.2%	93,130.6	103,731.2
Nonmegaregion	211.6	25.2	496.1	180.6	457.8	104.7	126.9	1,602.8	8.0%	18448.5	20,051.3
Total	1,149.6	479.7	3,784.2	1,647.7	2,669.2	1,146.6	1,326.5	12,203.4	9.9%	111,579.1	123,782.5

* By thousands of people.

Acc. = Accounting; Adv. = advertising; APS = advanced producer services; Ban./Fin. = banking/financing; Des. = design consultancy; Ins. = insurance; Logi. = logistics and management.

Table 4.11. Location Quotients Displaying Relative Strengths in APS Industries in U.S. Megaregions

	Accounting 2002	Accounting 2018	Advertising 2002	Advertising 2018	Banking/Finance 2002	Banking/Finance 2018	Design Consultancy 2002	Design Consultancy 2018	Insurance 2002	Insurance 2018	Law 2002	Law 2018	Logistics, Management 2002	Logistics, Management 2018
Arizona	0.98	0.89	0.58	0.59	1.07	**1.43**	1.17	0.93	0.88	**1.31**	0.72	0.80	0.82	0.95
Basin and Range	0.98	1.06	0.73	0.86	1.20	1.23	1.45	1.01	0.67	0.70	0.85	0.89	1.07	0.99
Northern California	1.10	0.89	1.01	1.10	0.87	0.93	1.33	1.12	0.86	0.69	1.05	1.01	1.01	1.06
Southern California	**2.41**	0.96	1.15	1.48	0.77	0.83	0.95	1.04	0.81	0.72	0.87	1.15	0.92	0.98
Cascadia	0.71	0.76	0.94	0.95	0.86	0.79	1.11	1.07	0.95	0.70	0.90	0.88	0.74	0.95
Central Plains	0.79	1.01	0.81	0.83	0.89	1.02	0.93	0.99	0.98	0.88	0.93	0.93	0.73	0.71
Florida	1.07	1.02	0.77	0.91	1.10	0.84	1.05	0.91	0.97	1.08	1.20	**1.42**	0.99	1.09
Front Range	0.83	0.91	0.68	0.82	0.93	0.97	**1.51**	**1.61**	0.96	0.96	0.97	0.98	1.09	1.21
Great Lakes	0.84	0.92	1.03	1.05	0.92	0.98	0.84	0.95	1.07	1.23	0.85	0.89	1.00	0.89
Gulf Coast	0.85	0.83	0.53	0.47	0.73	0.80	1.12	1.33	0.63	0.69	**1.23**	1.19	0.57	0.60
Northeast	0.87	1.12	**1.46**	**1.56**	**1.33**	1.24	1.05	1.07	**1.22**	1.02	1.19	1.36	**1.28**	**1.41**
Piedmont Atlantic	0.78	0.93	0.82	0.86	1.14	0.99	1.07	1.03	1.06	0.90	0.88	0.93	1.08	0.98
Texas Triangle	0.76	0.94	0.85	0.86	0.85	1.16	1.22	1.34	0.93	0.96	0.91	0.97	1.10	1.20
Nonmegaregion	0.82	**1.14**	0.54	0.32	0.80	0.81	0.73	0.68	0.79	1.06	1.10	0.56	0.61	0.59

Note: Numbers in boldface indicate the largest LQ value in the corresponding industry.

Table 4.12. Utility Patents in U.S. Megaregions*

	1990	2000	2010	2015
Arizona	194.7	336.5	332.2	397.4
Basin and Range	199.9	**757.3**	**565.7**	**555.7**
Northern California	**276.4**	**847.9**	**1,282.2**	**1,778.4**
Southern California	205.7	307.9	384.7	544.1
Cascadia	207.1	352.3	**756.8**	**827.0**
Central Plains	137.2	150.3	161.3	199.8
Florida	159.0	167.3	163.5	209.2
Front Range	**232.1**	**432.3**	437.8	551.3
Great Lakes	**252.1**	349.5	356.8	443.5
Gulf Coast	101.1	108.4	57.8	77.2
Northeast	244.7	345.0	382.7	458.8
Piedmont Atlantic	113.8	184.8	218.5	273.6
Texas Triangle	220.7	390.1	384.3	454.5
Megaregion Total	217.6	342.0	395.7	497.9
Rest of USA	79.5	107.0	122.5	144.5
Total	192.4	298.3	349.8	439.6

*Number of patents per million population.

Note: Numbers in boldface indicate the top three megaregions.

and consultants proportionally higher than the rest of the country. Florida had the highest concentration in legal services. Two megaregions, Northern California and Cascadia, which had the first- and third-highest GDP per capita among all megaregions (see table 4.6), did not rank the highest in any of the APS industries.

The APS industry analysis presented here suggests that the APS thesis may explain some megaregions' strength and performance in the global network. But it does not explain the full story. Megaregions vary greatly in their economic bases and specializations. Strategies and policies for megaregional economic development should be tailor-made, adapting to local conditions and relative strengths.

Technological innovation is another important indicator explored by researchers to measure regional and megaregional productivity and competitiveness. Florida, Gulden, and Mellander (2008) use data on patent activity as a proxy for technological innovation to identify and analyze megaregions around the world.

Table 4.12 reports utility patents (or invention patents, as opposed to design patents) filed by residents in megaregions from 1990 to 2015. Northern California stands out as the most innovative megaregion in the country owing to the information technology industries in Silicon Valley and the region's research institutions and universities such as Stanford and the University of California, Berkeley. Cascadia saw a rapid increase in patent applications from 1990 to 2015 owing to the expansion of firms like Amazon and Boeing. Interestingly, Basin and Range has become one of the top three most innovative megaregions since 2000. Several reasons may explain its high numbers of patent applications. First, Utah has many patent attorneys and patent agents, and Salt Lake City has the second-highest number of patent attorneys per capita (after Washington, DC) in the country. Second, Utah offers amenities attractive to startups and growing businesses. *Forbes* magazine declared Utah the "Best State for Business and Careers" in 2018 (Starner 2018). In 2019, the Federal Communications Commission selected Salt Lake City and New York City to develop innovation zones for research on implementing 5G networks (Federal Communications Commission 2019).

GROWING INEQUALITY

The United States has persistent economic inequality, and this has become a more urgent issue in recent years, particularly with the Black Lives Matter protests against racial inequality in 2020. Rising economic inequality is evidenced by the growing concentration of wealth in a small proportion of the population, the widening gap between white and Black Americans, and slow income growth for middle-class households relative to the upper-tier income group. The U.S. Census Bureau's 2020 report on income and poverty (Semega et al. 2020) shows that the top-earning 20 percent of households held 52 percent of all U.S. income in 2018. By comparison, in 1968, income earned by households in the top 20 percent accounted for 43 percent of the nation's total. The Pew Research Center reports that the difference in median incomes between white and Black households grew from $23,800 in 1970 to $33,000 in 2018. This rise puts the United States at the top for inequality among the advanced economies ranked by the Gini index. According to estimates by OECD, the United States had a Gini index of 0.434 in 2017, whereas the coefficients for other Group of Seven countries ranged from 0.392 in the United Kingdom to 0.326 in France (Parker, Minkin, and Bennett Pew Research Center 2020).

Similarly, significant inequalities both between and within megaregions continue to widen along with megaregional growth. Glaser (2007) notes a big gap in average household income for the year 2000, when the low end ($45,506), in the Gulf Coast, measured 35 percent less than the high end, in the Northeast ($70,158) and Northern California ($70,122) megaregions. Our analysis of per capita GDP reported earlier reconfirmed this between-megaregions gap and also revealed an accelerating trend. In 2001, the ratios of per capita GDP in Northeast and Northern California to that in Gulf Coast were 1.60 and 1.58, respectively. These two ratios increased to 1.68 and 1.78 in 2016 (using figures in table 4.6).

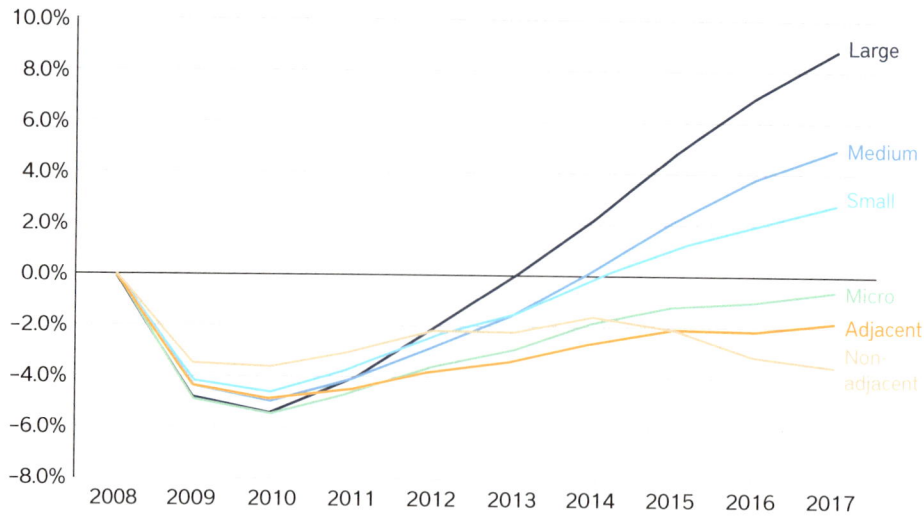

FIGURE 4.5 Percentage change in employment by community size, 2008–2017.
Source: Brookings Institution analysis of QCEW data.

The growing number of left-behind places reveals the geographic dimension of rising economic inequality. Atkinson, Muro, and Whiton (2019) identify the left-behind places as small communities that have experienced slow or negative employment growth since the 2008 Great Recession. Large metropolitan areas have recovered from the recession and are gaining an increasingly large share of the nation's employment growth (figure 4.5).

Global outsourcing and production digitalization contribute to the economic difficulties facing the left-behind places. Technological innovations have brought prosperity to and strengthened the competitiveness of larger cities and metros. Yet, the economic driving force associated with technological innovations has also contributed to the deepening divide between technology- and innovation-heavy cities and metros and those with less technology and innovation capacities within their own megaregions. A study by Brookings Institution researchers (Atkinson, Muro, and Whiton 2019) reports that, from 2005 to 2017, the five top innovation metropolitan areas—Boston, San Francisco, San Jose, Seattle, and San Diego—accounted for more than 90 percent of growth in the country's innovation sector. This increasing territorial polarization has left many places behind, resulting in economic stagnation and employment instability.

Tackling growing economic and social inequality calls for public interventions. Atkinson, Muro, and Whiton (2019) propose that the U.S. federal government step in to counter this regional divergence by designating 8–10 regional tech centers with federal funding. These centers would avoid the metros of existing technology hubs to spread across the nation's heartland. Each center would be supported through direct research and development funding of up to $7 billion over a 10-year period and receive other significant input, including workforce development funding, tax and regulatory benefits, business financing, economic inclusion, and federal land and infrastructure supports.

Megaregions present an intermediate scale between federal and local interventions to reverse the trend of regional divisions in inequality. Policies and investment decisions made collectively at the megaregional level can help internalize the externalities caused by local actions and competitions (Glaser 2007). Transportation is a typical area in which megaregionalism has its advantages because localities would benefit from regional transportation improvements, but individual communities do not have the right incentives to invest in the system beyond their jurisdictions. A megaregional approach could also help lead to more equal distribution of education and affordable housing opportunities, although the absence of existing megaregion-level institutions and legal structures may hinder the implementation of programs at this scale.

Sassen (2012) argues that a megaregion is of sufficient size to become an economic mega zone incorporating diverse types of agglomeration economies ranging from highly specialized APS sectors to fairly labor-intensive, medium- to low-wage manufacturing industries. Needs and capacities for economic diversity present megaregions with opportunities to alleviate inequality. For example, as Sassen (2012) suggests, the advanced economic sectors could redirect some of their supporting tasks, currently outsourced to low-cost countries, into megaregions' left-behind places that are closer to home.

CONCLUSION

Megaregions in the United States are changing and adjusting to growing globalism. An analysis of industrial specializations and export industries of U.S. megaregions finds that Great Lakes and Piedmont Atlantic are manufacturing megas, and Northern California and Cascadia have successfully transformed from manufacturing to service sector and similar industries. Three megaregions, Texas Triangle, Gulf Coast, and Central Plains, are still resource dependent but are gradually transforming to service industries. The remaining six megaregions are growing and strengthening in specialization of services.

In economic productivity, GDP per capita grew in all megaregion and nonmegaregion counties but had stronger growth in megaregions. Labor productivity, measured by GDP per worker, has been highest in Northern California, Northeast, and Cascadia since 2001. Productivity measured by GDP per unit of developed land was highest in Northern California, Southern California, and Northeast in both 2001 and 2016. The strength of APS industries, a measure of the knowledge economy, is only one reason behind U.S. megaregions' performance.

The United States is worst for economic inequality among the advanced economies of the world. Megaregions present opportunities to rectify income gaps between groups and bridge social inequality. To remain competitive, megaregions will need to adapt. The chapters that follow offer megaregional strategies and best-practice examples for tackling inequality and development challenges.

5

BUILDING ENVIRONMENTAL RESILIENCE AND ECOSYSTEM SERVICES

To fight for change tomorrow, we need to build resilience today.
—SHERYL SANDBERG

THIS CHAPTER OUTLINES THE PREDICTED EFFECTS from climate change. It then discusses solutions for coasts, urban areas, and large landscapes. Coastal and inland megaregions can use the 5R framework (resilience, resistance, restoration, retention, and retreat) to deal with climate change. Environmental planning in megaregions can apply the ecosystem services concept to the regions' large landscapes. Ecosystem services are those benefits humans derive from nature that have generally been regarded as free. These include regulatory services, such as bacteria decomposing waste and bees pollinating plants; provisioning services, such as food, water, and energy; supporting services, such as photosynthesis and nutrient cycling; and cultural services, such as the links between nature and art, recreation, and religion (figure 5.1).

U.S. MEGAREGIONS AND CLIMATE CHANGE

In the coming decades, every U.S. megaregion will face daunting—and in some cases, existential—threats posed by climate change. Ecological resources in inland megaregions will be stressed, and many plant and animal species will migrate northward. Human populations will also migrate out of megaregions made uninhabitable by extreme heat, drought, flooding, or fire dangers, potentially leading to widespread dislocation and migration like that from the Dust Bowl in the 1930s.

Extreme variation in rainfall patterns will cause riverine and urban flooding in some periods and places and severe droughts in others. Although the Great Lakes

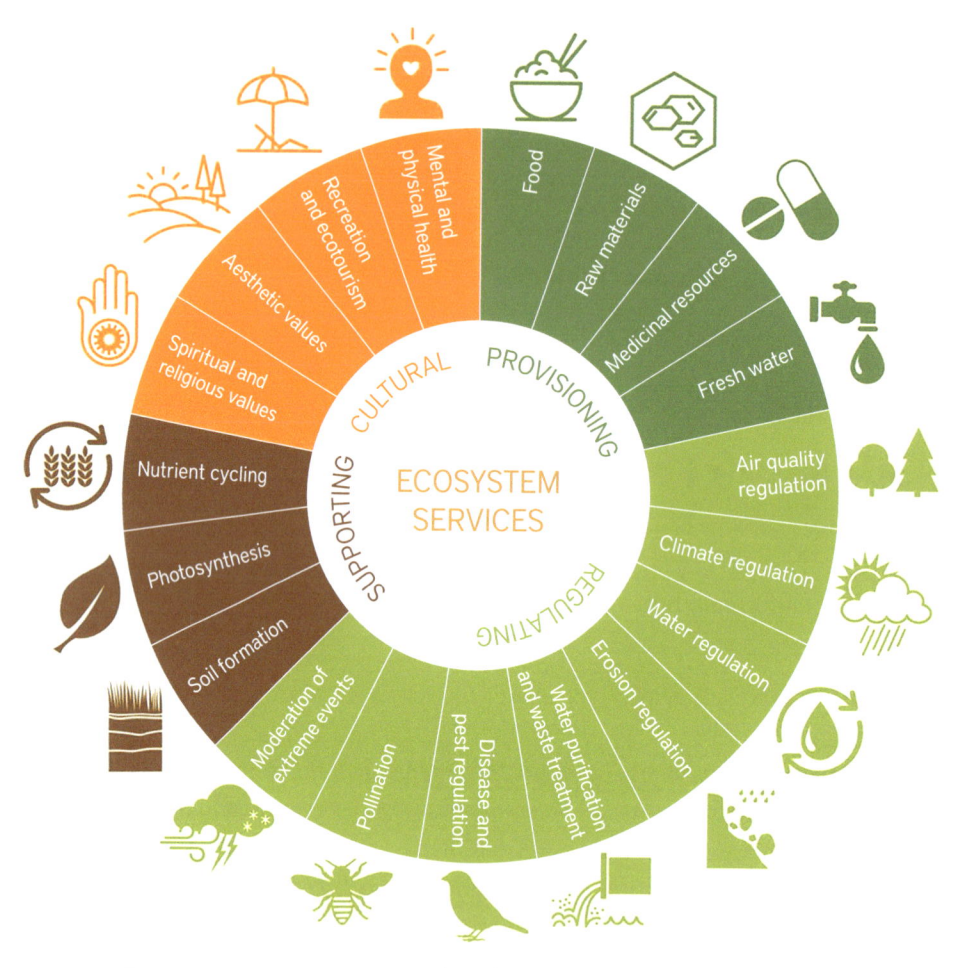

FIGURE 5.1 Ecosystem services. *Source: WWF (2020).*

megaregion has an abundant potable water supply, changes in rainfall regimes are causing extreme high water events and related coastal and urban flooding in lakefront communities. Rising temperatures will cause urban heat islands to intensify, making some portions of the Arizona Sun Corridor, Southern California, Texas Triangle, Florida, and Piedmont Atlantic megaregions nearly uninhabitable for much of the year. Those affected the most will be the poor, the elderly, and those with disabilities. Poorer neighborhoods across the nation have much less extensive tree canopies than other places, exacerbating the impacts of heat islands. In other places, higher temperatures will intensify forest and brush fires, like the catastrophic events in Australia, Northern and Southern California, and Cascadia in 2019, 2020, and 2021, and in Texas in 2011, 2018, and 2021. Climate change will also cause the extinction of some rare plant and animal species, and stress many others—particularly those that have difficulty migrating north as these changes unfold. In California, climate change will affect the wine industry and the nation's most productive areas for fruits and vegetables.

U.S. coastal megaregions will face these threats and additional ones caused by sea level rise and storm surges associated with major weather events. Sea level rise is a slow but inexorable threat to most low-lying coastal regions. Storm surges pose a special threat to megaregions on the East Coast and the Florida and Gulf Coast megaregions, all threatened by increasingly strong and frequent hurricanes, tropical depressions, and other coastal storms intensified by rising ocean temperatures. These events can have catastrophic impacts on coastal areas, resulting in loss of life and extensive property damage. Rapid changes in fisheries due to rising ocean temperatures are already being experienced—for example, commercial lobstering south of Cape Cod was eliminated in the 1990s. This threatens the economy of coastal communities already stressed by overfishing of species like cod and haddock and casts a cloud over the future of Maine's coastal villages and offshore islands and their residents, which depend heavily on lobstering for their economic viability. As the planet warms, the line where saline water meets fresh water in rivers will advance upstream in many rivers. For instance, the salt line of the Delaware River is moving from the area around Wilmington to near Philadelphia. If it continues to move upriver, this could threaten the drinking water of millions of people and the habitats of other species.

A 5R FRAMEWORK

Almost 95 million people—almost one-third of the U.S. population—live in coastal counties, and these places are among the nation's fastest-growing areas (U.S. Census Bureau 2019c). Tens of millions now live and work in low-lying places that have already been or will soon be classified as coastal flood zones. When people settled these areas, the ecosystem services that had been provided were ignored and destroyed. For instance, dunes and wetlands provide natural protection from storm surges. This is not new knowledge. The Dutch, for instance, have recognized the threat of North Sea storms to their low-lying country for centuries and protected and have fortified their coastline accordingly.

In a 1968 study, long before the refinement of computer mapping systems, the pioneering ecological planner Ian McHarg mapped the vulnerabilities of Staten Island and published his findings in *Design with Nature* (McHarg 1969). Through an ecological inventory and analysis, McHarg illustrated the places to avoid developing and those most suited for settlement. The study was largely ignored. The areas identified by McHarg in 1968 to avoid were the worst hit by Superstorm Sandy in 2012. Wagner, Mersin, and Wentz (2016) highlighted key lessons from McHarg's suitability analysis of Staten Island in the wake of Superstorm Sandy (figure 5.2). They found that if McHarg's suggestions had been followed, the damage from Sandy would have

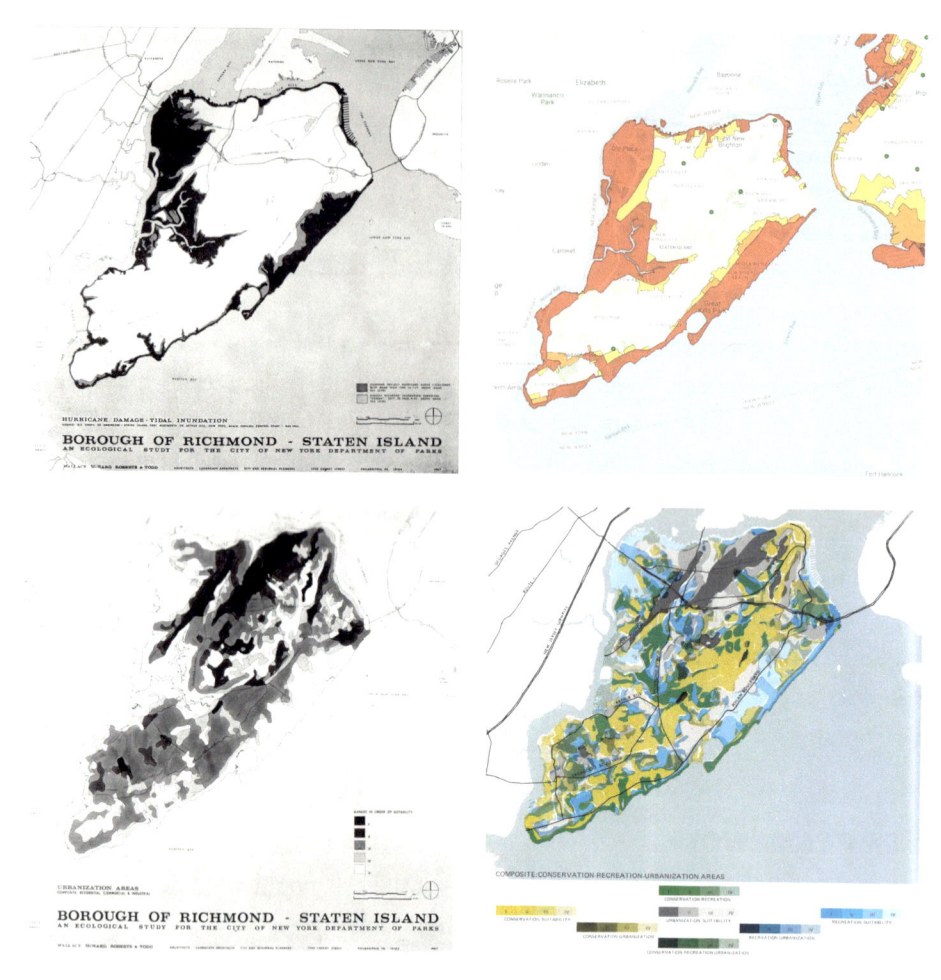

FIGURE 5.2 Staten Island plans and the Hurricane Sandy evacuation map. *Sources: Ian L. McHarg Collection, the Architectural Archives, University of Pennsylvania (top left, bottom left, bottom right); Aaron O'Neill (top right).*

been significantly reduced. Furthermore, they noted that urban pressures and inappropriate zoning led to the harm caused by the superstorm.

Many of these low-lying places, such as Lower Manhattan, downtown Boston, Philadelphia, Washington, DC, and Miami, have the nation's greatest population densities, highest land values, and leading economic productivity. They also hold the nation's most concentrated infrastructure systems, including airports and seaports and roads, trains, and subways. The increased frequency and severity of flooding in these areas will also inordinately affect low- and moderate-income households. In the New York metropolitan region, for example, 40 percent of the population currently living in the flood zone—residents of places like the Rockaways, Howard Beach, Queens, Red Hook, and Brooklyn and Jersey City, New Jersey—are low- and moderate-income households, 42 percent are nonwhite, and 49 percent are renters (Bowman et al. 2018).

Hurricane Katrina, Superstorm Sandy, Hurricane Harvey, and other storms this century have caused thousands of deaths, hundreds of billions of dollars in property damage, and tens of billions more in economic disruption. Catastrophic storms are now expected to be even more frequent and severe, and an expected increase in sea levels of at least six feet by the end of the century will cause even greater loss of life and more economic damage. Bold action is required to mitigate and prevent the harm to coastal communities.

We cannot look for simple solutions to these complex challenges. No one-size-fits-all strategy exists to eliminate or mitigate damage to densely populated shoreline areas. The 5R framework must be deployed in thoughtful ways to protect the communities and diverse geography of U.S. coastal megaregions. In these areas and their metropolitan zones, a layered defense will work best for flood prevention and mitigation to avoid loss of life and property damage as climate change transforms our world in the decades to come.

An additional R, recovery from damage, would cost less if federal flood insurance and disaster recovery programs incentivized the 5R framework for megaregions and their component metropolitan areas. Rather than spending tens of billions of dollars every year on disaster recovery, federal resources should instead be invested in the full range of activities needed to prevent or mitigate disasters in the first place. Flood insurance provisions that permit repeated reconstruction on flood-prone properties with federal payouts should be eliminated, replaced with a one-hit-and-you're-out provision. A federal bureaucracy created to oversee this transformation could become a proactive federal emergency mitigation agency. For example, after Superstorm Sandy in 2012, New Jersey established the Blue Acres Buyout Program to acquire flood-prone lands, initially with $300 million in federal disaster aid for at least 1,000 properties with willing sellers. The preserved lands create natural buffers against future storms and floods. In 2019, the New Jersey legislature provided ongoing funding for the program.

Resilience

The principle of resilience—that communities should become better able to withstand and recover from climate-related threats—has gained near universal support among planners and public policy experts. Resilience measures include a broad range of strategies, such as elevating structures and hardening electric power, water, and other infrastructure systems; improving communications and community support systems; and enhancing ecosystem services.

Resilience must be at the heart of measures to protect coastal regions from the effects of sea level rise and storm surges. Resilience measures make the most sense for sparsely populated barrier beaches and islands, seasonal communities, and medium- to low-density communities in flood zones. Outside the urban core district in the New York City region, for example, an offshore sea gate system could be implemented to protect the heart of the nation's largest urban region from storm surges, as discussed later. Outside this area, low-lying communities fronting the back bays—such as Freeport and Mastic Beach on Long Island's Great South Bay; Egg Harbor or Toms River fronting New Jersey's Barnegat Bay; or Rowayton, Connecticut, and Bayville, New York, on Long Island Sound—could use resilience strategies for protection and rapid recovery from flooding events.

Similar to coastal flooding, the prevention of urban and riverine flooding will also require a broad range of resilience strategies. Extreme rainfall, drought, heat waves, wildfires, and other climate-related threats will require additional measures. For instance, in February 2021, a catastrophic winter storm collapsed Texas's power grid. More than 4 million people lost their electricity, and some 14 million were left without potable water. The culprit was Texans' preference for an independent and unregulated power grid, natural gas, and free-market capitalism and denial of climate change (Baptiste 2021).

Resistance

Keeping the water out and the lights on in densely populated urban cores of coastal regions requires preventing or mitigating the flooding from storm surges and sea level rise. Major global cities in Europe and Asia—London, Rotterdam, Saint Petersburg, Singapore, Tokyo, and others—have constructed or are planning surge barriers (also known as hurricane, or typhoon, barriers, barrages, or sea gates) and related dike, levy, and fortified dune systems to prevent storm surges. Major population centers with several million residents in the Netherlands, including the entire Randstad urban megaregion, are protected by a system of high sea walls, surge barriers, and pumps. The Randstad includes both the nation's largest cities and its Green Heart, the thinly populated, major agricultural center of the nation. Several U.S. cities also have these systems, including post-Katrina New Orleans and three northeastern cities: Stamford, Connecticut; Providence, Rhode Island; and New Bedford, Massachusetts.

Many of these barrier systems, including those protecting the urban core of the Netherlands and London's Thames Barrier, were developed after multiple catastrophic flooding events occurred within a generation. All three of the hurricane barriers in northeastern U.S. cities were constructed after a relatively quick series of devastating storms—the 1938 New England hurricane and Hurricanes Carol and Hazel, both in 1954—caused widespread deaths and property damage in these cities.

All three northeastern flood prevention systems include movable barriers across harbor entrances and berms and levees designed to keep storm surges out of major population centers. All were built in the 1960s and 1970s, and although they were

FIGURE 5.3 London's Thames Barrier. *Source: Damian Moore, Flickr, image adjustments by Aaron O'Neill.*

designed to protect these cities from hurricanes, they are now routinely used many times every year to prevent damage from nor'easters and even extreme spring tides. When Hurricane Sandy struck the Northeast in 2012, all three barriers prevented flood damage within their bounds. Outside the barriers, nearby waterfront communities experienced widespread flooding, property damage, and loss of life.

London's Thames Barrier has a similar history (figure 5.3). This system was constructed after disastrous storm surges came up the Thames from the North Sea in 1948 and again in 1953, flooding densely populated, low-lying areas throughout the lower Thames Valley and central London. In the winter of 2013–2014, severe North Sea storms caused the Thames Barrier to be closed more than 50 times to prevent storm surges and to mitigate upstream flooding. It has closed more than 174 times since it was completed in 1984.

The technology behind surge barriers and sea gates—including movable barriers and berm and levee systems—is now proven, off-the-shelf engineering technology. Although local geotechnical conditions and environments may vary widely, given half a century of experience among diverse coastal and estuarine settings, the reliability of these systems and accuracy of cost estimation should also be high. Expedited environmental reviews and project delivery techniques, similar to those used for New York's new Tappan Zee Bridge, can build these systems in a matter of years to provide necessary protection for the nation's densest and largest population centers.

However, the price of these systems is high, generally costing hundreds of millions or even billions of dollars. For this reason, surge barriers and sea gates can be considered only in areas of high population density of high economic value and with high concentrations of vulnerable low- and moderate-income housing. For this reason, only a small portion of the total shoreline of low-lying coastal areas in the northeastern United States can be protected by these systems. But the districts with the nation's highest population density, greatest economic productivity, and highest land values, such as the urban cores of Boston, New York, Philadelphia, Baltimore, Washington, DC, and Norfolk, Virginia, could benefit from these systems. Flood-prone coastal areas of New York, Boston, and other cities include a high concentration of low-income and minority households, and barrier systems could protect some of the nation's most vulnerable populations, providing an additional justification for their large investments.

Flood Prevention and Mitigation in the New York Metro Region

The New York City metropolitan region is the largest urban area in the United States. Much of the region and many of its most densely populated areas and most valuable economic and infrastructure assets are increasingly threatened by coastal flooding and storm surges as projected increases in sea level and more frequent and intense coastal storms continue to arrive in the coming decades (figures 5.4 and 5.5). A barrier consisting of movable sea gates, similar to those of London's Thames Barrier or the Netherlands' Eastern Scheldt barrier, stretching from Breezy Point on the Rockaway Peninsula to Sandy Hook in New Jersey has been proposed.

At the landward ends of the barrier, berms would be built the length of these barrier beaches and tied into the mainland at their landward ends. Such berms could be naturalized into dune systems for aesthetic and wildlife protection, as is done with similar features on the Dutch coast. This entire system would provide flood protection to all low-lying population and employment centers, all three regional airports, and all seaports, tunnels, and other essential infrastructure lying in the core of the New York metropolitan region.

Openings would be provided for shipping channels and to preserve natural tidal flows in the Lower Bay and Hudson River Estuary. As in surge barriers protecting Saint Petersburg in Russia and Rotterdam, movable sections would permit shipping to access the Ambrose Shipping Channel and smaller shipping channels. A secondary barrier near the Throgs Neck Bridge at the western end of Long Island Sound would prevent flood waters from entering the East River. Smaller barriers may also be required for midsize cities in Connecticut, as well as across the channels entering the back bays on the South Shore of Long Island and New Jersey. Modeling conducted

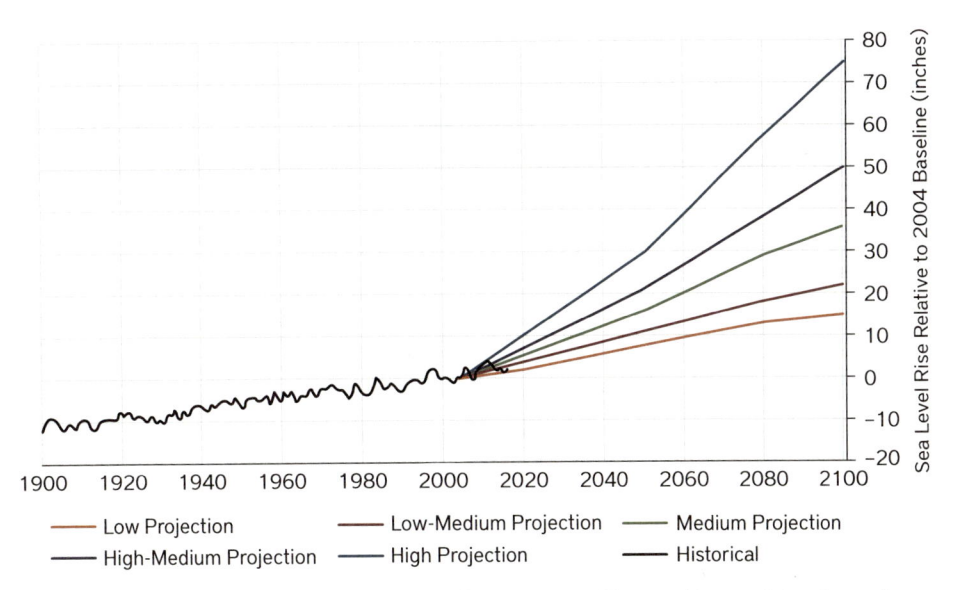

FIGURE 5.4 Sea level rise projections for New York City. *Source: Christian Termyn, Sabin Center for Climate Change Law, Columbia Law School.*

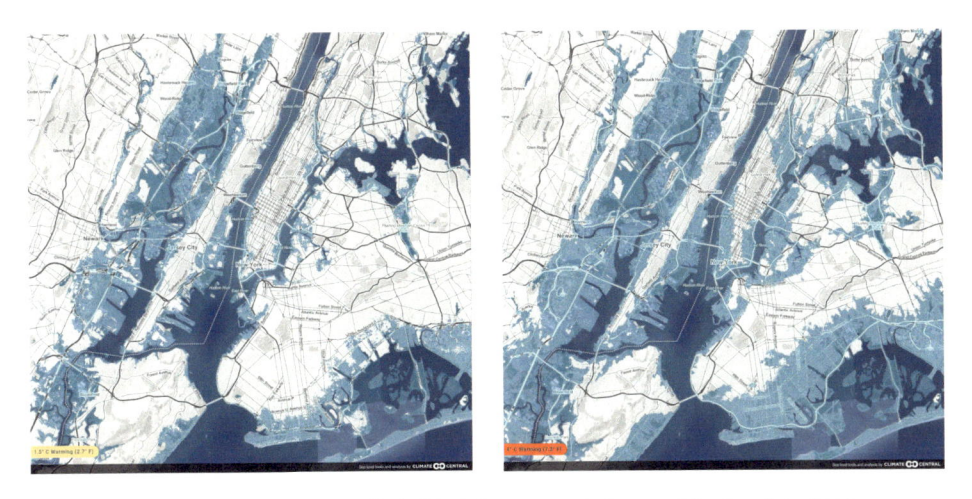

FIGURE 5.5. Sea level rise projections (light blue) for New York City neighborhoods by 2100 assuming 2.7°F (*left*) and 7.2°F (*right*). *Source: Climate Central.*

by Stony Brook University has determined that these barrier systems would raise water levels outside the barriers by only a few inches on the region's Atlantic coast and Long Island Sound (Bowman et al. 2021, 43–44).

Inside this barrier system, a set of low (three to six feet high) onshore berms, dunes, or levees would provide additional, layered defense for flood-prone communities and major infrastructure systems, including tunnel portals, airports, and sewage treatment plants. Restored and created wetlands, oyster beds, and other natural defenses could further reduce wave-induced flooding of low-lying areas (but not flooding from storm surges). As sea levels rise throughout this century, the offshore sea gates would be expected to close more frequently, as has been the case with London's Thames Barrier.

This barrier system would protect the vast majority of residents and economic activity at the core of the New York City metropolitan region, which contains the bulk of the region's $1.5 trillion economy, justifying the system's estimated $30 billion capital cost. Gaining support for this investment will not be easy. Some environmental groups oppose building any offshore barriers, fearing they would modify tidal and sediment flows, fisheries, and other natural systems. Proponents have responded that the system would be designed to minimize or eliminate these impacts.

In the absence of a regional strategy, the City of New York and other municipalities have decided to go it alone in proposing onshore barriers to protect vulnerable coastal communities. Ultimately, however, this approach will not protect the area from regionwide threats.

Flood Prevention and Mitigation in Other Cities

U.S. cities have already built or are considering the construction of similar systems. For example, New Orleans has a comprehensive flood prevention system, built by the U.S. Army Corps of Engineers in the aftermath of Hurricane Katrina's devastating flooding in 2005. Similar protection could be provided by surge barriers or movable sea gates in Boston, Philadelphia, Baltimore, Washington, DC, Houston, and other major metropolitan areas on the U.S. East and Gulf Coasts.

In metropolitan Boston, civic leaders and local government officials have proposed building a sea gate system like the one proposed for New York to protect the core of this densely populated region. As in New York, however, the City of Boston is pursuing its own system of onshore barriers to protect vulnerable communities, which leaves 14 other cities and towns facing Boston Harbor with no protection at all. And as in New York, some environmental groups have opposed building any offshore sea gates because of concerns about possible impacts on the ecology of tidal flows and the natural systems in Boston Harbor.

Restoration

In areas that cannot be protected by offshore surge barriers and sea gate systems, other techniques must be considered to protect low-lying communities from storm surges and sea level rise. Engineered dune systems can protect these places from storm surges and at lower cost than offshore barrier systems. The technology of environmental restoration has advanced significantly in recent decades. Protected, restored, or created wetlands, oyster reefs, and other natural systems can mitigate wave action. These systems could also provide environmental, wildlife protection, and recreational benefits and improve stormwater management and filter urban runoff. These ecosystem strategies are generally not effective in reducing storm surges, except where extensive networks can be established. Proposals have been made to build or restore wetlands, oyster beds, and other environmental systems in Boston Harbor (Yaro et al. 1987) and New York Harbor (Nordenson, Seavitt, and Yarinsky 2010). Ambitious programs of wetland restoration are also underway along Louisiana's Gulf Coast and in New York's Jamaica Bay.

Restoration can be a factor in design and approval of new projects. The Green Business Certification, Inc. SITES rating system can be helpful in this regard. Grounded in the ecosystem services concept, SITES represents the best practices in site-level design and rates projects on meeting water and soil quality standards, sustainable use of plants and materials, and site selection and design, beginning with the construction phase and continuing through site maintenance. SITES has already been adopted at all levels of the U.S. federal system: national, state, and local (Steiner 2020). At the federal level, the U.S. General Services Administration requires SITES in its vast holdings. The states of Rhode Island and Arizona have embraced SITES, as have New York City (its Department of Parks and Recreation), Chicago, and Austin. In Georgia, the Atlanta BeltLine requires SITES certification for all projects (Steiner 2020).

Retention

Extreme rainfall events and resulting riverine and urban flooding already threaten U.S. megaregions and their population centers. This trend will intensify as climate change continues. We can also expect more frequent and severe drought, like that being experienced in Northern and Southern California, the Arizona Sun Corridor, and across the southwestern United States. For this reason, rivers and streams in every megaregion must be preserved and, in some cases, reclaimed and redesigned to retain as much water as possible during both flood and drought periods.

Charles River Natural Valley Storage

An early prototype for metropolitan retention strategies is the Charles River Natural Valley Storage program, adopted by the U.S. Army Corps of Engineers in 1974. Since 1977, the corps has acquired more than 8,000 acres of undeveloped floodplains in the upper Charles Valley to prevent development that would have led to downstream flooding (U.S. Army Corps of Engineers 2017). The Charles is also one of the earliest examples of a river adapted to the Anthropocene epoch. From the 18th through the early 20th centuries, large areas of the Charles Estuary were filled to accommodate

Boston's development, creating neighborhoods like the Back Bay, Kendall Square, Cambridgeport, and Massachusetts Institute of Technology's riverfront campus. Frequent flooding of these and other nearby neighborhoods led the pioneering landscape architect Charles Eliot to create the Charles River Dam and Charles River Basin, essentially transforming the lower Charles River from a saltwater estuary into a freshwater lake. The parks, greenways, and parkways lining the river's edge, including the Charles River Esplanade and Embankment, are among Boston's most cherished and intensively used open spaces.

By the late 20th century, however, suburban sprawl encroached on the river's middle and upper reaches, which caused more frequent and severe flooding in the lower, urban portions of the Charles Basin. In response, the corps built a new and higher Charles River Dam, with six large diesel-powered pumps to discharge water from the basin into Boston Harbor during flood events. But even this would not have been adequate to prevent flooding if sprawl continued to pave floodplains in the river's upper reaches. Accordingly, the corps and the Charles River Watershed Association purchased floodplains in the middle and upper Charles Valley to retain them as natural storage areas during flood events. The Charles River Natural Valley Storage program now manages the area for wildlife habitat and recreational use.

This natural storage is complemented by the redesign of streets in nearby urban and suburban communities to create "green streets." The redesign replaces masonry curbs with swales that permit stormwater to saturate vegetated edges and soak into the ground, rather than shooting directly into catchment basins and nearby rivers and streams. Runoff from buildings and driveways during extreme rainfall events can also be diverted into groundwater or cisterns, instead of going into storm sewers, to prevent overflows of combined storm and sanitary sewers. The SITES rating system provides guidance on how this can be accomplished on a project-by-project basis.

Storage and Green Streets in Other Megaregions

The principles used in the Charles River watershed should be adapted to similar waterways across U.S. megaregions. Had this approach been taken to regional land and resource protection in the upper reaches of Houston's Buffalo Bayou, for example, the extreme flooding that accompanied Hurricane Harvey and other storms in that city could have been mitigated. Floodplain zoning should be mandated by state and local governments and incentivized by federal planning grants and reformed flood insurance provisions. Urban development in floodplains undercuts their flood storage capacity. Limiting development, in turn, could be complemented by acquisition of fee-simple interests or development rights in these areas.

Green streets design practices should also be universally adopted in megaregions across the country—again, perhaps encouraged by federal incentives. Existing public rights-of-way can be redesigned by narrowing travel and parking lanes, even while roadways remain completely functional and become safer as traffic is calmed by narrowed pavement. Transforming roadways began in the Pacific Northwest in the 1990s, in places like Vancouver, British Columbia; Seattle, Washington; and Portland, Oregon. The concept's origin dates to a 1997 article, "In Search of Cheap and Skinny Streets," by Terence Bray and Victor Rhodes. Bray and Rhodes (1997) determined that most urban streets could be narrowed to 18 feet from the usual 30-foot, or wider, paved area. This would create room for sidewalks and innovative stormwater detention designs, slow traffic, and save on construction and maintenance costs. These innovations should become standard practices in cities and suburbs across U.S. megaregions.

Retreat

Retreat by medium- and low-density population areas that are low lying and outside surge barriers may be the most effective response to anticipated future storm surges, severe coastal flooding, and sea level rise. Seasonal communities on low-lying barrier beaches and islands would be the first places to retreat. In the New York metropolitan region, for example, places like New York's Fire Island, New Jersey's Long Beach Island, and Connecticut's Fairfield Beach and Woodmont section in Milford should consider retreat. Retreat is expensive and difficult to implement; constructing a surge barrier would eliminate the need for the retreats underway or being contemplated in the New York region, such as in South Shore, Staten Island.

One of us, Bob Yaro, ran one of the nation's earliest retreat programs in coastal Massachusetts following the blizzard of 1978, February 8–10. This extreme nor'easter devastated east-facing barrier beaches along the length of the Massachusetts coastline, resulting in tens of millions of dollars in property damage and extensive loss of life. Yaro used state and federal disaster relief funds to buy damaged properties in the months immediately following the storm. Towns were reluctant to authorize the use of eminent domain for buyouts, except in communities where volunteer firemen had drowned attempting to rescue residents who had refused to heed evacuation orders. In other places, when the summer weather returned in June, owners were no longer interested in selling and decided to rebuild, arguing, "That will never happen again"— despite the frequent devastating storms on these barrier beaches.

ECOSYSTEM SERVICES AND LARGE LANDSCAPES

Every U.S. megaregion contains at least one—and in some cases many—large landscapes encompassing watersheds, river basins, mountain ranges, agricultural lands, seashores, or other special resources. In virtually every case, these resource systems span more than one political jurisdiction or even multiple states. Many of these places also encompass natural resources that make life in their megaregions possible, such as public water supplies, or desirable, such as attractive recreational or scenic areas that underpin a megaregion's self-image and quality of life. The pioneering regional planner and originator of the Appalachian Trail, Benton MacKaye, believed that access to three kinds of landscapes—urban, rural, and primeval—was essential to full human development (Anderson 2002; MacKaye 1928).

Large landscapes can and should also be protected and managed to conserve their exceptional assets and help address climate and biodiversity goals. Penn's landscape architecture chair Richard Weller has proposed creating a network of world parks to encompass entire ecosystems that in many cases span national boundaries. And the Harvard evolutionary biologist E. O. Wilson (2016) has proposed protecting half the planet with biosphere reserves designed to prevent mass extinctions, elaborated by Tony Hiss (2021). Meanwhile, President Joe Biden advocates protecting 30 percent of the land and water in the United States by 2030. Achieving these bold visions will require equally bold initiatives to plan for and manage these resources in an era of rapid climate, economic, social, and political change.

To promote a better understanding of large-scale landscape conservation techniques, the Lincoln Institute of Land Policy has organized the International Land Conservation Network's Large Landscape Peer Learning Initiative. Two of the large landscapes being studied by the initiative are in U.S. megaregions—the San Francisco Bay Area in the Northern California megaregion and the Appalachian Highlands in the Northeast megaregion. (The other two are the Patagonia and Mediterranean landscape regions.) Both U.S. regions have a long history of large landscape planning and preservation.

In the Northern California megaregion, decades of effective conservation advocacy and implementation have created what amounts to a permanent greenbelt and urban growth boundary around the urban core of the San Francisco Bay Area. These efforts began in 1968 with the creation of the Golden Gate National Recreation Area, which transformed hundreds of thousands of acres of former military lands into a national park, now called the Golden Gate National Park. Even before that, the Greenbelt Alliance has, since 1958, protected hundreds of thousands of acres as conservation land, forming an urban growth boundary for the region.

In the Texas Triangle, scholars at the University of Texas at Austin and citizens of Austin and San Antonio have advocated management of the Texas Hill Country to protect groundwater and surface water supplies for the metropolitan San Antonio and Austin areas and to protect the region's exceptional scenic, historic, and natural features. In addition to being beautiful, the Hill Country possesses some of the most plentiful groundwater resources in the nation, in the Edwards Aquifer. The voters of Austin and San Antonio have consistently approved taxes for protecting water resources and wildlife habitat. For instance, the Hill Country Conservancy has used these funds, plus private and federal resources, to purchase easements on thousands of acres of land over the recharge region of the Edwards Aquifer. In addition, the late UT Austin planning professor Kent Butler led the creation of the Balcones Canyonlands Preserve, a groundbreaking habitat conservation approach to protect endangered species. A joint undertaking by the City of Austin, Travis County, and the U.S. Fish and Wildlife Service, the preserve is one of the nation's largest, covering 32,000 acres, or almost 50 square miles. It protects two neotropical migratory songbirds and six invertebrates found in karst caves among other animals and plants. Beatley (1994) refers to the Balcones Canyonlands as the promise of a model regional approach for protecting endangered species.

By comparison, the Northeast megaregion contains dozens of large landscapes: upland, coastal, riverine, agricultural, forested, among others (see RPA and America 2050 2012). One of these, the Catskill Mountains, provides potable water supplies for more than 12 million people in metropolitan New York and Philadelphia. Others, like New York's Adirondack Park and New Hampshire's White Mountain National Forest, provide recreational resources for millions of Northeast residents. Running the length of the megaregion are the Appalachian Highlands and eastern deciduous forest, which had been mostly clear-cut in the 19th century but have now been largely reforested, in part because of the state and national forests and parks established in the early 20th century.

These resources can be managed to protect surface water and groundwater supplies, important scenic and recreational resources, and contiguous forest units critical to species migration. MacKaye proposed the creation of the Appalachian Trail in his 1928 book, *The New Exploration: A Philosophy of Regional Planning*. MacKaye's vision was to create a recreational trail surrounded by a preserved region of indigenous landscapes and cultures that could simultaneously function as a permanent greenbelt for the fast-growing cities of the Northeast. Only the trail itself came to be, but efforts are now underway to fully realize MacKaye's vision for the Appalachians. As Tony Hiss observes, MacKaye saw the Appalachians as a place of "strength and sanity" and had a vision to "think big, see more widely, take in it all" (Hiss 2021, 182, 183).

MacKaye believed that preserving the Appalachian Highlands was essential to the well-being of every resident of the Northeast and its crowded cities. To live a good, fulfilling life, in MacKaye's view, every human being needs access to three kinds of places: the town, the countryside, and wilderness. Whereas towns and cities form the foundation for our economy and society, the countryside and primeval places provide sustenance for the body and the soul. Preserving the Appalachians and the Appalachian Trail is not about recreation for the few and supplies of water and clean air for many but about the well-being of the 54 million people who live in the Northeast megaregion. To further this idea, MacKaye established the Wilderness Society and led its advocacy programs for many years. MacKaye (1940, 351) grounded his ideas and approach in ecology, observing, "Regional planning in short is applied human ecology." An Appalachian Trail Landscape Partnership was formed in 2015 to shape broader protections for lands abutting the northern end of the Appalachian Trail between New York City and Mount Katahdin in Maine, ensuring that MacKaye's vision will be sustained well into the future.

In the northern portion of the Northeast, the New England Wildlands and Woodlands project, led by the Highstead Foundation and the Harvard Forest, is working with states, regions, and local conservation groups to permanently protect 80 percent of the region's land area as forestland. A key step has been forming regional conservation partnerships—consisting of land trusts, public conservation groups, and concerned citizens—that advocate for both public and private measures.

Large Landscape Conservation in the Northeast

These activities build on a long tradition of large landscape conservation initiatives in the Northeast. In 1891, the New York State legislature designated an Adirondack preserve to prevent the complete clear-cutting of this 5-million-acre range of mountains and lakes in northern New York. Because the preserve was delineated by a blue line on maps, it became known as blue line preservation. The following year, the legislature created Adirondack Park and included a forever-wild provision for state lands in the park (Adirondack Park Agency 2021).

That same year, at the urging of the landscape architect Charles Eliot, the Commonwealth of Massachusetts established Boston's Metropolitan Park System, the first of its kind in the nation. The system was an outgrowth of Eliot's Emerald Necklace, planned with Frederick Law Olmsted. At the same time, most northeastern states established state park and forest systems—in many cases designed to restore abandoned farmland and clear-cut forests for the protection of wildlife, water quality, and recreational use.

In the 1920s, Eliot's nephew, Charles Eliot II, and Benton MacKaye proposed the Bay Circuit—the nation's first metropolitan greenbelt (figure 5.6). Their vision was to create a 110-mile-long network of parks and preserves ringing the Boston region, linked by pedestrian trails and a limited-access highway—what MacKaye called a townless highway. The project languished during the Great Depression and World War II. But in the postwar period, the state highway department embraced the highway portion of the Bay Circuit concept and built not a greenbelt but what became Route 128 (now Interstate 95)—metro Boston's inner beltway. Over time, parks and trails followed, encouraged by enabling legislation in 1954 and sustained

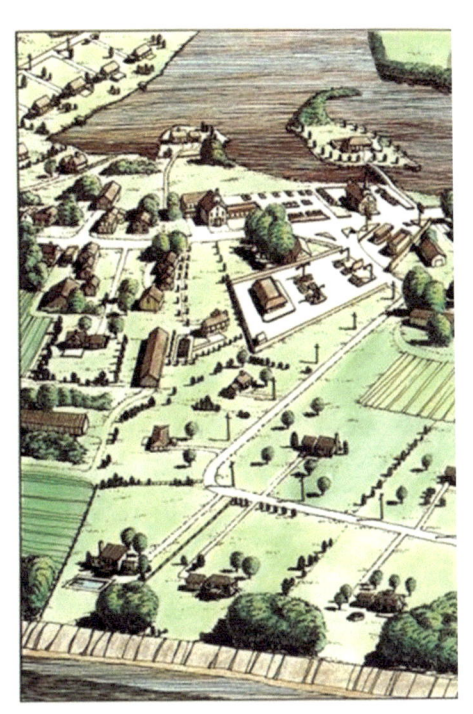

FIGURE 5.6 Depiction of the impacts of conventional development patterns on the characteristics of rural landscapes (a third image in the original triptych shows how creative development can minimize the visual impacts of development). *Source: Yaro et al. (1988).*

commitments of local, state, and private land conservation investments in the years that followed. Then, in 1982, the commonwealth committed funds to complete the Bay Circuit Trail and its network of conservation lands and established the Bay Circuit Trail Alliance to coordinate efforts.

Several regional landscape preservation initiatives have been undertaken across the Northeast and other megaregions since the 1970s. Many of these operate at a scale that can shape broader environmental conservation and climate strategies for large portions of the megaregion. Most also achieve their growth management and resource protection goals through state, regional, and local land use regulations and public and private land conservation measures.

An early example of this trend is the Adirondack Park Agency, which was created in 1971 to ensure that privately owned lands in the park—representing half the park's 5 million acres in the early 1970s—would also be protected. Its land management plan, adopted the following year, provided the agency with the authority to administer land use controls on public and private lands in the park. Since the agency's creation, it has worked with the Nature Conservancy and other private conservation groups, and New York State has acquired several hundred thousand acres of conservation land. As a result, there are both lands that have been acquired for conservation and lands with uses regulated.

Green-Line Parks

The so-called blue line concept for preservation has captured the imagination of conservationists and planners for well over a century. From the late 1960s through the 1990s, blue line preservation inspired a new generation of planners and conservationists—including us—to propose that similar parks, green-line parks, be established to protect threatened landscapes across the country.

Green-line parks and regulatory commissions for regional land use were established for Lake Tahoe (1969), the California coast (1972), the New Jersey Pinelands (1978), the Santa Monica Mountains (1978), and elsewhere. These early precedents would not exist if not for strong political leadership at the federal and state level. The Adirondack Park Agency, for example, could not have been established without the leadership of New York governor Nelson Rockefeller, and the New Jersey Pinelands Commission and National Reserve without Congressman Jim Florio of New Jersey. These and other early green-line parks and regulatory commissions, such as the California Coastal Commission and Tahoe Regional Planning Agency, required strong, top-down political leadership to found them and sustain them and their work over decades.

The impetus for national reserves decreased in the 1980s, with some notable exceptions such as Atlanta's ambitious BeltLine, which will eventually encircle the city. The Ronald Reagan administration and later administrations opposed further designation of these national reserves. Instead, the Jimmy Carter and Bill Clinton administrations created national heritage corridors and heritage areas, but these designations do not come with the same regional planning and regulatory tools that green-line parks had.

CONCLUSION

Climate change poses an existential environmental and social threat, one that endangers the ability of future generations to live safe and healthy lives and to prosper. Megaregions provide a scale to understand environmental systems and to take appropriate action to build resilience. Climatic, geological, and hydrological processes—the essential deep structures of places—occur over large landscapes. Animal migrations also occur at big scales, and those movements are being disrupted as the planet warms and flora adjust. The protection and enhancement of ecosystem services over large landscapes are essential for long-term resilience.

Understanding how to plan and design with nature has greatly increased over the last 50 years. There are lessons to be learned and built on from the Texas Triangle to

Cascadia and other U.S. megaregions. We can also learn from efforts in other nations, such as London's Thames Barrier and the Netherlands' Eastern Scheldt barrier. We have much work to do to build environmental resilience and ecosystem services. With sea levels rising; floods, wildfires, and extreme weather events increasing; biodiversity and prime farmland declining; and cities heating up, resilient and adaptive responses are not luxuries but necessities. The stakes are especially high for the most vulnerable populations—the poor, the elderly, and the disabled—and megaregional planning will help ensure a more just and equitable future.

6

CHANGING WORK AND TRAVEL PATTERNS IN U.S. MEGAREGIONS

A visionary starts with a clean sheet of paper, and re-imagines the world.
—MALCOLM GLADWELL

IN THIS CHAPTER, we explore the societal influences on commuting and the innovations in computing and in information and communications technologies (ICTs) and new mobilities that could affect how people work and travel, transforming the economic geography of U.S. megaregions. Technological advances and economic globalization have already had profound impacts on how people live, work, entertain, and travel. ICTs enable increasing numbers of employees to perform work duties without making physical trips, or at least making fewer commutes. Education is being similarly transformed, as many institutions offer an array of online learning options. People are taking advantage of the ICT-enabled work flexibility to live in one metro and work in a different one, enjoying the opportunities and amenities offered by both. Anecdotal evidence from the Texas Triangle megaregion suggests that a growing number of people live in Austin and work in Houston or vice versa through a combination of telecommuting and physical commuting. This chapter discusses these changing societal and technological trends and their implications for transportation planning and policy-making in the context of megaregions.

SOCIETAL FACTORS INFLUENCING TRANSREGIONAL COMMUTES

Understanding the reasons for people's choices of where to live and where to work helps explain commuting trends. ICTs enable workers to shorten the time spent commuting between work and home or make time spent commuting less wasteful (Mokhtarian and Salomon 2001).

Four trends have reshaped the social environment and people's daily life, which in turn influence commuting behavior: (1) increased numbers of dual-earner households; (2) advances in ICTs; (3) new concepts in work scheduling; and (4) people's changing attitudes toward travel.

More Dual-Earner Households

One important change in the American family since the 1960s has been the increase in women's participation in the labor market. According to the U.S. Bureau of Labor Statistics, women's labor force participation increased steadily between the 1960s and 1980s, then peaked at 60 percent in 1999. During and after the Great Recession, the rate declined slightly but still maintained a level of 56.7 percent in 2015 (Toossi and Morisi 2017). The pandemic has further affected these trends. The long-term consequences of the pandemic are unknown at this time. As more women earn college degrees, the number of career-oriented women rises. These more highly educated women are more likely to continue their careers after marriage. Consequently, the share of traditional one-earner households has been declining and dual-earner households have been on the rise. In 2007, 62 percent of households had two earners, compared with 24 percent of households with only one earner (U.S. Bureau of Labor Statistics 2009).

The growing number of dual-earner households calls into question the conventional interpretation of commuting behavior, which assumes that the commute of a single, main earner in a household determines residential location. But commuting decisions for two earners in a household are interdependent, and the two would attempt to minimize the overall commuting cost of travel time, money, and energy of both (Badoe 2002). In reality, dual-earner households face more complex situations than single-earner households in decisions on where to live and what job offers to accept (Sultana 2006). Living near the workplace of one partner may make a commute longer for the other (Hjorthol 2000; Turner and Niemeier 1997). In some other cases, couples in a dual-earner household may choose longer or shorter commutes because the entire family prefers certain housing and neighborhood amenities (Plaut 2006). Researchers have also found that dual-earner households tend to move less than single-earner households (Van Ommeren, Rietveld, and Nijkamp 1998). If the job market in one region cannot satisfy both partners, one partner may choose to commute a long distance to another region (Green 1997). The advent of high-speed rail in the United States could enable dual-earner households to more conveniently commute long distances, particularly if they are not required to make daily trips.

As more women began participating in the job market, researchers paid increasing attention to the gender difference in commuting behavior. General findings suggest that women still bear more housework responsibilities than men, especially in households with children, despite simultaneously playing a more and more important role in the workforce. Women on average receive lower wages and returns on commuting than men. For these reasons, they typically choose shorter commute times and distances than men (Clark, Huang, and Withers 2003; Hjorthol 2000; Plaut 2006; Turner and Niemeier 1997). In addition, women are more likely to use public transportation and have trip chains (in which work, shopping, and other activities are grouped into one trip) in the journey to work (Hjorthol 2000; Rose 2009). Although women usually dislike long-distance commuting, they may turn it into a positive experience by using the commute to make "a mental shift, [for] contemplation and relaxation" (Lyons and Chatterjee 2008, 194; see also Blumen 2000, 731; Rose 2009).

Whereas most partners in dual-earner households are making great efforts to coordinate their work and family life, many dual-earner households have adopted a "living apart together" relationship. The partners in these couples do not cohabitate in the traditional family form, instead pursuing careers in different regions with more employment options while maintaining interdependence (Levin 2004). The relationship of living apart together gives women a greater sense of autonomy and leads to a more balanced division of household work. It helps both partners separate work from leisure and increases the quality of their more limited time together (Holmes 2009). Instead of daily trips to local work, living-apart-together partners tend to make frequent weekly or monthly trips to the family home.

New ICTs

Living-apart-together relationships are an example of just one of many social benefits from new ICTs (Levin 2004). ICTs enable people to connect to each other when they are not physically together and could greatly affect people's face-to-face interaction and their need for travel. ICTs comprise five broad categories: (1) telecommuting; (2) teleconferencing; (3) teleservices such as teleshopping or telebanking; (4) mobile communications; and (5) electronic message transfer (Mokhtarian 2002; Salomon 1986). The COVID-19 pandemic greatly increased the incidence of telecommuting, and many workers in service industries chose to or were required to work remotely. The advent of reliable, low-cost, and high-quality teleconferencing services, such as Zoom, BlueJeans, and Google Meet, enabled this change. Many companies have decided to make at least some telecommuting a permanent aspect of their business after the pandemic.

Researchers have long realized the connection between ICTs and transportation (Gold 1979; Hardill and Green 2003; Mokhtarian 1990; 2002; Salomon 1985; 1986; Walls, Safirova, and Jiang 2007). The possible effects of ICTs on transportation include (1) substitution, because ICTs could reduce people's physical travel; (2) complementarity, because ICTs could either stimulate people to travel more or help people travel more efficiently; and (3) modification, because ICTs could change the time when people decide to travel without affecting the number or length of trips (Mokhtarian 2002).

Despite the consensus that connections between ICTs and transportation exist, there has not been agreement on the actual effects. For example, on the basis of several surveys in North America on teleconferencing practices, Gold (1979) concludes that teleconferencing would not reduce intercity travel in the 1980s but could eventually substitute for some intercity trips if more ICT systems were provided. In contrast, after examining people's attitudes toward ICTs and travel for work, shopping, and business, Salomon (1985) believes that people's desire for mobility would counterweight the substitution of telecommunication for travel. A more recent nationwide survey in Finland on telecommuting and commuting distance and frequency shows that the effects vary depending on commuting distance (Helminen and Ristimaki 2007). In addition, job types affect people's choices in telecommuting. Walls, Safirova, and Jiang (2007) find, on the basis of a survey in Southern California, that jobs in sales, education and other types of training, and architecture and engineering are more likely to have telecommuters.

Despite the inconclusiveness in findings on the relationship between transportation and ICTs, both telecommunication and travel are believed to be highly likely to continue to grow in the future. Telecommunications do permit great flexibility in making travel decisions such as whether, when, where, and how to travel (Mokhtarian 2002). Telecommuting provides people the possibility of working in places other than the office and during times other than regular working hours. Thus, long-distance commuting could become more acceptable when people have the choice to work at home for some days in a week.

Technological breakthroughs are also occurring in passenger transportation technologies, such as higher-fuel-efficiency cars, electric cars, autonomous vehicles, and high-speed rail. In 2008, more than 6,000 miles of new high-speed rail lines have been put into operation around the world (Campos and Rus 2009), most in Europe and eastern Asia. With speeds ranging from 100 to more than 300 miles per hour, high-speed rail is effective for linking places 100–500 miles apart (Leinbach 2004; Nash 2003). High-speed rail has the advantage of moving more passengers per hour than roads and at much higher speeds. Compared with air travel, it can free passengers from checking in and going through security screening and is more flexible in expanding passenger capacity (Nash 2003). In addition, high-speed rail is believed to be more environmentally friendly than auto and air travel because it operates mainly on electricity and produces little in carbon dioxide emissions. It consumes about

17 percent and 21 percent less energy per passenger mile than aircraft or automobiles, respectively, and is specially designed for noise abatement to reduce negative impacts on sensitive habitats (National Surface Transportation Policy and Revenue Study Commission 2007; Zaidi 2007).

The many supporters of high-speed rail consider it to have great potential for serving the needs of megaregions, in which the typical distance between metropolitan areas falls in the ideal operating range of high-speed rail. In turn, high-speed rail could transform interregional commuting patterns. For example, high-speed rail in the Texas Triangle connecting the four major metro areas at a speed of 430 miles per hour would reduce travel time by more than 70 percent. People could commute daily between any pair of cities in the triangle area in a reasonable amount of time (Zhang, Steiner, and Butler 2007). In a megaregion with high-speed rail, both households and companies could enjoy accessing more opportunities and resources in the megaregional environment than those available in individual metropolitan areas.

New Concepts in Work Scheduling

In recent years, employers have begun to allow employees greater flexibility in arranging their work times, not following a nine-to-five pattern but varying when they arrive at the office and leave. More than 25 million full-time U.S. workers, or 27.6 percent, somewhat varied their work hours in 1997 (Beers 2000). This flexible arrangement is more common for workers whose work can be conducted efficiently regardless of their start and end times, such as executive, managerial, or professional occupations (Beers 2000). Employees with more flexible work hours tend to work longer shifts (Hardill 2002). Furthermore, some employers have scaled down office facilities and equipped employees with laptops and ICT equipment to let them work from home, during travel, or from anywhere to reduce real estate costs (Hardill and Green 2003).

A compressed workweek offers another arrangement different from the traditional work schedule. Employees work fewer days in a week but have a longer workday (Hung 1996), resulting in fewer commuting trips and better use of leisure time. Compressed workweeks are especially attractive to long-distance commuters. Some research has indicated that in the United States most employees prefer compressed workweeks to the standard five-day workweek (Hung 1996; Ronen and Primps 1981; Zhou and Winters 2008). Employers also benefit from compressed workweeks: research has found that U.S. firms that implemented compressed workweeks reported increased morale and work efficiency (Hung 1996).

As people gain more flexibility in arranging work time and space, the day-to-day variability in commuting and work behavior could evolve. The typical-workday picture used in the current travel-demand analysis may not capture the true activities of many workers. For example, by varying work arrival time and departure time on the first and last days of a week and keeping a regular schedule the rest of a week, a person who adopts compressed workweeks will have a typical workweek instead of a typical workday. Thus, employers should discuss with workers allocating time weekly. Researchers have indeed recognized travel activity patterns that extend beyond the cycle of a single day (Doherty et al. 2002; Hanson and Huff 1988; Hirsh, Prashkea, and Ben-Akiva 1986; Jones and Clarke 1988). Generally, a one-week period could capture an individual's different daily patterns (Hanson and Huff 1988; Hirsh, Prashkea, and Ben-Akiva 1986).

Changing Attitudes Toward Travel

Travel is traditionally deemed derived demand. That is, travel is a consequence of people's desire to engage in activities in another location. For instance, commuting is done to get to the office and work. Mokhtarian and Salomon (2001) challenge this view, arguing that humans have the intrinsic will to travel and that travel itself could be the actual demand. It provides "the sensation of speed, the exposure to the environment and movement through that environment, the ability to control movement in a demanding and skillful way, the enjoyment of scenic beauty or other attractions of a route" (699). Sometimes, in the desire to travel, people may choose a longer route to their destination or even induce the demand for an activity. Mokhtarian and Salomon (2001) conducted a survey with more than 1,900 samples in three communities in the San Francisco Bay Area that confirmed their hypothesis of the positive utility of travel. More than half the respondents reported traveling "just for the fun of it" and agreed that the journey itself was part of the joy of travel (708).

Travel itself can bring enjoyment to people, but people can also do many activities while traveling (Lyons and Urry 2005; Mokhtarian and Salomon 2001; Ohmori and Harata 2008). The survey conducted by Mokhtarian and Salomon (2001) found that travel time was not generally considered only wasted time. Rather, people can use a bus or train journey for other activities, such as sleeping, reading, listening to music, playing electronic games, and working. ICTs further enrich travel activities by enabling people to communicate with people in other places and access the internet using mobile devices. An onboard survey in Japan conducted on standard trains and higher-grade liner trains, which provide more space and better services and privacy at an extra charge, indicated that people pay more to ride the liner trains to better use travel time. The survey also found that passengers were engaging in numerous types of activities on the trains, and some passengers with flexible work hours used the journey as working time (Ohmori and Harata 2008). Commuting time thus could become productive. In this case, public transportation would be valued more highly than driving. One of us commuted daily on the Metro-North Railroad from Connecticut to Grand Central Terminal in Manhattan for 25 years. The comfortable seating and then, later, Wi-Fi and cell phone service, along with lightweight laptops, iPads, and iPhones, made the entire round trip of more than two hours productive time.

For some, travel offers an alternative period of relaxation and free thought for a mental transition between origin and destination activities (Lyons and Urry 2005; Mokhtarian and Salomon 2001). Some people use the buffer created by the journey to switch roles from work to family life. Some commuters consider "long trips [to] represent 'the only time for thinking' they have, or 'the chance to catch up' on reading or other neglected but important tasks" (Mokhtarian and Salomon 2001, 702).

STUDIES ON LONG-DISTANCE COMMUTING

Some long-distance commuters choose to commute daily. These are workers who travel a significantly greater-than-average distance to get to work, and many often cross the boundary of a metropolitan region, either from one metropolitan region to another or to a nonmetro area. Others opt to live in a secondary home near their workplace and commute back to the primary home at weekly or longer intervals.

Job and Home Locations

Two economic theories attempt to explain how people select residential and work locations. According to the neoclassical model of urban residential location (Alonso 1964; Mills 1972; Muth 1969), households try to maximize their residential location utility, and the location decision is a trade-off between housing cost and transportation cost. This residential location model is based on the monocentric urban setting, in which land density and housing prices are lower farther away from a central business district than closer in. Thus, households may choose to live farther from the workplace and commute longer in exchange for lower housing costs and better living conditions. When a technological innovation decreases a community's transportation costs or the average household income increases, the urban periphery will expand as households find greater purchasing power and willingness to accept longer commutes. The residential location theory provides a basic explanation for a range of commuting behaviors, but it assumes a perfect market condition under which workers are fully informed and always able to choose the optimal commuting distance.

A contrasting body of economic theory, the search theory, suggests that workers have to continually search for jobs and dwellings to improve their position (Van Ommeren, Rietveld, and Nijkamp 1997; 2000). From the search theory point of view, commuting behavior is "determined by chance—the probability of receiving a job or residential offer at a certain distance—and a decision-making process—the decision to accept the offer" (Van Ommeren, Rietveld, and Nijkamp 1997, 404). According to the search theory, a longer-distance commute is often compensated by higher wages. With today's highly specialized workforce, labor markets cannot provide enough diversity in job options within a moderate distance of employee homes. This forces workers to commute a longer distance for the right job even when the travel cost is not fully offset by wages, thus avoiding costly job changes or home relocations (Sandow and Westin 2010; Van Ommeren and Rietveld 2007).

Intraregional Commuting

Research examining long-distance commuting within one metropolitan area, intraregional commuting, has been limited. Long-distance commuting has often been studied as excess commuting within one metropolitan region. Excess commuting is the deviation of the actual average commute from the theoretical smallest average commute given the spatial setting of residential and workplace sites in a metropolitan area (Horner 2002; Ma and Banister 2006). It is often used as an indicator of the overall geographic imbalance between jobs and housing in a city and is associated with unsustainable urban land use patterns.

One subset of literature on excess commuting concerns factors that contribute to long-distance commutes. In a comprehensive review of excess commuting research, Ma and Banister (2006) list many reasons examined by researchers since the 1980s that could prevent workers from finding jobs near their residential locations. They find that the most studied and well-established factor is the increased number of two-earner households, in which more obstacles exist for a pair of workers trying to optimize commutes than for a single worker. Homeowners tend to have higher levels of excess commuting than renters, and people who have relatively unstable jobs tend to accept longer commutes. Occupation variation and pay variation in a job market could also induce excess commuting. Transport subsidies such as employee parking allowances may encourage people to drive more. In addition, moving costs and rapid job turnover, neighborhood amenities and family life, and imperfect labor market information have all been examined as possible influences on excess commuting (Ma and Banister 2006).

Excess commuting is commonly deemed inefficient and unnecessary, so most of the literature has been concentrated on finding solutions to reduce it. Redistributing workers and encouraging mixed land use to achieve job and housing balance are the most commonly suggested policies (Ma and Banister 2006). However, these policies cannot effectively address all the intricate causes of long-distance commuting; the continuing complexity of household travel behaviors coupled with more advanced ICT applications could also weaken the power of policies that focus only on shortening journey-to-work trips. Thus, it is not surprising to see more excess commuting occurring.

Land use and transportation policies that attempt to reduce excess commuting and long-distance travel pose another question with respect to regional economic strength:

> [If] most workers actually worked in their residence county . . . [or other region unit], that would clearly be better for the transportation system in terms of congestion, but

would it be better for the region as an entity? . . . Isn't the strength—the hallmark—of a region based on its ability to provide a market in the millions? For example, an employer in a very specialized sphere located in a large region has a market of prospective employees measuring in the millions. This is also true of an exotic restaurant, great art gallery, or any specialty store. This suggests that transportation policies that would suppress longer distance travel and encourage short-distance trips are destroying part of what makes a big region a greater region. (Pisarski 2006, 150)

Excess commuting creates congestion and wastes energy, and it might indicate another problem: workers want access to larger markets for jobs or housing. When needs exceed the boundary of one metropolitan area, interregional commuting is inevitable. On the one hand, it is important to provide a better balance of jobs and housing in a particular region so that workers can live near their work. On the other hand, long-distance, interregional commuting should be further examined and solutions offered so that workers can do such commuting in a more sustainable way, thus creating a society in which people have more freedom in choosing where to live and work.

Transregional Commuting

Lee (1995; 1996) focuses on interregional long-distance commuting in the United States, investigating the motivations of long-distance commuters who traveled from homes in California's San Joaquin Valley to work in the San Francisco Bay Area. In this study, long-distance commuting is a journey over 45 minutes one way that crosses a metropolitan area boundary. Using the U.S. Census Bureau Public Use Microdata Sample 5 percent data, Lee concludes that a white, married male with a medium education level (but a relatively higher level than other commuters in the San Joaquin Valley) and who worked in the 1990s in construction, communications, or other public utilities field represented a typical long-distance commuter between the valley and the Bay Area.

Because census data do not provide detailed answers for behavior questions, Lee held four focus group discussions and conducted in-depth interviews with 40 interregional commuters. The respondents were contacted through the Bay Area regional ride-sharing agency. He discovered that the high cost of housing in the Bay Area was an important reason for these people choosing to reside in the more affordable San Joaquin Valley. A better living environment was a common reason for households with small kids. Some commuters preferred a rural lifestyle. Although they had some dislike for the driving, they became used to the commute. Lee concluded that the pull of the attraction of living in the valley was stronger than the push of repellent factors of living in the city, such as high housing costs or crime.

More recent studies on long-distance, interregional commuting have been performed by researchers in Europe. According to the literature, the number of long-distance commuters crossing municipal regions or even national boundaries has been steadily increasing in some European countries. Such commuting includes daily and weekly travel between home and work (Lyons and Chatterjee 2008; Sandow and Westin 2010). The literature concerned with this type of commuting is of two kinds. One group studies long-distance commuting from a travel behavior point of view and attempts to explain people's commuting decisions using quantitative methods. However, it does not distinguish between daily and weekly commuting but more often defines long-distance commuting as a work trip longer than 30–45 minutes. The other group pays special attention to weekly commuting. Studies in this group are typically performed by social or family life researchers and geographic researchers who examine weekly commuting's effects on family life and the connections between migration (change of home location) and weekly commuting.

Long-Distance Daily Commuting

A common method for studying long-distance commuting uses secondary data for developing regression models to scrutinize its causal effects (Öhman and Lindgren 2003; Sandow and Westin 2010; Titheridge and Hall 2006). Titheridge and Hall (2006, 60) analyze long-distance commuting in the Greater South East Region, a "global megacity region," of the United Kingdom (see also Hall and Pain 2006). Their study focuses on the East Corridor and the North Corridor radiating from London to the periphery of the region where rail service is available. Six models with dependent variables of commuting distance and mode were developed for each corridor for 1981 and 1991 on the basis of census data. They conclude that a lack of job opportunities near home was a significant reason for workers to choose a longer commute. In addition, they find that "higher social classes" traveled the longest distance (Titheridge and Hall 2006, 74).

The finding of Titheridge and Hall (2006) about the association of long-distance commuting with social class is confirmed by Sandow and Westin (2008), who asked 2,500 people in 2004 in four municipalities in a sparsely populated region of northern Sweden about their inclination and opportunity to commute. People with a high level of education, especially males working in the private sector, were more willing to accept longer commutes. The survey also reveals that 45 minutes one way is commonly the maximum that people accept as tolerable for daily commuting. The 45-minute time limit has been verified by other researchers (Levinson and Wu 2005; Öhman and Lindgren 2003; Sandow and Westin 2010; Van Ham and Hooimeijer 2009; Van Ommeren 1998); when a one-way commute is longer than 45 minutes, weekly commuting or migration may be preferred (Sandow and Westin 2008).

Sandow and Westin (2010) later conducted another study using 1995–2005 data gathered by Sweden's government to analyze the duration of long-distance commutes. They found that most long-distance commuters had been commuting long distances for many years, and economic incentive was important for them to sustain such long work trips. They concluded that because longer commuting provided more opportunities for all members in a household and was often associated with higher income, it tended to be a long-range mobility strategy rather than a temporary solution for households.

In the Netherlands, the determinants of long-distance commuting and intention for migration were examined by Van Ham and Hooimeijer (2009) using the 2002 Housing Demand Survey. Using three logistic regression models, Van Ham and Hooimeijer further proved the importance of individual and household characteristics to longer journeys to work. For example, long-distance commuters in the Netherlands commonly had higher incomes and higher levels of education. Although they found that homeowners were less willing to migrate for a job than renters, home ownership alone did not explain long-distance commutes.

Another long-distance commuting study in Sweden by Öhman and Lindgren (2003) used 1994 data. The results of their model were similar to the conclusions of other long-distance commuting studies. Yet, they uniquely addressed how the importance of social ties, both individual and social preferences and norms, and the accessibility and choice of transportation mode would all influence people's choice of longer commutes, although they did not include these variables in the model. Moreover, they distinguished three types of mobility patterns as "what people can do . . . must do . . . and want to do" (Öhman and Lindgren 2003, 6). What people can do depends on a society's access to transportation and communications technologies and an individual's physical ability, income, and information resources. What people must do to make a living and access services depends on the spatial setting of workplaces, housing and shopping in a region, social norms and values, and so on. What people want to do reflects people's free will and preferences, which might also be influenced by social norms. Then, long-distance commuting becomes the product of "can," "must," and "want" to mobility (Öhman and Lindgren 2003, 26).

Long-Distance Weekly Commuting

Workers who choose to take long work trips have the option of traveling between home and work daily or spending weekdays at the workplace and returning home for the weekend, which is called long-distance weekly commuting. When the distance between a workplace and a residence is too far to go every day, individuals have to commit to weekly commuting life when they need to or want to obtain opportunities far away from home without relocating. The literature on long-distance daily commuting discussed earlier does not distinguish these two types of long-distance commuting, although some researchers have mentioned them (Öhman and Lundgren 2003; Sandow and Westin 2010). Long-distance weekly commuters are few, and travel surveys for metropolitan transportation planning assume that individuals travel daily between a single fixed residence and single fixed workplace (Green, Hogarth, and Shackleton 1999a), which creates the major difficulty of having to separate weekly commuters from daily commuters. Most long-distance weekly commuting research has used small samples and qualitative methods.

The phenomenon of long-distance weekly commuting has mostly been investigated by researchers in the disciplines of geography and sociology. These two bodies of literature have emphasized different aspects of weekly commuting. Geographers study weekly commuting used to avoid migration and consider the social and spatial contexts. Sociologists focus on the effect of weekly commuting on family life and evaluate the satisfaction of such a lifestyle.

Long-Distance Commuting Versus Migration

Migration is "any permanent or semi-permanent change of residence, more meaningfully, a spatial transfer from one social unit or neighborhood to another, which strains or ruptures previous social bonds" (Zelinsky 1971, 225). Generally, migration is highly related to local labor market conditions. For example, wage differences between regions may motivate people to migrate to areas with higher wage levels to improve their living conditions. Unemployment due to occupation imbalance, lack of job skills, and uncertainty of job availability in a labor market may also force people to migrate (Oeberg 1995). In addition, individuals' backgrounds and experience could influence their migration intentions. For instance, a high level of education could prevent people from changing occupations but encourage them to change their residence location (Borsch-Supan 1990). People might decide to stay if their region has higher-quality physical infrastructure, such as diverse housing stock, a sophisticated transportation system, or an excellent education system (Oeberg 1995).

According to the late Penn State cultural geographer Wilbur Zelinsky (1971), our society has gone through five stages of mobility transition: in premodern times, society depended on traditional agriculture, then came stages characterized by massive migration flow, and migration flows today are absorbed by ICT systems (Oeberg 1995). Modern means of transportation have provided people higher mobility; advanced ICT systems give people access to information beyond geographic boundaries; and rising levels of affluence and education increase people's desire for better opportunities elsewhere. These factors make geographic mobility more possible, but humans have accumulated higher levels of physical capital and tend to build stronger bonds to a place. Neighborhood amenities, schools, city welfare, local social networks, and so on, tie people to a place. Long-distance weekly commuting resolves this dilemma by being an alternative to migration (Eliasson, Lindgren, and Westerlund 2003; Green, Hogarth, and Shackleton 1999a; Sandow and Westin 2008).

Long-distance weekly commuting between the regions of North East England and London were examined by the Policy Studies Institute in the mid-1980s and late 1990s (Green, Hogarth, and Shackleton 1999a; 1999b; Hogarth 1987; Hogarth and Daniel 1988). Between the late 1970s and 1980s, the north and south areas had a significantly uneven employment distribution. Many found jobs in the South East and London regions but remained living in the north. They commuted weekly principally because they could not find affordable accommodation near their work (Hogarth 1987). Hogarth (1987) and Hogarth and Daniel (1988) estimated that 10,000 people were long-distance weekly commuters. They distributed questionnaires on coaches and trains leaving London on a Friday evening for the North East region and found 105 long-distance weekly commuters. From those, they chose 25 for further in-depth interviewing. They also sought the opinions of some of these weekly commuters' partners, and they explored the attitudes of employers by surveying companies that had been advertising in the North East region for professional employees.

More than 10 years later, over 200,000 employees in England had workplaces beyond the daily traveling distance of their homes. Using the same method of questionnaires on trains and buses as Hogarth and Daniel (1988), Green, Hogarth, and Shackleton (1999b) found 115 long-distance weekly commuters, interviewed 25 of them along with some partners, and surveyed 48 companies. The surveys in both 1988 and 1999 related the increase of women in employment and the growth of dual-earner households to the phenomenon of long-distance weekly commuting. According to Hogarth and Daniel (1988) and Green, Hogarth, and Shackleton (1999b), one group of weekly commuters was pulled into weekly commuting because it provided them more prestigious employment opportunities and chances to further their careers. In addition, weekly commuting allowed them to retain their family home, an environment they preferred, where their partners had jobs, and their children attended school. This group of commuters saw benefits in such a lifestyle and appreciated the uninterrupted work time during weekdays. Another group was pushed into the lifestyle by layoffs or because the jobs were the only work available and they could not afford housing in the South East and London regions. Workers in this group deemed long-distance commuting a necessary evil to ensure the financial security of their family (Green, Hogarth, and Shackleton 1999b). A majority of the weekly commuters regarded commuting as long term, not temporary. Comparing the results of the two time periods, Green, Hogarth, and Shackleton (1999b) conclude that more pull factors contributed to commuting in the 1990s than in the 1980s. At the same time, employers had become more willing to accept long-distance weekly commuting by employees and permitted them more flexibility with the support of ICTs.

Commuting Couples: A New Family Form

Long-distance weekly commuting has attracted sociologists' attention because it created a new family form and partnership roles. The traditional couple relationship relies on cohabitation (Holmes 2009), and researchers had treated members in a family as a single unit in which the husband was the head of the family (Gerstel and Gross 1984). The historical reasons that separated couples typically involved men leaving home to work at sea, in the military, or in the oil and mining industries (Gerstel and Gross 1984; Holmes 2009). In more recent times, some careers require people, such as salespeople or politicians, to travel frequently. In most other cases, when a husband needed to move for work reasons, the wife followed, becoming the "trailing spouse" (Van der Klis and Mulder 2008). As more women participate in the labor market, more households have to manage careers for both partners, creating a new home format of commuting marriages or commuting couples.

One of the earliest studies in commuting marriage was conducted by Gerstel and Gross (1984, 2), who define the commuting marriage as "employed spouses who spend at least three nights per week in separate residences and yet are still married and intend to remain so." They question the suitability of nuclear families in contemporary society, in which the need for mobility in the labor market conflicts with the traditional pattern of a shared family home. Individuals had to find different ways to coordinate work and family life, and the commuting marriage became a solution to support the career pursuits of both partners (Gerstel and Gross 1984; Holmes 2009).

Since Gerstel and Gross's original study, other studies have further explored the topic. The method used by most of these researchers was a qualitative investigation. These researchers typically searched for respondents by nonrandom and snowball sampling techniques and conducted interviews examining the rationales behind the commuting marriage life, the meaning of separate homes and family roles for commuting couples, the benefits and stressors of a commuting marriage, and how to improve the commuting life.

This body of literature reports that reasons for a commuting partnership always include the work domain (Holmes 2004; 2006; Van der Klis and Karsten 2009a; Van der Klis and Mulder 2008). Most of the interviewees in these studies were professionals whose specialization in certain areas and high education levels left them with only small pools of job opportunities fitting their requirements (Van der Klis and Mulder 2008). Holmes (2004) in particular emphasizes the difficulty facing academic couples—the limited number of universities in one area made a commuting partnership highly likely, yet the flexibility of academic jobs counteracted the difficulty of such a relationship. Holmes (2006) also argues that professional jobs are necessary to maintain a commuting partnership because they offer sufficient money and flexibility to maintain two residences. In addition to work reasons, Van der Klis and Mulder (2008) address how the residential domain, such as lifestyle preference and housing market conditions, contributes to a commuting partnership.

Van der Klis and Karsten (2009b) investigate the meaning of the commuter residence to workers by interviewing 30 commuter couples in the Netherlands. They conclude that, because it was difficult for a commuting partner to establish a strong social connection near the commuter residence, the commuter would not typically consider the second residence as a true home and would totally separate work life at the commuter residence from family life at the primary residence. Thus, although more families are expected to commit to a commuter partnership in the future, Van der Klis and Karsten argue, contra Gerstel and Gross (1984), that the commuter partnership would not likely become an equal alternative to the nuclear family in the long run (Van der Klis and Karsten 2009b).

Because commuting couples usually spend at least half their lives separately, balancing work and family life becomes important. Van der Klis and Karsten (2009a) distinguish two types of commuting families: (1) traditional, in which the husband concentrates full time on paid work and the wife has no job or a part-time job and takes most of the responsibility for the housework; and (2) egalitarian, in which both partners participate in paid work and share the housework during weekends. The second family type reflects the changing role of women in contemporary U.S. family life. Some argue that wives in the commuting family still had more tasks than their husbands in household labor (Anderson and Spruill 1993), but other researchers believe women have gained a greater level of autonomy within a commuting partnership (Hardill 2002; Holmes 2004).

The commuting life has been found to have both rewards and strains (Bunker et al. 1992; Gross 1980; Hardill 2002; Van der Klis and Karsten 2009a). The most positive aspect of such a life is the enlarged geographic scale of job locations, and the most negative aspect is missing out on daily family life for a significant time (Van der Klis and Karsten 2009a). The perception of the commuting partnership could vary among different individuals under different situations. For instance, Gross (1980) concludes that older couples, couples married longer or freed from child-rearing responsibilities, and those among whom at least one partner had an established career might consider the lifestyle less stressful.

Furthermore, Bunker et al. (1992) compared the quality of life of 90 commuting couples with that of 133 single-residence, dual-career couples. Their study demonstrates that commuting couples express less satisfaction with their partner relationship and family life, but they, especially men, are more satisfied with their work life and appreciate the additional time they could reserve for themselves.

NEW CHALLENGES, NEW MOBILITY, AND NEW OPPORTUNITIES

The year 2020 may have a place as one of the watershed years in the span of the last 100 years, along with 1945, 1968, 1989, and 2001. The first pandemic in a century shaped an entirely new future for our country, its economy, and its social and political systems.

The pandemic forced emerging technologies to come together to create radically different patterns of remote work and business organization in the United States and throughout the industrialized world. Some of these technologies, such as high-speed rail, have been around for half a century or more, but Zoom, FaceTime, Google Meet, and other video conferencing services and on-call mobility services, such as Uber and Lyft, are relatively new. They promise to create a very different economic geography for metropolitan regions and megaregions as millions of workers and businesses find themselves unshackled from center-city work locations and long-distance commutes.

What will the lasting impacts of the COVID-19 pandemic be on business location, work, and travel patterns? And how can we shape and direct these changes to meet the economic, climate, and social justice goals of the United States?

Now, at this watershed moment, is the opportunity to shape an economic geography of less congestion, more equity, and more sustainability. Becoming carbon neutral and more land efficient in patterns of development and mobility will help achieve these goals. The new economy and settlement pattern must also reduce racial and spatial inequality.

COVID-19 Impacts

The pandemic lockdowns and economic collapse that followed exposed the inequality of U.S. economic and infrastructure systems, made more prominent by the mass demonstrations following the police killings of George Floyd, Breonna Taylor, and other African Americans. Whereas many white-collar workers could work safely from home during the pandemic, most essential frontline workers, many from minority groups, could not. This increased their exposure to the virus and resulted in far higher rates of death and hospitalization for Black and Latinx communities. Students in households with one or both parents at home and connected to high-speed broadband networks could continue their schooling via remote learning, but many students in inner-city and rural communities could not because they did not have a parent working from home or access to broadband, or both. This made it difficult or impossible for these students to keep up with their learning during the lockdown.

The COVID-19 pandemic lockdowns resulted in rapid adoption of remote work enabled by video conferencing, and this shift had surprising impacts that were felt almost immediately. Most firms in the business services, technology, media, and other white-collar sectors discovered that they could operate as efficiently with these new communications technologies as they had in traditional workplace settings.

One downtown Boston law firm, for example, reported that, even though the firm's offices were closed for several months in early 2020, efficiency did not suffer. Despite a major drop in greater Boston's economic activity during the shutdown, the firm's bottom line had been reduced by less than 5 percent. Staff found that working at home eliminated the need for time-consuming commutes and increased the amount of time they could devote to work—in some cases by a few hours daily. The firm decided not to add expensive office space in its high-rent Seaport district office tower and may even reduce occupancy because staff have continued to work mostly at home after lockdowns ended (D. McGarrah, senior partner at Foley Hoag, Boston, pers. comm., January 2021).

This firm is an example of what other firms and workers are experiencing in cities across U.S. megaregions. As of July 2020, an estimated 1 million jobs have already left New York City, and an estimated half million residents have left Manhattan. Similar trends are underway in many of the densest coastal cities that have been the epicenter of the nation's tech sector over the last few decades. Remember that a smaller but similar outmigration of jobs and residents from Manhattan followed the 9/11 terrorist attacks and New York's fiscal crisis in the 1970s. Despite predictions that these relocations would be permanent, these residents and firms (or their replacements) eventually returned to New York. This time may be different. Although it is too early to know the long-term impacts that the pandemic will have on residential and business locations, many of the lost jobs and residents will likely be replaced by a new generation of industries and their workforce. Even a modest reduction in jobs and residents in New York City could lessen congestion and the continued run-up in housing prices, which will further encourage these new industries to locate in the City.

The transportation sector as a whole is among those hit the worst by the COVID-19 pandemic. International travel restrictions have reduced air passenger volumes to a small fraction of the before-COVID level. Transit ridership in U.S. cities has declined dramatically since social distancing and working from home started (APTA 2021). Ridership shortfalls during the pandemic caused a fiscal crisis for transit agencies. As the economy opened back up in the summer of 2020, ridership on the New York region's subways and commuter rail lines began to recover, even though many commuters drove to work instead of taking transit for health and safety reasons. This modest return to center-city workplaces combined with increased commuting in single-occupant vehicles unfortunately increased congestion on arterial highways, despite overall reductions in travel.

Postpandemic Trends

Eventually, the pandemic will be under control, as has happened in the past with pandemics and epidemics such as cholera, Ebola, and SARS. Will life and business then return to normal? What are the implications of the COVID-19 pandemic for cities, regions, and megaregions? Scholars have reported some empirical findings, mostly on the short-term effects of the pandemic lockdowns—for example, travel restrictions, and school and work disruptions—but long-term impacts remain largely speculative.

Now that coronavirus vaccination is progressing, states and cities have lifted travel restrictions. Car and air travel have been coming back quickly, but public transit is still struggling. The long-term impacts of the pandemic on public transit could be devastating unless a concerted effort turns the crisis into an opportunity to reinvent public transportation services. With less automobile and transit use, air quality has improved in many places. Whether transportation can be reinvented to maintain better air quality and to produce less greenhouse gas emissions is one of the most important questions of our time.

Probably the safest assumption is that, as it becomes safe to travel again, as roadway congestion resumes, and as transit services recover, commuters will return to transit. But overall transit ridership may remain below peak levels of the 2010s because fewer workers commute daily to center-city jobs. This will be a healthy trend if it reduces crush-load commutes on subway, commuter rail, and light rail systems. But innovations in first- and last-mile connections and improved amenity and service levels will be needed to sustain transit ridership. Many transit agencies in Europe, Asia, and Latin America design their services with amenities and schedules to attract middle- and upper-middle income passengers. By contrast, most U.S. transit systems are designed to serve low-income workers, discouraging use by higher-income passengers. Improved amenities and schedules—along with better integration with the services of transportation network companies, transit services, and regional rail networks, as outlined later—will increase reverse-commute (from urban homes to suburban workplaces) and off-peak travel and increase efficient use of all these systems.

Whereas the travel modes involving space sharing have been affected negatively by the pandemic, micromobility modes—for instance, bikes, scooters, and walking—have risen (NACTO 2020).

Media reports have suggested that people and firms responded to the pandemic with spatial resorting. Millions of Americans moved away from big cities and dense metros in 2020 to escape the coronavirus (Popken 2020). Will the moves become permanent, or will those who left cities return after the pandemic is over? Many corporations are now operating online. Will they renew leases for offices and retain their downtown locations in the post-COVID time? Most believe that cities will rebound and that agglomeration economies will still matter. Generation Z, which is well educated, racially diverse, and technologically savvy, will become an urban demographic force and will likely demand more flexibility from employers. Employers will likely offer flexibility so that workers do not commute daily but do not work from home every day; they will operate in a hybrid mode, telecommuting a few days per week. Essential corporate functions will stay centrally located, primarily in downtowns. Other functions may move to suburban office parks or go online.

The COVID-19 pandemic has affected vulnerable populations and businesses more than others. The World Bank (2020) estimates that the pandemic eliminated years of antipoverty effects and drove about 100 million people back into poverty. Low-income adults and people of color experienced the most severe impacts from the pandemic, as reported by the Pew Research Center (Parker, Minkin, and Bennett 2020). The COVID-19 crisis hit women harder than men. Childcare closings and homeschooling forced many mothers to reduce their work hours or to quit jobs. U.S. Bureau of Labor Statistics data show that, in September 2020, 865,000 women had left the labor force—more than four times the number of men who left the labor force (Madowitz and Boesch 2020). Small businesses had fewer resources to withstand the pandemic crisis. Bartik et al. (2020) reported mass layoffs and closures because of it. They surveyed 5,800 small businesses in the United States and found more than 40 percent had closed by April 4, 2020. More closures followed.

For the post-COVID-19 era, many envision a plausible scenario of cities recovering and regaining their vibrancy. Regions would continue to expand, going beyond the metropolitan geography of the pre-COVID time. Expansion may accelerate with the growing adaptation of teleactivity and the demand for home office spaces, large yards, and natural amenities, but it could cause further sprawl. Inequalities by income, gender, race, ethnicity, and age and by geographic and digital dimensions are unlikely to improve by themselves. Public interventions could shape the process and outcome through strategic planning, infrastructure investments, and policy decisions with strong environmental and social commitments. Megaregions offer a sensible spatial platform for the needed dialogue and decision making.

Harnessing Emerging Technologies

Emerging technologies offer a means to reduce and, ultimately, eliminate metropolitan congestion.

- *Transportation network companies.* Uber, Lyft, and other transportation network companies use sophisticated algorithms to determine the shortest routes for their drivers and passengers. Dynamic congestion pricing and regulatory measures can incentivize similar routing methods for multipassenger vans and buses. This will provide multiple passengers with convenient travel times and routes during high-volume travel times on even the most congested streets and highways. This is analogous to the elevators now being installed in modern office buildings, which take large groups of users to adjacent floors, minimizing travel time and increasing efficiency. Mobile apps will inform travelers of a nearby bus or transit stop where other travelers to the same destination are congregated. Well-lit and climate-controlled stops will improve the quality of the experience for all. This will free up space previously devoted to travel lanes, on-street parking, and station area parking. Collectively, these measures will permit a complete transformation of the public realm in urban centers; at the same time, the first- and last-mile problems of transit use will be greatly diminished.

- *Dynamic congestion pricing and automated toll collection.* A handful of highways in the United States employ dynamic pricing to reduce congestion during peak periods. These systems charge tolls at amounts tied to congestion. The advent of automated toll collection systems makes it easy to implement congestion management systems on virtually any street or highway. Singapore has introduced an island-wide dynamic pricing system and uses toll collection to cross-subsidize the country's extensive rapid transit system. Similar systems could be adopted in U.S. metro regions.

- *Smartphones.* Every traveler can have access to real-time information on transportation prices, routes, travel times, and alternative modes. Smartphones will become the primary information portal to all the travel innovations outlined in this book. Sophisticated onboard, real-time information systems on every new automobile will also provide drivers with up-to-date information on routes, prices, and intermodal links. The universal use of smartphones also enables congestion management around the needs of individual customers.

- *Big data.* Rapidly collecting, analyzing, and using vast amounts of data about transportation demand, roadway use, vehicle locations, and so on, makes possible a fully automated and integrated multimodal transportation management system for every metropolitan region and megaregion.

- *Routing systems.* Most new vehicles in the United States today have built-in GPS and automated technologies that direct vehicles to the least congested route.

- *Autonomous and electric vehicles.* Urban automobile fleets do not yet have many autonomous or electric vehicles, but they could play an important part if their use is properly regulated and incentivized. Autonomous vehicles can make more efficient use of limited roadway capacity. They can also access transit stations without needing to park. They can reduce highway deaths and injuries caused by driver error, speeding, and drinking. Electric vehicles can reduce petroleum use and excess ground-level ozone, carbon monoxide, and nitrous oxides in air pollution hotspots. The reductions in air pollution due to the COVID-19 pandemic lockdowns demonstrate the quality-of-life benefits that reducing carbon-powered vehicles can provide.

- *Automated goods movement.* Lyon, France, and other European cities use sophisticated algorithms and road pricing to enable truckers to consolidate package deliveries and speed trucks to their destination in the most efficient ways. This results in fewer trucks making stops, relieving congestion in urban centers. These precedents can be adapted to U.S. trucking and parcel delivery services. And they will become essential parts of any congestion management system as online purchases continue to increase in coming years.

Autonomous Vehicle Adoption and Intercity Travel

A study explores the potential effects of autonomous vehicle (AV) adoption on intercity travel in the Texas Triangle megaregion. The study builds on the Texas Statewide Analysis Model to analyze changes in modal shares, vehicle miles traveled, and highway congestion under an assumed AV adoption scenario (Huang 2020).

The Texas Triangle contains 2,160 traffic analysis zones, which account for slightly less than half the total traffic analysis zones (4,667) defined in the Statewide Analysis Model for the entire state. The four major travel modes considered in the study were auto (AVs and conventional vehicles), bus, rail, and air. The study applied the standard four-step travel demand modeling procedure to estimate travel demand changes from the base year of 2010 to the forecast year of 2040, when adoption of AVs has led to an assumed 15 percent increase in total trips in addition to travel demand growth resulting from population and employment growth.

The study had three main findings. First, the introduction of AVs affects travel modes by changing trip distances. Travel by auto increases not only for one-way trips of less than 50 miles but also for long-distance trips of 100–700 miles. Trips by rail and bus decline for short-distance travel. The long-distance trip-by-auto increase comes largely at the expense of air travel. The auto mode gains the most among all modes, likely because of the reduced net cost of travel time offered by AVs. When travelers can reclaim partially or entirely a trip's time to use for productive activities or simply resting, this becomes an advantage compared with trip time that is a cost for other modes of travel.

Second, the changes in travel-mode trip distances are similar to the predicted changes in vehicle miles traveled (VMT), as shown in the first table below. AV adoption will redistribute VMT by major travel mode, increasing auto VMT by 70 percent and decreasing rail, bus, and air VMT. The second table below shows the geographic

Travel Modes and Vehicle Miles Traveled Before and After Adoption of Autonomous Vehicles

	VMT Before AV Adoption (billions)	VMT After AV Adoption (billions)	Change (%)
Auto	7.22	12.27	70.04
Rail	1.13	0.53	−52.98
Bus	6.91	4.85	−29.77
Air	12.94	5.82	−55.05

AV = autonomous vehicle; VMT = vehicle miles traveled.

Vehicle Miles Traveled in Major Texas Metros Resulting from Adoption of Autonomous Vehicles

	VMT Before AV Adoption (millions)	VMT After AV Adoption (millions)	Change (%)
Dallas–Fort Worth	865.96	1,560.21	80.1
San Antonio	297.09	432.88	45.7
Houston	814.67	1,328.25	63.0
Austin	410.55	624.77	52.2
Total	4,104.95	6,666.48	62.4

AV = autonomous vehicle; VMT = vehicle miles traveled.

distribution of VMT changes in four major metro areas in the Texas Triangle megaregion: Dallas–Fort Worth, San Antonio, Houston, and Austin. The larger metros, Dallas–Fort Worth and Houston, likely would experience greater VMT growth than the smaller Austin and San Antonio metros. These projected VMT changes indicate that the Texas Department of Transportation and regional and local agencies need to plan for AV technology infrastructure.

Third, highway congestion is likely to increase as a result of AV adoption, especially in large metros, on highways that are already heavily congested. Highways in the Dallas–Fort Worth region could suffer the most.

This study of the Texas Triangle presents a complex picture of the travel impacts of AV technologies. The auto mode is expected to increase the most by enabling people to travel more and by expanding its market share. The aggregate travel outcome, however, is alarming if total VMT and congestion likely increase after AV adoption. Planners and policy-makers must plan now to abate the negative externalities of AV-enabled additional travel, while embracing benefits brought by AV technologies such as safety improvements and increased use efficiency of roadway capacity and urban land.

CONCLUSION

Americans are experiencing rapid changes, embracing new technologies, or adopting new styles of living forced by events such as the COVID-19 pandemic. If these changes persist—a significant share of the workforce working from home or commuting perhaps once or twice a week to center-city offices—and if transit ridership resumes, a very different economic geography and more efficient mobility patterns could arise for U.S. megaregions. Such changes can address long-standing challenges facing these places—by reducing congestion, aiding the transition to a low-carbon and no-carbon economy and transportation system, reducing racial and spatial inequality, improving environmental quality, and more.

PART III
UNLOCKING THE ECONOMIC POTENTIAL OF MEGAREGIONS

7

THE GREEN MEGA DEAL

Change will not come if we wait for some other person or if we wait for some other time. We are the ones we've been waiting for. We are the change we seek.

—BARACK OBAMA

MEGAREGIONS CAN HELP ADVANCE IDEAS GENERATED BY the proposed Green New Deal in four areas: infrastructure, climate, social justice, and energy and the environment. This chapter summarizes the Green New Deal and discusses governance, finance, and implementation strategies to achieve goals in those four areas. Megaregional frameworks can contribute to advancing these goals. We propose a Green Mega Deal to complement the Green New Deal.

THE GREEN NEW DEAL

Let us green the earth, restore the earth, heal the earth.
—IAN L. MCHARG, *A QUEST FOR LIFE*

The name and goals of the Green New Deal are a clear homage to one of the most transformative, progressive eras in the history of the United States. Franklin D. Roosevelt led the nation out of the Great Depression through bold actions that lifted many people out of poverty and misery. As Goh (2020, 189) has noted, "The New Deal was not won or implemented at the stroke of a pen or in one legislative vote but as a sequence of acts and associated programs that, in each instance, expanded the powers of government in particular ways." Sadly, not all people benefited equally, and some groups were held back, such as Black citizens through redlining and other discriminatory measures.

The Green New Deal was introduced as a nonbinding resolution on February 7, 2019, in the U.S. House of Representatives by New York representative Alexandria Ocasio-Cortez and in a companion resolution in the Senate by Massachusetts senator Ed Markey (*Recognizing the Duty* 2019). On one level, the resolution addresses the existential challenge of human-induced climate change. On another, it acknowledges the social equity consequences of environmental injustice. In many ways, the resolution mirrors Pope Francis's remarkable 2015 encyclical *Laudato Si'*, in which he calls for an integral ecology to bridge climate change, environmental quality, and social justice.

Representative Ocasio-Cortez, Senator Markey, and their colleagues draw on the United Nations Intergovernmental Panel on Climate Change's 2018 *Fourth National Climate Assessment* to build their case for action: mass migrations, lost economic opportunities, wildfires, the decline of coral reefs, heat stress affecting millions, and the loss of the coastal infrastructure (Reidmiller et al. 2018). They acknowledge the United States' disproportionate role in the production of global greenhouse gases and the social consequences, especially for the poor, both nationally and internationally.

The nation must muster, Ocasio-Cortez, Markey, and their colleagues argue, a response with a level of urgency and resources comparable to that of the New Deal almost a century earlier. The resolution establishes five goals to be achieved over 10 years:

- Achieve net-zero greenhouse gas emissions through a fair and just transition for all communities and workers.
- Create millions of good, high-wage jobs and ensure prosperity and economic security for all people of the United States.
- Invest in the infrastructure and industry of the United States to sustainably meet the challenges of the 21st century.
- Secure for all people of the United States for generations to come: clean air and water, climate and community resiliency, healthy food, access to nature, and a sustainable environment.
- Promote justice and equity by stopping current, preventing future, and repairing historic oppression of Indigenous people, communities of color, migrant communities, deindustrialized communities, depopulated rural communities, the poor, low-income workers, women, the elderly, the unhoused, people with disabilities, and youth ("frontline and vulnerable communities") (McDonald 2019).

Although the Green New Deal has been opposed by most—Republicans and Democrats alike, including President Joe Biden and leaders in both houses of Congress—the objectives of the Green New Deal advocates and those of President Biden have many overlaps, especially in infrastructure, climate, racial justice, and energy and the environment.

A principal advantage of the megaregional scale is that issues can be addressed beyond the capacities of neighborhoods, cities, counties, and regions and, in some cases, beyond the borders of states and nations. This is certainly the case with infrastructure. In terms of governance, federal transportation funds are currently already funneled through regional governing or coordinating entities, often called councils of government, metropolitan planning organizations, or rural transportation planning organizations. The net-zero emissions goal of the Green New Deal requires reducing transportation emissions, which are 28 percent of total U.S. greenhouse gases. This will require investments in "zero-emission vehicle infrastructure and manufacturing ... clean, affordable, and accessible public transit; and ... high-speed rail" (McDonald 2019).

Several megaregions, such as Piedmont Atlantic, Northern California, and Great Lakes, already possess strong vehicle manufacturing capacities and are making zero-emission cars and trucks. This capacity could be expanded relatively easily. The Northeast megaregion has a highly integrated public transportation system that could be made more clean, affordable, and accessible and is replicable in other megaregions. At the same time, planning for high-speed rail is beyond the scope of regional governing or coordinating entities. The megaregion scale is ideal for high-speed rail, addressed in chapter 9. In addition, the Texas Triangle received its name long ago from the shape of the rail connections between Houston, San Antonio, and Dallas–Fort Worth.

Climate change mitigation lessens the harshness and pain of a warming planet. Mitigation measures include minimizing food waste to reduce emissions of heat-trapping greenhouse gases, managing refrigerants, conserving and restoring key ecosystems like rainforests, supporting small agricultural producers, promoting green energy, reducing the sources of greenhouse gas emissions, promoting energy efficiency, and encouraging renewable energy use. "Adaptation" refers to changing behavior, systems, and ways of life in response to climate change. Some responses are maintaining and creating refugia, promoting landscape connectivity, enhancing genetic diversity, facilitating community adjustments, and planning for disturbances such as hurricanes, flooding, and wildfires (figure 7.1).

Many of these strategies are beyond the scope of any single city or region. Cities and regions can make many crucial contributions, but megaregions have the scale to facilitate intergovernmental cooperation. For instance, the megaregion scale can be especially useful to conserve and restore key ecosystems, create refugia, promote landscape connectivity, and plan for climate disasters.

These actions will require leadership and action at all levels of government. Megaregions can help connect cities and regions within and across states. Certainly,

FIGURE 7.1 Submerged freeways and widespread flooding in Houston after Hurricane Harvey. *Source: Reuters/Richard Carson.*

national leadership is essential. To date, in the United States, the Green New Deal has been the clearest and most ambitious call to national climate action. What it will cost and who will pay for it remain unanswered. No action now will likely result in even greater costs in the future.

Some megaregions are better suited for large-scale mitigation measures than others. For instance, the Cascadia megaregion contains extensive areas of public lands. Thus, it lends itself to ambitious efforts to conserve and restore key ecosystems, especially forests. Other megaregions have more significant adaptation challenges, such as the hurricanes and sea level rise in the Gulf and East Coasts and wildfires in California (figure 7.2).

Climate change and inequality are inextricably connected. Although all megaregions have the most dramatic population and economic growth in the United States, not all expand equally, and megaregions contain disparities. These inequities will be exacerbated by climate change.

One of the key goals of the Green New Deal is to "create millions of good, high-wage jobs and ensure prosperity and economic security for all people of the United States" (*Recognizing the Duty* 2019, 5). In this regard, the proposition most echoes Franklin D. Roosevelt's New Deal. The resolution's authors envision that the transition away from fossil fuels and toward green, renewable energy will result in widespread job

FIGURE 7.2 Apple fire as seen from Route 243 in Southern California. *Source: istock.com/Rego Quintero.*

growth. Other climate mitigation and adaptation measures will also generate jobs. The New Deal's Tennessee Valley Authority had similar renewable energy and environmental management objectives. It and other New Deal programs lifted many from poverty and improved their lives. The Works Progress (later, Work Projects) Administration employed millions of people (mostly men) to construct public works and other projects. The Green New Deal seeks to similarly put a massive number of people to work, and this time with more gender and racial equity.

Currently, the U.S. economy is powered overwhelmingly by fossil fuels. Undoubtedly, the transition will require considerable innovation. Most of the great universities in the United States are in megaregions. The Ivy League is in the Northeast; the Big 10 is largely in the Great Lakes; and the Pacific 12 is mostly in California, Cascadia, and Arizona. Beyond these athletic conferences, which also support academic advancement, MIT, Johns Hopkins, the University of Chicago, Cal Tech, and all the top 10, even most of the top 20 and 30 academic universities in the United States, are in these same megaregions. Actually, most of the top 50 are in megaregions nationwide. Furthermore, these megaregion universities are also ranked among the best in the world. They have the capacity to continue to generate innovations in energy use and conservation, such as climate change mitigation and adaptation measures, and ways to create a more inclusive and fair society. President Biden has proposed increasing federal investments in research and development from $7 billion per year to

$300 billion over four years, with most of these funds focused on renewable energy research (*Economist* 2020).

As a result, megaregions have a strong leading-edge research advantage. Government research programs will play the leading role in promoting research into innovative technologies, and private venture capital will also play a significant role in commercializing these technologies. Most venture capital firms are in the Northern California and Northeast megaregions, which will help secure the pivotal position of these megaregions in transitioning the nation and the world to a postcarbon economy. Innovation is necessary to address climate change and to improve energy efficiency. Investments are needed into the "research and development of new clean and renewable energy technologies and industries" (*Recognizing the Duty* 2019, 12). Leading research universities and regional universities and community colleges can also respond to the Green New Deal's call for "providing resources, training, and high-quality education, including higher education, to all people of the United States" (11). This would help ensure that everyone is a full and equal partner in the benefits envisioned by the authors of the Green New Deal. Although social justice is unlikely to be resolved at the megaregion scale, best practices can be reinforced within and among megaregions.

As noted earlier in this chapter, transportation accounts for around 28 percent of U.S. greenhouse gas production. Buildings produce another 50 percent and account for nearly 50 percent of U.S. energy consumption (roughly 10 percent during construction and 40 percent in ongoing operations). As a result, the built environment presents the most significant opportunities for a greener future. As the sites of all the biggest cities on the planet, megaregions in the United States and internationally can lead the way. We need to address the fossil-fuel challenges in transportation and buildings. Reactions prompted by the Green New Deal to fossil fuels range from "abolish oil" (Martin 2020) to President Biden's advocacy for a softer transition from our current overreliance on petroleum-based fuels. In this case, the president and Green New Deal advocates have a similar position, because the resolution calls for a "fair and just transition" to renewable energy (*Recognizing the Duty* 2019, 5).

To achieve these ambitious goals, the built environment needs to be completely rethought, beginning with the design of ecosystem services. Instead of depleting them and passing along polluted air, water, and soils to future generations, we should consider how buildings and landscapes can incorporate and regenerate ecosystems services. For instance, we give little regard to urban wildlife habitat, despite the benefits it provides. Glass-clad skyscrapers kill thousands of birds annually. Beatley (2020, 5), in his thoughtful guide to creating bird-friendly cities, notes that birds "perform many important ecological functions, including pollination, seed dispersal, and

FIGURE 7.3 Depiction of a wildlife crossing to connect bifurcated landscapes. *Source: Jiaqi Suo/ Yaro-Steiner studio (Baum et al. 2019).*

nutrient cycling." For many people, birds were valuable companions during the pandemic. We enjoyed watching and listening to them. Similarly, roads result in the unnecessary loss of many animal lives in addition to human carnage. They should be redesigned to allow other species to move around as well, whether inside or outside city limits (figure 7.3).

Outside cities, climate reserves will both benefit other species and mitigate planetary warming by serving as carbon sinks. Megaregions provide the ideal scale for planning and locating these reserves. Since it was created by Congress in 1964, the Land and Water Conservation Fund has helped conserve thousands of acres of land across the United States. Under the 2020 Great American Outdoors Act, the Land and Water Conservation Fund received full and permanent funding for the first time since its establishment. This funding should be used and, if necessary, expanded to create climate reserves.

In 2020, the Landscape Architecture Foundation, the McHarg Center at Penn, the American Society of Landscape Architects, the Council of Educators in Landscape Architecture, and Columbia University Center for Resilient Cities and Landscapes organized the Green New Deal superstudio for studios from all built-environment design fields. Some 150 studios at 90 universities from 6 nations involving over 2,000 students and 150 faculty signed on for the superstudio between the fall 2020 and spring 2021 semesters (Green New Deal Superstudio 2021). The studios addressed both cities and countryside, taking on decarbonization as well as racial and economic justice. They built on the experience of the New Deal and precedents from design and planning history (figure 7.4).

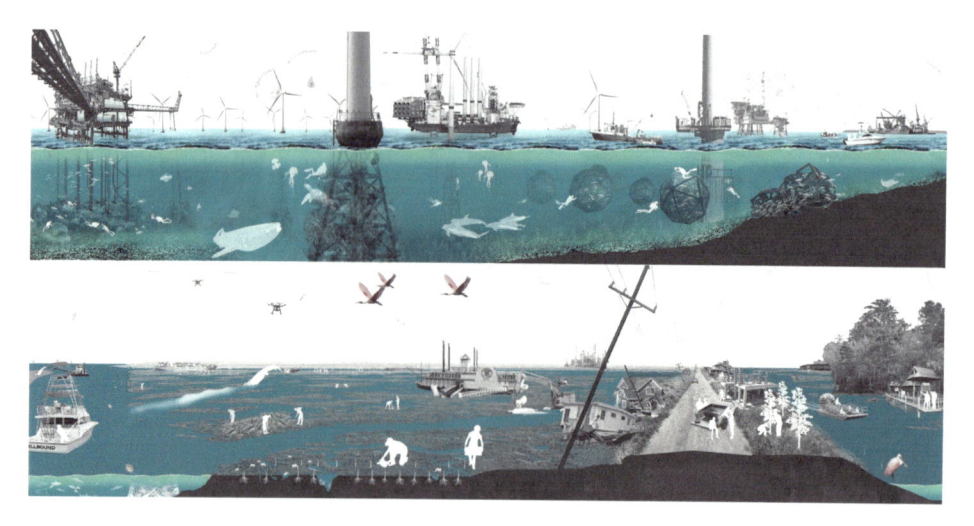

FIGURE 7.4 Student landscape design proposals to restore offshore and shoreline habitats of the Mississippi delta. *Source: Billy Fleming, University of Pennsylvania superstudio.*

The Northeast megaregion pioneered many historic innovations in urban design, such as the Fairmount Water Works in Philadelphia, the Emerald Necklace in Boston, and Central Park and the High Line in New York City. In the Piedmont Atlantic, the Atlanta BeltLine provides a good contemporary example. The Pacific Northwest and California pioneered several environmental planning innovations, including coastal zone management, environmental impact assessment, statewide planning, growth management, farmland protection, and the reduction of greenhouse gas emissions. In this context, the megaregions have fertile ground to advance green design and planning.

THE GREEN RECONSTRUCTION

National action such as that advocated by the Green New Deal is necessary to implement visions like those generated by the superstudio. This will involve climate reserves, climate change adaptations and mitigations, green infrastructure, efficient and clean energies, and ecosystem-services-generating settlement patterns.

In *Design with Nature Now* (Steiner et al. 2019), 25 real 21st-century projects from 21 nations illustrate how this can happen. The projects include large landscape protection, rising sea level response, freshwater protection, toxic land restoration, and urban growth management. Three examples of precedents for wider action are Room for the River in the Netherlands, Emscher Landscape Park in Germany, and the Yellowstone to Yukon Conservation Initiative in Canada and the United States.

Room for the River

The Randstad (ring or rim city) is the metropolitan conurbation of the four largest cities in the Netherlands: Rotterdam, Amsterdam, Utrecht, and The Hague. With 8.2 million people, the megalopolis is one of the largest in Europe, and it is one of the most densely populated places in the world. The cities are connected by a network of rail and highways. The area within the Randstad urban ring is dominated by farming, nature, and recreation. Known as the green heart, it is one of the most highly productive agricultural regions in the world. The Rhine River is the green heart's main artery. These metropolitan areas and the green heart, the entire population center of the Netherlands, sit behind a network of dikes and fortified levees.

The lowlands are famously below sea level, and the people have struggled with sea storms and river flooding for centuries. This struggle defines the Dutch culture and has led to a system for planning supported by science, engineering, and design. The modern Dutch national water management began after the colossal North Sea flood of January 1953. Dikes were breached in 89 places, resulting in over 1,800 deaths. The plan made in the wake of this tragedy promoted a massive nationwide project of engineering dams and dikes that took 25 years to realize.

The environmental movement of the 1970s and 1980s led to a new water management philosophy that promoted a balance of ecology and economy. This new perspective initiated the development of riverine habitats outside the dikes. After a period with relatively little flooding, in 1993 and 1995 the Rhine and other major rivers in the Netherlands experienced unprecedented flooding that caused widespread destruction and a massive evacuation of people and farm animals. In response, the Dutch government enacted a 2.3 billion-euro program for flood protection, especially as related to climate change (Steiner et al. 2019).

Room for the River is not a single project but an assembly of 34 projects along rivers throughout the Netherlands. Planned and built between 2007 and 2015, each project has two goals: flood abatement while safely increasing the carrying capacity of the major Dutch rivers and creating more attractive river landscapes (Steiner et al. 2019). The Dutch agency responsible, the Rijkswaterstaat, set out to achieve these goals by (1) improving dikes; (2) relocating dikes; (3) creating flood channels; (4) building water storage; (5) lowering groins; (6) returning reclaimed areas to the rivers; (7) restoring floodplains; (8) deepening riverbeds; and (9) removing obstacles. The 34 projects resulted in a major reconfiguration of the nation's hydrological systems and also more areas for recreation and wildlife.

Room for the River is an example of ongoing, national-level planning that transforms working landscapes and nature. Such planning is essential for the future of the Netherlands, especially vulnerable to climate change because of its low elevation. An interdisciplinary team from Wageningen University and Research has proposed a nature-based future for 2120 (Baptist et al. 2019). In addition to climate adaptation, the proposal addresses an energy transformation, the transition to more sustainable agriculture, biodiversity restoration, and urbanization. The basic idea is for nature to take the lead in future planning.

Rhine-Ruhr and IBA Emscher Landscape Park

The Emscher Landscape Park in the Ruhr region of Germany presents an outstanding case of devising green infrastructure as a spatial framework to help transform former mining and steel communities into a well-connected, vibrant city-region.

The Rhine-Ruhr is the largest urban agglomeration in Germany. Three rivers flow through the Ruhr region, the Ruhr to the south, the Lippe to the north, and the Emscher between; all feed into the Rhine River to the west. The riverbanks offer home to 53 towns and cities in a territory of approximately 1,715 square miles, and the rivers and their tributaries form natural boundaries between the communities. These communities first flourished in the late 19th century and again in the post–World War II period, owing to the Ruhr Valley's rich coal resources and high production of steel and iron. After the 1960s, however, the region's economy collapsed because of rapidly declining demand for coal and steel products. Half the region's mining workforce (nearly 500,000) lost jobs between 1957 and 1967, and a quarter of the steel workers were unemployed between 1977 and 1986. The Ruhr Valley had a troubled economy, contaminated land, polluted waterways, and a ravaged landscape.

In 1989, the state of North Rhine–Westphalia provided 5 billion deutsche marks to revitalize the Ruhr Valley. The revitalization plan centered on the Internationale Bauausstellung Emscher Park (International Architecture Exhibition Emscher Park; IBA Emscher Park), a model of experimental urbanism beginning in early 20th-century Germany and used five times in other German cities before 1989. Whereas previous IBAs focused largely on architectural improvements, IBA Emscher Park had a regional and ecological outlook. Economic impetus was the basis for ecological upgrading of a region framed by a system of river corridors. The system is formed from the main east–west corridor along the artery of the Emscher River and seven north–south corridors along other river tributaries and open spaces. To implement the spatial concept, the IBA Emscher Park plan had seven project objectives: reconstruction of the landscape; ecological restoration of the Emscher River system; development of Rhine–Herne Canal as an adventure space; promotion of industrial cultural heritage as a national treasure; provision for employment in the park; new forms of housing; and new options for social, cultural, and sports activities.

LEGEND

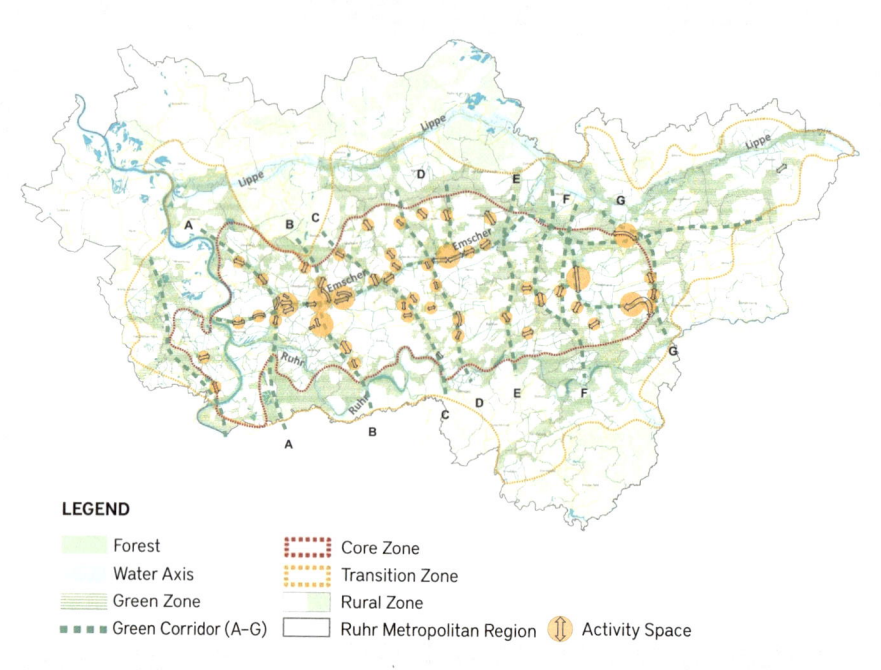

Forest	Core Zone	
Water Axis	Transition Zone	
Green Zone	Rural Zone	
Green Corridor (A–G)	Ruhr Metropolitan Region	Activity Space

Regional Open Space Concept for the Ruhr Metropolis.
Source: Regionalverband Ruhr/Ruhr Regional Association, Essen, Germany.

The activities of IBA Emscher Park lasted 10 years, between 1989 and 1999, with state-provided funding. Among the major infrastructure projects completed are six decentralized sewage treatment plants and about 200 miles of underground sewer lines. These and other ecological rebuilding efforts transformed Emscher River from the sewer tunnel for the Ruhr region into a system of greenways. The region's rivers and their tributaries no longer function as boundaries as they did in the past. Instead, they are shared amenities that bond the individual communities throughout the region. IBA Emscher Park selected about 100 collieries, blast furnaces, and industrial complexes and preserved them as symbols of the region's industrial culture. Many of the old factory spaces have been repurposed to attract artists and art education, in addition to visitors, to the area.

IBA Emscher Park as a regional greening initiative played a critical role in regenerating the Ruhr region. Today, the Ruhr region is home to 5.1 million people and 22 universities that specialize in green industries—for example, arts and design, R&D for bio- and nanotechnologies, new material science, and renewable energy. The region continues to perform as a pivotal node in the national and international transportation network. Duisburg, for instance, is the world's largest inland harbor. It is a key transshipment point for container-carrying ships on Europe's inland waterways and a rail terminus point connecting to China's Belt and Road project, the new Silk Road. In 2017, the Ruhr region received a new branding, *Stadt der Städte*, City of Cities, after public campaigns for reimaging the Ruhr Valley.

Yellowstone to Yukon

The Yellowstone to Yukon Conservation Initiative, established in 1997, is a long-range conservation plan to connect wildlife habitat across a vast megaregion of different land uses. Wildlife corridors for seasonal wildlife migrations open pathways that allow species to adapt to climate change over the long term (Steiner et al. 2019). The Y2Y corridor spans 2,000 miles and encompasses over 500,000 square miles. The initiative comprises over 200 organizations, First Nations, private landowners, and government entities, united to promote environmental science, maintain and restore degraded land within the corridor, and advise and address development that does not harm other species.

These projects offer hope that we can build a greener, more equitable, and healthier future. Another world is possible. Without leadership and decisive action, climate-related threats will only worsen. In one example, more people are moving to parts of the United States—especially in the California and Cascadia megaregions—that are the most susceptible to wildfire. As people are priced out of cities, they move to places likely to burn, thus increasing risks for everyone (Gopal and Buhayar 2019).

We describe next a megaregional approach, a Green Mega Deal, that can help identify the places most suited for settlement and then direct investment to those places while protecting forests and rangelands.

TOWARD A GREENPRINT FOR MEGAREGIONS

The great turning points in U.S. history—for example, 1776, 1861, and 1932—will come to include 2020 because the nation faced the worst global pandemic in a century, the deepest economic collapse since the Great Depression, and the Black Lives Matter demonstrations against racism in U.S. society—one of the largest and most sustained protest movements in the nation's history. At the same time, the United States and its megaregions faced other threats:

- Climate change and its related dangers of sea level rise, severe storms, heat waves, wildfires, drought, and intense rainfall events.
- Failing infrastructure after decades of disinvestment in highways, railroads, airports, flood control, electric power distribution, and water and sewer systems.
- A dysfunctional political system, with Congress and the White House gridlocked over even the most fundamental governmental responsibilities.
- Growing risks to global security and increasing great-power competition as the United States' position as the largest national economy in the world sharply declines after a century and a half.

Recognition grows that the United States must take bold action to address these troubles and to provide Americans with health, safety, security, and prosperity regardless of race, national origin, or geographic location. The nation's megaregions are home to four of five Americans and an even larger share of the national economy, thus reforms and investments to ensure the future success of the 13 U.S. megaregions will determine whether the United States can meet these challenges.

How can the nation and its megaregions get back on track? A new level of federal, state, and local leadership, establishment of new institutions, and reinvention of existing ones are required. Also, several trillion dollars in transportation and environmental infrastructure, broadband, alternative energy systems, and climate adaptation and mitigation measures are needed to transition over the next two or three decades to a low-carbon economy and then one that is carbon-free.

How can the nation institute these reforms and make these investments while recovering from the deepest recession in nearly a century? Not since Franklin D. Roosevelt's New Deal has there been a comparable effort by the federal government to tackle economic, social, and environmental challenges of this scale. The answer now as in 1932 is that it will be imperative to rebuild whole sectors of the U.S.

economic, transportation, energy, and water systems in each of the U.S. megaregions. A 2022 version of the New Deal must be created to deliver reforms and investments. Overcoming the deep political divisions in the nation's capital will require that an infrastructure and climate investment strategy be seen as benefiting all corners of the country. And given the central role the 13 U.S. megaregions play in the nation's economy, these policies and investments could and should be organized around the special needs of these places.

BUILDING ON THE GREEN NEW DEAL

In recent years, several public policy groups and elected officials have looked to FDR's New Deal as the precedent for steps needed today. In 2006, a Green New Deal, proposed by the Green New Deal Task Force of the Green Party, had the goal of decarbonizing the U.S. economy by 2030 through a carbon tax and other means. This ambitious proposal also had a broad range of initiatives that went beyond climate and greening measures to include a universal job guarantee and living minimum wage, a single-payer health insurance program, and free public college.

Senator Markey and Representative Ocasio-Cortez's 2019 nonbinding congressional resolution called for a national Green New Deal incorporating these and other progressive provisions, which invokes the memory of FDR's New Deal. There now appears to be broad public support for its climate initiatives. In a similar vein, Senate Democrats have also proposed a Better Deal, which calls for a $1 trillion investment in infrastructure, $15 national minimum wage, labor reforms, and other elements of a populist economic agenda.

Although President Biden has not endorsed the Green New Deal, he has proposed investing $2.3 trillion in climate, alternative energy, and infrastructure initiatives, such as a national high-speed rail network. However, until this book, a proposal such as this has not been discussed in the context of U.S. megaregions. Support grows for the most important infrastructure project needed for the long-term success of U.S. megaregions: high-performance intercity rail. High-performance rail could be incorporated in a 21st-century version of FDR's New Deal. When the New Deal was proposed by FDR in 1932, it was not a fully fleshed-out reform agenda but a series of initiatives that evolved over time. Some of the most progressive elements of the New Deal, such as Social Security and unemployment compensation, were not adopted until the third year of FDR's first administration, when there was greater public and political acceptance for these progressive measures.

Importantly, both the Green New Deal and the Better Deal proposals do not address the nation's economic geography and the new mobility and work patterns forming in the aftermath of the COVID-19 pandemic. In particular, they lack any reference to the needs of megaregions and the policies and investments needed to ensure that these places that are the drivers of the U.S. economy can take full advantage of the efficiencies and synergies inherent in megaregional economies and mobility systems. They also lack provisions to address the needs of communities and regions that have been left behind in the nation's prosperity over the last half century—and in particular, the needs of African American communities that have been discriminated against for generations.

For this reason, we propose a set of Green Mega Deal initiatives for the United States that would complement or overlay whichever version of the Green New Deal or Better Deal that is adopted by the Biden administration and Congress in 2021. We call it a Green Mega Deal to invoke FDR's New Deal while acknowledging the green commitment by young progressives. "Mega" refers to the scale of implementation, and that it is indeed a "big deal," or "BFD," the off-color term Joe Biden used to describe the passage of the Affordable Care Act (Stolberg and Pear 2010).

To succeed both politically and practically, a Green Mega Deal program should also strive for (1) economic recovery in short- and long-term employment; (2) reinvestment in infrastructure and communities; (3) social and racial equality; and (4) climate and alternative energy reforms at the national, megaregional, and metropolitan scales. These initiatives would be designed to achieve a broad leveling up of left-behind regions and communities in much the same way as the New Deal did. The Green Mega Deal should provide targeted strategies and investments needed to address the racial and economic equality goals of the Black Lives Matter movement. Like FDR's New Deal, the Green Mega Deal should be driven by the spirit of experimentation to determine which strategies and investments achieve the best results. Under this approach, programs and agencies that did not perform would be dropped and new initiatives would take their place.

The transformation of these systems and places will require bold investments in transportation and alternative energy infrastructure, urban housing and amenities, higher education, research, and other activities. Given the extraordinary cost of these investments, they must create multiple benefit streams—in common parlance, "two-fers," three-fers," and "four-or-more-fers"—that provide crosscutting economic, job creation, climate, energy, social and racial equality, and other benefits. These investments should also heed the pandemic's business and residential location and travel patterns and the opportunity the new patterns could provide to create more balanced and equitable markets for housing, labor, and transportation systems.

Finally, making these investments will require that the federal government take an activist role in financing and delivering these investments in partnership with state and local governments and in establishing new planning and special-purpose delivery institutions at the megaregional and metropolitan scales. Some of these institutions will need to span megaregions in whole or in part to deliver projects that benefit multiple states and regions. The entire effort should aim for breakthrough and innovative strategies that transform megaregions and the entire country. These could be comprehensive measures to control metropolitan congestion, address affordable housing and climate change, build high-performance intercity and regional rail networks, and rebuild the economies of left-behind cities and regions. These are outlined in greater detail later, and in chapter 8 we show how they can come together to transform one megaregion—the Northeast—for the better.

LEARNING FROM THE NEW DEAL

President Biden and several prominent members of Congress have invoked FDR's New Deal when considering the reforms needed today. But what are the most important lessons that the New Deal can offer to shape policy, investment, and institutional design decisions for similar initiatives in the 2020s?

To begin with, today's economic, social, and political crises rival those facing FDR as he assumed the presidency on March 4, 1932. The week before his inauguration, banks failed in dozens of states, adding to national despondency as the Great Depression deepened and unemployment exceeded a quarter of the workforce. In his inaugural address that day, he summed up what faced his new administration:

> Our greatest primary task is to put people to work. This is no unsolvable problem if we face it wisely and courageously. It can be accomplished in part by direct recruiting by the Government itself, treating the task as we would treat the emergency of war, but at the same time, through this employment, accomplishing greatly needed projects to stimulate and reorganize the use of our natural resources. (Roosevelt 1933)

As they contemplate adapting New Deal programs to our current circumstances, planners and politicians can learn important lessons from those programs (such as what to do and what not to do). These investments should be designed not only to stimulate jobs but also to help achieve a leveling up of the U.S. economy that will revitalize communities and regions that have been left behind amid prosperity elsewhere in the nation. Many rural states and regions would be among the prime beneficiaries of this initiative because they have missed out on the prosperity seen by coastal regions over the last three decades. These overlooked areas have also been among the places hardest hit by the dislocations associated with the COVID-19 pandemic.

FDR's New Deal created massive public works employment programs across the United States that helped pull the country out of the Great Depression. Even more important, these public works investments helped create the modern economic geography of the United States and transform its formerly underdeveloped regions into post–World War II economic powerhouses.

Alphabet Soup: WPA, PWA, CCC, and Others

The New Deal and its alphabet soup of agencies had a profound impact across the United States. Several million workers were given employment during the height of the Great Depression, and they left a legacy of public works that continues to benefit the whole country. Many of these initiatives were created by executive order of the president—a precedent for President Biden as he seeks to break political deadlocks with a divided Congress.

One of the largest New Deal public employment programs was the Works Progress Administration (WPA), which built 40,000 new and 85,000 improved buildings, including 5,900 new schools; 9,300 new auditoriums, gyms, and recreational buildings; 1,000 new libraries; 7,000 new dormitories; and 900 new armories (Federal Works Administration 1946, 5). Another New Deal public works agency, the Public Works Administration (PWA), contracted projects through private construction companies and had an equally large impact. Between 1933 and the beginning of World War II, FDR's New Deal put hundreds of thousands of Americans to work rebuilding every aspect of the nation's infrastructure. Projects ranged from sidewalks, parks, and schools to airports, bridges, roads, and waterways. In effect, these projects enabled much of the defense buildup that made America the "Arsenal of Democracy" during the war and the postwar boom that followed.

Collectively, these projects were transformational for whole cities and regions, particularly where there was leadership from visionary federal, state, and local officials. The New Deal's Rural Electrification Administration, for example, built electric power networks across the rural United States and established electric power cooperatives that continue to deliver power to 12 percent of U.S. households.

Central Texas illustrates the revolutionary transformation made by New Deal investments. In this formerly isolated, rural area surrounding Austin and San Antonio, the New Deal's Rural Electrification Administration brought low-cost electricity to isolated Texas Hill Country farms and villages that had been without (Caro 1982). Dams provided potable water supplies, irrigation for agriculture, flood prevention, and hydropower, and created major recreational resources at Lake Lyndon B. Johnson (named for the area's young congressman), Lake Travis, and elsewhere. Schools, sidewalks, parks, and playgrounds provided needed public facilities. Public universities received new dormitories, classrooms, and libraries, as did the University of Texas at Austin, which also gained its iconic Tower, or Main Building. All-weather highways connected isolated towns with nearby cities, and farm-to-market highways carried farmers' crops to urban customers. In part because of these investments, Austin today is one of the United States' most successful tech centers.

In the largest U.S. urban region, New York City and its metropolitan area, an even greater transformation was realized by New Deal infrastructure investments under the direction of the master builder Robert Moses (Caro 1974). The Triborough and Whitestone Bridges; the Midtown and Lincoln Tunnels; the Grand Central, Northern State, Southern State, and Taconic State Parkways; Jones Beach and dozens of other state parks; several hundred city parks and playgrounds; tens of thousands of units of public housing; and the Central Park Zoo were built. New York City mayor Fiorello LaGuardia also used WPA funds and workers to build the Independent Subway System and LaGuardia Airport.

Another New Deal agency with profound and lasting impacts on the U.S. landscape was the Civilian Conservation Corps. The CCC built or restored facilities in thousands of national, state, and municipal forests and parks, including roads, bridges, campgrounds, and beaches, employing over 3 million people in these efforts over several years.

The New Deal's Resettlement Administration built dozens of model rural communities and three model greenbelt suburban towns in Maryland, Ohio, and Wisconsin for farming families displaced by the Dust Bowl. It also employed tens of thousands of displaced farmers to create firebreaks and do other conservation work. The New Deal's Public Housing Administration and Federal Housing Administration built hundreds of thousands of public housing units and created low-interest, long-term mortgage programs benefiting millions of middle-class homeowners. The FHA continues to provide federally insured mortgages to homeowners across the United States.

The New Deal was not focused just on buildings and physical infrastructure. It also put thousands of unemployed writers, playwrights, actors, and artists to work producing public art and theater, documenting historic resources, and writing local and state guides. Altogether, they were responsible for creating 200,000 murals, sculptures, and other works of art for public buildings, schools, and outdoor spaces across the country.

The planning arm of the New Deal, the National Resources Planning Board, chaired by Frederic Delano (FDR's uncle and one of the founders of New York's RPA), also set forth plans for major infrastructure and public employment activities, such as a network of national toll roads and free roads, which provided the template for the postwar Interstate Highway System (discussed later). The board also promoted the creation of state and regional planning agencies to develop priorities for infrastructure and economic development at each level. In one of its final acts in 1943, the National Resources Planning Board outlined postwar education and housing benefits to demobilized service members that became the GI Bill of Rights. The GI Bill provided free higher education and low-interest mortgages to millions of veterans, which underpinned a generation of postwar prosperity for the United States. Throughout the New Deal, these activities were driven by FDR's insistence on continual innovation and experimentation—he wanted to try every kind of investment and employment program to see which created the greatest number of jobs and the most lasting value. If a project did not succeed within a few years, it was dropped and replaced by other innovative projects.

Unexpected Benefits of New Deal Infrastructure Mega Projects

The New Deal, while making vast investments across the United States, gave special attention to regional infrastructure and economic development projects in several underdeveloped areas of the country, including the Southeast, Southwest, and Pacific Northwest. These projects produced almost unlimited supplies of inexpensive hydropower and potable and irrigation water in formerly isolated and arid regions. New Deal construction of roads, airports, electric power distribution, and other infrastructure in these regions enabled the emergence of the Sunbelt and the cities of Atlanta, Knoxville, Las Vegas, Los Angeles, San Diego, and others. Similar New Deal infrastructure, energy, and water projects made possible the development of Seattle, Portland, and other cities in the Pacific Northwest.

These infrastructure projects were behind the rapid defense buildup in the late 1930s and 1940s that helped make the United States the Arsenal of Democracy, in FDR's slogan, during World War II. The New Deal's Tennessee Valley Authority, for example, built hydropower, irrigation, navigation, and flood control systems, as well as roads and bridges. It even built new communities and oversaw related economic development activities across an underdeveloped seven-state region. Much of this area had never recovered from the devastation of the Civil War, more than six decades earlier.

Then, as World War II approached, this region, with its Tennessee Valley Authority–enabled low-cost hydropower and extensive public water supplies, became one of the world's largest centers for aluminum and aircraft manufacturing. The Tennessee Valley Authority also became a focal point for the Manhattan Project, with the Clinch River reactor and newly built city of Oak Ridge at the center of atomic research and uranium refinement. Two atom bombs that Oak Ridge produced were dropped on Japan in 1945, which surrendered a few days later. The United States became a world leader in nuclear power, nuclear physics, technology, and science.

In the Southwest, several large Colorado River hydropower and water supply projects, including the Hoover, Parker, and Imperial Dams and the All-American Canal, fed the growth of this arid region as well as Los Angeles, San Diego, Las Vegas, and Arizona's desert cities. These projects also made the Imperial Valley one of the most productive all-season agricultural districts in the United States. Once again, low-cost electricity made this area a focal point to produce aircraft, ships, and other components of the wartime Arsenal of Democracy.

In the Pacific Northwest, the New Deal's Bonneville Power Administration built dam, irrigation, and navigation projects for yet another formerly isolated, mostly rural area, turning it into one of the most prosperous U.S. regions. Boeing's wartime production of B-17s and B-29s benefited from low-cost aluminum and water produced by the region's hydropower projects.

Lessons for Today's Planners from FDR's New Deal

A similar approach to innovation and experimentation makes sense for today as the Biden administration undertakes a 21st-century version of New Deal public employment, infrastructure development, and leveling up of the nation's left-behind cities and regions. The lessons are wide ranging.

Local Leadership and Special-Purpose Delivery Agencies

New Deal regional development programs were proposed by local officials and business and civic leaders, then financed and built by the federal government. In most cases, special-purpose delivery agencies were established to plan and deliver these complex, multibillion-dollar, and multiyear projects, and in the case of regional development agencies, these were intended to be rooted in the places they were designed to serve. This is like the U.K. government's new agency, Transport for the North, which delivers Northern Powerhouse Rail and other important infrastructure investments in the north of England.

Many of the New Deal's most effective programs involved partnerships with local governments, in New York and other places, through locally controlled public authorities with their own municipal and revenue bonding powers. This enabled limited federal investments to be multiplied through capture of tolls, user fees, and other revenues.

California recently adopted legislation authorizing municipalities and counties to finance projects through Enhanced Infrastructure Financing Districts, which can sell revenue bonds to capture the value created by public infrastructure investments. This concept could also be adapted to the rest of the United States. Investments in building and safeguarding infrastructure, energy, and natural resources can transform the economy of left-behind regions and communities.

Promoting a Culture of Innovation in Government

Another feature of FDR's leadership, in both the New Deal and later in planning for wartime defense production, was to establish new agencies to carry out these missions. The best and brightest from industry and academia were recruited to run the agencies, bringing much-needed innovation to them. In many cases, multiple agencies were established to carry out similar programs, but only those that succeeded were kept and the others were terminated.

Many of today's federal and state agencies have been hollowed out by decades of budget cuts and multiple layers of red tape. Attracting talented people to public service can reinvent these bureaucracies around the Green Mega Deal initiatives outlined here. An approach similar to the New Deal's radical experimentation in delivering public services will be essential today if any of the initiatives outlined in this chapter are to be successfully implemented. Creative reforms of permitting, procurement, project delivery, and labor practices will be needed to ensure that projects are delivered on time and on budget.

Energy Production and Distribution

The New Deal's regional development projects involved low-cost hydropower, or in the case of the Tennessee Valley Authority, a mix of hydro- and fossil-fuel-generated power production. In each case, the power produced by dams and power plants was distributed by electric cooperatives or government-subsidized distribution systems, such as the Rural Electrification Administration (Malone 2008). A similar process could subsidize universal broadband networks in rural and urban communities. The 21st-century version of these programs will be based on carbon-free, alternative energy production—from wind, solar, geothermal, tidal, wave, or other sources—and distributed systems for power generation and storage, all part of a broader strategy to decarbonize the U.S. energy supply and economy.

Water Management

All the New Deal regional development projects included flood control, irrigation, and public water supply initiatives. The 21st-century version of the New Deal could target regional development projects on climate-related flood control measures to address coastal, riverine, and urban flooding. Regional development projects could conserve water resources as droughts become more frequent and rainfall patterns more widely variable. Urban waterways and natural areas could be restored and made available for flood prevention, recreation, and wildlife habitat.

Further, many urban water supply and waste management systems in U.S. megaregions and beyond are at the end of their useful lives and now pose significant hazards to public health and natural resources. Hundreds of thousands could be put to work rebuilding and modernizing these systems. Many older cities in the Northeast and Great Lakes megaregions and elsewhere have out-of-date combined storm and sanitary sewers that overflow even in minor rainfall. These systems should be replaced with separated storm and sanitary sewers. Also, current stormwater management systems should be replaced by updated green infrastructure systems that retain stormwater to recharge groundwater, rather than directing it into nearby waterways.

Cities in U.S. coastal megaregions must adapt to climate change. Layered defense systems consisting of, where appropriate, offshore movable sea gates to protect against storm surges and onshore dikes or berms to deal with sea level rise would provide protection. In addition, wetlands, oyster beds, dunes, and other systems can be restored or constructed to address wave action and improve water quality and ecological health.

Environmental Conservation

The New Deal's CCC made large- and small-scale improvements in municipal, state, and national parks and forests. In addition, the U.S. Department of Agriculture invested billions in soil conservation and improved agricultural practices. FDR also added more than 100 new units to the national park system and a network of monuments, battlegrounds, historic sites, and the Washington, DC, park system (NPS 2020). A 21st-century Green Mega Deal initiative could create a network of national climate reserves made of forests, grasslands, wetlands, and other natural areas that would capture carbon, enable species to migrate as climate change unfolds, and put tens of thousands of young people to work to create and manage these resources.

Skills Training, Education, and Culture

New Deal projects constructed or renovated thousands of schools across the country. New Deal workers received skills training that they could use long after they had left these public construction projects. And the GI Bill, mentioned earlier, provided millions of World War II veterans with higher education and trade skills. A 21st-century Green Mega Deal could give workers immediate jobs in public works, environmental restoration, housing, and other activities and also skills for longer-term employment in growth industries. Apprenticeship programs and targeted skills training in community colleges could collaborate with companies that are reshoring, or returning to the United States, their manufacturing.

Mobility Systems

The New Deal built or improved thousands of miles of roads across the United States. New Deal planners also proposed a national limited-access system that became the postwar Interstate Highway System (described later). A Green Mega Deal program could reconstruct segments of the interstate system and other roads that have exceeded their use-by dates. The rebuilding can create urban-friendly highways by eliminating bottlenecks and reducing safety hazards. These roads could also be rerouted to urban communities' advantage by undergrounding, relocating, or in some cases, replacing them with surface boulevards or arterial roads.

Housing and New Communities

The New Deal built hundreds of thousands of public housing units across the United States and pioneered in creating greenbelt towns that became templates for postwar suburban development. These projects put large numbers of the unemployed to work but also produced much-needed low-cost housing. The New Deal's Federal Housing Administration and the Veterans Administration housing programs provided low-cost, long-term, government-insured mortgages for tens of millions of Americans. Later, broader federally insured mortgage programs further expanded homeownership in the late 20th century.

This assistance was not distributed evenly, however. Most New Deal housing programs used redlining and other measures to reinforce patterns of racial segregation and discriminate against African Americans. The effects of these and related urban renewal and highway programs continue to be felt today in the social and economic isolation of Blacks and other racial minorities in U.S. cities. Federal housing programs have further failed to meet the needs of millions of low- and moderate-income households after federal support for public housing was replaced with inadequate rental assistance programs by the Ronald Reagan administration. Over succeeding decades, these assistance programs have shrunk, leaving millions poorly housed or unhoused.

A Green Mega Deal housing initiative could preserve large quantities of rental housing where foreclosures occur and restore these units as permanently protected affordable housing under the control of nonprofit housing sponsors. Additional affordable units could be made available by converting underused hotels into supportive housing for homeless people. Existing public housing projects—many of them dating back to the New Deal and the early post–World War II era and now in desperate need of renovation—could be restored and converted into mixed-income developments, again putting hundreds of thousands to work building these projects.

INSTITUTIONAL AND FINANCIAL ISSUES

Most New Deal spending was financed through U.S. Treasury debt, and the national debt increased by 50 percent between 1933 and 1936, despite federal public works spending being supplemented by municipal and revenue bonds secured by tolls and user fees. It seems very unlikely that investment on the scale needed for a 21st-century version of the New Deal could be achieved solely through current institutional arrangements, existing federal departments, and local authorities. The New Deal was not just about spending public money but about creating government institutions to lead change energetically with a can-do attitude.

Federal transportation investments in the United States have declined since the 1990s because Congress cannot find agreement on increases to national gasoline taxes. The shortfall has been partly replaced by increases in state gas taxes and municipal bond and revenue bond financing. In most cases, these commitments have been authorized by voters at the local or state level, but they are not enough.

Today's historically low interest rates and readily available capital make it possible to finance a 21st-century version of the New Deal through the sale of U.S. Treasury debt, the vast majority of which would be purchased by international investors and sovereign wealth funds. In effect, the rest of the world would be investing in rebuilding U.S. infrastructure for a more productive worldwide economy. If projects are carefully selected and designed to unlock the economic potential of U.S. megaregions, debt service would be more than covered by future increases in employment, household and business income, and the federal tax revenues the income would generate.

Because the entire program of borrowing would create economically valuable national assets, not fund consumption or social welfare, future income streams from those assets—such as high-speed railways—could be sold or leased to international wealth and pension funds, thus reclaiming all the debts. Robert Moses used these techniques to build his enormous New Deal–era bridge, tunnel, and park projects in New York.

A project on the scale of FDR's New Deal and wartime innovations will require a step change in institutional arrangements, capabilities, and funding and a reversal of many of the attitudes, ideologies, and assumptions that have prevailed in the last decades. FDR's election and his program were driven by near economic collapse and the loss of middle-class wealth in the Great Crash and ensuing Great Depression, just as President Theodore Roosevelt's earlier Progressive program and his Square Deal reforms had been driven by hugely widening inequalities. In both times, voters had an incentive to look for radical change. Perhaps the changes caused by the COVID-19 pandemic will allow another time of reform.

The scope for an economic stimulus to consumption and asset prices, through tax cuts, further central bank purchases of government bonds (quantitative easing), and interest rate cuts, seems at best limited. But it is investment that is needed, not consumption: investment in resilient health systems, decarbonization, sustainable and secure energy supply, food security, climate change resilience and adaptation, and perhaps most of all, infrastructure.

The central focus must remain on the needs of those hurt the most by the pandemic's economic disruption. Reform, FDR argued, "must build from the bottom up and not the top down . . . [and] puts faith in the forgotten man at the bottom of the economic pyramid" (Roosevelt 1932, 625).

A GREEN MEGA DEAL PROGRAM

Instead of just patching up the existing failing, 100-year-old infrastructure, energy, and environmental systems that most regions depend on, we need to invest in new low-carbon and carbon-free mobility and environmental infrastructure networks for the next century of success and prosperity. This will not be easy—we have heard for decades, from a national government unwilling to provide necessary leadership or financing, that investing in these systems is futile.

The last time the United States built a transformational infrastructure system—the Interstate Highway System—there was similar public and political resistance to the tax increases needed to pay for it. To build public support, in 1954, President Dwight Eisenhower appointed a blue-ribbon panel chaired by the retired war hero General Lucius Clay and consisting of a group of eminent business and labor leaders. The Clay Committee dusted off the national limited-access highway plan first proposed by the National Resources Planning Board in 1938, but this time they presented the argument that interstate highways were needed for national defense, highway safety, and economic growth. This won support from business, civic, and labor leaders and powerful industries that stood to gain from the investment, such as petroleum, automobile, rubber, and construction. Congress passed the National Interstate and Defense Highways Act of 1956 and its authorization of federal gas tax increases needed to build the system.

The interstate highways made possible the automobile-oriented U.S. metropolitan regions and a fivefold increase in U.S. GDP over the half century following completion of the interstate in 1970. This highway system did more to shape the post–World War II economy and metropolitan landscape than anything else. The 1956 National Interstate and Defense Highways Act

> was to do more to shape the lives of the American people than any other law passed since 1945. It reinforced the ascendancy of the private car over all other forms of passenger transport; it made continental bus services fully competitive with the already declining railroads; it boosted freight carrying by truck; it gave great impetus to black emigration from the South, and a huge boost to the automobile, engineering and building industries, thus helping to stimulate the prosperity of the sixties; by encouraging car-ownership it encouraged car utilization, thus stimulating the spread of the population into vast sprawling suburbs, where only the car could get you to work, to the shops, to schools, entertainments and voting-booths. (Brogan 2001, 611)

Unfortunately, the Clay Committee, the Eisenhower administration, and Congress did not extend their thinking to consider a balanced, multimodal national transportation system of roads, rail, aviation, and other modes. And they paid no attention to the kind of settlement pattern that would be produced by the interstates. In the absence of effective urban and regional planning, these highways produced three generations of mindless suburban sprawl instead of coherent, inclusive patterns of development.

Urban segments of the interstate system also destroyed or damaged hundreds of low-income and minority urban communities. Bob Yaro's father, for example, grew up in the 1920s in a poor community on Home Avenue, in the central Bronx. Bob was always puzzled that he could never find this street on a modern map of the Bronx. Then, one day, he came across a 1920s map of the borough and discovered that Home Avenue was in the future right-of-way of Robert Moses's Cross Bronx Expressway. It became one of hundreds of similar low-income communities obliterated by urban interstate highways.

The redlining provisions of Federal Housing Administration lending policies combined with exclusionary local zoning provisions to discriminate against low-income, working-class, and minority households. These provisions produced the highly segregated patterns of metropolitan development that are part of today's Black Lives Matter protests.

Although critics at the time, such as Lewis Mumford, predicted many of these outcomes, their warnings went unheeded. Alex Marshall revisits a Mumford essay:

> [Mumford] starts his essay with these lines: "When the American people, through their Congress, voted a little while ago for a $26 billion highway program, the most charitable thing to assume about this action is that they hadn't the faintest notion of what they were doing." [Mumford] was concerned that soon it would be "too late to correct the damage to our cities and our countryside, not least to the efficient organization of industry and transportation, that this ill-conceived and preposterously unbalanced program will have wrought." (Marshall 2010)

Upon entering office in January 2021, one of President Biden's first actions was to propose the $2.2 trillion American Jobs Plan, the most ambitious infrastructure program in decades. It included a major commitment to intercity passenger rail but only limited funding for high-speed rail. This was despite Biden's campaign commitments to building the world's best high-speed rail system.

The White House and a group of moderate Republicans and Democrats worked to create bipartisan support for this investment program. In 2021, the Senate and House adopted the Infrastructure Investment and Jobs Act, which provided for only $550 billion in new funding—in effect deleting three-quarters of Biden's original program. Most of the $66 billion earmarked for passenger rail was directed to repair the Northeast Corridor, and $12 billion of it was directed to conventional intercity rail projects in other areas of the country (White House 2021). President Biden signed the bill into law in November 2021. Democrats are expected to enact a

$1.8 trillion human infrastructure program that could include a limited amount of funds for high-speed rail.

Both the Infrastructure Investment and Jobs Act and a related reconciliation package will fall far short of Biden's original commitment to high-speed rail, disillusioning progressive groups and climate, infrastructure, and Green New Deal advocates about the scope of this infrastructure investment program. This could create the opportunity for a second and more ambitious commitment to these needs in the future—the Green Mega Deal. Further, the White House and Congress have chosen to work through existing agencies and institutions, many of which lack the capacity for innovation and expedited delivery of major projects. This is a radical departure from FDR's demand that New Deal programs be designed to achieve "bold, persistent experimentation" during the New Deal (Roosevelt 1932, 646).

To build public and political support for the Green Mega Deal, the Biden administration should consider creating a 21st-century version of the Clay Committee. Its rationale for these investments and reforms, like the Clay Committee, should feature national defense, public health and safety, and economic growth. Whereas the 1950s national defense concerns centered on Cold War competition with the former Soviet Union, the top foreign policy concern in the 2020s and beyond will be investing in national defense to compete with China. A robust national economy will be needed to finance future defense expenditures.

Today's public safety and public health concern is the immense toll that automobiles take on passengers and pedestrians. Automobiles kill around 90,000 Americans every year—about 40,000 deaths in car accidents and an estimated 50,000 more from long-term exposure to air pollution emitted by cars (Manjoo 2020). Two million additional Americans are hospitalized every year because of car crashes.

Investments in rail, air, and auto and truck transportation and other infrastructure will lay the foundation for economic growth in the 2020s and beyond and be the key to increasing Americans' household incomes and standard of living for decades to come, in much the same way the interstate highways did in the late 20th and early 21st centuries. These investments have further potential benefits: creating short- and long-term jobs, addressing climate change, improving social and racial equality, reducing congestion, making housing more affordable, and leveling up left-behind communities and regions.

Instead of a single, blue-ribbon panel, at least three panels will be needed for (1) transportation; (2) environment, climate, and energy; and (3) urban and regional development. It will also be essential to consider the kinds of land use, housing, and other outcomes we wish to create with the Green Mega Deal's proposed infrastructure systems. For example, do proposed intercity, regional rail and rapid transit networks promote relatively compact settlements linked by these rail networks? What housing and land use policies will ensure that these places provide a range of housing types and prices, making them accessible to all incomes and demographics?

To succeed politically and economically, Green Mega Deal plans and investment proposals must begin creating millions of jobs to build these projects. Long-term employment and economic growth must follow that addresses the nation's spatial, economic, and social inequities; climate change (both adaptation and mitigation); rapidly escalating metropolitan housing prices, displacement, and homelessness; and crushing congestion.

As the Clay Committee did in the 1950s, it will be necessary to produce a compelling national map to demonstrate that the entire country will benefit from these investments:

- High-speed rail and high-performance intercity rail routes in most, and perhaps all 13, megaregions.
- Regional rail networks in the 10 (or even 20) largest metros, similar to the RPA's T-REX (Trans-Regional Express; Barone et al. 2018) proposal for metro New York and TransitMatters' (2018) regional rail proposal for metro Boston, and modernized rapid transit and light-rail transit networks in the nation's 50 largest metropolitan areas.
- Renovation, replacement, or undergrounding of substandard and unsafe urban components of the Interstate Highway System and, in some cases, replacement of these roads with at-grade urban boulevards.
- Airport upgrades and enhanced connections with rail.
- Metropolitan water management that, for example, modernizes potable water, wastewater, and stormwater management systems.
- Metropolitan climate adaptation and mitigation, including reducing the impacts of storm surges and sea level rise on urban centers and retreating from flood-prone, low-density areas.
- Modernized inland navigation systems across the center of the country for the Ohio, Tennessee, Missouri, Mississippi, and other major river systems.
- Expanded and modernized systems of global gateways, such as the airports, seaports, and international border crossings on the Mexican and Canadian borders.
- New or expanded land grant university and federal agency campuses in designated growth centers in left-behind regions.
- New technology hubs in each megaregion.

MAKING IT HAPPEN

The process has three steps. The first is leadership. The Biden administration could invoke FDR's legacy to call for a broad national rebuilding and job creation initiative to pull the nation out of the current economic crisis, which would also help left-behind cities and regions, further climate strategies and social and racial equality, build affordable housing, and reduce congestion. This could be presented by the White House as the "moral equivalent of war," requiring a wartime-type mobilization of resources to combat this economic challenge. The White House might also call for a second "American Century" to sustain the nation's place as the world's largest economy and create opportunities for coming generations of Americans (Luce 1941). At its core, this program would address climate change, with both mitigation and adaptation measures, to make the United States a global leader in climate advocacy.

Megaregions will be at the forefront of this initiative, given their predominant role in U.S. economic, innovation, and mobility systems. They are also home to the majority of the nation's minorities and immigrants and where they can become fully integrated into the nation's economy and society. Megaregion-scale high-speed and high-performance rail networks, alternative energy, and landscape preservation systems would be at the heart of national infrastructure, energy, and climate initiatives.

The second is an assessment of national infrastructure investment needs organized by sector, mode, and geography. This could be completed by metropolitan planning organizations and collaborative groups at the megaregional scale, perhaps in partnership with national business, civic, and other groups, such as the American Association of State Highway and Transportation Officials, the American Public Transit Association, the American Planning Association, the American Society of Civil Engineers, the American Society of Landscape Architects, the American Institute of Architects, and the U.S. Chamber of Commerce.

The third is financing. Much of this program could be financed through the sale of U.S. Treasury bonds on international markets, primarily to sovereign wealth funds and international investors. With today's interest rates at all-time lows, investors will be rebuilding the capacity of the U.S. economy and infrastructure system at the lowest possible cost. The debt service on these bonds could be financed through the additional federal tax revenues generated by employment and income growth resulting from these investments.

A portion of the capital cost and operating expenses associated with these investments could be financed through user fees—tolls, fares, water and sewer fees, and other charges to the people benefiting most from these investments. State matching contributions could also be financed through user fees, with the federal contribution representing the bulk of required capital costs. Finally, value creation and capture systems, like California's Enhanced Infrastructure Financing Districts, could cover state and local financing costs for key infrastructure investments. These investments could also be financed through a modest carbon tax that would have the additional advantage of incentivizing transition from carbon-based fuels to renewables.

Early action or demonstration projects should be identified and carried out as soon as possible to illustrate the efficacy and value of these investments. Locally initiated projects can demonstrate the projects' transformational potential. Several U.S. megaregions, for example, have initiated or proposed high-speed rail projects, which were previously stymied or scaled back by the absence of federal support. These projects could be completed on an expedited basis to demonstrate the value of similar projects in other megaregions.

NATIONAL, METROPOLITAN, AND MEGAREGION: PLANNING AND INSTITUTION BUILDING
National Planning and Policy Guidance

As FDR's administration did with the New Deal, the federal government, states, metropolitan areas, and megaregions should create institutions to shape investment, economic development, climate, and social equity strategies. A planning agency will be necessary to oversee this whole process. Remarkably, not since 1943, when the National Resources Planning Board was abolished, has the United States had a national long-range planning and policy coordinating group.

The absence of a U.S. planning group can be embarrassing. Several years ago, Yaro led a World Bank–sponsored metropolitan planning initiative for the Colombian government. The Yaro team's final presentation was held in the 21st-floor conference room of the national planning agency's new high-rise headquarters overlooking downtown Bogotá. Following Yaro's presentation, the head of the national planning department—a cabinet-level minister—asked him where the headquarters for the U.S. national planning department was in Washington. The answer, of course, is that there is no such agency and has not been one for more than three-quarters of a century. The United States is virtually alone among developed countries in not having a national policy and planning body. So much for U.S. exceptionalism!

A Green Mega Deal planning agency could be established by statute or by executive order of the president, as FDR's National Resources Planning Board was in 1933. This agency would oversee national infrastructure and climate and related policies and investments, but it would leave broad discretion and initiative to metropolitan and megaregion-scale agencies to administer their own activities. An agency to administer trillions of dollars of infrastructure, climate, energy, and related investments is essential.

Megaregional Plans

Each megaregion should have plans for addressing its major systems—principally intercity and regional rail, climate and energy policies and infrastructure, and large landscape and water management systems. Megaregion-scale planning functions could be carried out through collaboration among metropolitan planning organizations or new public and nonprofit organizations operating at this scale. The Northern Powerhouse Partnership—a nongovernmental organization for planning regeneration of the North of England—could be a precedent for some U.S. megaregions. These agencies will need an official role in the planning process and teeth to carry out plans. Plans could also be developed and administered by special-purpose delivery agencies, like the United Kingdom's Transport for the North. This agency develops and carries out plans for major transportation investment in the north of England, in collaboration with the Northern Powerhouse Partnership.

Megaregional plans should cover the following:

- Comprehensive climate adaptation, such as green solutions to stormwater management, innovative wastewater treatment, and flood prevention and mitigation, but that also includes the creation of national and megaregional carbon reserves in large protected forest, grassland, wetland, and other landscapes.
- Reinvigoration and remagnetization small and midsize cities and left-behind communities and regions in megaregions across the country.
- Carbon-free, alternative energy production and distributed power generation and storage systems.
- High-performance intercity and regional rail networks.
- Rebuilding or relocation of interstate highway links that cause the most damage to urban communities in terms of public health and economic dislocation.
- Investments in roads, rail, airports, public universities, federal employment centers, and other activities to revitalize left-behind cities and regions across the country.

Megaregional plans should explore technology hub locations in each megaregion. In the United Kingdom, the Northern Powerhouse Partnership and its cabinet-level minister have proposed that an "MIT of the North" be established to create a new tech hub in the north of England to compete with the current Oxford-Cambridge-London tech axis in southern England (Evans 2020).

Similar initiatives have been proposed for the United States, where the nation's innovation technology sector is concentrated in only a handful of places, and this overconcentration is accelerating. Four megaregions—Cascadia, Northern California,

Texas Triangle, and Northeast—already have major innovation sector tech hubs in such places as Seattle, Silicon Valley, Austin, and Boston. The Brookings Institution and the Information Technology and Innovation Foundation have proposed that 8–10 technology hubs be created in other areas of the country (Atkinson, Muro, and Whiton 2019). The goal should be to have at least one such hub in each megaregion, probably connected to an existing research university.

Metropolitan Strategic Plans

At the metropolitan level, strengthened and reconstituted metropolitan planning organizations or new nongovernmental planning groups would be responsible for creating plans similar to the Fourth Regional Plan by the RPA (2019) for metropolitan New York and California's Blueprint strategic plans for Los Angeles, the Bay Area, and other major urban regions (Caltrans 2015).

These plans would need to address a broad range of policy and investment concerns and not just transportation issues, as most metropolitan planning organizations do today. Metropolitan plans should promote affordable housing across metropolitan regions and eliminate the overconcentration of jobs and population that have caused the rapid run-up in housing prices in recent decades and that have promoted gentrification and homelessness in minority communities. Other components should be the following:

- Regional rail, urban transit, and congestion management.
- Climate, carbon reduction, and alternative energy strategies.
- Regional parks and regreening and brownfield reclamation.
- Social, economic, and environmental justice investment.
- Reinvigoration of left-behind communities.
- Provision of universal broadband.
- Infrastructure investment needs and their financing.
- Governance and institutional reform.

State Plans

Whether states would need to adopt their own plans is unknown because most of the action would be occurring at the regional and megaregional levels. States and their governors will want a role in coordinating metropolitan plans. In particular, it may be necessary to identify legislative priorities that can be met only at the state level. In dozens of places across the country, however, metropolitan regions encompass portions of two, three, or more states. Several megaregions enfold portions of two or more states.

Promoting Collaboration Between Levels

The basic principle that should guide this planning process is subsidiarity: plans should be developed and implemented at the lowest level commensurate with the issue being addressed. For example, intercity rail networks should be planned at the megaregional scale and involve metropolitan regions because these systems serve both. Metropolitan water systems and climate strategies should be managed at the metropolitan level. And decisions about where to place stop signs on city streets or site playgrounds should remain the responsibility of local governments.

In keeping with the federal system, this entire process should be managed on an incentive basis, in which federal funds would be provided to state, metropolitan, and megaregion-level agencies when they complete plans that are consistent with federal goals. States, regions, and megaregions could opt out of the system but would forgo significant amounts of federal support.

To deliver projects on time and at a reasonable cost, agencies responsible for implementing major investments may need to reform permitting, procurement, labor practices, and project delivery. Currently, major U.S. infrastructure projects cost more than what European and Asian countries pay for comparable projects. The additional costs are due to inefficient and outmoded permitting, procurement, and labor practices, and project delivery systems commonly used in the United States.

CONCLUSION

The Green Mega Deal framework should be overlaid on the climate and infrastructure investments included in the Infrastructure Investment and Jobs Act and the budget reconciliation package of 2021. These are expected to fall far short of the needs described in this book. The initiatives outlined here would help advance the policies, investments, and institutions necessary to secure the future success of the 13 U.S. megaregions and their 260 million residents. To build what is needed requires a WPA 2.0 as envisioned by Drake (2016).

The multitrillion-dollar spending plans from the administration and Congress must meet the specialized investment needs of megaregions and provide high-performance intercity rail, climate adaptation and resilience strategies, megaregion- and metropolitan-scale congestion management, and affordable housing. As noted earlier, the Infrastructure Investment and Jobs Act should be seen as only a down payment toward these needs. A second and much more ambitious set of investments will be required to achieve these goals. These measures should also adapt existing mobility systems and settlement patterns to accommodate the sweeping changes now underway in work and travel behavior. Finally, they must promote opportunities for every community and every racial and ethnic group to succeed in the new economy of the postpandemic era.

For some ballpark estimates of funding levels for the needs discussed in this chapter, consider the following:

Rebuilding urban interstates	$500 billion
Rebuilding rural roadways and interstates	$100 billion
Installing intercity high-speed rail and high-performance rail	$1 trillion
Bringing urban transit into a state of good repair	$200 billion
Greening infrastructure	$500 billion
Improving urban parks, protecting metro public watersheds, and restoring brownfields	$100 billion
Protecting from storm surges and urban flooding	$300 billion
Managing urban traffic management and regreening urban roads	$200 billion
Building or updating airports and seaports	$200 billion (with higher private sector leverage ratio)
Installing universal broadband	$50 billion
Creating climate reserves and restoring landscapes	$300 billion
Implementing alternative energy and distributed power systems	$500 billion
Financing planning and institution building	$100 million
Total	$4 trillion to $5 trillion

8

A STRATEGIC PLAN FOR THE NORTHEAST MEGAREGION

Cities, like dreams, are made of desires and fears, even if the thread of their discourse is secret, the rules are absurd, their perspective deceitful, and everything cancels something else.

—ITALO CALVINO

THE NORTHEAST IS THE NATION'S OLDEST MEGAREGION and arguably its most politically complex. The Northeast is defined by its history, geography, and economy. Growing racial, economic, and social divisions threaten its future prosperity. These divisions are further exacerbated by climate change and decaying infrastructure. This chapter outlines a proposal for a Northeast megaregion transportation system and related institutional and governance systems. It also describes adaptation and mitigation measures for climate change that the Northeast needs to take.

DEFINING THE NORTHEAST MEGAREGION

From the beginning of the republic, the Northeast megaregion has been the principal engine of the U.S. economy. Today, the Northeast has the largest population and economy of any U.S. megaregion, with more than 61 million people and a $4.5 trillion economy. Its major metropolitan centers are the drivers of U.S. governance, finance, media, biomedicine, pharmaceuticals, manufacturing, education, insurance, energy, communications, and innovation. It is also home to the world's largest concentration of top-ranked global research universities and teaching hospitals—perhaps one of its most important competitive assets. In addition, many major philanthropic foundations are headquartered in the Northeast megaregion. The Northeast megaregion has an innovation economy second only to that of Northern California. Its five largest metropolitan areas—New York, Boston, Philadelphia, Washington, DC, and Baltimore—have more than two-thirds of the nation's total transit ridership.

The Northeast is the nation's most complex megaregion, consisting of portions of 14 states and thousands of municipalities. No government institutions encompass all or even most of the Northeast, and the collaboration among the states has been limited. The U.S. Constitution makes collaborative efforts difficult by requiring that most multistate initiatives be authorized by an interstate compact (see chapter 10) approved by participating state legislatures and the U.S. Congress. Obtaining collective agreement on initiatives facing the whole Northeast is rare; just how rare is illustrated in the following: In 2008, the RPA led an advocacy campaign in support of the Passenger Rail Investment and Improvement Act. This legislation authorized federal investments in Amtrak, its Northeast Corridor, and a proposed national high-speed rail network. To promote its adoption, the RPA led a coalition of more than a dozen major business groups, representing cities and regions stretching from Boston to Washington, DC. Despite foot-dragging from the White House and Congress, in the end, the entire 26-member U.S. Senate delegation from Maine to Virginia voted as a bloc in support of the bill when it was going through Congress. This was possibly the most agreement ever achieved in the Northeast. When Bob Yaro was asked to discuss this achievement with the RPA's board of directors, he highlighted the uniqueness of this accomplishment. Yaro argued that not since the ratification of the Bill of Rights by the Northeast states more than two centuries earlier had a similar consensus been achieved. He was interrupted by Kenneth Jackson, board member and distinguished Columbia University historian, who said, "You're wrong—New York voted against the Bill of Rights."

MAJOR CHALLENGES FACING THE NORTHEAST

The COVID-19 global pandemic, which began in early 2020, by November 2021 had killed more than 750,000 Americans. Indigenous Americans, Black Americans, and older citizens were disproportionately affected. More than 130,000 deaths occurred in the Northeast (Worldometer 2021). The ensuing global economic collapse produced mass unemployment and vast numbers of business failures not seen since the Great Depression. By April 2020, unemployment rates across the Northeast skyrocketed, exceeding 16 percent in New York and 17 percent in Rhode Island. Although these rates declined rapidly over the ensuing year, they remained significantly higher than in the rest of the country (Mena 2021). That pandemic year was also when most Americans started thinking of climate change in the present, not the future, tense. Record-breaking numbers of climate-induced or climate-intensified wildfires struck Northern and Southern California and Cascadia. Pine barrens landscapes in New

Jersey, Massachusetts, and New York are susceptible to similar wildfires. The Atlantic hurricane season produced the largest number of hurricanes and tropical storms in history, and many of these intensified because of record-breaking water temperatures in the North Atlantic and Gulf of Mexico, which had catastrophic impacts on the Gulf Coast, Texas Triangle, Northeast, Piedmont Atlantic, and Florida megaregions. Extreme drought and record heat also struck much of the country, particularly in the Front Range, Basin and Range, Arizona Sun Corridor, Southern and Northern California, and Cascadia megaregions. Several northeastern states experienced their warmest summer months in history.

Compounding the pandemic, economic, and climate-related disasters was the surge of public support for the Black Lives Matter movement in the aftermath of George Floyd's and Breonna Taylor's murders. The pandemic and climate-induced disasters only added to the troubles of minority communities already reeling from economic inequality across the Northeast and other megaregions. After adjusting for age, the numbers reveal that 3.4 times as many Blacks and 3.3 times as many Hispanics died from COVID-19 as whites (APM Research Lab 2021).

Growing Racial, Economic, and Social Divisions

The Northeast's major urban centers—except Baltimore—experienced significant population and employment growth in the quarter century leading up to the 2020 COVID-19 pandemic. Although this growth resulted in significant increases in household income and municipal, state, and federal tax rolls, these benefits were not evenly shared with the large concentrations of poor African American, Latinx, and immigrant residents in all five metropolitan areas. Children in poor minority households in inner cities and small communities were placed at an extreme disadvantage compared with their middle-class and suburban peers when schools moved to remote learning during the COVID-19 pandemic. This was due to the inadequacies of broadband networks in poor communities across the megaregion. These disadvantaged groups bore the brunt of both the pandemic and its economic impacts, including losses of jobs, education, travel, health care, and other benefits, as well as housing evictions and increases in crime and drug addiction. These disproportionate impacts were at the heart of months of racial justice protests in many northeastern cities in 2020.

Beyond its five major metropolitan areas, the Northeast also contains a network of hundreds of older, midsize urban centers—places like Scranton and Allentown, Pennsylvania; Camden and Paterson, New Jersey; Poughkeepsie and Newburgh, New York; Waterbury and New Britain, Connecticut; Providence, Rhode Island; Springfield and Fall River, Massachusetts; Brattleboro, Vermont; Manchester, New Hampshire; and Lewiston-Auburn and Bangor, Maine—many of which never recovered from the loss of manufacturing in the 1970s and 1980s. These places are home to millions of working-class, disabled, and minority residents with lower household incomes and higher rates of unemployment than the rest of the Northeast and nation. They have also become increasingly detached from each other and from the Northeast's major metropolitan centers because regional rail service has deteriorated—or in many places, collapsed—since 1970 and because interstate and arterial highways have become more congested.

The Northeast's current economic geography is defined by a governance system in place since the 17th century and transportation policies and investments in place since the mid-20th century. Since the adoption of the 1956 National Interstate and Defense Highways Act, the nation's and the Northeast's transportation policies and investments have focused on building limited-access highways in the rapidly expanding metropolitan areas. These roads enabled these places to become the sprawling and congested automobile-oriented places that they are today. Adding discriminatory national and local housing and tax policies to the Northeast's highly Balkanized municipal governance system produced a sum of metropolitan regions where race, income, and geography are highly correlated and highly segregated.

Climate Change

Climate change threatens the Northeast's cities and their residents with coastal storm surges and sea level rise, urban and riverine flooding, threats to drinking water, and more frequent severe rainfall events, droughts, and heat waves. Major urban centers experience heat islands, the effects of which are worse in poor neighborhoods because there are fewer trees. These conditions are expected to become more frequent and severe as the century progresses, undercutting the livability and safety of northeastern cities, suburbs, small towns, and rural areas.

Maintaining the integrity of large natural systems that permit species to migrate northward as climate change unfolds has been hindered by low-density suburban sprawl and warehouse distribution centers. Residential sprawl into wooded areas could also increase the potential for property damage and loss of life if the region begins to experience the massive wildfires that have struck California, Cascadia, Australia, and portions of the United Kingdom, Portugal, and other European countries in recent years.

Traffic Congestion and Housing Costs

Significant population and employment growth in these metro regions in recent decades have caused extreme highway congestion and uncontrolled escalation of housing prices and commercial rents. High prices make it more difficult to attract the young, well-educated people necessary to the megaregion's innovation economy and increase rates of displacement, homelessness, and financial distress for households in inner-city minority communities. However, these trends could be fundamentally altered by changes brought by the COVID-19 pandemic: the growth in telecommuting has reduced travel, people are shopping even more online, and remote learning could continue to grow after the pandemic ends. These changes will reduce highway congestion and also reduce rents and housing prices. The rise in work from home brought on by the pandemic could also work to the advantage of the Northeast's midsize cities if rail networks can better connect them to each other and to the megaregion's major metropolitan centers.

Decaying Infrastructure

Infrastructure broadly refers to the frameworks that hold the nation together, such as roads, sewer lines, childcare facilities, and high-speed broadband. It is the backbone of megaregions and garners considerable attention from policy-makers. The Northeast has the nation's oldest infrastructure. With the highest population density of any U.S. megaregion, it also is more dependent than any other on rapid transit and commuter rail networks, which have experienced decades of disinvestment. In 2018, the American Public Transit Association reported that bringing the Metropolitan Area Transit Authority system of Washington, DC, to a state of good repair would require $6.6 billion. Restoring Philadelphia's Southeastern Pennsylvania Transportation Authority and Boston's Massachusetts Bay Transportation Authority systems to a state of good repair would cost $7.3 billion and $5 billion, respectively (Sisson 2018). The tight fiscal constraints on these systems and on New York City's Metropolitan Transportation Authority system have been compounded by the pandemic and the resulting reductions in farebox receipts and tax and toll revenues.

The existing intercity rail services of the New England–downstate New York region could best be described as a low-capacity rail network. They are slow, infrequent, unreliable, expensive, and uncoordinated between modes and do not serve most of the region's midsize cities at all. The region's commuter rail services are geared to serving weekday journey-to-work trips to big-city central business districts and are slow, infrequent, and unreliable for other travelers and at other times and days. These systems are fragmented and limited in the travel markets that they serve.

Urban segments in the Interstate Highway System are now 60 or more years old, and many aging, elevated structures require substantial reconstruction or replacement. Nearby low-income and minority communities breathe high levels of small particulates produced by diesel exhaust, which increases rates of asthma and pulmonary and cardiovascular disease. In the straitened fiscal condition of most states and cities in the aftermath of the pandemic, these investments cannot be made without a significant commitment of federal resources.

Global Competitiveness

The major export industries that drive the Northeast's economy—including biomedicine, information technology, media, manufacturing, higher education, and financial and business services—compete globally for customers and talent. The megaregion's competitors in Europe and Asia are served by—or are planning—modern, intercity high-speed rail and high-performance regional rail systems that reach the networks of scientists, researchers, and professionals who create competitive advantage in these industries. After six decades of proposals to create high-speed rail service in the Northeast, little has been done. In addition, proposals for modernized regional rail networks for metro New York and Boston are totally unfunded.

A STRATEGIC PLAN FOR THE NORTHEAST

To respond to these known threats and anticipate future ones, the Northeast should create the nation's first megaregion-scale plan. The planning process would be useful to other U.S. megaregions when creating their plans. It is entirely appropriate that this process emerge in the Northeast first. From Philadelphia's revolutionary Fairmount Water Works, built between 1812 and 1872, to the Regional Greenhouse Gas Initiative of 2005, the first U.S. cap-and-trade program for power plant carbon emissions and a 10-state cooperative effort, the Northeast has a long tradition of large-scale planning and infrastructure development.

Constructing a more equitable, prosperous, and sustainable economy will require comprehensive action on a broad range of fronts, with policies and investments in mobility, education, economic justice, energy, environmental protection, housing policy, governance, and tax reform. The decline of most of the region's midsize cities could be reversed with economic development, such as fostering creative disruption through a partnership between existing firms and start-ups, developing and recruiting talent needed by firms, and building a creative habitat that enhances each city's distinctive character and assets. The most fundamental reforms will transform the Northeast's economic geography by better connecting its major metropolitan areas and providing currently isolated and left-behind communities with equal access to the economic opportunities of the entire megaregion. This can be done with a high-speed and high-performance rail network for the entire Northeast, connecting every midsize city and its hinterlands to each other and to major metropolitan centers. With this network, every community will have equal access to the innovation economies that are now concentrated in only a handful of dense urban centers.

A high-speed and high-performance rail network would help expand housing access for communities across the Northeast. It would connect neighborhoods with large minority populations to job markets across the megaregion while also reducing pressures for gentrification and displacement in these communities. Midsize cities, many of them currently left behind and with large minority populations, could attract new jobs and residents with accessibility to metropolitan employment. Most have lost a significant portion of their populations and employment since 1970, leaving tens of thousands of acres of vacant and derelict land and buildings. These could be repurposed to create new housing opportunities for current and future residents.

Cities and suburbs that get stations on the network could be required to adopt inclusionary zoning ordinances as a condition of receiving improved rail service. Zoning and other land use and building regulations could be revised to promote finer-grained, smaller-scale housing development suitable for self-builders and small contractors. Land now devoted to station-area parking could be repurposed for the construction of mixed-income housing.

The northern half of the megaregion encompassing downstate New York and the six New England states could be served by a network called North Atlantic Rail. Several attempts have been made since the 1960s to preserve and upgrade the Northeast Corridor. The most significant was in 1988, when Senator Daniel Patrick Moynihan removed several sections of the corridor from the proposed privatization of CONRAIL assets and transferred them to Amtrak's control (*Tax Exempt Bonds* 1988). The states of New York, Connecticut, and Massachusetts then purchased portions of the rail corridor; and now almost the entire corridor between Washington, DC, and Boston, Massachusetts, is in public ownership.

In the southern half of the megaregion, a second high-performance rail network, called Mid-Atlantic Rail, would serve seven states and the District of Columbia, stretching from New York City south to Virginia. The spine of both networks would be Amtrak's Northeast Corridor transformed into a high-speed rail line stretching from Washington, DC, to Boston. Mid-Atlantic Rail's components would parallel those of North Atlantic Rail: the high-speed Northeast Corridor; high-performance, intercity services connecting all the region's midsize cities with each other and with the Northeast Corridor; and regional rail networks serving metro Philadelphia and the Washington-Baltimore region.

NORTH ATLANTIC RAIL

North Atlantic Rail (NAR) is a proposed high-performance passenger rail network serving the seven-state New England–downstate New York region. This region already has more than two-thirds of U.S. rail ridership and a strong rail culture. The NAR network is a $105 billion investment that will provide not only transformational mobility but also economic development and climate resilience benefits for the entire seven-state region. The network has three components:

- A high-speed rail (200 mph or faster) service between Boston and New York City.
- A high-performance intercity rail network, providing frequent, reliable, reasonably priced, and fast (80–110 mph) service connecting all the region's midsize cities to each other and the high-speed rail route.
- Modernized regional rail networks around metropolitan Boston and New York City.

Completing this network would be modernized rapid transit and bus rapid transit systems in each major metropolitan area. Transportation network companies such as Uber and Lyft will provide first- and last-mile connections to transit stations, reducing the need for station-area parking, which in turn would further expand opportunities for new transit-oriented housing and employment near transit stations. Also, the routing algorithms used by these companies could be adapted to reduce costs for multipassenger services.

The New England–downstate New York area is home to 11 percent of the U.S. population and the source of 14 percent of its GDP. It has an economy of more than $3 trillion—larger than that of California and all but five countries. The engines of this economy are metro Boston and New York City—two of the world's most dynamic places. The second-tier cities—midsize, former industrial cities—have lost a significant share of their population, employment, and tax base since 1980 and have become increasingly disconnected, as highways, commuter rail networks, and airports become highly congested and unreliable. Achieving the rebirth of these cities requires passenger rail links that directly connect these places with each other, with the region's economic engines, and with the airports serving these cities—Green, Bradley, Manchester, Portland, and MacArthur airports, in addition to Boston's Logan and New York–area airports. It also requires a comprehensive set of job training, technology transfer, urban regeneration, and housing strategies in cities across the region. Importantly, many of these strategies are programs already in place or being developed.

Rather than simply a rail infrastructure project, NAR is more properly framed as a rail-enabled economic development strategy. Connecting this economy and its research universities with all the region's cities, the NAR network will create an integrated market for labor, capital, and ideas. The whole will be greater than the sum of its parts, likely surpassing the United Kingdom in GDP to become the fourth-largest economy in the world. High-performance rail will be fast, frequent, reliable, networked, and priced to attract a broad range of riders. This modern, high-performance network will unify currently separate housing and labor markets into the world's largest innovation network. Building the network will put hundreds of thousands to work in the immediate aftermath of the COVID-19 pandemic. Its operation will reduce congestion on the region's highways and passenger rail lines and expand housing markets and commute sheds to slow rapidly escalating housing prices, in addition to promoting land-efficient, transit-oriented development. The fully electrified rail network will be powered by renewable energy sources, significantly reducing carbon and air pollution. Its proposed inland route between Boston and New York will not be threatened by sea level rise or storm surges.

NAR's Origins and Future

First proposed in 2017, the plan for NAR emerged from a research studio at Penn's Weitzman School of Design called Rebooting New England. Now called the North Atlantic Rail Initiative, it is led by prominent business, civic, government, and academic leaders from across the New England–downstate New York region. Since 2017, roundtable workshops on this proposal have been held across New England whose participants were municipal, state, and federal officials and business, civic, academic, and philanthropic leaders. Three key points emerged from these discussions:

- Participants have expressed strong agreement with the problem statement and support the solutions described in this chapter.
- Each state has identified the need for one or more priority rail investments but lacks funding or the critical mass of benefits to justify the cost. Combining these rail projects into the first phase of a comprehensive high-performance rail network adds value to each project and makes state and federal financial support more likely.
- Roundtable participants have volunteered to participate in upcoming NAR advocacy and planning efforts.

The existing North Atlantic Rail Alliance could become the basis for a North Atlantic Partnership, a nongovernmental economic development organization that would forge local partnerships with municipal governments and business, civic, and academic leaders and coordinate initiatives for the whole region. The partnership would provide long-term leadership across state boundaries and through election and business cycles.

Three-Phase Development

The NAR initiative has broken the project into three phases. Components of all three phases can be initiated simultaneously to expedite economic and employment benefits. The first phase (figure 8.1), building high-priority rail projects, should include the planning and design of the entire system (figure 8.2), with full public consultation and review, leading to the reservation of rail rights-of-way where needed and confirming the strategic value of early-phase investments.

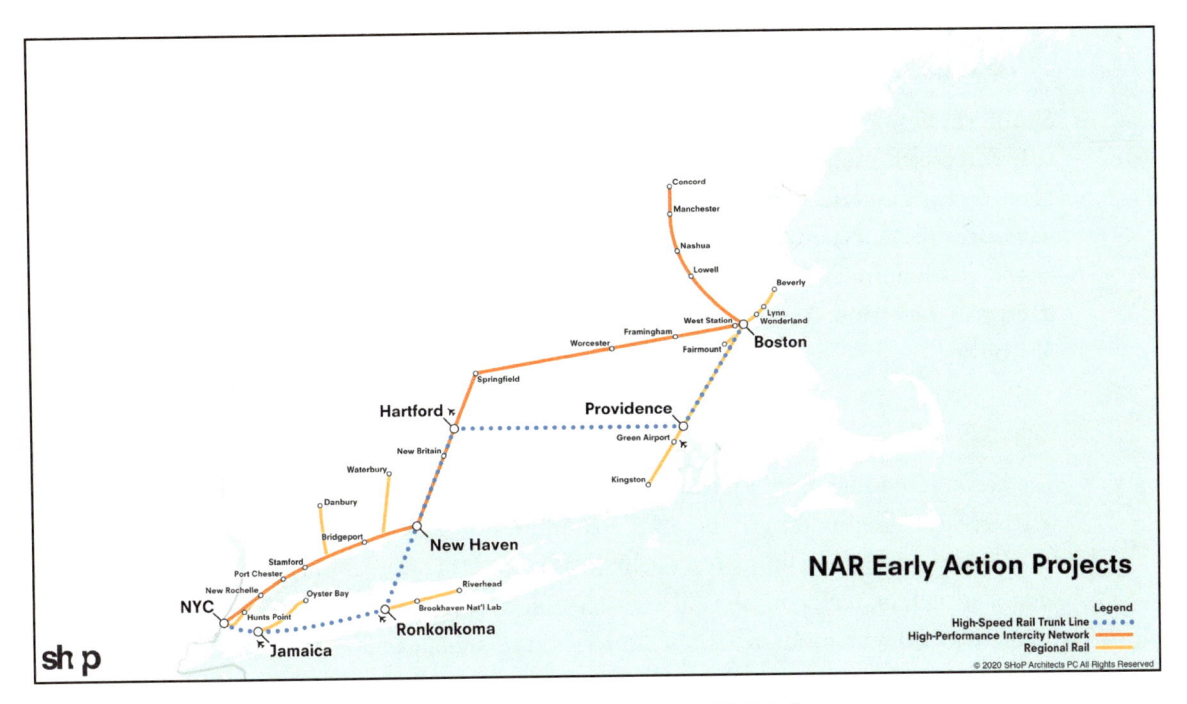

FIGURE 8.1 North Atlantic Rail's early action projects. *Source: SHoP Architects.*

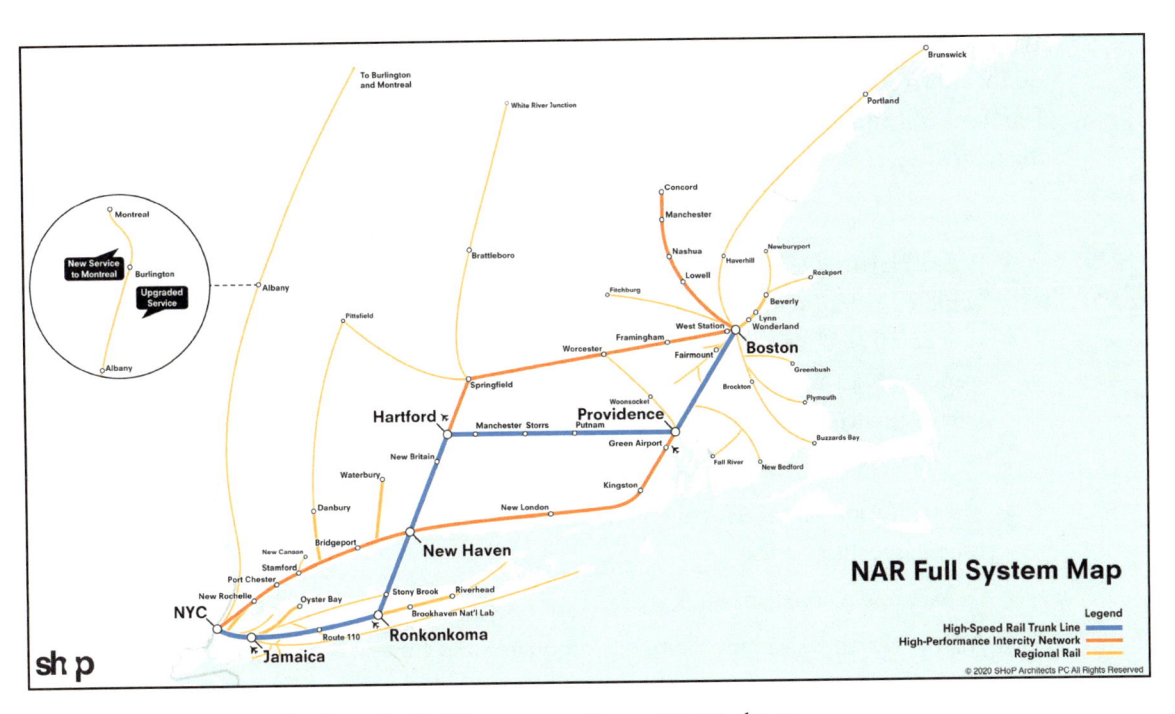

FIGURE 8.2 North Atlantic Rail's full system map. *Source: SHoP Architects.*

A STRATEGIC PLAN FOR THE NORTHEAST MEGAREGION | 215

Phase 1: Early Action Projects

Southern New England states have identified high-priority early action projects that will create a foundation for the ultimate seven-state New England–downstate New York high-performance rail network. Planning and preliminary engineering have already been conducted on most of these projects. Expediting major portions would put hundreds of thousands to work during and following the COVID-19 pandemic recession. These projects have an estimated total construction cost of $35 billion.

Connecticut

The New Haven Line from Manhattan to New Haven, Connecticut, is the most intensively used commuter rail line in the country. But in recent years, travel times have increased, and reliability has declined as a result of decades of deferred maintenance, such as replacing several century-old, movable bridges. Investments in bridge replacement; modernization of interlocking, signal, and power systems; and additional tracks in key locations will improve reliability and reduce travel times between New Haven and Manhattan from the current 120 minutes to 66 minutes. Stations with high-level platforms, which eliminate train stairs, and multimodal connections will be built in the Bronx. An intermodal station will be constructed in Port Chester, New York, to connect Westchester Bus Rapid Transit Service, linking White Plains and the Interstate 287 office corridor to the New Haven Line. Additional improvements will be made in the Hartford Line to expand service between Hartford and Springfield. New services and development opportunities will include the following:

- Frequent, bidirectional, local, high-performance rail service within Connecticut.
- A new Hartford Hub Transit Center and related downtown redevelopment that could be paired with Interstate 84 reconstruction and achieve better integration of rail and bus services for the Hartford metro area including the bus rapid transit service to Manchester, Vernon, Storrs (the location of the University of Connecticut), and Hartford's western suburbs.
- Synchronized rail-transit connections to Bradley Airport.
- Electrification of the Hartford Line and upgraded Hartford Line and Shore Line East rolling stock.
- Departures every 30 minutes at peak times, 60 minutes at off-peak on all routes.
- A New Haven pulse hub (demand responsive and timed transfer) permitting easy transfers from trains on the coastal and inland routes.

- Waterbury rail and bus connections to Bridgeport and New Britain–Hartford integrated with New Haven and Hartford Line rail schedules that run at consistent intervals (clock-face schedules).
- Faster and more frequent rail service to Stamford, Connecticut; New Rochelle, New York; and both Penn Station and Grand Central Terminal in Manhattan.

Rhode Island

Rhode Island's early action project will upgrade the existing Northeast Corridor alignment to provide frequent, reliable, 45-minute regional rail service from several places in the state to Boston's South Station. This project adds track capacity and high-level platforms in several Rhode Island and Massachusetts stations, including Providence, Green Airport, and Attleboro; improves power systems; and expands tracks and platforms at Boston's South Station. A new rail service will provide a limited-stop express service within Massachusetts between Boston's South Station and Providence and will continue onward to serve stations within Rhode Island between Providence and Westerly, including T. F. Green Airport.

Massachusetts: Greater Boston

The Bay State's early action projects will begin the transformation of the Massachusetts Bay Transportation Authority commuter rail network into a modern metropolitan rail system. The MBTA already has plans to electrify and build high-level platforms on the Fairmont, Worcester, and Lynn Lines. NAR funds will complement these investments by electrification and station modernization along the rest of the MBTA commuter rail network inside Route 128 (especially to Franklin and Needham to make the Readville–Back Bay corridor all electric) and electrification of the Worcester Line to downtown Worcester. Other projects are the following:

- Selective realignment addressing speed and capacity needs for express services while building on planned capacity expansion at Boston's South Station.
- Expanded capacity at Route 128 Station.
- Increased capacity at Canton Junction.
- Potential additional track capacity between Readville and Boston.
- Potential metropolitan rail and rapid transit integration with new interchanges on the Worcester Line–Green Line interchange at Riverside and other locations.
- Planning for integration of northside and southside regional rail services.

Western Massachusetts

Top priorities for western Massachusetts are creating East-West Rail, a high-performance rail connection from Springfield to Worcester, and improving the existing Worcester–Boston rail line with 80-minute travel times from Springfield to Boston. Springfield's restored station will become a pulse hub for east–west and north–south rail service in the region. A new bus rapid transit network will connect all the region's major population and employment centers to Springfield Station. Palmer's historic train station will become an intermediate stop on the Springfield–Boston route and a focal point for downtown revitalization.

The Danbury branch of Metro-North between South Norwalk and Danbury, Connecticut, will receive speed improvements, electrification, and selective installation of double tracks to allow more frequent bidirectional service. This will set the stage for and improve the value of future restoration of the Berkshire Rail service between Danbury and Pittsfield. Similar upgrades should be made on the Waterbury branch.

Northern New England: Vermont, New Hampshire, and Maine

Although the MBTA has not considered a link between Boston's North and South Stations to be a top priority for Greater Boston's rail network, it is essential to incorporating northern New England into the region's rail network. Construction of the link will transform North and South Stations from highly congested stub-end terminals into efficient through-running stations. This will enable major growth in rail service on the entire metropolitan Boston network with less terminal expansion at North and South Stations. With this new rail link, the Downeaster service and regional rail trains from Maine and New Hampshire and MBTA trains from the North Shore and northern suburbs will be able to run through to all major employment centers in Boston, including the Financial District, Seaport, Back Bay, and Longwood Medical Area. The link will eliminate difficult transfers for passengers who currently must walk or take two-seat transit or taxi rides between these stations.

Construction of the link will improve the performance and increase the value of the proposed extension of the Downeaster service to Lewiston-Auburn, Maine, and extension of the current Haverhill Line commuter service to Nashua, Manchester, and Concord, New Hampshire. In addition, Amtrak's Valley Flyer service will be extended from Greenfield, Massachusetts, to Brattleboro, Vermont, and possibly on to White River Junction, serving southeastern Vermont and southwestern New Hampshire.

Amtrak's intercity rail service on the Northeast Corridor will be expanded and improved in this phase of the program. Capacity on the existing corridor will be increased to an hourly Acela service and a regular hourly Northeast regional service north of New York City. These hourly services will connect at New Haven for trains following the upgraded inland route between New Haven and Boston via Hartford,

Springfield, and Worcester or via the extended Valley Flyer route. Selected regional trains could operate direct from New York via the inland route. Trip times for all trains between New York and Boston will decrease, and service reliability will improve.

Engineering and right-of-way acquisition should include studies of alternative solutions for high-performance rail service between New York and New Haven and between New Haven and Boston. This will be necessary to inform good investment decisions for Metro-North, Long Island Railroad, Hartford Line, Worcester Line, western Massachusetts, South Coast, and Greater Boston services. These studies will also aid regionwide right-of-way preservation and selective acquisition and rail banking in phase 1. They should also locate property for yard and shop facilities.

Phase 2: High-Speed Rail System

Phase 2 could be initiated simultaneously with construction of the phase 1 investments. Phase 2 NAR investments will build the high-speed rail (160–225 mph) spine from Manhattan to Boston.

Two possible routes exist between the East River in New York City and New Haven. One route mostly follows the existing Amtrak Hell Gate Line between Long Island City, Queens, and New Rochelle, New York. The line would have four tracks and be upgraded for higher speeds and to provide separate tracks for local and non-stopping trains. A grade-separated junction and expanded hub station would be built at New Rochelle, and new high-speed tracks would be built approximately parallel to the New Haven Line between New Rochelle and at a point to be determined in western Fairfield County, Connecticut. The remainder of the New Haven Line would be upgraded to increase speed on the express tracks, eliminate bottlenecks, and bypass slow-speed curves at Bridgeport, Connecticut.

The second route would run east on Long Island, via a new right-of-way between Long Island City and Jamaica, Queens, then on new high-speed tracks approximately parallel to the Long Island Rail Road main line between Jamaica and Ronkonkoma. At Ronkonkoma, the route would turn north and follow a utility right-of-way to Port Jefferson, where a 17-mile tunnel would connect to the existing Amtrak Northeast Corridor in Milford, Connecticut. This tunnel and its rail service would bring Long Island into the heart of the Northeast Corridor, ending its isolation from New England's employment centers and strengthening its connections to Manhattan.

Both routes would have difficulties in right-of-way acquisition and potential community and environmental impacts, but either route would deliver major mobility and access benefits for travelers in the respective corridors. A detailed technical analysis and an extensive public review and consultation are required to select a route between New York City and New Haven.

Both existing and new rail rights-of-way will connect New Haven to Hartford, and a new high-speed alignment will connect Hartford to Providence. A new rail tunnel under downtown Hartford could be combined with the proposed realignment and undergrounding of Interstate 84. From Providence, the route can use Amtrak's existing right-of-way to get to Boston. The estimated travel time between Boston and New York will be approximately 100 minutes via the Long Island route and 140 minutes via the New Haven Line. The Long Island route would bring everywhere in the region to within an hour's travel time of either Manhattan or downtown Boston, or in the case of Hartford, both.

Related to this work is Amtrak's Gateway Project, which, when approved by Congress, will fund the modernization and expansion of New York's Penn Station, the completion of two new tunnels under the Hudson River, and the restoration of the North River Tunnels, built in the first decade of the 1900s, under the Hudson. Together with NAR and proposed upgrades to New Jersey Transit's commuter rail network, this project will provide the capacity needed for high-speed and high-performance rail services serving the entire New York–New Jersey–Connecticut metropolitan region.

Phase 3: Connecting the Dots, Completing the Network

The third and final phase of NAR will connect all New England's midsize cities with each other. Elements of this phase could occur simultaneously with phases 1 and 2. In phase 3, Amtrak's Downeaster service, now between Brunswick, Maine, and Boston, could be extended to Bangor and Rockland, Maine, with the metropolitan rail service extended from Boston to Nashua, Manchester, and potentially on to Concord, New Hampshire.

Regional Rail Networks

When the rest of the United States lost commuter rail services in the 1950s and 1960s, the Northeast's major urban centers retained some. The New York metropolitan region invested heavily in commuter rail, and its three rail authorities—the Long Island Rail Road, Metro-North Railroad, and NJ Transit—are the most heavily used commuter rail networks in the country, carrying nearly a million daily passengers before the COVID-19 pandemic (Wikipedia, *The Free Encyclopedia* 2021). Similar systems serve metropolitan Boston, Philadelphia, and the Washington-Baltimore-Virginia-West Virginia metropolitan areas. For the most part, however, these systems are designed to serve one market only: a daily commuter service to and from downtown employment centers. They provide limited or no reverse-commute, inter-suburban services, or through-running services.

Government and civic groups in Boston and New York City have proposed that these commuter rail networks be transformed into regional rail networks, providing more frequent off-peak, reverse-commute, and through-running services and frequent service between suburban centers. In Boston, MBTA has proposed a $29 billion modernization and expansion plan for the region's century-old commuter rail system. Components of this plan, which has support from the civic group TransitMatters, include electrifying the entire network; building high-level platforms; providing 30-minute services between suburban centers and 15-minute services in denser communities; providing peak, off-peak, in-bound, reverse, and through-running services; and integrating currently separate networks north and south of Boston via a new north–south rail link (TransitMatters 2018).

In its 2019 *Fourth Regional Plan*, New York's RPA recommended that the region's existing commuter rail system be transformed into a "T-REX" (transregional express) network (Barone et al. 2018) with features similar to those proposed by Boston's MBTA in 2018 (figures 8.3 and 8.4).

Implementation of this network, estimated to cost $60 billion, will require a renewed state and federal commitment to infrastructure investment, given the need of an additional $50 billion or more just to bring the existing transit networks of the New York Metropolitan Transportation Authority and NJ Transit to a state of good repair.

Transforming Urban Highways

A number of U.S. cities are proposing that urban segments of the interstate highway system be redesigned or removed, since they are highly congested, in need of significant reconstruction, and are damaging to public health and the quality of life in adjacent low-income communities.

Several Northeastern cities propose removing or transforming the most damaging and decrepit of these highways. In New York City, for example, the city is working with the New York State Department of Transportation to transform the elevated Sheridan Expressway in the Bronx into an at-grade boulevard. In Syracuse, New York, the Department of Transportation is replacing an elevated section of Interstate 81 with a surface boulevard and reconstructed street grid (New York State Department of Transportation 2021).

Boston's $14 billion Big Dig project depressed the elevated Interstate 93 Central Artery highway, reconnecting downtown Boston with the formerly isolated waterfront and Seaport districts. The project decongested downtown and led to 1,000 acres of formerly derelict waterfront becoming Boston's innovation district. The project rebuilt century-old infrastructure systems. Although widely derided for escalating costs (from an original estimate of $3.5 billion) and mission creep, as the scope of the project grew during its decade-plus planning and construction period,

FIGURE 8.3 Proposed modernized commuter rail system for Boston.
Source: Massachusetts Bay Transportation Authority.

so did its benefits. The Big Dig transformed the economy of the city and surrounding metropolitan region.

Similar transformations are needed in dozens of cities across the Northeast. Elsewhere in the United States, there are proposals to cap or remove interstates in Austin, Saint Paul, New Orleans, and Atlanta.

The most ambitious of these plans is a proposal to undo the damage done when Interstates 84 and 91 were bulldozed through downtown Hartford, Connecticut, in the 1950s and 1960s (figure 8.5). Hartford400 seeks to seize the economic and

FIGURE 8.4 Proposed Regional Express Service map. *Source: Regional Plan Association.*

FIGURE 8.5 Hartford400 vision for a new River Road capping Interstate 91 through downtown Hartford, Connecticut and reconnecting the city to its waterfront. *Source: Doug Suisman.*

A STRATEGIC PLAN FOR THE NORTHEAST MEGAREGION | 223

Hartford400: Transforming the Connecticut Valley and Its Capital City

During the 19th and early 20th centuries, the Connecticut Valley was the Silicon Valley of its age—a national and global hub of finance, manufacturing, and innovation. With this prosperity came so much urban investment that in 1868 Hartford resident Mark Twain wrote, "Of all the beautiful towns it has been my fortune to see, this is the chief" (Darbee 1959).

In the mid-20th century, urban upheaval and disinvestment and a host of ill-conceived transportation and urban renewal projects undermined the region's broad prosperity. The World Population Review (2021) ranked Hartford as one of the nation's 10 poorest cities in 2021. Neighboring towns like East Hartford, Manchester, and New Britain have large populations of low-income, Black, and Latinx residents who suffer from persistently high rates of unemployment, shortened life expectancy, and disproportionate health and economic impacts from the COVID pandemic.

Highway construction in the 1960s devastated Hartford by extending Interstates 91 and 84 through the city's downtown, cutting off the region's major employment center from adjacent neighborhoods, notably the North End and its mostly Black residents. Interstate 91's riverfront alignment further isolated the city from the Connecticut River waterfront, and the Interstate 84–91 interchange and East Hartford's sprawling "mixmaster" of an interchange consumed acres of valuable land and dampened economic development. The absence of a beltway forced large volumes of bypass traffic gracelessly through rather than around downtown. The result is a bottleneck that is the second worst in New England and among the worst in the country. It creates an economic choke point for passengers and goods across New England, undercutting the economic potential of all of Connecticut and the nearby areas of Massachusetts and Rhode Island.

The absence of modern intercity rail and the deterioration of regional rail since the 1960s has further isolated the Connecticut Valley's housing and labor markets from those of nearby Springfield and New Haven and from metropolitan Boston and New York, constraining the economic potential of the entire New England–New York megaregion.

Hartford400 is a bold yet pragmatic vision to transform, decongest, and revitalize the heart of the Connecticut Valley and the state's capital city by 2035, the 400th anniversary of Hartford's founding. The initiative directly addresses the region's persistent racial, economic, and physical divisions and climate concerns. It is backed by a coalition of government, civic, and business groups from the region and advised by some of the nation's leading planners, engineers, and urban designers.

Hartford400 proposes to reconnect Hartford's North End and Asylum Hill with downtown Hartford by relocating portions of I-84 into a decked-over trench and place other sections in a new tunnel. Relocation of two interchanges, the congested interchange of I-84 with I-91 in downtown Hartford and the sprawling interchange in East Hartford, will free up prime urban land for development. The plan will restore Hartford's riverfront by depressing a portion of I-91 and creating a new at-grade River Road and waterfront park with pedestrian and bicycle links. Hundreds of acres of highway ramps and parking lots will become well-designed, traffic-calmed boulevards. The city will be protected from climate-related flooding by reconstructing Hartford's failing 80-year-old Connecticut River levee. A new Union Station intermodal transportation hub will allow underground alignment for NAR's New York City–Boston high-speed rail route, the Hartford Line, and bus rapid transit and intercity bus lines

Hartford400's proponents are seeking support from Governor Ned Lamont and the Connecticut and other New England congressional delegations. Altogether, Hartford400 is expected to cost approximately $20 billion, funded through the Biden administration's proposed national infrastructure and climate investment program. In August 2021, the president's proposal to invest $20 billion in urban highway relocation projects like Hartford's was reduced to $1 billion in the Infrastructure Investment and Jobs Act adopted by the Senate. If enacted by Congress, a portion of these funds could be used for engineering, design, and environmental reviews for the Hartford400 plan. Hartford400 could become a flagship initiative in Biden's national investment program, bringing short-term infrastructure jobs, long-term economic transformation, sustainable mobility, climate adaptation, and racial and social justice to the 1 million residents of the Connecticut Valley and its capital city.

mobility opportunities of the proposed NAR network, which will place Hartford and neighboring Springfield and New Haven at the heart of the Northeast's new high-performance intercity rail network. With this system in place, Hartford will be 50 minutes from New York City and Boston and 20 minutes from New Haven and Springfield, putting the city in the center of the region's transformed economic geography.

NAR Financing

Building the NAR network is estimated to cost $105 billion over a 20-year period. Initial funding for NAR could be provided by the federal government through the bipartisan Infrastructure Investment and Jobs Act as well as the reconciliation budget bill debated by Congress in fall 2021, both of which include rail fundings. Although the federal government's current proposal is to fund this entire program through tax increases and redirection of COVID-19 recovery funds, the high-speed rail and other components of this program could be financed through the sale of 20- or 30-year U.S. Treasury bonds, purchased by sovereign wealth funds and overseas investors, whose effective interest rates are currently well under 1 percent. The increased federal tax revenues as the region's economy grows would meet the debt service requirements. In effect, the rest of the world would rebuild New England–downstate New York's infrastructure and production capacity. The federal contribution would be a tiny fraction of the annual amount ($47 billion) that is the difference between what this region sends to Washington and what it gets back in federal expenditures.

Alternatively, financing could be modeled on that for the Interstate Highway System, in which states provide 10 percent and federal grants 90 percent of costs. It would also be possible to have sovereign wealth funds—overseas investment funds of foreign governments—finance a portion of the cost. This approach is being used by Texas Central, the proposed Dallas–Houston high-speed rail route, where the Japanese government is committing 50 percent of the project's cost. In return, the project will use Japanese Shinkansen train sets and other equipment. This approach, however, would add considerably to the project's cost, leading to higher fares and preventing some of the intended users from riding NAR. Public-private partnerships—in which private investors finance some or all of a project's costs—would increase financing costs even more. This, in turn, would further decrease ridership and undercut its economic benefits.

All global competitors to the United States—a total of 26 countries—already have high-speed intercity rail services, and virtually all have been fully financed by national governments or sovereign wealth funds. International experience also strongly suggests that the intercity and regional rail services on this network can become operationally self-sufficient, requiring little or no ongoing public subsidies. Metropolitan services—high-performance, intercity trains running on the network's tracks—may still require operating subsidies, but they will enable the region's midsize cities and their environs to become much more productive and generate additional state and federal tax revenues.

One such strategy is the Northern Powerhouse initiative, through which the U.K. government is investing upward of $160 billion to revitalize the economy of several older industrial cities in the North of England. The Industrial Revolution began here, and the region went through the same deindustrialization that U.S. legacy cities did in the post–World War II era. It also has strong historical ties to New England and its legacy cities.

Northern Powerhouse is constructing two high-speed rail lines: High-Speed 2, which will provide fast and frequent connections between London and the North, and High-Speed 3, which will connect all the smaller northern cities to each other. These will form the core of a network of improved rail and road connections throughout the North, unifying housing and labor markets across the whole region. A new agency, Transport for the North, will plan, build, and operate these transportation improvements. This major rail investment program has remained a high priority in the United Kingdom for both major political parties through multiple changes in government and through its exit from the European Union. A new nongovernmental organization, the Northern Powerhouse Partnership, is coordinating these investments, with a broad array of job training, technology transfer, urban amenity, local transport, and governance reform initiatives needed to rebuild the economies of the region's cities.

NAR Governance

In addition to forming a North Atlantic Partnership out of the North Atlantic Rail Alliance, as described earlier, the alliance proposes that Congress should establish a North Atlantic Rail Corporation as a joint venture between federal and state governments to manage the financing, building, and operation of this multistate transportation network. The U.K. Transport for the North is one of many international precedents.

A North Atlantic Rail Corporation could expedite designing and building rail projects, reduce overall project costs, and increase accountability to Congress, the White House, and participating states. It could use public-private partnerships to deliver and manage many elements. The corporation would design and build components of the rail network and collaborate with existing agencies, such as New York's Metropolitan Transportation Authority, the MBTA, Amtrak, and state departments of transportation to design, build, and operate key components of it. The corporation would be analogous to the Tennessee Valley Authority or Bonneville Power Administration, both established during the New Deal to advance infrastructure and economic development projects in multistate regions. The North Atlantic Rail Alliance is working with the region's congressional delegation to gain authorizing language for the project so that preliminary engineering, design, and environmental reviews can proceed in 2022–2023. Early action demonstration projects can proceed in the ensuing years. NAR has gained broad support from congressional, municipal, business, and civic leaders from across the Northeast that could lead to authorization and funding for the project in coming years.

NAR Project Delivery

The estimated cost of NAR, $105 billion, and construction period, 20 years, were developed by a research team at Penn with advice from rail industry experts at international engineering and planning firms. These estimates assume that innovative permitting, procurement, construction supervision, and labor practices are used, so that unit costs will total only three times those of comparable European and Asian railroad projects. Recent Northeast Corridor and California High-Speed Rail Authority projects had costs that were five times as high as comparable European and Asian rail projects because they did not use these innovative practices.

Delivering the whole NAR program on time and at reduced cost requires the following:

- A North Atlantic Rail Corporation to manage the project from planning and design and through construction.
- Up-front financial commitments for the whole project to avoid starting and stopping, which adds significant costs.

An Economic and Climate Justice Rationale for NAR (Bergstrom 2020)

Every node of NAR is amplified by connection to the larger network and has its agglomeration advantages, its critical mass, and its economies of scale. This is not just a physical rail network; it is a set of rail-enabled economic relationships, across the whole megaregional geography rather than just one of its metros, that can serve as a platform for economic transformation and for the creation of a just and green economy. The networked megaregion will make personal networks larger and more dynamic, shaped by the churn of workers and firms across the whole economic geography.

A firm in Hartford would be an hour from either New York City or Boston, with access to all the talent in those cities and the cities between them. A Hartford resident would be within a one-hour commute of all the jobs in the megaregion. NAR would shrink the megaregion such that it takes the same time to travel by train across the corridor as it now takes to cross the Hartford metro by car.

NAR will enable a rebalancing of the megaregion's mobility system, shifting passenger movements to rail, thereby creating capacity on the highway system for freight and other uses, such as tradespeople who cannot practically use rail. It will rebalance the economic relationships between the two global cities and the smaller cities between them. NAR would distribute jobs and housing more evenly across the whole megaregion. New York City and Boston have become overconcentrated, too big, too costly, and too congested to be sustainable on their own.

The small cities of New England and downstate New York could evolve into the next version of a city, as largely self-built, maker communities that are engines of innovation and upward mobility. For example, many of the small cities between New York City and Boston have large areas of surface parking lots within walking distance of their rail stations. These areas could serve as the canvas for a creative habitat made by self-builders and small developers combined with young talent and start-ups, immigrants, and existing, mostly nonwhite neighborhood residents. This is an opportunity for local wealth creation and for closing the wealth gap between whites and nonwhites.

These self-built creative habitats could also be the location of micromanufacturing. Additive manufacturing processes have the potential to eliminate economies of scale for certain kinds of products, meaning that manufacturing could return to urban neighborhoods, where it was located for most of history. How can some of the work in live-work developments be about making things in small manufacturing shops rather than just studios or lofts? Could this expand the middle rungs of the job ladder–the middle-wage jobs, now mostly public servants like police and firemen and teachers?

The COVID-19 quarantine revealed that the current economy is out of balance: at one end, mostly low-paid essential jobs in health care and food production and distribution at a workplace; at the other end, higher-paying nonessential jobs that can often be done from home. Typically, a higher-paying job requires a college degree, whether or not the college degree is necessary to do the work.

Middle-wage jobs and maker communities that are engines of innovation and upward mobility could come from breakthrough ideas that exploit the opportunities in crises. As a region and as a nation, we now face five simultaneous crises: (1) the pandemic; (2) a deep economic recession; (3) a demand to end racial and economic injustice; (4) the climate emergency; and (5) attacks on fundamental democratic institutions and norms from within and abroad.

Reducing our carbon footprint while reducing income inequality relies on relocalizing and shortening the chains of supply and distribution and on building local wealth and redistributing it in a circular rather than extractive business model. Relocalization logically happens in the megaregion rather than the state or the city or the metro, because megaregions have population and land to operate as largely self-contained ecological and economic systems, with long job ladders and local wealth creation. Megaregions have sufficient sources of local supply, large enough local demand, a local critical mass of firms and talent, and vast local reservoirs of ideas and capital. NAR will create the platform for this economic transformation in the New England–downstate New York area.

- Expedited permitting, possibly using the dashboard process initiated by the Obama administration, for the project's environmental review. Simultaneous agency reviews and stakeholder engagement would identify environmental and community impacts.
- Innovative procurement, such as design-build, best-value procurement, and breaking the project into bite-size components. Furthermore, ensure that designs are standardized for all key components to reduce costs.
- Project labor agreements that eliminate traditional practices and work rules that result in delays, inefficiencies, and redundant work forces and ensure availability of the skilled workforce needed to build the project.

A precedent for the procedures proposed here is New York's Governor Mario Cuomo Bridge (originally called the Tappan Zee Bridge). This project was managed with accelerated permitting conducted by the Federal Highway Administration, and design-build, best-value procurement being conducted by an independent state authority, the New York State Thruway Authority. From Governor Andrew Cuomo's decision to proceed with the project to a construction start took 15 months, and the whole project was completed within seven years for $3.98 billion, a fraction of the originally projected cost and a fraction of the time required under traditional permitting, procurement, and project delivery procedures (New York State Thruway 2021).

CLIMATE CHANGE ADAPTATION AND MITIGATION

The plan for the Northeast, in addition to its transportation vision of NAR, aggressively pursues both adaptation strategies to anticipate climate change impacts and mitigation strategies to reduce the megaregion's carbon footprint. A projected six feet or more of sea level rise by 2100 will threaten coastal cities from Norfolk, Virginia, to Portland, Maine. Severe rainfall events will cause urban and riverine flooding in communities across the Northeast. Extreme droughts will test the limits of urban water supply systems. Urban heat islands will threaten the health of millions of poor, minority, and elderly residents. According to Shaw, Lustgarten, and Goldsmith (2020), areas of the United States will experience "compounding calamities," in which "a number of issues stack on top of one another." Most hurricanes, for example, produce storm surges and urban flooding in cities along the coast and riverine flooding caused by excessive rainfall in inland rural areas.

The Northeast's cities and landscapes are already experiencing the impacts of climate change:

- Tornadoes and other severe storms have struck with increased frequency and ferocity in New England and other northeastern areas in recent years in places that have never experienced storms of this kind. Superstorm Sandy struck communities from Virginia to New England in 2009, producing the lowest atmospheric pressure ever recorded in the North Atlantic and a 14-foot storm surge in New York Harbor.
- In 2007, an extreme rainstorm dropped four inches of rain on New York City in less than two hours, flooding most of the city's subway system.
- Since 2010, northeastern cities and states have experienced 9 of their 10 hottest years. In Philadelphia, for example, in the last half of the 20th century, the city averaged three days a year when the temperature was above 95 degrees. The city now forecasts that Philadelphia could exceed this between 17 and 52 days a year, depending on the degree to which the world limits greenhouse gas emissions.
- In 2014, Boston experienced the greatest amount of snowfall (108 inches) in its history, and three years later it experienced four nor'easters in a row, causing extensive coastal and urban flooding.
- In 2021, Hurricane Ida caused extensive urban and riverine flooding across the Northeast, causing dozens of fatalities and major property damage.
- Invasive insects, such as the southern pine beetle, and other pests are spreading north with climate change, threatening the survival of the Northeast's forest ecology.

Climate and Energy

The Regional Greenhouse Gas Initiative (RGGI), the cap-and-trade program mentioned previously, has already resulted in significant reductions in power plant carbon emissions across the Northeast. The 10 RGGI states have joined with three other northeastern states and Washington, DC, in a parallel initiative—the Transportation and Climate Initiative (TCI)—to reduce tailpipe emissions from automobiles and trucks (Transportation and Climate Initiative 2021).

In much the same way that RGGI provides states with resources to incentivize installing insulation, using alternative energy, and other steps to reduce demand for carbon fuels, TCI incentivizes the purchase of electric vehicles, investment in transit systems, and other measures to reduce carbon production from the transportation sector. These outcomes would be achieved through a wholesale tax on vehicle fuels, adopted by the District of Columbia and the 13 participating states (Connecticut, Delaware, Maine, Maryland, Massachusetts, New Hampshire, New Jersey, New York, North Carolina, Pennsylvania, Rhode Island, Vermont, and Virginia). Like RGGI, TCI is implemented through collaborative action among participating states, not a congressionally authorized interstate compact.

With both RGGI and TCI in place, the Northeast will have many of the tools to create a postcarbon energy system and economy—regardless of policies in the rest of the country. Northeastern governors can also take bold action to electrify vehicle fleets—for example, by following California's lead to prohibit sales of petroleum-powered cars after 2035. The Northeast has an abundance of non- and low-carbon resources on which to build its alternative energy future:

- *Offshore wind.* In 2017, Rhode Island opened the Block Island Wind Farm, the nation's first offshore wind facility, producing 30 megawatts from five turbines. It was built by the Danish wind power company Ørsted, which has plans for other wind farms off the Massachusetts, Rhode Island, New York, New Jersey, and Virginia coasts (Ørsted 2021).
- *Hydropower.* The megaregion has an abundance of hydropower generation and the potential for more. In addition, Hydro-Québec has been selling excess power to New England and New York since 1996. Its proposed 1,200-megawatt Central Maine Power line will dramatically expand its ability to distribute power in the Northeast (Hydro-Québec 2021).
- *Solar.* More than a quarter of a million homeowners in the Northeast—12 percent of the U.S. total—have installed solar power systems, incentivized in part by RGGI-funded subsidies and state electric utility regulations (Solar Energy Industries Association 2021). Although the region is not the sunniest place in the nation, it has potential for considerably more solar power.
- *Tidal, or lunar, power.* The Northeast has enormous amounts of energy from tidal flows and wave action. Coastal New York and the New England states have some of the highest tidal ranges and strongest tidal currents in the United States. Tidal energy is powered by the sun and moon's gravity acting on the earth and has the advantage over solar energy in that predictions for peak lunar power

potential are for thousands of years, whereas solar power potential cannot be accurately predicted for even a week in the future. In the 1930s, President Franklin D. Roosevelt proposed building the world's largest tidal power project in the Passamaquoddy region of Maine and New Brunswick, where the Bay of Fundy tidal range is more than 20 feet. With the advent of World War II, the plans were dropped. In 1984, Nova Scotia opened North America's largest tidal power project, the 20-megawatt Annapolis Royal tidal turbine plant. Plans are now underway for floating tidal turbines in the Bay of Fundy (Davie 2019). But discussing lunar power can be tricky. Coauthor Bob Yaro was on an alternative energy panel with U.S. senator Bob Menendez. When Yaro mentioned the potential of lunar power, Menendez grimaced and moved away. An experimental tidal power plant has operated in New York's East River for several years, and Verdant Power recently installed three of its newest type of turbines at the Roosevelt Island Tidal Energy site (Verdant Power 2021).

- *Biomass.* Despite centuries of urbanization, the Northeast remains one of the most heavily forested regions of the country. The land area of all but three states in the megaregion (Delaware, Maryland, and New Jersey) is more than 50 percent forested, and nearly 90 percent of the northern New England states is covered with forests. For this reason, perhaps the oldest energy source in the Northeast is its abundant supply of firewood. Across the Northeast, wood remains the fastest-growing heating fuel. The 2010 census reported that households heating with wood increased by 122 percent over the previous decade in Connecticut and by 96 percent in Maine and Rhode Island (Alliance for Green Heat 2011).

Preserving Ecosystems

The plan for the Northeast proposes a network of climate preserves. The New Jersey Pinelands National Reserve was the first of its kind and is a model for federal, state, and local cooperation and governance. Established by Congress in 1978, the reserve encompasses 1.1 million acres in southern New Jersey. The reserve is home to 500,000 people and 22 percent of the state's land area. It includes parts of seven counties and all or part of 56 municipalities. This vast oak-pine forest, called a pine barrens, is characterized by small- to medium-sized pines and is underlain by the huge Kirkwood-Cohansey Aquifer System. In addition to being an important source of water for Pinelands residents, the aquifer provides fresh water to the Delaware River. The congressionally mandated reserve led to New Jersey enacting the Pinelands Protection Act and the establishment of the Pinelands Commission in 1979. The commission's board is composed of federal, state, and local members. They are guided by the Pinelands Comprehensive Management Plan, adopted by the commission in 1980 and approved by the New Jersey governor and the U.S. secretary of the interior the following year. The plan established both preservation and protection areas.

The plan is based largely on a McHargian inventory and analysis of the Pinelands' ecology and human history. The plan determined suitability for various land uses by balancing conservation and development. Since its inception, the commission has done an admirable job protecting the groundwater, agricultural, plant, animal, and historical resources of the region.

The New Jersey Pinelands National Reserve provides an example for a national climate reserve system that will also preserve the Northeast megaregion's ecosystem services, including drainage basins, estuaries, river valleys, mountain ranges, and coastlines. Such a network is essential for the United States to capture vast amounts of carbon to achieve national and global climate goals.

It is possible to envision several kinds of climate reserves needed to protect key resource systems:

- *Water supply reserves*—areas with public water supplies, including surface and groundwater sheds.
- *Ecological reserves*—areas containing rare or endangered plant or animal communities or species habitats, such as those threatened by climate change.
- *Coastal reserves*—flood-prone waterfront areas adjoining wetlands and uplands, including barrier beaches and islands that are already largely natural or that may become depopulated as a result of retreat strategies.
- *Riverine and wetland reserves*—areas that flood frequently or that are expected to become flood prone because of severe rainfall in the future or headwater areas that can retain floodwater and prevent downstream flooding.
- *Ridgeline reserves*—ridgelines and mountain ranges with rare or endangered ecosystems or significant recreational or scenic resources.
- *Forest reserves*—areas heavily forested or suitable for reforestation to protect unique plant communities or that are or could become major carbon sinks.
- *Agricultural reserves*—highly productive farmland close to population centers for assured supplies of close-to-home food in decades to come.
- *Geneways*—contiguous belts of undeveloped land for species retreat as climate change progresses.

To identify the areas needed for protection, we need to begin with climate: What is it now, and what will the temperatures and precipitation be in the future? We then need to understand the regional geologies and geomorphologies to understand what areas will be underwater or under threat of ocean surges in the future. A comprehension of climate and geology leads to an awareness of groundwater and surface water systems. These abiotic processes interact with living organisms to form soils. Some soils are much better than others for producing food and must be protected for food security. Soils and microclimates combine with terrain to create habitat for plants and animals. We then need to understand how people have historically used these biophysical processes to create their settlements.

In the Northeast megaregion, coasts and fall lines (divisions between the Piedmont and coastal plain) have been especially valuable for human settlements from the times when Indigenous people dominated to the present. For instance, coasts and fall lines were important fishing resources for Native Americans. With European colonization, settlements along the coasts where rivers drained into the ocean facilitated trade. The rivers provided fresh water. The fall lines became ideal for manufacturing, which gave birth to the Industrial Revolution in North America. With global warming, these low-lying areas are under increasing threat from rising tides and storm surges. In addition, freshwater supplies are endangered as salt fronts move upstream. As a result, climate reserves are necessary to protect people from storms and to ensure drinking water for future generations.

In addition to protecting areas prone to storm surges and flooding, the prime agricultural land and forests need to be protected and expanded. Farms are essential for food security. Climate change adds urgency to protecting areas with prime soils and promoting the best conservation practices to limit erosion. As in the New Jersey Pinelands, other Northeast forests are vulnerable to wildfires. This is exacerbated by both climate change and ill-conceived exurban housing. Wildfires may be more accurately called climate fires. Several environmental organizations have called for planting more trees both in forests and in cities. Although planting trees in itself will not fix climate change, it has many ancillary social and environmental benefits, such as ameliorating urban heat islands. In addition, protecting existing forests does help mitigate climate change.

BirdLife International, the Wildlife Conservation Society, and the World Wildlife Fund have taken on this challenge in the Trillion Tree Initiative. They promote a three-pronged approach: ending deforestation, improving protection, and advancing restoration. This initiative complements efforts to restore an urban forest canopy in the Northeast's cities to reduce urban heat islands and improve urban air quality, livability, and public health.

One of the most ambitious land conservation initiatives now underway in the Northeast is the Wildlands and Woodlands Project, which proposes protecting 70 percent of the landscape of the six-state New England region as forest and farmland. A key objective of this program, which is being sponsored by the Harvard University Forest and a Connecticut-based philanthropy, the Highstead Foundation, is to promote the preservation and establishment of mature forests as carbon sinks.

Wildlands and Woodlands aims to create a network of both public and private lands, funded by voluntary and public actions. Portions of these lands could be incorporated into the national climate reserve system. Management of these lands and public access would create jobs, much as the Depression-era Civilian Conservation Corps created work for unemployed men in the 1930s.

Layered Defense Against Storm Surges and Sea Level Rise

All five of the Northeast megaregion's major population centers are on the coast and subject to storm surges and sea level rise. Boston, New York, Philadelphia, and Baltimore began as colonial seaports and trading centers. The location of Washington, DC, was the conscious decision by our first president to place the new national capital on the Potomac River. These cities expanded with extensive landfills in the 18th, 19th, and early 20th centuries, and most—from Boston's Seaport to Washington's Anacostia River—are already experiencing increasingly frequent flooding. Most of these places were built on unconsolidated fill, which means that, during flood events, water percolates up through the soil to the surface even before rising floodwaters inundate these areas. So, simply building onshore levees may not protect them from flooding.

Hundreds of smaller cities and towns and numerous summer resorts on barrier beaches and islands also sit on the Northeast coast. Altogether, several million northeastern residents live and work in low-lying places that have been or will soon be classified as coastal flood zones. Both the National Academy of Sciences and MIT researchers predict that the New York region will face more frequent and severe hurricanes in the years to come (Fountain 2020). Rather than poorly defined resilience strategies, the more fine-grained 5R toolbox (resilience, resistance, restoration, retention, and retreat), described in chapter 5, offers real solutions. New York's experience following Superstorm Sandy in 2012 suggests how northeastern metropolitan centers can address the dual concerns of storm surges and sea level rise.

Sandy Sea Gate System

Hurricane Sandy caused 96 deaths, more than $79 billion in direct damages, and many months of disruption to the region's infrastructure and economy (figure 8.6). Immediately following Sandy's devastation of the New York–New Jersey region in October 2012, the New York–New Jersey–Long Island Storm Surge Working Group (SSWG), a coalition of more than 30 prominent government and civic leaders, environmental and social scientists, engineers, architects, and planners was convened by the SUNY Stony Brook oceanographer Malcolm Bowman. The SSWG has proposed a $60 billion layered defense system to protect the New York–New Jersey metro region from recurrence of the devastating flooding that accompanied Sandy:

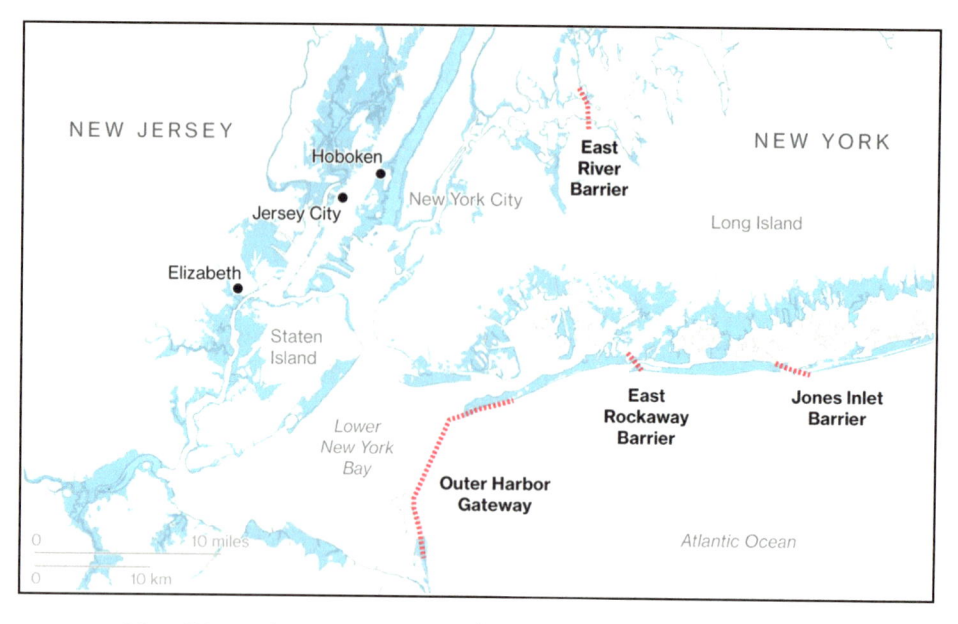

FIGURE 8.6 Map of New York City region flooding (light blue) after Hurricane Sandy (dotted red lines show proposed future storm barriers). *Source: Federal Emergency Management Agency, National Institute for Coastal and Harbor Infrastructure.*

- *Two offshore movable sea gates.* The first of these, the Outer Harbor sea gate, would extend from Sandy Hook, New Jersey, to Breezy Point, New York, a five-mile stretch of mostly shallow water (except for navigation channels). Larger movable gates, like those protecting shipping channels in Rotterdam and Saint Petersburg, would protect the entrance to the Ambrose Channel shipping lanes. Two existing smaller channels close to the two shores maintained for fishing vessels and other small craft would also have movable gates. All gates would be closed only before forecasted major storm surges or at low tide and to allow stormwater and sewage discharges to function properly without backup during storm surge events, remaining open the rest of the time to minimize disruption of tidal and sediment flows, and fish and mammal migration and to preserve the ecological health of the Hudson and other rivers. When closed, water levels outside the barriers would increase by only a few inches. The second, a mile-long East River sea gate, near the Throgs Neck Bridge, would block storm surges from Long Island Sound from entering the harbor. Additional short movable sea gates across the Rockaway Peninsula, Jones Beach and Fire Islands, and other eastern inlets on the south shore of Long Island would prevent flooding of back bays and densely populated waterfront communities.
- *Fortified dunes.* Built with stone or concrete cores along the length of the Sandy Hook and Rockaway Peninsula and along the barrier beaches on the south coast

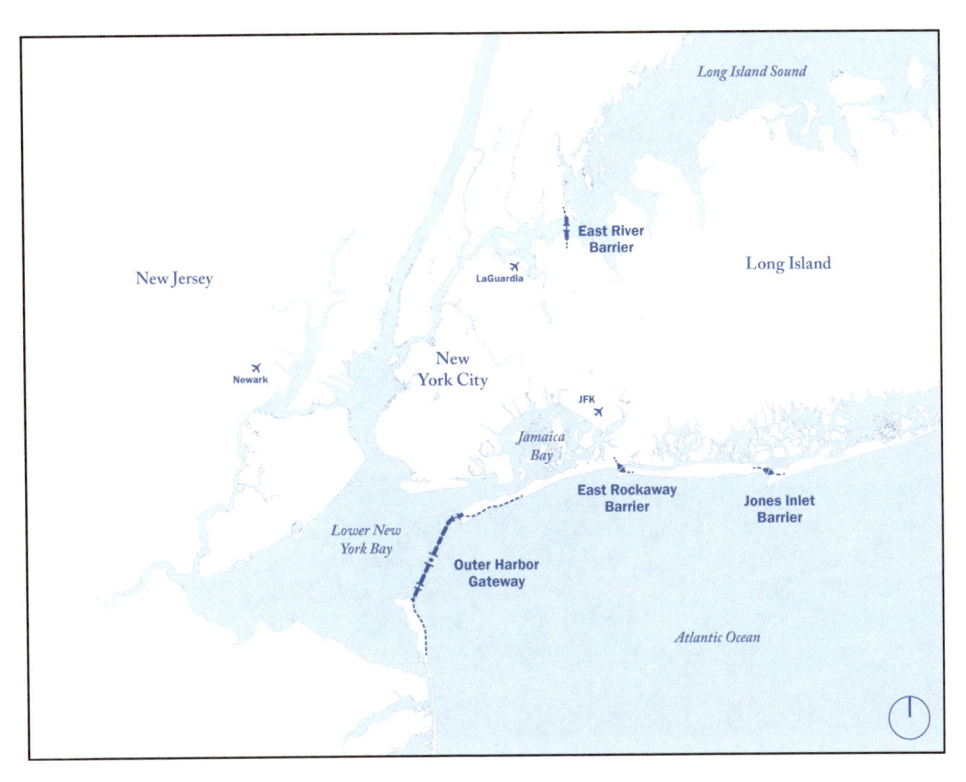

FIGURE 8.7 Sandy Sea Gate system map. *Source: Justinesk/CC BY-SA 4.0/Wikimedia.*

of Long Island, these dunes would be stabilized with dune grasses; they would appear and function as natural dunes but would possess immense strength. These hidden fortifications would better protect densely populated communities, maintain coastal inlets and barrier islands, and minimize overtopping of storm surges into the interior.

- *Low onshore dikes and seawalls.* Low-lying communities and infrastructure would be protected from sea level rise (but not from storm surge itself) and more frequent but less severe coastal storms and spring tides by dikes and seawalls.
- *A network of restored natural systems.* Restored and created wetlands, oyster beds, and dunes would protect coastal communities from wave action and improve estuarine quality.

The SSWG's ultimate goal is to seek special federal legislation similar to that used to build New Orleans's flood barrier system, which would direct the U.S. Army Corps of Engineers to expedite the design and construction of the Sandy Sea Gate system (figures 8.7 and 8.8). With support from the region's congressional delegation, it may

A STRATEGIC PLAN FOR THE NORTHEAST MEGAREGION | 239

FIGURE 8.8 Storm surge barrier near Massdijk, Netherlands, showing design similar to that proposed for the Outer Harbor Sea Gate in New York. *Source: Michiel Verbeek/CC BY-SA 3.0/Wikimedia.*

also be possible to include funding for this effort in President Biden's proposed multitrillion-dollar national climate and infrastructure proposal.

Layered Defense for Other Northeastern Metropolitan Regions

Similar systems of layered defense could be used in Boston, Philadelphia, Baltimore, and Washington, DC, to protect their dense urban centers. Discussions are underway in Boston about the merits of a regional sea gate system like New York's proposed Sandy Sea Gate. Like New York, the City of Boston, with support from researchers at UMass Boston, has chosen a go-it-alone approach that will protect its downtown, the Seaport district, and other vulnerable urban core communities from storm surges and sea level rise. In response, a coalition representing 14 other communities fronting Boston Harbor is being mobilized by former state senator Bill Golden (who initiated cleaning up Boston Harbor in the 1980s) to advocate for a regional sea gate system. Three smaller New England cities already have barrier systems in place (see chapter 5). All were constructed following several devastating storms between 1938 and 1954 and have protected these cities from storm surges for more than half a century.

In outlying, low-density coastal communities, a combination of onshore levees, constructed dunes, and elevated streets and structures could give protection before sea level rise requires relocation of residents and infrastructure. And in very low-density barrier beach, island, and back bay communities, it may make sense to proceed now with the relocation of vulnerable residents and properties.

As described in chapter 5, Bob Yaro ran an ambitious program to acquire storm-damaged properties in the immediate aftermath of the February 1978 nor'easter. Within months after stormwaters receded, however, political support for widespread buyouts of barrier beach homes also dissipated. This has implications for managing sea level rise and the more severe storms and storm surges in decades to come.

CONCLUSION

Preparing the Northeast megaregion for the coming decades will not be easy. Since the 1970s, Americans have been led to believe, as Ronald Reagan famously said in 1981, "Government is not the solution to our problem, government is the problem." For the most part, Americans are unwilling to raise taxes, tolls, fares, or user fees to pay for essential public infrastructure investments. Further, Americans have also lost confidence in their ability to build large-scale infrastructure projects or to manage or intervene in large natural systems. In part, this is because current environmental and other permitting requirements take years to complete, and conventional design-bid-build procurement procedures and traditional labor practices add years and billions to the time and cost of delivering major projects.

President Biden's American Jobs Plan proposed investing $2.2 trillion in infrastructure and climate initiatives, but the amount was reduced to $1.2 trillion in the bipartisan Infrastructure and Jobs Act enacted by Congress and signed into law by President Biden in November 2021. Of this amount, only $550 billion represented new spending. Much more will be needed to rebuild all the Northeast's existing infrastructure and to build the systems needed for the climate, mobility, racial justice, and other challenges the megaregion will face in coming decades. The success of the projects and initiatives outlined in this chapter hinge on adopting innovative permitting, procurement, labor practices, and project delivery techniques that can cut costs and completion times. New York's new Governor Mario Cuomo Bridge was built in record time and below original estimated costs by using these strategies. It can be done if we find the political will. Many of these initiatives also depend on northeastern states collaborating in new ways across political boundaries. Governors collaborated and slowed the COVID-19 virus's progress and then worked together on plans to reopen the economy. This suggests that the states can find common ground on important issues.

9

HIGH-SPEED AND HIGH-PERFORMANCE RAIL

I've logged more than 2,100,000 miles on Amtrak.
—JOE BIDEN

HIGH-SPEED RAIL (HSR) AND HIGH-PERFORMANCE RAIL (HPR) can play a critical role in unlocking the economic potential of U.S. megaregions. HSR systems are designed to be fast, frequent, and affordable. The fastest of these trains cruise at 220 miles per hour on dedicated tracks. This chapter explores the potential of these networks in advancing mobility, social equity, public health, safety, and climate resilience in U.S. megaregions—home to more than 80 percent of the nation's residents. It discusses the merits of both types of rail systems and calls for the creation of a federal agency for interstate passenger rail development. The agency would plan and deliver a system of HSR and HPR, in partnership with the states and multistate development authorities organized at the megaregion scale. The chapter considers the ways that this new rail network will contribute to the travel, work, and business location patterns emerging in the post-COVID-19 pandemic era.

WHY NOW?

Although construction of HSR in the United States was first proposed almost six decades ago, until now this has never been a high priority on the nation's to-do list. Now, with Joe Biden's election, for the first time in living memory, the United States has a president who is making construction of a national HSR network a national imperative. In particular, Biden has identified HSR for Amtrak's Northeast Corridor as one of his personal priorities. Biden has spent much of his life commuting on intercity trains and has firsthand knowledge of both the merits and the shortcomings of the existing U.S. rail network. When our Weitzman studio of Penn graduate students went to the White House in 2010 to present their plan for Northeast HSR to then–Vice President Biden, he told the Penn team, "I've been waiting 40 years for this proposal." The Infrastructure and Jobs Act, adopted by Congress in 2021, includes $66 billion for passenger rail investments, but most of these funds will be reserved for state of good repair in the Northeast Corridor and conventional rail projects elsewhere in the country. However, the funds can and should be used to design the next generation of HSR and HPR projects in the nation's megaregions. So now is the time to act to build HSR systems in the Northeast and in megaregions across the country.

HSR alone, however, will not meet the mobility and economic development needs of all U.S. megaregions. Instead, many will require development of hybrid passenger rail systems, which combine elements of HPR and HSR operations. An example of these networks is described in chapter 8, with its discussion of the proposed North Atlantic Rail network serving the New England–downstate New York portion of the Northeast megaregion.

DEFINING HSR AND HPR NETWORKS

In the European Union, HSR trains have operating speeds of 155 mph or more on new, dedicated lines or 125 mph on upgraded rail lines (ITF 2014). Only one rail route in the United States, the Northeast rail corridor, approaches this level of service, but the trains achieve these speeds only on short segments of the 453-mile-long corridor and average only 84 mph between Boston and Washington, DC. In China, Japan, France, and other countries, new HSR services routinely achieve 200 mph or higher, which should become the standard for HSR routes in the United States. In most U.S. megaregions, which currently have little or no passenger rail service, the goal should be to create hybrid networks that incorporate both HSR and HPR services.

One definition of HPR, such as that by advocates for the North Atlantic Rail network (see chapter 8), is that they are networks with the following attributes:

- Fast, with speeds of 80–110 mph, which can cut travel times between major cities by 50 percent or more.
- Frequent, with headways (distance between trains) ranging from 15–30 minutes during peak travel periods to hourly.
- Reliable, with high levels (over 95 percent) of on-time performance.
- Affordable, with fare levels for all income groups, ranging from moderately priced coach seats to high-priced business-class seats and cross subsidization.
- Fully integrated with other rail, transit, and bus services to create megaregion-scale networks.

- Safe, with high levels of passenger safety compared with highway travel; almost no fatal accidents have occurred on international HSR routes since the first of these services opened more than half a century ago.

In addition to these attributes, a combined national HSR and HPR network would provide further benefits: Trips between cities 200–600 miles apart could be diverted from overcrowded airports and highways to rail. Major urban centers would be decongested, and compact urban development could occur in smaller cities. National unity would be promoted by strengthening mobility, economic, and political connections among regions. Rail systems promote efficient land use and development in and around compact urban centers and train stations. Rail uses one-quarter of the amount of energy per passenger mile than do airplanes and private automobiles. Japan's Shinkansen trains use one-sixth as much energy per passenger miles as automobiles and one-quarter as much as airplanes (Todorovich and Hagler 2011). HSR and HPR can be powered with renewable sources, reducing carbon production and promoting climate resiliency. France's HSR trains, for example, are powered entirely by nuclear power. Finally, HSR and HPR provide a broad range of economic benefits, as described later.

HSR'S ESSENTIAL ROLE

HSR is the mode of choice in megaregional mobility systems around the world because these regions are too large for their cities to be easily accessed by automobile and too small for cities to be efficiently accessed by air. Indeed, HSR is uniquely suited to U.S. megaregions, which range from 300 to 600 miles across, for achieving agglomeration benefits among the multiple metropolitan areas that are the building blocks of megaregional economies.

HPR and HSR lines could transform the economic geography of megaregions and all their component communities, leading to economic revitalization of hundreds of small and midsize cities that could use their new accessibility to gain a critical mass of jobs and talent equal to that of major metropolitan centers. These rail networks could also address the current overconcentration of jobs and residents and the excessively high rents in major urban centers, especially as workers and employers in the post-COVID era choose to live and work in smaller cities and suburbs but want access to larger metropolitan labor markets. Knowledge workers and others could expand their networks of productive contacts exponentially across more than one metropolitan area, adding to the productivity of everyone in the region.

These outcomes can be enabled by building HSR corridors in most U.S. megaregions that connect cities of different sizes, with service plans for multiple markets. Nonstop connections between major urban centers would be supplemented by more frequent intercity rail services with stopping patterns that serve smaller centers along the way.

DEVELOPMENT OF HSR AROUND THE WORLD

The world's first HSR route was Japan's Tokyo–Osaka Shinkansen line, which opened in 1964 with 130 mph service, later increased to 177 mph. Japan's HSR network now serves every major city in the country, which has integrated housing and labor markets across much of Japan.

Japan's lead was followed by Italy's Milan–Rome route in 1977. Then France launched an HSR route connecting Paris to Lyon in 1981. Germany opened a route in 1991 between Hamburg and Munich via Frankfurt. In 1992, Spain connected Madrid with Seville and then with most major cities in Spain, furthering national unity goals. Since then, HSR routes have extended to more than 20 European nations, and plans are underway to extend these services into the Baltic countries and elsewhere in Eastern Europe. With very few exceptions, these systems have been financed by national governments, often with support from the EU.

In Asia, South Korea and Taiwan followed Japan's lead in building national HSR networks, and then China initiated the world's most ambitious HSR building boom, extending over 23,000 miles by 2020, at an estimated cost of $300 billion. This system is expected to grow to 24,000 miles by 2025 (Nunno 2018).

As of 2021, nearly every highly industrialized country—the United States not among them—has built HSR routes. More than 27 countries in Europe, Asia, and North Africa, including Turkey, Saudi Arabia, Morocco, and Kazakhstan, already have HSR routes; other developed and developing countries are building or planning HSR routes, including Canada, Australia, India, Indonesia, Malaysia, Vietnam, Singapore, Russia, South Africa, and Brazil.

A precedent for HSR in the United States is High Speed 1 in the United Kingdom (figure 9.1). Half the capacity of this HSR route is devoted to high-speed Eurostar intercity trains linking Paris, Brussels, and Amsterdam with London. Javelin high-speed commuter trains use the other half of High Speed 1 capacity. Javelin trains originate in nine small and midsize cities in Kent on Victorian rail lines (figure 9.2). Many of these cities saw decades of economic and population decline because of poor rail connections to London but have been transformed by their 140 mph Javelin service to London Paddington station, which opened in 2009.

ECONOMIC AND OTHER BENEFITS OF HSR

Trillions of dollars have been invested in HSR by nations around the world. Although their capital cost is huge, so are their economic, social, climate, and political returns. Economic benefits for cities and megaregions include higher wages and productivity, long-term job growth, deeper labor markets, expanded tourism and visitor spending, direct job creation both during and following construction, higher wages and productivity as

HSR in Europe

European countries have a long history and extensive networks of rail-based transportation systems. The first generation of HSR lines in Europe, built in the 1980s and 1990s, aimed at increasing service capacity and decreasing journey times on intercity routes within country borders. SNCF, the national French railway, operated Train à Très Grande Vitesse between Paris and Lyon beginning in 1981 at a maximum speed of 162 mph, marking the birth of Europe's second national HSR network. In subsequent decades, French lines and services expanded, connecting Paris with major cities across France, including Marseille, Lille, Bordeaux, Strasbourg, Rennes, and Montpellier, and with neighboring countries (Belgium, Luxembourg, Germany, Switzerland, Italy, Spain, and the Netherlands). Spain's HSR service, Alta Velocidad Española, started in 1992, later than the French service, but it

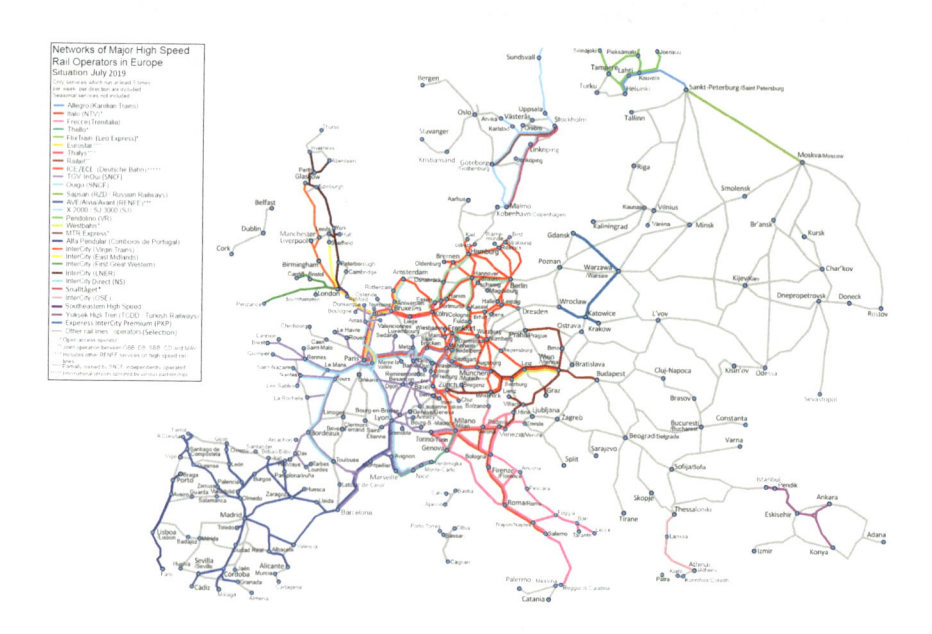

High-speed rail networks built or in planning in Europe. *Source: Bernese Media/ CC BY-SA 3.0/Wikimedia.*

operated at the higher speed of 193 mph. Spain's HSR expanded much faster than in other European countries. By 2017, Spain operated 10 HSR lines with more than 2,000 miles of track (Statista 2019).

As of 2018, nine major European countries (including the United Kingdom) operate HSR services (155 mph or faster) in a total network of 5,564 miles (Statista 2019). European HSR presents two distinguishing features. One is the high degree of integration with existing conventional rail services. France and Germany use existing rail lines in addition to dedicated HSR lines. The other feature is the integration of HSR networks across Europe. In the early 1990s, the European Commission adopted the Trans-European Transport Network (TEN-T), a plan to coordinate and invest in major transport infrastructure improvements to primary roads, railways, inland waterways, and ports (air, sea, and inland). The Trans-European High-Speed Rail Network is an essential element of TEN-T. EU directives defined the HSR network and provided EU funding to support the construction of most cross-border railway lines.

The evidence is ample on HSR services enhancing people's mobility across Europe. The broader economic and environmental impacts, however, are context specific. Empirical studies have shown a general consensus on HSR investment effects. HSR's effects on elevating economic productivity, inducing consumption (e.g., for tourism), and shaping urban and regional form show a large variability across studies (Blanquart and Koning 2017). A 2018 study estimates that, upon the completion of core projects between 2017 and 2030, TEN-T (including HSR and all other transport projects) would employ 800,000 workers, or 7.5 million person-years of jobs. The core projects would add to GDP growth by 1.6 percent in the EU and to carbon dioxide emission reduction by 26 million tons (Schade et al. 2018).

HSR in Japan and South Korea

Japan is known for being the birth country of modern HSR. Its first HSR line (bullet trains, or *shinkansen* in Japanese) began services in 1964, connecting Tokyo and Osaka over 320 miles on dedicated rail tracks. Currently, nine HSR lines with 1,655 miles in total track length serve 22 major cities, stretching across Japan's three main islands. An additional 595 miles of HSR tracks are under onstruction or planned. Traveling up to 177 mph, Shinkansen has maintained a remarkable safety record. In over 50 years of service, Shinkansen has had no passenger fatalities due to operational accidents.

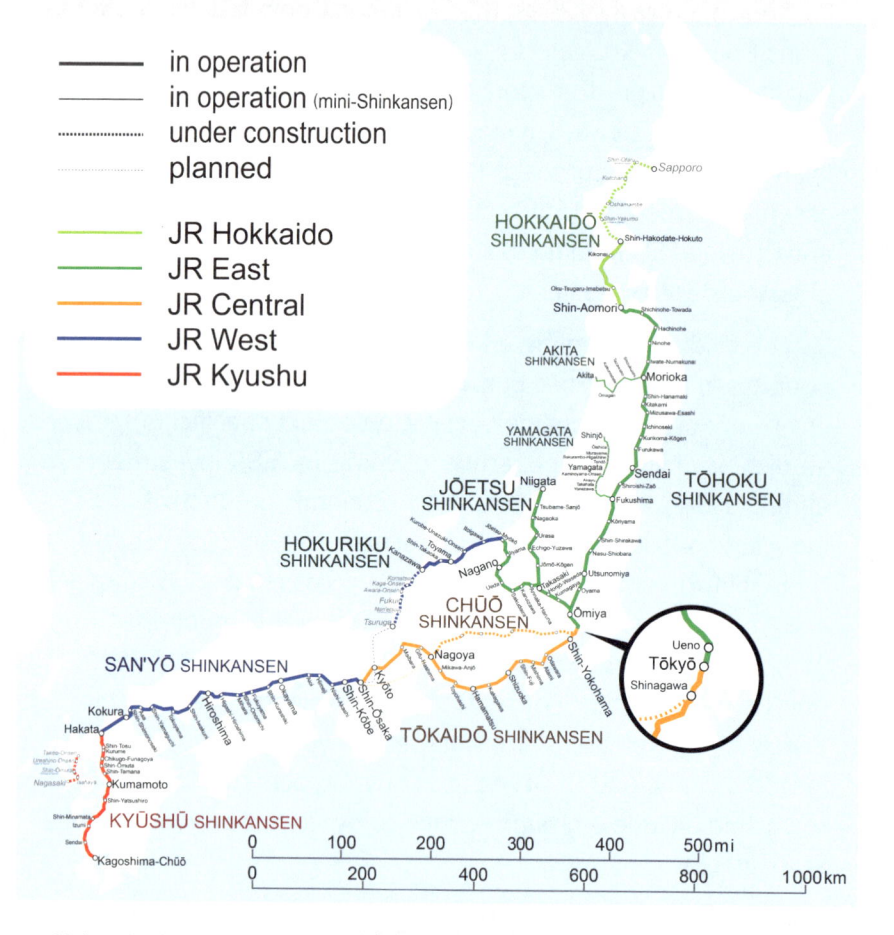

Network of Japan's high-speed (Shinkansen) rail lines.
Source: Hisagi/CC BY-SA 4.0/Wikimedia.

Network of high-speed rail lines in South Korea. *Source: Chugun/CC BY-SA 4.0/ Wikimedia.*

South Korea's first HSR service, Korea Train eXpress (KTX), started in 2004, connects the country's two largest metro areas, Seoul and Busan, and the cities between them. The 230-mile Seoul–Busan corridor serves more than two-thirds of South Korea's total population. Before 2004, the Gyeongbu Expressway and Korail's Gyeongbu Line provided roadway and conventional rail links for people and business along the corridor but suffered from severe congestion, prompting the national government to explore new forms of transportation. A second Seoul–Busan railway was proposed as early as 1972. The HSR version of the Seoul–Busan Gyeongbu Line came in the mid-1980s. Yet, construction of the HSR line did not start until 1992 and was further delayed because of the Asian financial crisis. Twelve years later, the Seoul–Busan Gyeongbu Line began its passenger services at an operating speed of 180 mph. As of 2020, South Korea operates multiple HSR lines over a network of 1,200 miles (at 100 mph or higher).

HSR services in Japan and South Korea share several characteristics. First, they attain high ridership. Shinkansen carries more than 420,000 passengers on a typical weekday. KTX had 586 million passenger trips between 2004 and 2016 in a country of just over 50 million people. Reliable and convenient services offered by Japan and South Korea HSR operators have made HSR competitive relative to air and cars. Second, HSR's role in urban and regional expansion is evident in the cities they serve. Empirical research from Japan shows that Shinkansen has affected location decisions of real estate, commerce and services, and public administration firms (Hayashi et al. 2017). Many HSR station areas have become attractive nodes that feature convenient retail, office, and business services enjoyed by people who live nearby or travel through. Third, HSR development and operation have generated positive social, economic, and environmental impacts, although the magnitude varies by city and station. Services by HSR in Japan and Korea have shrunk the space-time distances between cities and regions, expanded market potentials, and contributed to economic productivity gains and transportation emission abatement. Using historical data from 1981 and 2006 for 47 prefectures in Japan, Wetwitoo and Kato (2017) confirm that prefectures with HSR services were more productive than those without. Koh and Yang (2018) report that rural townships adjacent to KTX stations experienced an increase, 10 percent over 10 years, in local economic activities attributable to KTX access.

HSR in China

China currently operates approximately 23,500 miles of HSR lines (China Ministry of Transport 2021; China State Council 2021; see also Jones 2021). The country's HSR system will continue to expand, as shown in the blueprint by China Railway Group released in 2020 (*Global Construction Review* 2020). According to the plan, China will build an additional 21,000 miles of tracks for HSR operations designed for speeds of 155 mph or higher by 2035. HSR has had a profound impact on the way people work, live, and do business in China. Nowadays, people can make weekend trips between Wuhan and Beijing easily and conveniently. Many business travelers prefer high-speed rail to air because of its on-time performance and their productive use of travel time on the train. The conventional trains still run, with some leaving the origin city in the evening and arriving at the destination city the next morning. These train services are convenient for those who want to avoid the expense of lodging. HSR was first adopted by the tourism sector and then expanded to other industries as well. It appears that people are increasingly taking advantage of HSR services by finding jobs beyond the cities where they live; they commute daily or weekly, maintaining their homes in the cities where their spouses work, their children go to school, and their close relatives and friends reside.

Investing in HSR is part of China's national development strategy. The central administration aims at a twofold development goal for HSR: improving surface transportation to accommodate fast-growing mobility demand, especially for intercity and interregional travel, and supporting national economic growth and urbanization. Coupled with the national HSR plan is a national spatial strategy for development of city-cluster regions. These regions contain multiple large or super large cities and an array of intermediate-sized cities or counties and their hinterlands, forming an economic geography similar to megacity regions in Europe or megaregions in the United States.

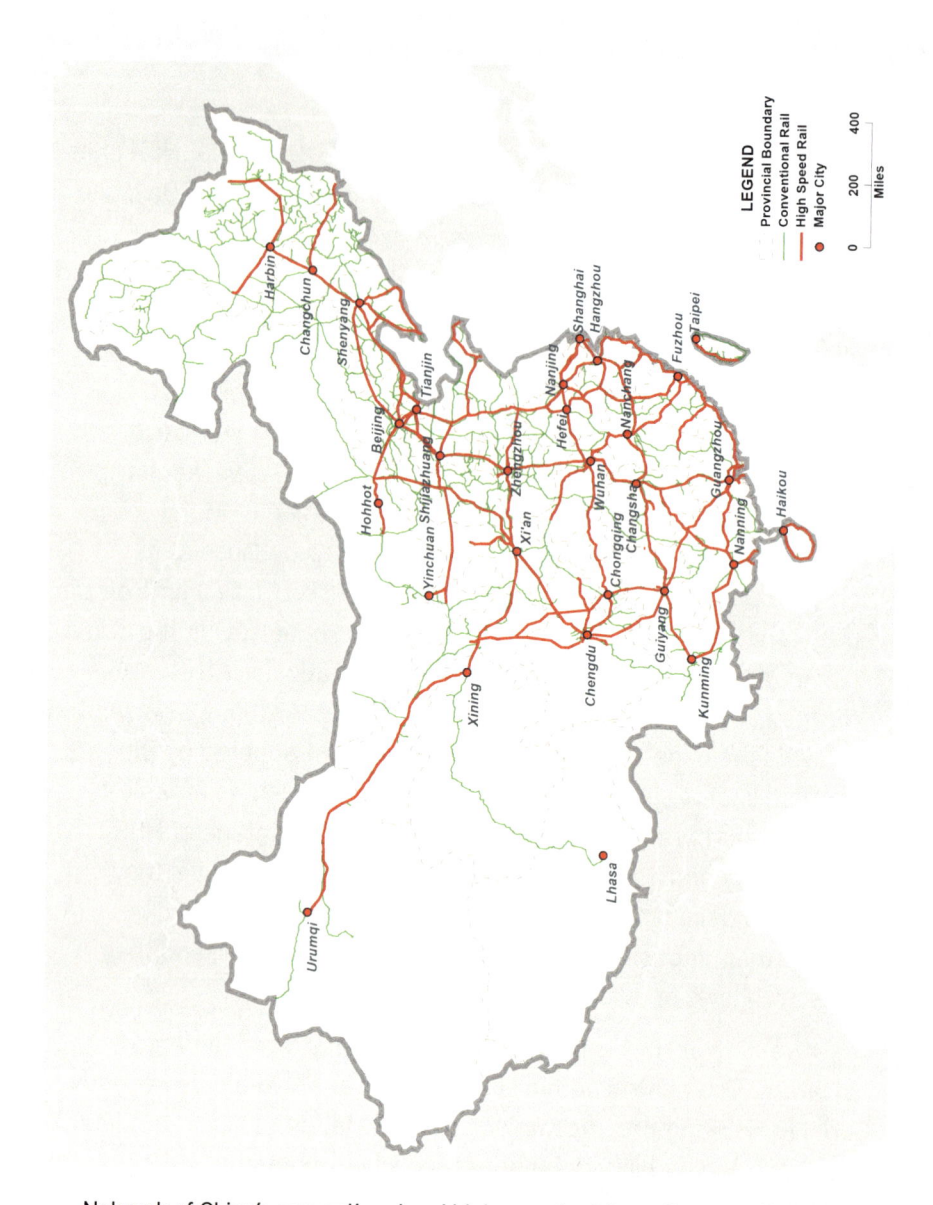

Network of China's conventional and high-speed rail lines. *Source: Ming Zhang.*

China has long practiced spatial planning at the national and local scales to achieve broad goals of economic and social development. A chief policy goal of this spatial planning is to achieve a balanced development across the national territory. China's Urban and Rural Planning Act mandates a city-town system plan for municipalities aimed at regional integration of different-size cities. After 2000, the policy focus shifted to fostering coordinated development of all sizes of cities and gradually adopted the concept of urban rings (analogous to metropolitan areas in the United States), which then evolved to become city clusters in the 2014 update to national spatial development. A city-cluster region includes multiple previously defined urban rings. The policy update promotes a new type of urbanization that preserves farmland and ecologically sensitive areas and concentrates future urbanization in a set of carefully delineated clusters of metropolitan regions (Groff and Rau 2019).

The National Development and Reform Commission, which is responsible for developing national Five-Year Plans and resource allocations, leads the city-cluster regional planning efforts. As of 2019, the State Council of China had formally approved the plans for 11 city-cluster regions. Plans for the remaining eight city-cluster regions are still in the works. HSR investment was part of the national infrastructure development plan to support China's national spatial policies (NDRC 2009; 2016). The early version of the HSR network plan, in 2004, emphasized connecting provincial capital cities and other major cities (CGCPRC 2005). HSR development accelerated after 2008 when the State Council issued China's economic stimulus plan to counter the worldwide economic recession (NDRC 2009). As the national HSR grid takes shape, HSR networks will expand to connect prefecture- and county-level cities throughout the country by 2035.

labor markets expand, urban revitalization and station area development, creation of technology and expertise that can be exported to other countries, and larger agglomeration economies in megaregions that create long-term competitive advantage for the cities, regions, and megaregions that the HSR serves.

One indication of how these economic benefits could be translated into political support occurred when coauthor Bob Yaro's Penn studio first proposed the $100 billion HSR transformation of the Northeast rail corridor in 2010. When Yaro presented the project and its benefits to the conservative Republican chairman of the House

FIGURE 9.1 High Speed 1 train in the United Kingdom. *Source: iStock/Sterling750.*

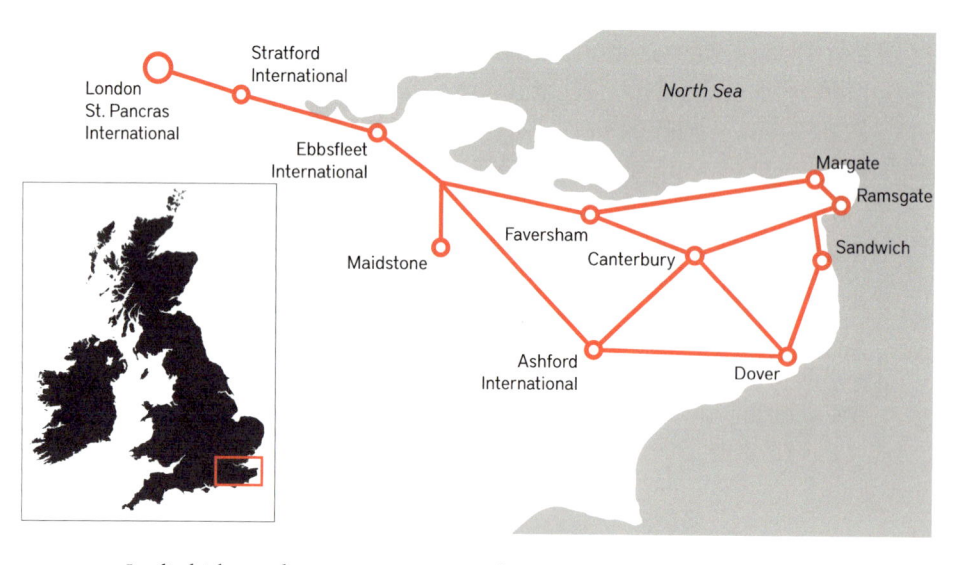

FIGURE 9.2 Javelin high-speed commuter route in southeast England. *Source: Charles E. Weber II.*

Transportation and Infrastructure Committee, he responded, "We're spending that much every few months on the war in Iraq; why wouldn't we invest a comparable amount to rebuild the economic potential of our most productive megaregion?"

Extensive research has been conducted on the economic benefits of HSR in Europe and Asia. One of the most authoritative empirical research projects was carried out by Peter Hall and Chia-Lin Chen (2009) at University College London. In a series of articles and essays, they document the extensive benefits (as quantified by rising employment, household incomes, housing prices, and other measures) that the United Kingdom's 85–110 mph rail service, initiated in 1985, provided to cities brought within one- and two-hour travel times of Central London. This research found that nearly every city brought into the London orbit by HSR gained population, employment, and other economic benefits. They note, however, that improved rail services were necessary but not sufficient to transform the economy of a handful of cities with concentrated poverty and other urban ills.

Another principal reason for investment in HSR by China, Taiwan, Korea, the United Kingdom, and other countries has been the role these systems can have in rebalancing national economies. In effect, HSR can promote growth in less developed areas that gain HSR service; businesses and individuals can relocate to these places because they have access to the workforce and employment opportunities formerly available only in major cities. In 2019, for example, U.K. prime minister Boris Johnson committed his government to building two HSR projects costing a total $160 billion as a platform for his national leveling-up campaign. Recall the High Speed 1 service, discussed earlier, which connects London with Europe. The High Speed 2 will connect London with the north of England, and the High Speed 3 will connect major cities across the North with each other and provide linkages to the transregional High Speed 2 service.

All these countries have also invested in infrastructure, housing, and amenities in smaller cities to help promote development in these places. A countervailing concern, however, is that HSR will enable workers and businesses to relocate from smaller cities to newly accessible large places, as service workers seek the bright lights, work, and social opportunities available in larger cities. This concern was expressed to Yaro a few years ago by the president of JR Kyushu, the rail company that serves Japan's southernmost island. They had just completed the new HSR route linking Fukuoka—Kyushu's largest city—and Kagoshima—a midsize city at the island's southern end. Despite neither being fluent in the other's language, he and Yaro had an animated discussion about the economic benefits HSR would provide to Kyushu. When Yaro asked him whether the new rail line would draw jobs and residents from smaller cities like Kagoshima into Fukuoka, he responded by pursing his lips and making a sucking sound—like sucking on a straw. When asked if he meant that the new route would draw economic activity away from Kagoshima and other smaller cities on the island to Fukuoka—the "giant sucking sound" (Porter 2019)—he answered in the affirmative.

We believe that, with trains running in both directions, jobs and residents will flow to the places that provide the best package of quality of life, talented workforce, well-priced housing stock, and amenities. Small and midsize cities gaining HSR services need to focus on sustaining or creating these attributes if they are to take full advantage of their access to HSR. And national and metropolitan governments need to provide the resources required to create these attributes in smaller, less well-developed cities.

WHERE HSR WOULD WORK IN THE UNITED STATES

HSR should not be built everywhere in the United States. Only the nation's megaregions have the population density and economic geography that can support and make good use of the mobility that HSR can provide. The United States should be building HSR lines between Chicago and Indianapolis, for example, or from Vancouver, British Columbia, to Portland, Oregon, but it should not be creating HSR routes between Chicago and Los Angeles.

In 2011, Peter Hall wrote that U.S. megaregions are

> ideally suited to HSR as a competitor to air, with the major cities spaced along linear corridors over distances up to 500 miles, served by some of the world's most trafficked (and hence most profitable) short haul air corridors. Elsewhere—first in Japan and now in Europe—HSR has quickly seized the lion's share of traffic along analogous corridors. Tokyo–Nagoya–Osaka, Paris–Lyon–Marseille, London–Manchester, Paris–Brussels–Amsterdam, and Madrid–Zaragoza–Barcelona. There is no reason to believe that the result will be different on corridors such as Washington–New York–Boston or San Francisco–Los Angeles. (Hall 2011, 352)

HSR services should be used to create new competitive advantages in the major cities and megaregions of the United States. They should also be designed to rebalance the economy of the country and of individual megaregions—promoting development in underperforming areas and decongesting the largest, most congested, and highest-priced large cities. Left-behind areas in the Northeast, Great Lakes, Southern California, and other megaregions have not benefited from the prosperity of major cities like New York, Chicago, and Los Angeles. These include places like Scranton and Bethlehem, Pennsylvania, Waterbury, Connecticut, and Springfield, Massachusetts, in the Northeast; South Bend, Indiana, Akron and Dayton, Ohio, in the Great Lakes; and Fresno and Bakersfield in Southern California. These places could gain new residents, jobs, and prosperity as a result of the new connections to larger, more successful cities that HSR and HPR would offer. This would provide a special advantage for Black, Latinx, and recent-immigrant communities who live in these outlying places by giving them access to employment and wealth-creation opportunities.

Fortunately, there are advantages as well as disadvantages to being late to the global HSR party. The United States can learn, for example, from Asian and European HSR precedents

- what kinds of institutions work best to expedite planning delivery and management of HSR routes;
- which technologies, speeds, and service plans work best;
- how HSR services can be integrated with classic intercity rail and regional rail networks;
- how to build effective economic development strategies on top of HSR investments to revitalize underperforming cities and regions; and
- what the merits are of joint development at station sites, of downtown versus suburban station locations, and what strategies to use to integrate HSR with regional rail and transit services.

Major disadvantages to being late to the HSR party will be difficult and expensive to overcome. Among these are that rights-of-way have not been protected from development, adding to the financial and political costs of building these routes now.

OBSTACLES TO A U.S. HSR NETWORK

The United States is just about the last developed country to build HSR but not for a lack of vision. U.S. senator Claiborne Pell (D-RI) proposed creating the world's first HSR route in the U.S. Northeast rail corridor in 1962, and he also proposed a new public authority to own, operate, and invest in the corridor. Pell's proposal was translated into the 1965 High-Speed Ground Transportation Act, which aimed to cut in half, to fours hours, the travel time on the corridor from Washington to Boston. This investment was to be financed by long-term, tax-exempt bonds guaranteed by the federal government. However, a combination of bureaucratic and political foot-dragging and the financial collapse of the Pennsylvania and New Haven Railroads doomed the entire project (Lyon 1968).

Despite Pell's vision and the government's good intentions, Amtrak's Northeast Corridor and its intercity rail service have never flourished, limping for more than half a century from one hard-fought annual appropriation to another, typically with just enough cash to keep the entire system from collapsing. Unfortunately, although infrastructure had bipartisan support for much of the last century, beginning in the 1990s, some Republican politicians began to oppose these investments.

For this reason, appropriations have been tied to Republicans' demand that Amtrak's national network break even on the back of its one profitable route—the Northeast Corridor. Consequently, fares on Amtrak's Northeast Corridor regional trains—and especially on its premium Acela service—have soared. Until recently, profits from the Northeast Corridor have been used to cross subsidize congressionally mandated long-distance trains in the rest of the country. Amtrak has not had the funds needed to maintain the Northeast Corridor, much less build HSR service, and speeds on Acela trains average only 84 mph between Washington and Boston. Although the federal government has starved intercity rail in the Northeast Corridor and across the country, it lavishes hundreds of billions on direct and indirect subsidies to commercial aviation and the national highway, rail's competing modes.

In the absence of federal support for HSR, individual states and private investors have proposed building these systems as business propositions. Attempts to build HSR routes in Texas and Florida in the 1980s ran afoul of Texas governor George W. Bush and Florida governor Jeb Bush, who killed these proposals to the relief of airlines and their other corporate supporters.

In 2008, the California legislature approved Assembly Bill 3034, authorizing $10 billion for construction of the state's HSR network. Later that same year, an America 2050 internal memo, written by Yaro, proposed a national HSR network serving U.S. megaregions (figure 9.3).

The Obama administration and a Democratic Congress included $8 billion for HSR in the $831 billion 2009 American Recovery and Reinvestment Act. An additional $2 billion was appropriated by Congress for this purpose in 2010. The Federal Railroad Administration produced its own proposal for a national HSR network and proceeded to distribute these funds to projects across the country—in Ohio, Wisconsin, Florida, and California, but not in the Northeast Corridor.

For political reasons, Republican governors in the first three states canceled these projects, and the California project failed to secure necessary federal funds to complete even an initial operating segment in the state's rural Central Valley. After an additional $1 billion was added to the federal HSR program in 2010, the new Republican Congress terminated further appropriations for the program and attempted to claw back commitments to California's HSR program.

The bipartisan Infrastructure and Jobs Act signed by President Biden in November 2021 includes $66 billion for passenger rail, mostly for state-of-good-repair improvements in the Northeast Corridor. Up to $12 billion of this amount could be used to design and build HSR projects in several US megaregions and to undertake HSR demonstration projects. The authors believe that once these projects are put into service and Americans gain first-hand experience with the benefits of HSR, they will demand that these systems be built out across the nation's megaregions. As a next step, the federal government should issue a request for proposals from the states or groups of states representing the nation's megaregions. Proposals should include HSR spines for states' rail networks and HPR routes to connect small and midsize cities.

Other countries offer multiple templates that could shape the U.S. HSR network. For the HPR components of these systems, the Swiss Federal Railways' pulse system (demand responsive and timed transfer) comes closest to the ideal when planning these networks for U.S. megaregions. Although the Swiss railways do not seek to achieve global HSR standards for speed, they do provide reasonable and assured

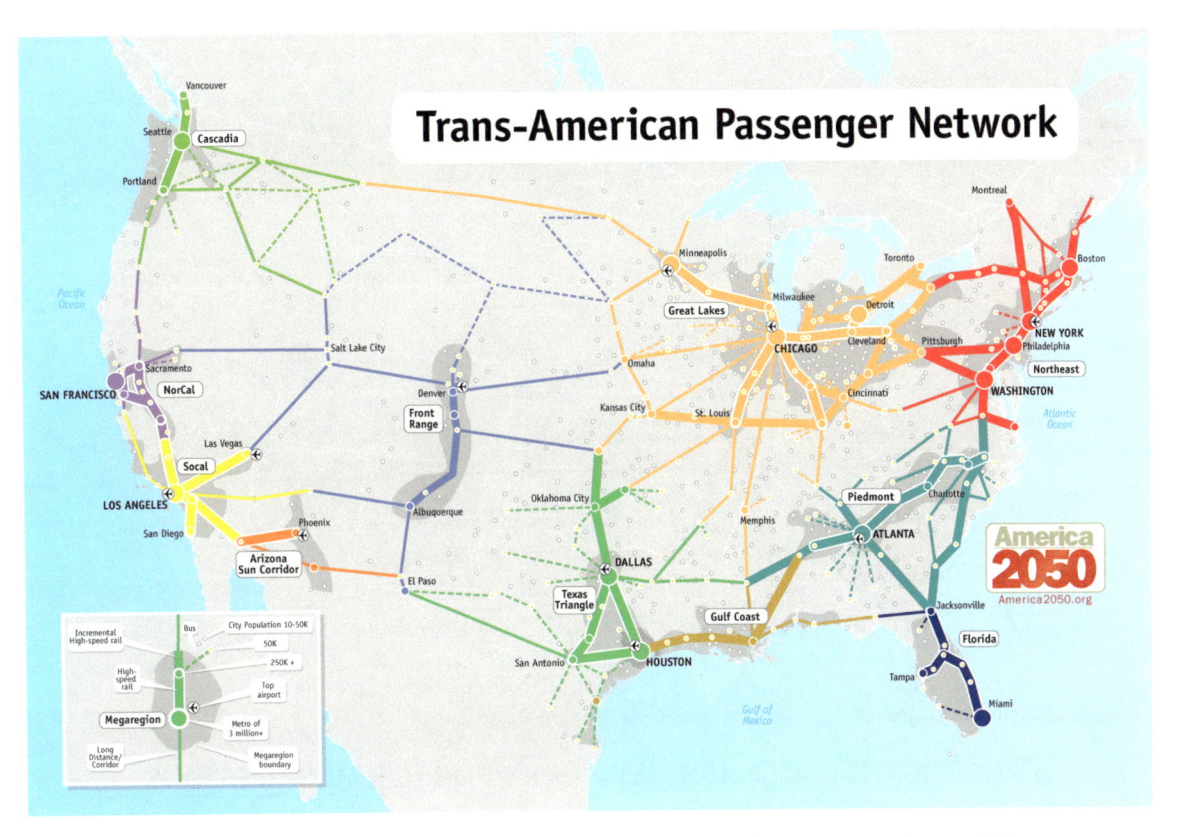

FIGURE 9.3 Proposed trans-America passenger network in the United States. *Source: America2050.org, Regional Plan Association.*

travel times between major centers, with frequent services on hourly, half-hour, or quarter-hour schedules depending on the route. (Their motto is "Not as fast as possible, but as fast as necessary.") Most important, they provide convenient transfers at hub stations to connecting trains, trams, buses, and other services. Switzerland's national rail system achieves high levels of ridership in a wealthy nation with population densities comparable to those of many U.S. megaregions, with only moderate operating subsidies (Peterson 2016).

By contrast, today, even in the Northeast, which has the most extensive intercity and commuter rail networks in the United States, there is little, if any, coordination between Amtrak's intercity services and commuter rail networks. Consequently, passengers making connections between these services often find themselves stranded at stations waiting for the next connecting train—which may be hours later. Even within major metropolitan areas, including New York, Boston, and Chicago, there are no through-running trains across these regions. Passengers wishing to make rail journeys across these regions must make time-consuming and often difficult transfers between different trains and even networks to complete these trips (figure 9.4).

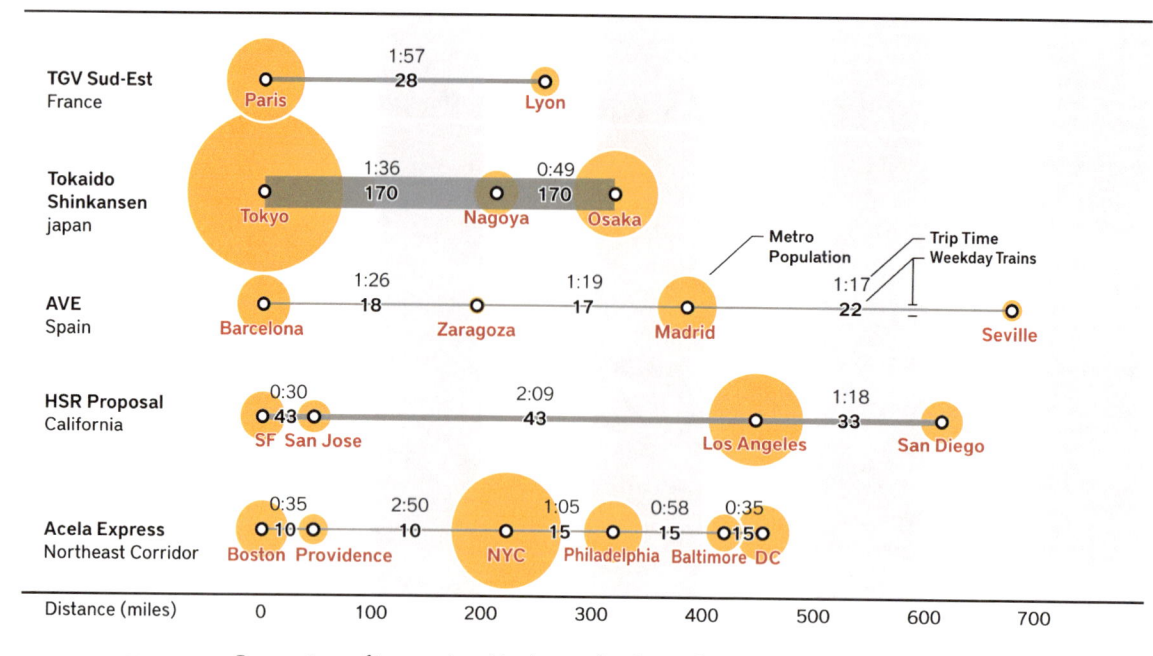

FIGURE 9.4 Comparison of international high-speed rail corridors with California's proposed rail system and Amtrak's Northeast Corridor. *Source: courtesy Robert Lane.*

DESIGNING HSR AND HPR NETWORKS FOR U.S. MEGAREGIONS

Critics have long argued that with lower population densities and higher car ownership, U.S. cities and regions are fundamentally different from nations with HSR and HPR networks. The reality, however, is that several U.S. megaregions have population densities and economic geographies that are comparable to European nations with successful HSR networks. The experiences in both Europe and Asia have been that high-quality, well-integrated rail services can compete successfully with automobiles and airplanes, particularly as these alternate modes become more congested and inconvenient.

Further, in most of the country, major airports (at least prepandemic) and stretches of the interstate highway system within megaregions are approaching or have already exceeded their capacity limits and are gridlocked for several hours every day. Building HSR and HPR networks will decongest these facilities to make room for essential long-distance travel and goods movement.

With global precedents in mind, a U.S. HPR system should be designed as integrated networks serving each megaregion, with the following components:

- *HSR spines.* Connecting major metropolitan centers within megaregions to each other, two-track spines could provide four to eight trains per hour. In most U.S. megaregions—as in much of Europe—midsize cities lie between major urban centers, and an additional 8–10 trains per hour could connect intermediate stops along each route. A precedent for this kind of service is the High Speed 1 line in the United Kingdom and its Javelin high-speed commuter service, described earlier (Francis 2017).

- *HPR routes.* HSR alone is not sufficient to meet the mobility needs of the nation's megaregions and, in particular, of the small and midsize cities that do not lie on HSR routes. In a Weitzman School studio workshop in Manchester, England, in October 2017, the British planner Jim Steer offered this aviation planning analogy: If air transportation plans had only one superbly designed airport, that airport would be a great monument, but as a transportation network it would be useless. Complementing this first airport with a second one would be a big improvement, opening fast connections between two places. Build three airports, and you would add enormously to the utility of the whole system. Build a network of well-designed airports and provide fast, frequent, reliable, and well-priced service on these routes, and that is a highly functional and desirable system (J. Steer, pers. comm. 2017).
- *Integrated HSR and HPR networks.* With this aviation planning analogy in mind, rail networks for the largest U.S. megaregions should include both HSR spines and connecting HPR networks. These should be designed to link all the megaregion's small and midsize cities with each other and the HSR network, providing frequent, 80–110 mph services.
- *Regional rail.* Major metropolitan areas (such as New York, Boston, Philadelphia, Washington, Chicago, Houston, Dallas–Fort Worth, Denver, Seattle, Los Angeles, and San Francisco) should also be provided with regional rail networks. Precedents for these systems include newly expanded regional rail networks in Paris, London, and Tokyo. Recent regional rail proposals for U.S. cities include the Massachusetts Bay Transportation Authority and TransitMatters' proposal for Boston (TransitMatters 2018), the RPA's proposed T-REX system for New York (Barone et al. 2018), and the High Speed Rail Alliance's CrossRail proposal for Chicago (High Speed Rail Alliance 2021).
- *Local transit, bus, and bus rapid transit systems.* Nonrail systems can complete the utility of these networks.
- *Shared mobility systems.* The final component in these comprehensive mobility systems should be decongesting urban road networks by increasing use of shared mobility systems, such as those provided by transportation network companies like Uber and Lyft. These companies use algorithms to provide passengers with alternatives to single-occupant automobiles that could be adapted to eliminate the first- and last-mile problem that has bedeviled transit users for centuries. These services can also eliminate the need for most station-area parking and create new opportunities for intensive transit-oriented development in these locations. These innovations are described in greater detail in chapter 6.

Rail Networks in Balanced Transportation Systems

Building HSR and HPR intercity and regional urban transit networks alone will not meet the mobility needs of the nation's megaregions. The backbone of every megaregion in the 21st century will be a balanced multimodal transportation system:

- International airports and seaports are the global gateways for commerce and passenger travel. Before the pandemic, most airports in major U.S. cities were approaching or had already exceeded their carrying capacity limits; decongesting these facilities by diverting short-haul routes to HSR will help, but even with this diversion, additional runway and terminal capacity will be needed in many places.

- Limited-access and local highway networks are also approaching their capacity limits and end of life in most U.S. metro regions. Major investments will be needed just to maintain existing systems. Automated vehicle technology (described in chapter 6) will improve use of these systems as part of comprehensive congestion management systems.

- Navigation systems in coastal and inland river regions need major investments. The United States has one of the most extensive inland and coastal navigation systems in the world. Reforms are needed in shipping regulations to permit additional bulk cargoes to travel on these routes.

- Rail freight networks in the United States are already among the world's most efficient but will require additional capacity and connectivity in coming years.

Federal Leadership and Financing

Because of their high capital costs, long payback periods, and complex engineering, HSR routes are nearly always financed and built by national governments. Attempts have been made to use public-private partnerships, such as the U.K. government for the High Speed 1 connecting the Channel Tunnel to London's St. Pancras International, and some of these projects have failed. High Speed 1 had to be completed by the U.K. Department for Transport when its public-private partnership collapsed because of unanticipated engineering and financial risks. The private sector has an appropriate role in financing and operating these systems, however. Upon its completion and following years of successful operation, High Speed 1 was leased for a 30-year period to a consortium led by Ontario Teachers' Pension Plan. The U.K. government expects to recover its capital investment possibly within 60 years.

For this reason, unless the U.S. government makes a similar strong national commitment to financing HSR, these projects will not proceed, or their designs will be compromised by longer travel times, higher fares, limited stops, and suburban terminal locations.

Despite President Biden's campaign commitments to build HSR, the bipartisan Infrastructure and Jobs Act signed by the president in November 2021 did not include funding explicitly dedicated to HSR projects, despite efforts by congressional leaders in both houses to include $205 billion for these projects. Instead, $66 billion was provided for state-of-good-repair investments in the Northeast Corridor and for Amtrak and state-led conventional rail projects in other areas of the country. Importantly, up to $12 billion of this amount could be directed to HSR projects. In addition, Democratic Congressional leaders have included $10 billion for HSR projects (defined as achieving speeds greater than 186 mph) in the reconciliation budget bill. As noted, both programs could be used to complete engineering, design, and environmental reviews on several HSR projects and to fund demonstration projects. It should be noted, however, that these funding levels represent a tiny fraction of the amount needed to build HSR networks across the nation's megaregions.

Some of these funds could also be directed to proposed privately initiated HSR intercity rail projects in Florida, Texas, and Nevada, which could transform these projects into world-class rail networks, with HSR speeds and travel times, center-city station locations, easy transfers to regional rail and transit services, and safer, grade-separated routes.

Delivering a National HSR Network

To expedite design and construction of a national HPR and HSR network, Congress should establish a new public authority, with a name such as the U.S. Interstate Passenger Rail Development Corporation and authority to coordinate development of the national network. This agency could promulgate national design and engineering standards to reduce costs and ensure interoperability of components across the whole country. In China, standardized designs and engineering standards reduced construction costs by one-third compared with other Asian and European projects and expedited construction schedules for the national system (Lawrence, Bullock, and Liu 2019). Working with state and multistate partners, the new federal entity should seek to complete construction of a national system within a generation. A small, independent, and highly skilled staff would operate the corporation under the direction of a board appointed by the president and Congress. It would be authorized to contract with outside engineering, design, and construction firms to finalize plans for the national network in collaboration with the states and multistate megaregional partnerships.

The agency should be authorized to cut through the red tape of federal permitting, procurement, and other procedures. It should work with the states and new multistate partnerships to plan the national network and submit these plans to Congress for approval within one year of the agency's establishment. Congress should then authorize 20- and 30-year bonds for the entire estimated cost of this system and appropriate the construction funds necessary to complete the initial phase of the project. It will be essential to manage this process outside Congress's normal, annual authorization and appropriation processes, to ensure that the whole program stays on track and is not subject to political intrigue.

For megaregions located entirely within a single state, the agency could partner with the states and special-purpose entities, like the California High-Speed Rail Authority, to finance, design, build, and operate these projects. Where megaregions encompass portions of two or more states, the federal government could work with the states to establish multistate, public development authorities, as has been proposed for the North Atlantic Rail project in New York and New England.

Private Sector and Public-Private Partnerships

Two U.S. HSR projects are now being planned as public-private partnerships: the Texas Central Rail project linking suburban Houston with Dallas and the Brightline West route linking Apple Valley, California, to suburban Las Vegas. Both routes cross lightly populated lands and will involve joint development projects at suburban stations to help offset their capital costs. Both also propose to be financed in part through tax-exempt federal and state bonds (Vartabedian 2020). The Texas Central project is adopting Japanese Shinkansen technology and is being financed in part by Japanese government sovereign wealth funds (Smith 2018).

A third privately financed and developed project, Florida's Brightline, is being funded in part through proceeds from station-area joint development projects and in part through tax-exempt bonds. Its trains operating between Miami and West Palm Beach are limited to 79 mph because of frequent grade crossings, where more than 40 deaths have occurred in the train's first two years of service. An extension of this service is now being planned to Orlando. With a federal financial contribution (and equitable distribution of costs and profits between the federal government and its private sponsor, the private equity firm Fortress), this service could be improved with grade separations, track and signal modernization, and electrification to provide true high-speed service connecting central and south Florida with stops in Miami, Fort Lauderdale, West Palm Beach, Orlando, and Tampa (Brightline 2021).

Bringing these services into central business districts or locations where they can connect with regional rail and mass transit networks would be highly desirable but not essential. Many HSR stations in Japan, France, Germany, China, and other countries are in suburban areas, often with an extensive overbuilding of transit-oriented commercial, retail, and residential development, and cross subsidies from commercial and retail development. Much of Japan's Shinkansen system, for example, is built around the edge of city stations, many of them sited on former rail yards that have been converted into major urban development projects led by the privatized Japan

Rail companies themselves. Commercial and retail operations on these sites help cross subsidize operating expenses on Shinkansen services.

Nearly everywhere in the world, however, suburban stations have connections to local, regional, or national rail services, which is not yet a feature of the Texas, Las Vegas, or Florida projects. There will also be multiple opportunities for participation by the private sector in the development of these and other rail development projects. Project sponsors could, for example, have design-build partnerships with collaborations of engineering and construction firms to design and build these projects or segments of the projects. They could also contract with private operators to maintain the systems once completed, as the U.K. Department for Transport has with its High Speed 1 HSR project. In some cases, it may be appropriate to collaborate with class 1 freight railroads to deliver portions of this system that are colocated on existing rail rights-of-way. Private investors could also be brought in for codevelopment of electric power, broadband, and other utilities on publicly owned rights-of-way. Finally, private companies could operate some of the trains on these routes, competing with Amtrak and state or regional rail operators for customers.

HSR AND HPR IN THE POST-COVID-19 ERA

Whether the changes in work and travel patterns of the COVID-19 pandemic will be sustained once the virus is contained is unknown. It appears that most businesses will return to a hybrid pattern of work, with employees working at home a few days a week and returning to offices perhaps once or twice a week or even less frequently. It is also likely that, freed from onerous daily commutes to center-city offices, many workers will choose to relocate to more distant and less expensive suburban areas.

Dense urban centers, however, will continue to attract workers and employers. Younger workers will probably continue to seek center-city locations to take advantage of the social and cultural activities available in these places. Workers in centrally located offices will also continue to grow their networks of contacts—essential to innovation and productivity, particularly in advanced technology sectors. Development of cutting-edge products and technologies will require transfers of tacit knowledge only possible through face-to-face interactions. Some workers will also continue to seek the stimulation that comes with high-density live-work environments that can be found only in large cities.

The HSR and HPR networks proposed here could establish these patterns, allowing workers to travel longer distances once or twice weekly to center-city offices. Some businesses will also choose to move some of their offices to satellite locations, which could also be organized around these rail networks. If smaller cities can provide greater social and cultural opportunities and a broader range of housing types, prices, and densities, they may attract workers and residents who might previously have chosen to live and work in larger urban centers.

A related question is whether the big technology centers, like San Francisco, Seattle, and New York, that drove the expansion of the innovation economy in the first two decades of the 21st century will continue to play this essential role in the U.S. economy in the coming years. In October 2020, an article in the *Washington Post* pondered "whether the pandemic would diminish the dynamism and allure of New York and other 'superstar cities' like it. This elite class of American cities, including San Francisco, Los Angeles, and Washington, DC, is made up of densely populated economic powerhouses with deep reserves of talent and wealth. But without an office to report to, their relatively high costs of living become harder to justify, especially as technology and necessity have opened pathways to work pretty much anywhere" (Shaban 2020).

Construction of HSR and HPR networks in U.S. megaregions would also foster new tech centers in other places, because they create their own critical mass of knowledge workers and start-up companies needed to join this small club of superstar cities. This, in turn, could provide the foundation for a broader leveling up of cities and regions of the country that have been left behind in the growth of national prosperity in recent decades.

CONCLUSION

HSR and HPR networks are essential elements of megaregional transportation infrastructure in Europe and Asia. Existing institutions and financing levels will not be sufficient to create similar networks in America's megaregions. The 2021 Infrastructure and Jobs Act, with its focus on state of good repair in the Northeast Corridor and slow trains in other places, will not achieve this goal. However, a small portion of these funds could be used to provide a downpayment towards this goal, by financing engineering, design, and demonstration HSR projects that lead to future major investments in these networks. With this goal in mind, Congress should make an ongoing multibillion-dollar commitment to HSR and HPR and establish a new public authority for interstate passenger rail to build out this national network. In the absence of this institutional reform and financial commitment, the United States will never be able to build the intercity rail networks that U.S. megaregions require to compete globally and achieve climate and racial and social justice goals in decades to come. In the next chapter, we discuss governance reform and innovation options for U.S. megaregions.

10

GOVERNING U.S. MEGAREGIONS

The dogmas of the quiet past are inadequate to the stormy present. The occasion is piled high with difficulty, and we must rise—with the occasion. As our case is new, so we must think anew, and act anew. We must disenthrall ourselves, and then we shall save our country.

—ABRAHAM LINCOLN

THIS CHAPTER PRESENTS THE GOVERNANCE REFORMS AND innovations that U.S. megaregions will need to realize their full potential in the 21st century. Creating national, megaregional, and metropolitan governance systems will require a reinvention of the federal system and a nationwide program of innovation and experimentation unlike any that the country has undertaken since the New Deal almost a century ago. Like the New Deal, the Green Mega Deal will require new public agencies and reinvention of existing bureaucracies—many of which have become sclerotic and mired in bureaucratic inertia and red tape after generations of policy drift.

The success of these efforts will determine whether President Biden's Build Back Better initiatives can enable the country and its megaregions to achieve his administration's ambitious goals to strengthen the U.S. economy, transform its mobility systems, realize climate goals, increase racial and social equity, and enhance environmental quality.

REINVENTION FOR A GREEN MEGA DEAL

The country demands bold experimentation. It is common sense to take a method and try it. If it fails, admit it and try another. But above all try something.

—FRANKLIN D. ROOSEVELT

FIGURE 10.1 Texas Triangle at night (photo taken by Expedition 36 crew members from the International Space Station). *Source: NASA.*

Nowhere in the country do we currently have effective governance systems for the nation's megaregions. For those megaregions entirely or largely within the boundaries of single states—Florida, Texas Triangle, and Northern and Southern California— the states can create the necessary institutions and governance systems to address the development of climate adaptation strategies, water quality and quantity, high-speed and high-performance rail systems, and other network-scale issues (figure 10.1).

Even in these places, however, improved coordination across state lines and, in some cases, national borders will be required. The first maps of U.S. megaregions, prepared by teams at Penn and the RPA from 2004 to 2006, identified the strong economic and transportation connections of several U.S. megaregions with adjoining areas of Canada and Mexico. This book examines exclusively the U.S. portions of megaregions because of the difficulty of integrating demographic and economic data across national boundaries. This is another place where the U.S. Census Bureau could help, by coordinating data sets with its Mexican and Canadian counterparts.

Southern California, for example, will need to coordinate plans, policies, and investments for high-speed rail and water resources with the neighboring states of Nevada and Arizona, as well as Baja California in Mexico. Northern California has clear connections with Cascadia. The Texas Triangle will need to coordinate its high-speed rail plans with Oklahoma's Tulsa and Oklahoma City regions, as well as with northeast Mexico. Florida has similar ties with Caribbean nations and with Central and South American nations.

However, the nation's nine other megaregions—which incorporate portions of multiple U.S. states and portions of Canada and Mexico—will be starting almost from scratch in creating effective governance systems.

Compounding this challenge is that dozens of major metropolitan regions that drive the economy of U.S. megaregions—including Boston, New York, Philadelphia, Washington, DC, Chicago, Saint Louis, Cincinnati, Kansas City, and Portland, Oregon—incorporate portions of two or three states. All these places depend on multiple systems that operate at the metropolitan scale: transportation networks, water supplies, large natural resource systems, housing and economic development, racial inequality, and others. They all need to address climate change at the metropolitan or megaregional scale. None has effective governance systems to plan for, manage, or invest in these activities.

The decades-long deterioration and near collapse of greater Washington's metro system illustrates the difficulty. Construction of this metro system, which serves the District of Columbia and extensive nearby areas of suburban Virginia and Maryland, was largely financed by the federal government during the Lyndon Johnson administration. Since then, the system has not had sustained maintenance funding from the district or the participating states. Reliability and safety have deteriorated, and fatal accidents and severe service disruptions have caused loss of public confidence and ridership. It is now, in the words of the U.S. House of Representatives Committee on Oversight and Reform, in a "death spiral of disinvestment and declining service" (House Committee on Oversight and Reform 2019).

Although every U.S. metropolitan region has an officially constituted metropolitan planning organization or council of governments, not since the 1980s have most regional bodies had real authority to address metropolitan issues. Most are handicapped by federal regulations that limit their responsibilities to transportation issues alone and even prohibit them from proposing transportation investments in which costs exceed available revenues. It has now been nearly a half century since these shortsighted limitations were put in place, and revisiting this issue is long overdue.

The hyperlocalism of government in many megaregions presents further difficulties. The Northeast megaregion has thousands of municipal governments and service districts, often with overlapping jurisdictions and taxing powers and, in the case of service districts, limited public accountability. Although this highly decentralized system places government close to the people it serves, the structure limits opportunities for effective regional and megaregional planning and operates with low levels of productivity and accountability. This, in turn, leads to higher tax rates and lower service levels than in other parts of the country. In addition, the highly decentralized land use regulatory system in the Northeast and other megaregions lends itself to exclusionary zoning practices that further disadvantage poor and minority residents. These practices reinforce and maintain conditions created by past racist policies, particularly redlining. As racism is reinforced, so, too, are environmental destruction and the general uglification of the U.S. landscape.

One example of extreme localism is the governance of Greater Boston's Metropolitan Area Planning Council, which encompasses 101 municipalities. The council's governing board is structured so that every community has nearly the same level of representation—from exurban Essex, with a population of fewer than 4,000, to Boston, with 700,000 residents. Meanwhile, in Connecticut, several boroughs are still governed by wardens and burgesses—feudal titles abolished in England centuries ago.

Governors and state legislators have a critical role in this reinvention. They will need to be convinced of the benefits for each participating state and for the rural areas both within and beyond their boundaries. Rural communities have sway in Congress and state legislatures. The 13 U.S. megaregions comprise portions of 44 states and the District of Columbia and are represented by 88 U.S. senators and most of the U.S. House of Representatives. These megaregions include extensive rural areas. In addition, the states outside the megaregions (Alaska, Hawaii, Montana, Nebraska, North Dakota, and South Dakota) link to the megaregions through economics, food, energy, minerals, transportation, and recreation. One of the most ambitious and innovative natural resource megaregional efforts, the Yellowstone to Yukon Conservation Initiative (see chapter 7), is grounded outside the urban-based megaregions.

SUBSIDIARITY: A BASIC PRINCIPLE TO SHAPE GOVERNANCE REFORM

Governance systems should be reformed or reconstituted to better meet the needs of U.S. megaregions by the principle of subsidiarity, meaning that issues should be addressed at the lowest level that can effectively manage them. Here are some examples, from the bottom up:

- Traffic signs, sidewalks, and neighborhood parks should be sited by local or municipal governments.

- Regional water and sewer facilities should be operated by metropolitan water and sewer districts that correspond with boundaries of public water supply watersheds and related natural systems.

- Planning for metropolitan land use, housing, and economic development should be performed by strengthened metropolitan planning organizations or regional councils of government with capacity and accountability to manage these systems. Metropolitan planners should, for example, address regional housing and social and racial justice needs. Some regional bodies—San Diego County Association of Governments (SANDAG) in California and Portland Metro in Oregon—already have these responsibilities.

- Metropolitan transportation system authorities should have power to raise the revenue through taxes, tolls, fares, and so on, needed to manage the systems. Northern California's Metropolitan Transportation Authority comes closest to this ideal, with its ability to plan for, invest in, and manage road, bridge, and rail networks in the nine-county region around San Francisco, Oakland, and San Jose.

- Metropolitan governments or service districts should coordinate the systems that function at the metropolitan scale. The federal government could encourage combined authorities to manage activities such as transportation, economic development, urban regeneration, climate adaptation, and similar issues at the regional level. An international precedent is the combined authorities of the United Kingdom's major metropolitan centers. These elected authorities, with responsibility for managing metropolitan infrastructure, public health, housing, economic development, and other systems, are created through voter initiatives, after passage of 2009 legislation. They are led by elected mayors and councils of center cities and inner-ring suburbs. The Metropolitan Council in Minneapolis–Saint Paul has had many of these responsibilities for decades. A second U.S. precedent is Oregon's Portland Metro; however, its authority does not reach across the Columbia River to Vancouver, Washington, or other distant portions of the metropolitan region.

- Management of statewide infrastructure and natural resource systems, such as roadways, coastlines, and wetlands, is a logical responsibility for state governments. Oregon and Hawaii have effective state-level infrastructure planning systems.

- Management of megaregion-scale natural systems and climate adaptation strategies should be the responsibility of public authorities empowered by the federal government and states to operate at this vast scale. Voluntary collaboratives of states can be established. Construction and operation of large-scale natural or infrastructure systems—for example, high-speed rail networks or metropolitan water supplies—will require public authorities to carry out these responsibilities. The proposed North Atlantic Rail Corporation, described in chapter 8, could show the way.

CREATING MEGAREGION AUTHORITIES

Article 1, Section 10, Clause 3 (the compact clause) of the U.S. Constitution requires that multistate agreements be ratified by Congress. This clause authorizes multistate initiatives for infrastructure and economic development and natural resource management across state boundaries. Under this provision, the federal government has authorized several multistate authorities to promote economic development in isolated, left-behind rural regions. These include the Appalachian Regional Commission for a 13-state region stretching from Mississippi to New York, the Delta Commission for an eight-state region in the lower Mississippi Valley, and the Northern Border Commission for a four-state (New York, Vermont, New Hampshire, and Maine) region along the Northeast's northern border with Canada.

Several other federal-state compacts manage multistate natural resource systems, such as the four-state (New York, New Jersey, Pennsylvania, and Delaware) Delaware River Basin Commission and the Upper Colorado River Commission (Wyoming, Utah, Colorado, and New Mexico) and the two-state (Washington and Oregon) Columbia River Gorge Commission. The Red River Basin Commission consists of three states (Minnesota, North Dakota, and South Dakota), one province (Manitoba), and two nations, the United States and Canada, plus First Nations. The Great Lakes Commission also includes parts of Canada and the United States and 10 states and two provinces.

States have played a pivotal role in the creation and operation of all these multistate collaborative institutions. In the U.S. federal system, states must continue to play a central role in creating new megaregion-scale governance systems.

The Biden administration could expedite job creation in building and managing major infrastructure and climate adaptation initiatives by following the approach of the New Deal, as discussed in chapter 7. The multistate economic development, energy, and natural resource management authorities established then included the Tennessee Valley Authority, Bonneville Power Administration, and the Colorado River Project.

Modern examples exist for nonstatutory ways for states to collaborate. Two such are described in chapter 8. The first is the Regional Greenhouse Gas Initiative, a cap-and-trade program created through a memorandum of understanding among its 10 northeastern member states, which did not seek congressional approval. The U.S. Supreme Court has allowed this and other multistate agreements rather than quashing them by applying a literal reading of the compact clause of the Constitution ("Compact Clause" 2007). The second initiative is an offshoot of the first. The Transportation and Climate Initiative of 13 northeastern states and the District of Columbia will reduce carbon emissions by 25 percent from the transportation sector.

In 2008, Congress established the Northeast Corridor Commission to manage investments in the corridor. The commission includes representatives of eight states along the corridor (Massachusetts, Rhode Island, Connecticut, New York, New Jersey, Pennsylvania, Delaware, and Maryland), the District of Columbia, the Federal Railroad Administration, and Amtrak. The commission spent years hammering out a cost allocation formula between the states and Amtrak over maintenance costs on the corridor. However, the commission does not have the authority to operate or make direct investments in the corridor.

Models of Cross-Jurisdiction Collaboration: Interstate 10 Corridor Coalition

The Interstate 10 Corridor Coalition is a voluntary partnership formed in 2016 by the departments of transportation of four states in the U.S. Southwest: California, Arizona, New Mexico, and Texas (Arizona Department of Transportation n.d.). The coalition aims at improving safety and operational efficiency for freight (truck) and passenger movement on I-10 along the corridor of approximately 1,680 miles.

I-10 is the southernmost cross-country route of the national interstate grid. Its full length stretches 2,460 miles, traversing the southern and southwestern states of the Sunbelt. It serves five of the 13 U.S. megaregions. A third of I-10 lies in Texas, but then there are "Miles and Miles of Texas" (according to the song by the band Asleep at the Wheel), and El Paso is closer to San Diego than to Houston. I-10 carries high and growing volumes of passenger and freight traffic as the population grows rapidly and the economy

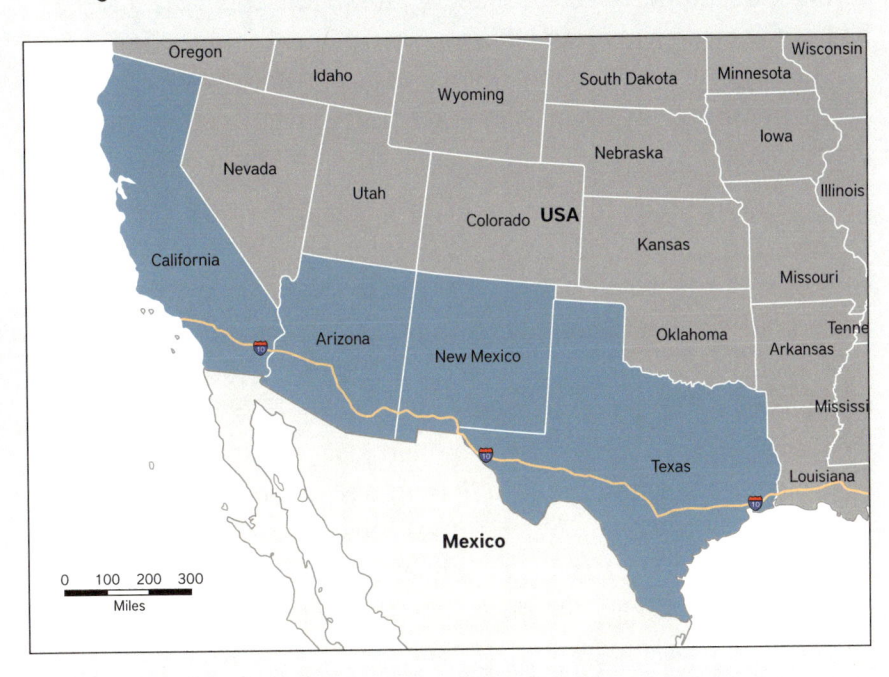

Interstate 10 corridor coalition map. *Source: Ming Zhang.*

Rush hour traffic on Interstate 10 approaching the Spaghetti Bowl in downtown El Paso, Texas. *Source: istock.com/bwancho.*

expands strongly in the Sunbelt states. Some segments of I-10 have become heavily congested. The I-10 segments in Texas and Arizona ranked as the third and fifth, respectively, most dangerous highways in the United States in 2015–2017 (Schmidt 2019).

Although federal funds paid for much of their construction, interstate highways are owned and managed by the states they cross. Dividing responsibilities for the interstate highways by state has led to complexity in managing emergency response, law enforcement, and roadside services. The Interstate 10 Corridor Coalition aims to improve cross-state coordination of technology; standards of practice; and protocols for applications in permitting, parking, platooning (grouping or flocking of freight vehicles), and inspections that better support freight movement along the corridor. Similar applications will also be developed to better serve passenger movement for integrated, connected vehicle information sharing. The coalition also partners with the transportation manufacturing and technology sectors to develop and test products and services for operations and management.

The Interstate 10 Corridor Coalition won a federal grant in 2019 to develop an information service and management system for smart truck parking. The system will detect and disseminate information on real-time parking availability at 37 public truck parking locations along the corridor to help truck drivers and dispatchers optimize operational schedules, improve safety by reducing roadside and ramp parking, and lower emissions and fuel consumption by spending less time searching for parking spaces.

MANAGING MEGAREGION-SCALE SYSTEMS

Several types of large systems should be planned or administered at the megaregion scale:

- *Interstate high-speed rail, high-performance rail, and transportation networks.* As discussed in chapter 9, interstate transportation systems are often best financed and built by national governments.
- *Multistate natural resource systems.* Protection and restoration of drainage basins, estuaries, mountain ranges, and ecoregions could be achieved through federal incentives or coordination of state protection programs, as is already being done with the Chesapeake Bay Program. The Chesapeake Bay Program is a partnership authorized by Congress in 1983 that includes Maryland, Virginia, and Pennsylvania, the District of Columbia, and the U.S. Environmental Protection Agency. The program was established to reduce pollution and restore natural systems in this multistate estuary but has repeatedly missed targets for reductions in nitrogen pollution in the bay. Participating states and environmental groups have sued (Wheeler 2020). Multistate regional commissions with their own powers to regulate pollution and deliver restoration programs is another idea. The Lake Tahoe Commission is a bistate (Nevada and California) model for this kind of collaboration.

- *Large-scale economic development and revitalization.* Projects for left-behind communities and regions include the Appalachian Regional Commission, Delta Commission, and the recently formed Northern Border Regional Commission along the Canadian frontier in upstate New York and northern New England. These examples operate outside U.S. megaregions in nonmetropolitan areas but are a template for similar initiatives in megaregions with a special focus on economic development and job creation. To be effective, these new entities would require a significant increase in funding levels, above that of the regional commission precedents mentioned here.
- *Climate adaptation and mitigation initiatives.* Protection against storm surges and sea level rise in coastal metropolitan regions, creation of national and regional climate reserves, and preservation or restoration of large interstate estuaries and rivers, such as the Connecticut River, Hudson River Estuary, Delaware Basin, Chesapeake Bay, and Suwannee River in Georgia and Florida, require megaregion-scale management. For more than two centuries, the U.S. Army Corps of Engineers has been charged with responsibility for major coastal public works, including channel dredging and shoreline protection on barrier beaches and islands and the operation of the entire inland navigation and flood control programs on the Mississippi-Missouri River system. In recent years, the corps has become mired in bureaucracy and politics that have limited its ability to act decisively to protect coastal and inland cities from storm surges, sea level rise, and flooding (figure 10.2). An exception is New Orleans, where the corps completed, on time and on budget, the $14 billion Great Wall of Louisiana to protect New Orleans from a repeat of the devastating floods of Hurricane Katrina in 2005. However, the wall protects the city only from Category 3 storms. To expedite similar programs in other vulnerable coastal cities in the nation's seven coastal megaregions, it may be necessary to establish new megaregion-scale authorities to plan, build, and operate flood prevention or mitigation projects for major metropolitan areas in these places.

Recognition of megaregions by the U.S. Census Bureau, in much the same way that it recognizes metropolitan regions and organizes and collects data on them, would make the necessary planning and administration easier. Without that recognition, several alternative processes are available. One option is congressionally authorized interstate compacts of federal-state partnerships. The states could also create these partnerships voluntarily, without prior congressional authorization, as was done with the Northeast's Regional Greenhouse Gas Initiative. Partnerships could form collaborations among adjoining metropolitan planning organizations. And finally, independent, not-for-profit organizations could assume coordination. A precedent is the United Kingdom's Northern Powerhouse Partnership, discussed in chapter 8.

FIGURE 10.2 Aerial view of a flooded solar power station with dirty river water in rainy season. Source: istock.com/Bilanol.

MUNICIPAL AND SCHOOL FINANCE REFORM

The Biden administration has made reckoning with racial and social inequality a major national priority. Undoing the effects of long-standing federal, state, county, and municipal policies that promote inequality will not happen overnight. To succeed, these efforts will require a restructuring of municipal tax and school finance systems in several megaregions. For example, the Northeast's highly Balkanized governance system—with its thousands of municipalities, many of them acting like self-governing republics—contributes to the megaregion's racial and economic inequality. Most municipal services are financed through property taxes, which contributes to the problem because of extreme inequality in tax rates and a disparate quality of services between well-off—and usually predominantly white—suburbs and often poorer and predominantly Black and Latinx nearby cities and suburbs.

Local government and taxation systems in most of the Northeast are relics of the 17th-century English colonial system. They are highly fractured and have little relevance to many economic, climate, public health, and other challenges now facing the megaregion of the 21st century.

In New England, most local governance is by town meetings—in which the governing body includes every adult resident of the community. Part-time elected select boards provide day-to-day administration, and voluntary part-time boards and committees run most town affairs, including planning and zoning, finance, education,

Collaboration on Cross-Metropolitan Transportation Planning

Two groups in the Texas Triangle megaregion, the Capital Area Metropolitan Planning Organization (CAMPO) in the Austin region and the Alamo Area Metropolitan Planning Organization (AAMPO) in the San Antonio region, collaborated to develop biregional enhancements to mobility in the greater Austin–San Antonio region.

The cities of Austin and San Antonio are about 80 miles apart. The two regions have been growing rapidly. Census data indicate that the two may merge into one combined metro. Population projections show that, by 2045, the two regions' combined population would be like that of the Dallas–Fort Worth area. Interstate 35, which goes through the hearts of the two metro areas, already suffers from chronic congestion yet would need to carry even more traffic with this growth. The demographic trend and the increased economic interactions and traffic between the two metropolitan areas call for transportation planning and investment decisions to be made beyond individual jurisdictions. CAMPO and AAMPO partnered with the Texas Department of Transportation to perform the Capital-Alamo Connections Study in 2017–2019 (TxDOT 2019).

The study considered the Interstate 35 corridor and major parallel facilities in the combined 12-county area (Cohen 2018). The joint study team organized public workshops, interested-party meetings, and one-on-one interviews to identify the critical challenges and urgent needs. The team also analyzed regional growth patterns and trends in terms of population, land use, and passenger and freight movement up to 2050. Finally, the team developed plans and policies that are organized in short-, mid-, and long-term implementation time frames by recommendations for regional coordination, integrated corridor management and intelligent transportation systems, modal options, priority transportation corridors, and arterial improvements. Main strategies for the long term are to develop combined planning

> documents, establish an interregional transit coalition, participate in interregional coordination for rail freight relief efforts, establish redundancy in regional traffic management centers, deploy technologies to support connected vehicle systems along major travel corridors, use emerging technology to move people and goods within the regions, equip arterials with connectivity capabilities to accommodate new technologies, and nurture the extension of the local and relief arterial networks to enhance mobility and connectivity among growing regions.

conservation, and public health boards. Although this system can be the most democratic form of government in very small rural communities, in larger places, where only a small fraction of the public appears at annual town meetings, it becomes one of the least democratic systems. The system retains strong political support, however, because of widespread public disdain for distant public authorities—a relic of the region's Revolutionary past.

Thousands of special service districts across much of the Northeast further fracture governance. These bodies are responsible for every kind of service, including schools, libraries, fire protection, and water and sewer systems—but are unaccountable to voters. Consequently, taxpayers in much of the Northeast can receive tax bills from their borough, village, town, county, state, and a plethora of special service districts. In response, New England states have essentially abolished county government, other than for oversight of courts and jails. This extremely localized and distributed governance system means that, with layer upon layer of government, tax rates are significantly higher in the Northeast than in other parts of the country and that service levels are highly correlated with community wealth and race.

CITY-COUNTY CONSOLIDATION, METROPOLITAN SERVICE DISTRICTS, AND COMBINED AUTHORITIES

Several U.S. regions—including Miami, Louisville, Indianapolis, Charlotte, Jacksonville, and Memphis—escaped this Northeast problem by consolidating city and county governments. In Texas and other southwestern states, cities have broad annexation powers that allow them to incorporate growing suburbs and move their tax base within city limits. However, none of these places are in the Northeast. The last city-county consolidations there—in places like Philadelphia, Boston, and New York—occurred more than a century ago, and there is little political support for similar actions today. An approach with a better chance of gaining broad political support in the Northeast is creation of metropolitan service districts. Portland, Oregon, and Minnesota's Twin Cities both have institutions to manage regional planning, water and sewer systems, convention centers, and other regional activities, with considerable success.

The United Kingdom's combined authorities, described earlier, are elected to manage regional responsibilities—in some cases, police and fire services for center cities and inner-ring suburbs. The move to combined authorities has been encouraged by the U.K. government, which provides financial incentives and devolved authority to these institutions. In the United States, the federal or state governments could provide similar incentives for the creation of metropolitan service districts or combined authorities in megaregions.

EDUCATION AND TAX REFORM

Education policy is beyond the scope of this book, but education finance is highly relevant to any discussion on reducing racial and economic inequality.

Underfunded and poorly performing schools in many minority and low-income communities contribute to pervasive, systemic racial and economic inequality in metropolitan areas across the country. Although many factors contribute to poor school performance, two key contributors are the highly localized system of school finance and administration in much of the country. An additional problem is the frequent de facto segregation of mostly white suburban school populations from mostly Black and Latinx populations in urban and inner-ring school districts. Across the country, nearly half of school funding comes from local government, and 80 percent of these revenues come from municipal property taxes (Reschovsky 2017).

Overreliance on property taxes has more pernicious effects in the Northeast megaregion than in other parts of the country, given its Balkanized municipal governments and school districts. Schools are likely to be organized and funded at the county level in parts of the South, but in the Northeast, schools are more often organized and funded at the municipal level or, in some places, regional school districts at the subcounty level. Thus, poor communities in the Northeast with lower property values have less property tax revenues to invest in their schools.

To rectify this situation, some northeastern states have taken steps to equalize school funding across districts. The state of Vermont has assumed a larger share of school finances. In Pennsylvania, a legislative proposal to eliminate local property taxes to finance schools failed by a single vote in the state senate in 2017 (Reschovsky 2017). Connecticut has been forced by the state supreme court decision *Sheff v. O'Neill*, 238 Conn. 1, 678 A.2d 1267 (1996), to invest state finances in underperforming urban school districts and create magnet schools that can voluntarily integrate urban and suburban schools. After more than 30 years and several billion dollars in state investments, however, the Hartford school system is more segregated than it was before the *Sheff* lawsuit to integrate Hartford's schools was filed in 1989 (De la Torre 2017). School finances contribute to underperforming segregated schools but are by no means the only factor behind their failure.

If the Northeast and other megaregions are to reform their highly segregated schools and housing markets, they will need to also reform school finance and administration. This could be done through assumption by state or federal government of a larger role in school finance and by regionalization of school districts to encompass both mostly white suburbs and mostly minority cities and inner-ring suburbs. None of this will be easy, however.

USER FEES AND VALUE CAPTURE SYSTEMS

Several trillion dollars of deferred infrastructure investments will be required to restore existing infrastructure systems and build the capacity required in megaregions across the country. To achieve this goal will require an all-hands-on-deck approach to financing and rebuilding infrastructure, with contributions from every level of government, the private sector, and the citizens using and benefiting from these investments. Further, the challenge will be not only to build these systems but also to operate and maintain them to prevent a repeat of the patterns of disinvestment that have brought U.S. infrastructure to its current dilapidated state. This will require a broad range of user fees—utility rates, tolls, fares, value capture systems, and other measures.

ENHANCED INFRASTRUCTURE FINANCING DISTRICTS

One of the significant innovations in infrastructure finance in recent years has been California's Enhanced Infrastructure Financing Districts (SB 628). The act took effect in 2014, authorizing municipalities and counties—and groups of these entities—to form public finance authorities that can finance, build, and operate infrastructure projects through a value-capture system (California Association for Local Economic Development 2021). Public finance authorities determine a base level of taxes collected before an investment is completed and then collect the increment in taxes resulting from the investment. Public finance authorities are also authorized to borrow against this anticipated increment to finance construction of proposed improvements. These projects create value through strategic infrastructure investments that increase economic activity and tax collections and then capture a portion of that value to finance the investments.

CONCLUSION

Governing U.S. megaregions and financing needed investments in megaregion-scale infrastructure, alternative energy, climate adaptation, water systems management, and other measures require new systems. Templates for these innovations already exist in many parts of the United States and overseas but need adapting to the specific circumstances, politics, and ecologies in each megaregion. Overcoming bureaucratic inertia and political foot-dragging will not be easy. For multistate megaregions, governors and state legislators will resist the creation of new agencies beyond their control. Even megaregions contained entirely or mostly within one state will have to overcome considerable resistance to the innovations proposed here. These reforms will require powerful federal leadership and financial incentives to mobilize all levels of government and all sectors of society.

PART IV
RETROSPECT AND PROSPECT

11
REFLECTIONS

BOB YARO
Regional Planning and Land Conservation Experience

Bob Yaro's journey as an urban and regional planner began with the first Earth Day in 1970, when he helped coordinate activities at Wesleyan University in Middletown, Connecticut. While still a student, he became an intern at the Midstate Regional Planning Agency in Middletown, where he worked for Yale urban planning professor Walter Harris. Following graduation in 1971, he became a city planner in New Britain, Connecticut, and created a citywide open-space plan, including restoration of the historic Walnut Hill Park in the city's center, an 80-acre park designed by Frederick Law Olmsted and Calvert Vaux in 1870. In 1973, he became a planner for the Boston Redevelopment Authority with responsibility for citywide open space planning and park design. He participated in planning for restoration of the Boston Common and Public Garden and the Olmsted Park System in preparation for the 1976 bicentennial celebration.

In 1976, following completion of his master's degree in city and regional planning at Harvard, he was appointed chief planner and then deputy commissioner for the Massachusetts Department of Environmental Management (DEM, now the Department of Conservation and Recreation). He led efforts to invest more than a quarter-billion dollars in land conservation projects, including preserving a 54-mile-long section of the Appalachian Trail and the Holyoke Range mountains in western Massachusetts, preserving the Boston Harbor Islands, and creating a network of waterfront parks along the length of the state's coastline.

Yaro and DEM began to experiment with complementary techniques in land conservation and local and regional land use planning. Yaro decided to identify the most significant lands requiring conservation. And even though in the 1970s and 1980s, conservation easements were a relatively new tool, it was clear that the purchase or donation of development rights could become an efficient land conservation tool—particularly if public access and management were not necessary. The fast-growing land trust movement and programs for the farmland purchase of development rights also presented critical partnership opportunities for broader land conservation initiatives.

DEM identified high-priority natural, scenic, and historic landscapes and resources statewide for conservation:

- *Endangered species and rare plant communities.* In partnership with the Nature Conservancy, DEM established the Massachusetts Natural Heritage Program for the most significant rare species habitats and plant communities.

- *Scenic and historic landscapes.* Harry Dodson, DEM's chief landscape architect, created the Massachusetts Landscape Inventory, the nation's first statewide classification and inventory of scenic and historic landscapes. Dodson was assisted by a distinguished advisory panel that included Neil Jorgensen, a landscape historian at Wheelock College; Ernie Gould, director of the Harvard Forest; Hugh Davis, professor of regional planning at the University of Massachusetts, Amherst (and Benton MacKaye, disciple); and Gordon Abbott Jr., director of the Trustees of Reservations, the nation's oldest land trust.

- *Scenic rivers.* DEM environmental planner Katharine Preston conducted the state's first statewide inventory and assessment of scenic river corridors and initiated the designation of scenic rivers.

- *Coastal reserves.* DEM staff surveyed the entire Massachusetts coastline to identify lands suitable for acquisition by the state and municipalities as conservation areas and initiated an ambitious program of coastal land acquisition, doubling the number of sites accessible to the public in less than a decade.

- *Historic urban landscapes.* DEM staff surveyed industrial landscapes, city parks, and town commons, and it worked with the Massachusetts Association of Olmsted Parks to identify parks designed by Frederick Law Olmsted and his colleagues. The resultant 14-city State Heritage Park program protects historic urban landscapes and structures. Other programs based on the survey are the Olmsted Historic Landscape preservation program that restored Olmsted parks in more than a dozen cities and a program to restore important city squares and town commons.

DEM used these inventories to build support for increased state conservation, including a $184 million state land conservation program in 1983. Despite having literally hundreds of millions of dollars to invest (at a time when land values were relatively low and this bought a lot of land) and having set clear priorities for land conservation, it became clear to Yaro and others that it would not be possible to protect large portions of the state's most scenic and natural landscapes from rampant suburban sprawl.

For this reason, DEM adopted regional plans and land use regulatory schemes. Under the state's new scenic rivers statute, which Yaro administered, DEM had the authority to unilaterally impose protective orders (deed restrictions) on lands within 300 feet of the river's edge. But when it came time to designate the North River as the state's first scenic river, Yaro wanted to build more public support for this designation. To do this, he invited the head of Maine's Saco River Commission to a meeting of town officials and residents to discuss protecting that watershed's scenic, natural, and recreational resources. When local officials demanded that a similar commission be created for the North River, DEM readily agreed. Given support from all six towns in the area, necessary legislation was quickly enacted, and in 1978, the North River Commission was created to protect one of the state's most important tidal rivers.

Real estate interests opposed the commission's creation, arguing that it would reduce property values. However, just the opposite occurred: property values within the commission's jurisdiction increased significantly because of the additional security the protective orders provided. This sequence—initial skepticism and opposition, based on fears of loss of control and reduced property values, followed by public support and increased property values—has played out repeatedly across the country for other regional land conservation and land use regulatory systems.

In 1982, DEM established the Connecticut Valley Action Program to promote land conservation in the Massachusetts section of the valley. Yaro hired Terry Blunt, former executive director of the Connecticut River Watershed Council, to lead the program. For 28 years, until his death in 2010, Blunt led the program's wide-ranging and highly effective efforts to protect the valley's important agricultural and riparian lands and its scenic character.

That same year, Yaro proposed a land bank for Nantucket funded by a 2 percent real estate transfer tax to bankroll land conservation and historic preservation. The tax was later increased to 4 percent and also funded affordable housing. Yaro proposed this tax at a forum held to discuss Nantucket's future, and instead of being invited to take the first boat off the island, he and his proposal received near unanimous support from town officials and businesses. The island's powerful real estate and business interests embraced the proposed legislation out of concerns that the island could become overwhelmed by speculative second-home development. In the ensuing months, Yaro worked with Bill Klein, then director of the Nantucket Planning and Economic Development Commission, to gain support from the town meeting, which is Nantucket's form of city council, and the state legislature, which created the Nantucket Land Bank in 1983. This became the precedent for legislation for community preservation in Massachusetts, New York, and other states in the Northeast.

Working with the Trustees of Reservations and the Nantucket Conservation Foundation, the Nantucket Land Bank has protected half the island's land area. These efforts have been complemented by the adoption of sophisticated zoning and other tools to prevent large-scale subdivision in the island's coastal areas and central moorland district. These efforts and the work of an island-wide historic district commission have preserved Nantucket's scenery and groundwater resources, prevented overdevelopment, and led to some of the nation's highest property values—yet more evidence for the economic benefits of regional land conservation and land use regulatory programs.

In 1985, Yaro became a professor at the University of Massachusetts, Amherst, and the following year he obtained special legislation to establish the university's Center for Rural Massachusetts, which he led in partnership with Gordon Abbott Jr., who had just retired as director of the Trustees of Reservations. The center promoted smarter patterns of growth in rural and exurban communities across the commonwealth through improved land use planning and other means. In 1986, the center initiated the country's first smart growth initiative, Growing Smart in Massachusetts (and coined the term *smart growth*), and enlisted the support of Governor Michael Dukakis and First Lady Kitty Dukakis in its work. In 1988, the center published *Dealing with Change in the Connecticut River Valley*, written by Yaro, Randall Arendt, Harry Dodson, and Elizabeth Brabec. This book presented triptychs of visual simulations of alternative, conventional, and smart growth strategies for typical landscapes across the valley. It also included a set of model bylaws that could be used by towns to promote the smart growth alternatives illustrated in the book.

Over the next 20 years, Terry Blunt's Connecticut Valley Action Program advocated for adoption of smart growth bylaws by dozens of communities in the valley and across the commonwealth. Several of Yaro's students became town planners, land trust officers, state officials, or consulting planners and landscape architects, and they worked to implement smart growth across the region. Improved town plans and regulations were complemented by state and local land conservation programs, such as the purchase by the Massachusetts Department of Agricultural Resources of development rights for thousands of acres of prime agricultural lands across the valley, the state's most important agricultural district. Tens of thousands of additional acres have been protected by four highly effective land trusts: the Kestrel, Franklin, and Hilltown Land Trusts and the Valley Land Fund (which merged with Kestrel in 2011). Blunt, Dodson, and Yaro were all cofounders of these land trusts. In addition, Gordon Abbott went on to organize the Land Trust Exchange, which later became the Land Trust Alliance—a nationwide coalition of land trusts.

Supported by Center for Rural Massachusetts resources, UMass faculty and students have worked on local and regional smart growth, land conservation, and economic development plans across the commonwealth. The center also organized town planning institutes to train town planners and planning board members in dozens of rural and suburban towns, in partnership with the university's cooperative extension service.

In 1988, Yaro and the Center for Rural Massachusetts worked with Armando Carbonell (then executive director of the advisory Cape Cod Planning and Economic Development Commission) to create the Cape Cod Commission. CRM also worked with Don Connors, a Boston attorney, and former U.S. senator Paul Tsongas on this initiative. The commission was authorized to create a regional plan for this exceptional coastal region, with the requirement that town plans and regulations in the region must be consistent with the regional plan. The commission was also authorized to designate districts of critical planning concern and regulate developments of regional impact. Since its inception, the commission has prevented overdevelopment of the Cape's sensitive landscapes and has protected the region's sole source aquifer. It also became a model for a new generation of locally initiated and controlled bottom-up regional commissions across the Northeast megaregion.

Yaro, Carbonell, Tsongas, and the *Boston Globe* editor in chief Tom Winship also organized 1000 Friends of Massachusetts, a statewide advocacy group for state and local smart growth policies and programs, in 1988. Simultaneously, the center's staff worked with state senator Carmen Buell—who was also a trained regional planner—to create and staff the Commission on Growth and Change in the Commonwealth. The commission developed pioneering state smart growth policies supporting local and regional planning initiatives.

In 1989, after the *New Yorker* magazine published a profile by staff writer Tony Hiss of Yaro and his work at the Center for Rural Massachusetts, Al Appleton, commissioner of the New York City Department of Environmental Protection, asked Yaro to speak at Belleayre Mountain Ski Area in the Catskill region of upstate New York about his regional land conservation work in the Connecticut Valley and on Cape Cod (Hiss 1989). Appleton wanted Yaro to explain how these concepts could be adapted to protect New York City's upstate watersheds, which were then being threatened by unplanned suburban and rural sprawl. This planted seeds that would lead several years later to an innovative program to protect the watersheds.

Then, in the fall of 1989, Yaro was asked by the RPA to lead its Third Regional Plan for the New York metropolitan region, which he agreed to do. What began as a two-year assignment became a quarter-century commitment to the RPA, the Third Regional Plan, and *A Region at Risk*, a documentary book of the plan, coauthored by Yaro and Tony Hiss, in 1996. A key feature of the Third Regional Plan was its proposed regional reserves—large landscapes administered by regional land use regulatory commissions to protect the region's surface water and groundwater public water supply systems, threatened by suburban sprawl and second-home development.

When the RPA began work on the Third Regional Plan, the tristate region already had a regional reserve in place—the New Jersey Pinelands National Reserve, established by an act of Congress and implemented by state legislation in 1978. This reserve was imposed on the Pinelands region through concerted federal and state action. By the early 1990s, it was widely assumed that this kind of top-down regional commission could not be replicated in an era when federal leadership on land conservation was absent and when state officials were less willing to impose similar protective measures on rural regions. For this reason, the RPA promoted replication of the Cape Cod bottom-up model of regional planning for its new generation of regional reserves. The first of the tristate region's reserves to be established was the 100,000-acre Long Island Central Pine Barrens, administered by the Central Pine Barrens Commission, established by an act of the New York State Legislature in 1993. As on Cape Cod, preservation of the region's sole source aquifer was an important driver of this initiative.

Yaro and other RPA staff participated in a broad coalition of environmental, business, and civic groups to establish the commission, and subsequently the RPA drafted its innovative management plan and the nation's first regional transfer of development rights system. As a result of the bottom-up process used to create the Pine Barrens commission, the three participating towns, Suffolk County, and the region's legislative leaders all strongly supported it, smoothing the way for state legislation to be enacted under Republican governor George Pataki's leadership.

Then, in 1997, a second reserve was established through a similar bottom-up process, this time for New York City's 1-million-acre upstate public water supply system, under the leadership of Mike Finnegan, an attorney on Governor Pataki's staff. The RPA and a broad coalition of environmental and community groups worked with Finnegan, the city's Department of Environmental Protection, local officials, and residents to create an innovative system to protect the city's watershed from inappropriate development, agricultural runoff, and failing septic systems. This, in turn, enabled the city to obtain a waiver from federal Clean Water Act requirements that municipal water supply systems be filtered. To obtain this waiver, the city committed to making a $1.4 billion investment in land conservation, improvements in municipal wastewater treatment systems in watershed communities, and reductions to pollution entering the city's upstate reservoirs. But because of the waiver, it avoided spending $13 billion to build a filtration plant that would annually cost hundreds of millions to operate. New York continues to have the largest unfiltered public water supply in the country, benefiting its 9 million users.

The RPA then advocated for creating a fourth regional reserve, this one in New Jersey's Highland region. Led by Joe Maraziti, chairman of the State Planning Commission, the new New Jersey Highlands Council was empowered to develop a regional master plan to guide development and preserve open spaces and water resources in this

859,000-acre region, which contains the public water supplies for millions of North Jersey residents.

What Has Yaro Learned?

From his experience over decades of working to protect large landscapes and advance other public policy goals, Yaro concluded that a key to success is to not only have a compelling vision that inspires action but also stay focused on political realities. In Theodore Roosevelt's admonition, "Keep your eyes on the stars, but your feet on the ground" (Safire and Safir 1982, 164). This was good advice in the late 19th century, and is valid today. In addition, success depends on patience, persistence, and perseverance. Yaro learned that it might take years, or even decades, to achieve his objectives.

Finally, it is important to seek allies with diverse interests and create coalitions of unlikely partners to build political support. The coalition behind the creation of the Long Island Central Pine Barrens protection plan, for example, included the Long Island Association business group, the Pine Barrens Society, the Nature Conservancy, and the Long Island Homebuilders Institute. Although each of these groups had its own narrowly defined special interest, they came together around a shared interest to protect this 100,000-acre groundwater and ecological preserve. Generally, it is enlightened self-interest, not altruism, that motivates people to take action on difficult environmental and land conservation initiatives. A focus on public health—in particular, public water supply protection—is a motivator. People get the connection between their health and what comes out of their water taps. A concern for public health and disease prevention was one of the reasons for the creation of Frederick Law Olmsted's urban parks in the 19th century, and along with climate change, it remains a prime motivator for action in this postpandemic time.

Protecting large landscapes and their resource systems requires the following provisions:

- The public must perceive a threat to an important resource system or landscape—for example, a public water supply system. Loss of life from floods, fires, or other extreme weather events can galvanize public support for protecting the resource or protecting and restoring landscapes. Our new understanding of the critical role that large landscapes have in advancing global climate efforts can also underpin public support for actions needed to protect these places.
- A regional conservation or planning agency must have authority from the state or federal government to protect the resource system; further, municipal or county plans and land use regulations must be consistent with and designed to implement the regional plan.
- Federal, state, local, and private land conservation programs with dedicated revenue streams and staff are needed to protect the most significant lands,

using the entire land conservation toolbox of fee-simple and less-than-fee preservation techniques.
- Leadership is needed to initiate and sustain these programs, skilled staff to administer them, and effective outside advocates to support them.
- Public understanding of and support for local, regional, and private initiatives must be maintained. Creating and managing reserves is not enough—they must be protected in perpetuity from attempts to restrict conservation efforts. Determined advocacy groups cannot forever fend off attacks.

MING ZHANG
Journey to Megaregion Study

Zhang's interest in megaregions can be traced back to the late 1980s, when he made a case study of Beijing for his master's degree at Tsinghua University, Beijing. It was a time when China's economy had begun to take off under the open-door policy, and Chinese cities were set to expand rapidly. Beijing, like other major cities in the country, faced severe housing shortages, infrastructure degradation, and insufficient public services after decades of disinvestments. Population and economic growth placed additional pressures on Beijing to expand physically. Zhang's mentor, Professor Liangyong Wu, suggested he examine the problems facing Beijing from a regional perspective, investigating the development characteristics at the urban-rural edge of the city.

This challenged Zhang both analytically and logistically. Having received primarily architectural training in college, Zhang did not have the knowledge or skills for a typical regional analysis. Remote sensing data were not yet available, and aerial photos were restricted. For transportation, all that Zhang could afford was a used bike, and the limited bus service was not adequate for making circumferential field trips around Beijing. Zhang decided to take a low-tech approach. On April 22, 1988, Zhang celebrated his birthday with a test-run biking excursion to northern Beijing. The following day, he rode his bike for about 50 miles in 13 hours, stopping to take more than 400 photos of development conditions along the urban edge of Beijing. The low-tech, slow-mobility trip was eye-opening. Zhang observed a part of the metropolis that was unimaginable to him from walking around the university campus, the shopping districts, or tourist centers like Tiananmen Square.

The trip around Beijing led Zhang to begin studying cities as regions. Cities in China are administrative territories consisting of a continuous landscape from a highly urbanized center to the rural villages and farmland surrounding the center. The transition from urban to rural (and vice versa) was gradual. Other parts of the world, as Zhang observed years later in the United States, display similar gradients in the urban landscape. Today, however, territorial boundaries are not the brick walls of ancient days; they exist in legal or administrative documents and in people's minds.

These boundaries define territories of responsibilities and identities and also create jurisdictional or psychological barriers that resist between-territory interactions and integrations.

After graduating from Tsinghua, Zhang accepted a teaching job at Huazhong University of Science and Technology in Wuhan, the capital city of his home province of Hubei. Wuhan, in central China, is at the intersection of China's north–south railway that runs between Beijing and Guangzhou (Hong Kong) and the east–west waterway on the Yangtze River (between Shanghai and Chongqing). Wuhan's central location gives it national importance for highway, waterway, and railway transportation.

Zhang's travel experience in China, starting in his college days and to the present, attests to the country's mobility improvements and regional transformation facilitated by major transportation investments, especially high-speed rail networks. Zhang grew up in a rural area about 90 miles east of Wuhan. In the early 1980s, when Zhang attended Tsinghua University, a one-way trip from his home to Beijing required two days: a four-hour bus journey to Wuhan, an overnight stay in Wuhan, and then a 22-hour train ride from Wuhan to Beijing covering the last 760 miles. The railway between Beijing and Wuhan was China's first long-distance line, built in the last decade of the Qing dynasty. The line, then called the Peking–Hankou Railway, started passenger service in 1906. The line's infrastructure and operations have been upgraded many times since then. In the early 1980s, the train cruised at about 50 miles per hour. At this speed, Zhang's trip from Wuhan to Beijing lasted nearly a full day. Because of the distance and the limited travel options, Zhang could afford only two trips home per year, during the winter and summer breaks. In the 1990s, fast trains made fewer stops and reduced the trip time by a few hours. By the turn of the century, the fastest train serving the Wuhan and Beijing route took approximately 10 hours.

The arrival of high-speed rail has redefined China's space-time geography. China's first service started in 2008, connecting Beijing with Tianjin over a 70-mile track, mainly to serve the 2008 Olympics. In the following year, China's first long-distance, interprovincial high-speed rail line began operating between Wuhan and Guangzhou in southern China. On December 26, 2009, Zhang, joined by his son, rode the high-speed train on its inaugural day. The 660-mile trip took about three hours. Three years later, in 2012, high-speed rail service between Wuhan and Beijing commenced, running parallel to the 100-year-old conventional railway and compressing the trip time to around four hours. By the end of 2020, China was operating a high-speed rail network of more than 23,000 miles.

At Huazhong University in Wuhan, Zhang hosted Peter Seidel, a visiting professor from Cincinnati, Ohio. Seidel was a protégé of Ludwig Mies van der Rohe and Ludwig Hilberseimer and practiced architectural design early in his career. Later, as his environmental consciousness grew, Seidel dismissed van der Rohe's glass-wall designs and started writing and teaching as adjunct faculty on designing and planning for environmentally sound and socially integrated communities, calling himself an environmental architect-planner. Seidel introduced to Huazhong University students the urban-belt planning project he had proposed in the late 1960s. An urban belt consists of connected circles along a transportation corridor for both mass rapid transit and freeway. Each circle centers on a transit station, has a radius of walking distance from the station, and is of relatively high population density. Open landscape separates the circles from each other, and green wedges penetrate into the core of each circle. Seidel was hired to implement the project in Cincinnati during the Lyndon Johnson administration's Model Cities program, but the Richard Nixon administration terminated that program. Zhang was enamored with the urban-belt concept and realized years later that it was the precursor to transit-oriented development, a model popularized worldwide some three decades later. Great plans and designs cannot become reality without great timing.

While teaching planning at Huazhong University, Zhang continued his inquiry into rural-urban development with case studies of small cities around Wuhan. Increasingly, however, he felt he lacked sufficient theoretical and analytic tools to disentangle the more complex regional puzzles before him. He decided to pursue further education and training. Seidel introduced Zhang to the planning program at the University of Cincinnati. Zhang liked Cincinnati, both as a place to live and as a lab for studying planning in the setting of a market economy and private land ownership. He learned that Cincinnati was the first U.S. city to have a comprehensive plan approved and adopted into law by a city council. What impressed Zhang the most during his short stay in Cincinnati was the village of Greenhills, in the northern suburbs of the Cincinnati metro area, which Zhang did a case study of for a term project. Greenhills was one of just three greenbelt towns built in the Greenbelt Towns program under Franklin Roosevelt's New Deal. From a bird's-eye view today, one can hardly distinguish Greenhills from other suburban communities in terms of their physical layouts of curvilinear streets and cul-de-sacs, which many have blamed for increased auto dependency in U.S. suburbs. From his field trips to Greenhills, Zhang learned that the planning and design of Greenhills followed garden-city principles and neighborhood-unit norms. The layout featured walking and biking networks that connected the ends of cul-de-sacs and separated nonmotorized movements from motor vehicle flows. This network, however, had been eliminated in most surrounding neighborhoods. To Zhang, it was the elimination of the protected pedestrian and bike network, not the street curvature and cul-de-sacs per se, that heightened suburban automobility. Decades later, a protected pedestrian and bike network has made a comeback, hailed by the new urbanist designers.

After a year's study in Cincinnati, Zhang transferred to the State University of New York at Albany. The program at SUNY Albany attracted Zhang because of the opportunity to earn a graduate certificate in geographic information systems (GIS) and spatial analysis when completing a master's degree in regional planning. The additional technical skills garnered for Zhang his first job in the United States. He worked as a GIS specialist at the Rockefeller Institute of Government in Albany. Zhang helped create the institute's first GIS lab, providing support to its researchers in data processing and mapping. This job exposed Zhang to research on place-based federal initiatives—for example, the Empowerment Zone and Enterprise Communities programs. After two years' work at the Rockefeller Institute of Government, Zhang wanted to do more than data processing and mapping. He decided to pursue a Ph.D. and thus quit his job and entered the Massachusetts Institute of Technology (MIT).

A teaching and research assistant opportunity at MIT brought Zhang back to his initial interest, the megalopolis. In 1999, Zhang joined an MIT team led by Professors Tunney Lee and Ralph Gakenheimer for a planning studio project that explored cooperative strategies for Hong Kong and its neighboring cities in the Pearl River Delta region. This was just two years after the transfer of Hong Kong's sovereignty to China under the "one country, two systems" framework. Although the political and social divide between Hong Kong and the mainland remained wide, the economic interactions between the two sides quickly grew. Business, trade, and light-industrial sectors were particularly keen to lower physical and administrative cross-border barriers.

The MIT team first investigated the existing constraints and future potentials facing the Delta region. They then developed five scenarios and analyzed each scenario's implications for the region as a whole and for its constituent cities and communities. Coordinated integration turned out to be the best option. Cities on the mainland were eager to boost their economies but lacked expertise and access to the international market. Hong Kong had those. Hong Kong, in turn, had severe development constraints because of shortages of land, housing, labor, fresh water, and other resources. The vast mainland had those. Economic integration everywhere has often been complicated and delayed by political controversies, and nearly all major projects for expanding the Hong Kong–China cross-border links ran into political resistance. A couple of controversial projects were the Hong Kong–Shenzhen Western Corridor, the high-speed rail extension from Shenzhen to West Kowloon of Hong Kong, and the bridge linking Hong Kong, Zhuhai, and Macau. After decades of joint efforts, these projects, and many others, have been completed and have been serving the Delta region and beyond.

Zhang's teaching career in the United States started at Texas A&M University. During his three years in College Station, two projects increased Zhang's awareness of the importance of cross-jurisdiction coordination for addressing growing regional challenges. One was the Urban Mobility Report led by Tim Lomax. The project assesses and annually reports highway congestion and the economic costs to major U.S. cities and metropolitan areas. Congestion continues to worsen across the country, yet public interventions have been ineffectual. The other project was research led by Michael Lindell and funded by the National Science Foundation to develop a decision support system for evacuation management in the Gulf Coast region. From this project, Zhang gained field knowledge on disaster planning by joining the research team to interview the county emergency response coordinators in southeast Texas and Louisiana.

In 2004, Zhang accepted a job offer from the University of Texas at Austin, where Fritz Steiner was dean of the School of Architecture. The first Penn studio took place the same year, which led to the rediscovery of Jean Gottmann's megalopolis, occurring across the United States in a new century and relabeled as *megaregion*. The following year, the megaregion scholars at Penn invited schools to join the megaregion research network by contributing case studies of their home megaregions. Steiner asked the Texas faculty if anyone would be interested in studying the Texas Triangle megaregion. Zhang, along with his colleague Kent Butler, joined Steiner. To learn from the European spatial planning experience, the U.S. megaregion network, led by Bob Yaro and Armando Carbonell, organized a charrette in Madrid, Spain, in 2006. Zhang, Butler, and 13 Texas students participated in the Madrid charrette, where they were joined by two other university teams, from Penn and the University of Michigan.

In the subsequent years, Zhang has continued his exploration of megaregion concepts and development in the United States and across Asia and Europe. His concentration has been on transportation in the Texas Triangle. Whether the Texas Triangle qualifies as a single megaregion has caused debate. Some scholars identify two or three separate megaregions in the triangle area. Regardless of how many megaregions there are, the commonly agreed challenge facing the Texas Triangle is how to accommodate its future population growth, projected to double by 2050; and the associated demand for travel, housing, and resources. Zhang and his team estimate that the total travel demand in the Texas Triangle would likely reach 1.12 trillion person-miles by 2050. Close to 70 percent of it would be by high-speed travel, and air transportation would not be able to keep up. Accommodating this travel demand would require innovative transportation solutions such as high-speed rail, hyperloop, and increased telecommuting.

The choice of transportation technology has implications in the long run for how cities and regions will physically expand and how much land and resources will be consumed. From a close examination of Texas's records of highway construction and satellite images taken between 1979 and 2002, Zhang and his team found that over 80 percent of urbanized area was within two miles of a highway in the Austin area. A 1 percent increase in road length was associated with approximately a 5 percent increase of urbanized land. The urbanization decreases by nearly 45 percent per one-mile increase in distance from the highway. In another study of the Gulf Coast megaregion, Zhang and his team reported that the per capita traffic volume in 2050 would be double the 2010 level. The total volume of passenger and freight traffic would grow much faster, to four times as high in 2050 as in 2010.

Transportation vulnerability becomes obvious during extreme weather events. Hurricane Katrina in 2005 devastated New Orleans and other communities along the Gulf Coast. The storm displaced more than 1 million people, about one-fifth permanently. Many displaced Louisiana residents fled to Texas. Three weeks after Hurricane Katrina's landfall, Hurricane Rita threatened the Gulf Coast and Houston. About 3 million people evacuated before Rita's landfall. Two families, Zhang's friends, fled Houston to seek shelter in Austin. The 170-mile trip took more than 12 hours. Routes from Houston to Dallas also saw gridlock, lasting more than 20 hours for many families. These events demonstrated how vulnerable a car-dependent infrastructure is in the event of disasters like hurricanes. Building resilience to mitigate a disaster's effects cannot be done by individual cities and counties alone. Megaregion thinking is critical for local communities to improve resilience.

Zhang's studies of megaregions extend to other countries as well. China's high-speed rail development and megaregion planning efforts lured him to collaborate with Chinese scholars sharing his interests. He and Liwen Liu of Jiangxi Normal University, China, examined the effect of high-speed rail on mobility, accessibility, and productivity (Liu and Zhang 2018). The study analyzed data for 266 prefecture-level cities from 2006, before high-speed rail, and from 2014, with high-speed rail. They found that high-speed rail reduced city-to-city travel times by an average 45 percent, or 589 minutes. Access disparity within most city-cluster regions decreased, whereas the between-region gaps remained. The study estimated high-speed rail elasticity of productivity per capita at 0.28 nationwide. A follow-up study examined high-speed rail impacts on small and midsize cities in the mid–Yangtze River city-cluster region. The study found that an integrated multimodal system that included high-speed rail would provide the cities the most travel-time savings and accessibility gains. The transformative impacts of high-speed rail are clear in coastal megaregions, such as the Yangtze River Delta city-cluster region centered on Shanghai. Zhang and his collaborator Jie Xu from Tongji University surveyed passengers and found evidence of economic and spatial integration between the constituent cities and metros in the Yangtze River Delta megaregion (Xu et al. 2019).

High-speed rail generates direct and wider impacts, as evidenced in Europe and Asia. Expected and realized high-speed rail effects vary among counties with different development histories and contexts. In European countries where rail transportation has long served intra- and intercity travel, high-speed rail is an evolution in services for mobility and access. In Asian countries, high-speed rail arrived when personal mobility was low. Japan, for example, opened the world's first high-speed rail line in 1964, when it had about 80 motor vehicles for every 1,000 people. This was also the case in China, where vehicle ownership was about 80 per 1,000 people when the country launched its high-speed rail services in 2008. For ordinary Chinese citizens, high-speed rail elevated personal mobility for intercity travel by a huge margin. In contrast, the United States has high personal mobility when measured by vehicle ownership (more than 800 per 1,000 people). High personal mobility coupled with extensive air transportation networks creates high barriers for high-speed rail to enter the U.S. passenger service market. The successful high-speed rail experience seen in European and Asian countries cannot be transferred wholesale to the United States. However, this does not mean that high-speed rail or high-performance rail has no market at all. The alarm over climate change demands creative thinking to reduce dependence on cars and reduce greenhouse gas emissions from the transportation sector. In most countries that have high-speed rail, the government has made the investment, but innovative business models are emerging to finance and operate high-speed rail services. One example is the Dallas–Houston high-speed rail project being developed by the company Texas Central.

The many examples and variety of efforts from around the world have motivated Zhang to coordinate international exchanges and learning on megaregions and to actively participate in them. In 2012, Zhang organized an international symposium on high-speed rail in Wuhan, with participant scholars from 12 countries or regions. In 2013, Zhang arranged for and accompanied a planning delegation from China to visit the RPA in New York City. The delegation of high-profile scholars and planners was specifically interested in the America 2050 work. Professor Liangyong Wu of Tsinghua University has been researching the Greater Beijing area, now named the Beijing-Tianjin-Hebei City-Cluster Region, for over 40 years. Zhang has stayed in touch with Wu and attended multiple symposiums organized by Tsinghua, including one in 2014, when Bob Yaro gave a keynote speech on U.S. megaregion efforts.

In 2015, the U.S. Department of Transportation released its plan "Beyond Traffic 2045: Trends and Choices." The plan highlights the significance of megaregions to the nation's future. In 2016, the Department of Transportation issued an open call for proposals to create consortiums through its University Transportation Center program authorized by the 2015 federal Fixing America's Surface Transportation Act. Zhang and his colleagues at UT Austin partnered with the teams from Penn, Texas Southern University, and Louisiana State University to submit a proposal with a central theme of megaregions. The team won a grant, and hence the creation of the Cooperative Mobility for Competitive Megaregions (CM_2). Since 2016, CM^2 has funded more than 60 research projects and supported more than a dozen symposiums or workshops. This book is one of CM^2's culminating projects.

As part of fulfilling its education mission, CM^2 supported international workshops on megaregions. The first one took place in Manchester, United Kingdom, in 2019, offering an excellent opportunity to learn from the Northern Powerhouse initiative and the UK 2070 study (UK2070 Commission 2020). In early 2020, right before the COVID-19 pandemic, a joint team of UT Austin and Penn students and faculty visited the Randstad and Rhine-Ruhr region. The Netherlands' Room for the River program and the Ruhr's branding strategy as the City of Cities offered enlightening lessons for other megaregions around the world.

What Has Zhang Learned?

- Cultivate the habits of visionary thinking, communication, and persistence. These traits are needed when addressing the challenges cities and regions face from the very nature of megaregions—for instance, traffic congestion, pollution, and socioeconomic inequality. Population growth and movement, technological advances, and politics (from local to global) add dynamic forces to the mix, as do extreme weather events and pandemics.
- Learn from international experience. Successes such as the transformation of the Rhine-Ruhr or implementation of high-speed rail in Asia should be studied for their valuable lessons, but they cannot be simply copied and pasted to other regions and countries. Megaregions are global geographic phenomena that share many characteristics, but each has a unique history and geosocial setting.
- Build the megaregion knowledge base. Scholars like Patrick Geddes and Jean Gottmann described the megalopolis decades ago, yet contemporary knowledge on megaregions is limited. Whether theoretical, empirical, or a collection of best practices, knowledge is the basis for megaregional planning, strategic investment, and policy. Megaregional governance needs particular research attention. Megaregions cross jurisdictional boundaries. How can federal agencies help? U.S. federal precedents are the Tennessee Valley Authority and interstate highways (successes) and the Greenbelt Towns and Model Cities programs (failures).

FREDERICK R. STEINER
Regional Planning and Land Conservation Experiences

Fritz Steiner began his planning journey as an undergraduate cooperative-education (alternating academic quarters with on-the-job quarters) student from the University of Cincinnati working in a new community in Ohio beginning in 1970. He worked for an idealistic homebuilder, Don Huber, and a crusty Harvard-educated landscape architect, Gerwin Rohrbach, who taught him the basics about public hearings, urban design, and site design. In a time of social turmoil—the civil rights movement, Vietnam War protests—Steiner discovered Ian McHarg's *Design with Nature* while helping organize a book fair at the first Earth Day. Designing with nature resonated with him, having grown up hiking in the open space created by Arthur

Morgan's Miami Conservancy District. Steiner thus determined to go to the University of Pennsylvania and study with McHarg.

As graduation from Penn neared in 1977, Steiner sought to reenter practice with his new ecological understanding. He had not planned on becoming an academic, but the opportunity arose to help create programs in landscape architecture and regional planning at Washington State University with Ken Brooks and others. Inspired by his co-op background in practical work and the example of Mao Tse-tung, who believed knowledge begins with practice, Steiner joined the staff of the Whitman County Regional Planning Commission one day a week during the academic year and full time through the summers. This put him on the front lines of the farmland preservation movement in the Pacific Northwest and nationally.

Washington State University is in the highly productive and highly erodible Palouse region of eastern Washington and northern Idaho. Led by planners Bill Wagner and Jack Kartez and commission chair Norm Hatley, the regional planning commission adopted a plan, which was then approved by county commissioners. The plan and its implementing ordinances zoned the entire county for agricultural use. New development was permitted only adjacent to cities and towns. New rural housing had to adhere to strict suitability requirements that included avoiding prime farmlands and environmentally sensitive areas. This late 1970s plan and its implementation ordinances has stood the test of time and remains largely in place. Steiner wrote and produced a film about farmlands preservation, became involved at the origin of the American Farmland Trust, went to the Netherlands as a Fulbright scholar at Wageningen University to study landscape planning there, and worked with state senator Phil Talmadge on what eventually became the Washington Growth Management Act of 1990.

Meanwhile, Steiner's academic career was going just fine, and he was awarded tenure and promotion to associate professor. He decided that, to continue to develop as an academic, it would be wise to pursue a Ph.D., and he returned to Penn in 1983. McHarg invited him to coordinate the Landscape Architecture and Regional Planning 501 studio, where the basics of reading landscapes were taught by a team of environmental and social scientists, landscape architects, and planners. After the end of his first year of doctoral studies, he took a summer job with the National Park Service. The Philadelphia office of the Park Service, under the leadership of Glenn Eugster, had become a leader in the green-line park movement. With Eugster, Cecily Corcoran Kihn, and others, Steiner worked on the Blackstone Heritage Corridor Conservation Plan in Rhode Island and Massachusetts, where he met Bob Yaro for the first time.

Steiner also homed in on a dissertation topic under the direction of his chair, Ann Louise Strong, a leading environmental attorney. He focused on soil conservation in the Palouse region and across the nation. This work would influence reform in the U.S. Department of Agriculture and programs for conservation reserve and conservation easements. He met many dedicated Agriculture officials in the process, including Lloyd Wright. Wright was designing a suitability rating system for farmlands, LESA (land evaluation and site assessment), and enlisted Steiner to help.

From Washington State, Steiner moved to the University of Colorado at Denver in 1987 and then to Arizona State University in 1989. He worked on several large-scale planning initiatives in the Front Range of Colorado, the Verde River Valley of Arizona, the San Pedro River in Mexico and the United States, and the Phoenix metropolitan area. For instance, with the Phoenix planning department, he helped develop a plan for conservation and development for the northern 20 percent of the city (some 110 square miles). At Arizona State, his most frequent teaching and research collaborator was landscape architect Laurel McSherry, who significantly influenced his approach to design and planning. Steiner also became a fellow of the American Academy in Rome, where he studied Italian provincial-level planning. Both editions of his *The Living Landscape* had been translated into Italian, and the volume informed a new provincial planning law. Steiner was interested in how his book was being adapted in provincial planning in one of the oldest Western cultures.

In 2001, Steiner became dean of the School of Architecture at the University of Texas at Austin, but he remained involved in on-the-ground planning and design projects. For example, he was involved in the five-county Envision Central Texas initiative, the Hill Country Conservancy, research about the Texas Triangle, the creation of the Waller Creek Conservancy (now the Waterloo Greenway Conservancy), the new City of Austin comprehensive plan (the first approved in three decades), and a new campus plan for the University of Texas. Meanwhile, Tsinghua University in Beijing was establishing a landscape architecture program, with Laurie Olin as its first chair. Olin enlisted Steiner to join him, and Steiner had more opportunities to work with Chinese colleagues in their large-scale planning efforts.

In 2016, Steiner returned to Penn as dean of the Stuart Weitzman School of Design. Among other projects, he has helped establish the Ian L. McHarg Center for Urbanism and Ecology and organized activities around the 50th anniversary of the publication of *Design with Nature*. Working with Richard Weller, Karen M'Closkey, Billy Fleming, and Bill Whitaker, Steiner was part of Design with Nature Now, a project that resulted in three exhibitions, a book, and an international conference that opened on the summer solstice of 2019, officially launching the McHarg Center.

What Has Steiner Learned?

Dwight Eisenhower once said that "plans are useless, but planning is indispensable" (1984, 1516). A plan is but one artifact of planning. Successful planning yields many other results. Ideas from the planning process, realized in the built environment, result in better places for people to live, work, study, recreate, and worship. Lives are transformed.

From his national and international experiences in planning at the megaregional scale, Steiner has learned the following lessons:

- A good planner seeks out everything possible that has been recorded about the planning area. Study the history of the place, previous plans, existing laws, maps of everything, and scholars' research on the natural environment and the human cultures there. Places are layered with meaning. People have settled them with hope that sometimes has been realized, other times not. They have left accounts of their settlement and recorded their plans and expectations.

- Think in geological time. The planet predates humans, but this age is the Anthropocene epoch, in which human activity has significant effects on Earth's weather, geology, and ecosystems. Consider the consequences of a plan for future generations.

- Learn from past planning failures and successes. Every community has its share of both. A good planner not only identifies what worked and what did not in past plan but also ascertains what led to those outcomes. Failures often involve lack of citizen support. Conversely, positive results frequently flow from informed political leadership ready to act when opportunity presents.

- Be bold and visionary but humble. "Make no little plans," the architect Daniel Burnham (1910, 5) stated in a 1910 London speech: "They have no magic to stir men's blood and probably themselves will not be realized. Make big plans; aim high in hope and work." Among others, Jane Jacobs (1961) and Robert Caro (1974) have documented the folly of big plans that were too big and not grounded in the desires of citizens. An ideal plan strikes a balance between high aspirations and firm grounding.

- Illustrate plans generously with photographs, drawings, maps, and diagrams. People are visual creatures. Illustrations clarify complex ideas and illuminate process outcomes. Good planners possess graphic sophistication or appreciation.

- Be adaptable and flexible. Things never go completely to plan. A good planner compromises, especially on small matters (and knowing what is not important is an art in itself). However, remain loyal to core values and be prepared to walk away from situations that are unethical.

- Early successes help realize a plan's goals. Such success can be credited to the effectiveness of the planning process. Conversely, early failures are not helpful. Sometimes a project or policy envisioned in a plan falls flat because of opposition, controversy, or expense. By the way, be sure to take credit for the successful project or policy. Also, own the failures.

- Keep planning. Humans are planners. That fundamental trait applied to shaping communities affects how future generations plan and live their lives.

12

MEGAREGIONS AND THE NEXT "AMERICAN CENTURY"

All of us are called, each to his own measure of capacity, and each in the widest horizon of his vision, to create the first great American Century.

—HENRY LUCE, *LIFE MAGAZINE*, FEBRUARY 17, 1941

IN 1941, JUST BEFORE THE UNITED STATES entered World War II, Henry Luce proclaimed the 20th century to be the "American Century." Whether the 21st century becomes the second great American century will be determined by the success of the nation's megaregions.

In the 21st century, the United States may no longer have the world's largest economy for the first time since 1870, when U.S. GDP surpassed that of Germany and the United Kingdom. China is expected to surpass the United States in GDP within the next 5 to 10 years because of decades of declining investments in U.S. infrastructure and lagging productivity growth—and unless Americans rise to this challenge, we will no longer have the economic resources needed to sustain our standard of living and advanced research base or to support a robust defense establishment.

In 1956, at the height of the Cold War, strengthening the economy and national defense were two of the reasons the Clay Committee recommended that President Eisenhower and a Republican Congress raise taxes to build the National Defense and Interstate Highway System (see chapter 7). This investment helped create U.S. metropolitan regions. It also underpinned a fivefold increase in GDP over the next five decades and enabled the United States to make defense investments needed to win the Cold War. It is time for similarly bold action today but, this time, focused on activities and investments for U.S. megaregions to reach their full potential, in much the same way that the interstate highways enabled the growth and success of metropolitan regions in the mid-20th century.

The nation's megaregions will determine whether the United States can compete with China and other growing economies and sustain its high standard of living. The 13 U.S. megaregions are home to more than 80 percent of the nation's population and close to 90 percent of its economy. They are home to its innovation economy and most of its major research universities, teaching hospitals, and national laboratories. Unleashing the creative capacity of these places will allow them to continue to be engines for the prosperity of the whole country throughout the 21st century and beyond.

U.S. megaregions are also home to more than 80 percent of the nation's growing Black, Latinx, and immigrant populations, many of whom are not part of the economic and social mainstream. If the places where they live can achieve a zero-carbon economy and adapt to climate change, the rest of the country can, too. And finally, sustaining the livability and vitality of U.S. megaregions will determine the future standard of living and quality of life enjoyed by the next generations of Americans for decades to come.

To finance and deliver needed investments in megaregion-scale infrastructure, alternative energy, climate adaptation, and other measures will require new governance and public finance systems and new levels of innovation and public entrepreneurship not seen since the New Deal nearly a century ago. Fortunately, the templates for these innovations already exist in many parts of the United States and overseas, but they must be adapted to the unique circumstances and politics in each megaregion. Overcoming bureaucratic inertia and political foot-dragging in adapting the models will not be easy. The political reality is that for multistate megaregions, many governors and state legislators will resist creating agencies that will be beyond their control. Even megaregions contained within one state may have considerable resistance to the innovations proposed in this book. With megaregions encompassing portions of 44 states, however, it should be possible to mobilize congressional leadership around the investments and institutional changes proposed here.

Rebuilding the nation's infrastructure and economic capacity will require the full range of financing options, including taxes, tolls, fares, and other user fees; for long-term investments, it will require judicious use of deficit financing. But not tax cuts. Since the Reagan administration, Republican presidents and talking heads repeat the mantra that prosperity depends on cutting taxes. What is the result? Economic inequality grows, and funding is not there for critical investments in both physical and human capital. We have not, for example, built a new international airport since Denver opened its airport a quarter century ago. But U.S. competitors in Europe, Asia, and the Middle East have either modernized and expanded or built dozens of airports. As noted in chapter 9, the United States has not built a single high-speed rail line, but virtually every other developed and developing country in Europe and Asia has built entire high-speed rail networks.

Creating institutions and implementing reforms will require bold federal leadership and financial incentives to mobilize all levels of government and all sectors of society. We should look for inspiration to FDR's New Deal, whose programs were enacted during a similar period of economic, social, and political turmoil. FDR's commitment to large-scale innovation and experimentation transformed the economy and landscape of the country. The United States still benefits from this legacy, and almost a century later, it is time to do it again.

Americans have always turned major political and economic catastrophes into opportunities for reform, investment, and innovation. The combination of the COVID-19 pandemic and the unprecedented economic, racial, and political unrest is the catalyst for today. Achieving the goals outlined in this book requires that we rise above narrow partisan politics and the social wars that have distracted Americans for much of the last half century. The $550 billion of new funding in the Infrastructure Investment and Jobs Act (of the total $1.2 trillion) signed by President Biden in November 2021 should be seen as a down payment toward this goal (White House 2021). And even if current proposals for high-speed rail projects like North Atlantic Rail are not funded now, this act can enable engineering, permitting, and early action demonstration projects for this and other priority initiatives. By enabling these and other strategic investments in America's megaregions, we can ensure a bright, prosperous future for this and ensuing generations of Americans.

ACKNOWLEDGMENTS

THIS PROJECT WAS MADE POSSIBLE BY a grant from the U.S. Department of Transportation, which established the Cooperative Mobility for Competitive Megaregions (CM^2) consortium. CM^2, directed by Ming Zhang of the University of Texas at Austin, is a partnership of four universities: UT Austin, the University of Pennsylvania, Texas Southern University, and Louisiana State University. We very much appreciate the support from Sandra Ciarletta, CM^2's assistant director for administration. UT Austin master of landscape architecture (MLA) student Charlie Weber did an amazing job providing editorial support and whipping the manuscript into shape.

A number of students at UT Austin assisted in the book project in 2019–2020. Nadia Carlson helped create a database on the U.S. metropolitan planning organizations and provided valuable information for chapter 2. Nicole McGrath compiled population and economic census data for the analyses presented in chapters 3 and 4. Yang Li assembled six national travel surveys for the generational travel analysis in chapter 2. Ziqi Liu calculated the Gini index of household income inequality in U.S. megaregions for chapter 3. Yantao Huang conducted the study on autonomous vehicle adoption in the Texas Triangle in chapter 6 with funding support from CM^2.

At Penn, Michael Grant, Kait Ellis, and John Caperton were most helpful. Penn MLA student Aaron O'Neil assisted with selecting photos and securing permissions. We also value Erick Guerra's and John Landis's leadership for the Penn portion of the CM^2 consortium.

The Lincoln Institute of Land Policy made this book possible; and we appreciate the help and guidance from Maureen Clarke, Emily McKeigue, Madeleine Donachie, Anthony Flint, and George McCarthy. Thanks to Armando Carbonell for the terrific foreword. We are grateful for the amazing copyediting undertaken by Mary Ann Short, and we thank Deborah Grahame-Smith and Susan Geraghty, project editors at Westchester Publishing Services, for their assistance with production. We value the aesthetic acumen of Sarah Rainwater, who designed the wonderful book cover. We value the insights and suggestions from Barbara Faga and Ethan Seltzer, who reviewed the manuscript for the Lincoln Institute.

On December 3–4, 2020, we discussed the project in a workshop. We appreciate the involvement and advice from the workshop participants: Lisa Aultman-Hall, Kip Bergstrom, Armando Carbonell, Susannah Drake, Billy Fleming, Yonah Freemark, James Garland, Amy Kim, Carol Lewis, Lisa Loftus-Otway, Carlos Martin, Beth Osborne, Leslie Richards, Catherine Ross, Megan Ryerson, Bryan Rodda, and Ethan Seltzer.

REFERENCES

Adirondack Park Agency. 2021. "History of the Adirondack Park." https://apa.ny.gov/about_park/history.htm.

Alderson, A. S., and F. Nielsen. 2002. "Globalization and the Great U-Turn: Income Inequality Trends in 16 OECD Countries." *American Journal of Sociology* 107(5): 1244–1299. https://doi.org/10.1086/341329.

Alliance for Green Heat. 2011. "2010 Census Shows Wood Is Fastest Growing Heating Fuel." *Biomass Magazine*, October 10. http://biomassmagazine.com/articles/5849/2010-census-shows-wood-is-fastest-growing-heating-fuel.

Alonso, W. 1964. *Location and Land Use: Toward a General Theory of Land Rent*. Cambridge, MA: Harvard University Press.

Anderson, E. A., and J. W. Spruill. 1993. "The Dual-Career Commuter Family: A Lifestyle on the Move." *Marriage and Family Review* 19(1–2): 131–147.

Anderson, L. 2008. *Benton MacKaye: Conservationist, Planner, and Creator of the Appalachian Trail*. Baltimore: Johns Hopkins University Press.

APM Research Lab. 2021. "The Color of Coronavirus: COVID-19 Deaths by Race and Ethnicity in the U.S." *American Public Media*, March 5. https://www.apmresearchlab.org/covid/deaths-by-race.

APTA (American Public Transportation Association). 2021. "The Impact of the COVID-19 Pandemic on Public Transit Funding Needs in the U.S." Prepared by EBP US, Inc. January 27.

Arizona Department of Transportation. n.d. "Interstate 10 Connects People, Businesses, States and More." https://i10connects.com/.

Atkinson, R. D., M. Muro, and J. Whiton. 2019. "The Case for Growth Centers." (December). https://www.brookings.edu/wp-content/uploads/2019/12/Full-Report-Growth-Centers_PDF_BrookingsMetro-BassCenter-ITIF.pdf.

Badoe, D. 2002. "Modelling Work-Trip Mode Choice Decisions in Two-Worker Households." *Transportation Planning and Technology* 25(1): 49–73.

Bailey, R. G. 1983. "Delineation of Ecosystem Regions." *Environmental Management* 7: 365–373.

Banerjee, T. 2009. "Megaregions or Megasprawls? Issues of Density, Urban Design, and Quality Growth." In *Megaregions: Planning for Global Competitiveness*, ed. C. L. Ross. Washington, DC: Island Press.

Baptist, M., T. van Hattum, S. Reinhold, M. van Buuren, B. de Rooij, X. Hu, S. van Rooij, N. Polman, S. van den Burg, G. J. Piet, T. Ysebaert, B. Walles, J. Veraat, W. Wamelink, B. Bregman, B. Bos, and T. Seines. 2019. *A Nature-Based Future for the Netherlands in 2120*. Wageningen, Netherlands: Wageningen University and Research.

Baptiste, N. 2021. "It's Not Just Texas. The Energy Meltdown Can Happen in Your State, Too." *Mother Jones*, February 24. https://www.motherjones.com/environment/2021/02/its-not-just-texas-the-energy-meltdown-can-happen-to-your-state-too/.

Barnett, J. 2020. *Designing the Megaregion: Meeting Urban Challenges at a New Scale*. Washington, DC: Island Press.

Barone, R., J. Whitmore, J. Zupan, E. Roach, A. Henry, C. Jones, D. Simons, B. Oldenburg, and D. Shin. 2018. "Trans-Regional Express (T-REX)." (April). https://rpa.org/work/reports/trans-regional-express-t-rex.

Bartik, A. W., M. Bertrand, Z. Cullen, E. L. Glaeser, M. Luca, and C. Stanton. 2020. "The Impact of COVID-19 on Small Business Outcomes and Expectations." *Proceedings of the National Academy of Sciences* 117(30): 17656–17666.

Baum, A., L. Culp. I. Lingenfelter, Y. Yuan, J. Moodie, J. Suo, Y. Wang, and N. Reid. 2019. "New Prospects for New England." Philadelphia: Department of City and Regional Planning, University of Pennsylvania.

Beatley, T. 1994. *Habitat Conservation Planning: Endangered Species and Urban Growth*. Washington, DC: Island Press.

———. 2020. *The Bird-Friendly City: Creating Safe Urban Habitats*. Washington, DC: Island Press.

Beers, T. 2000. "Flexible Schedules and Shift Work: Replacing the '9-to-5' Workday?" *Monthly Labor Review* 123(6): 33–40.

Bergstrom, K. 2020. "An Economic and Climate Justice Rationale for NAR." Unpublished report prepared for the North Atlantic Rail Alliance.

Blanquart, C., and M. Koning. 2017. "The Local Economic Impacts of High-Speed Railways: Theories and Facts." *European Transport Research Review* 9(12). https://doi.org/10.1007/s12544-017-0233-0.

Blumen, O. 2000. "Dissonance in Women's Commuting? The Experience of Exurban Employed Mothers in Israel." *Urban Studies* 37(4): 731–748.

Blumenberg, E., B. D. Taylor, M. Smart, K. Ralph, M. Wander, and S. Brumbagh. 2012. "What's Youth Got to Do with It? Exploring the Travel Behavior of Teens and Young Adults." UCTC-FR-2012-14. Los Angeles: University of California Transportation Center. https://escholarship.org/uc/item/9c14p6d5.

Bock, M., R. Fleischer, M. Merritt, P. Patel, P. Russell, E. Welch, J. Winslow, and R. Yaro. 2016. *Toward a Regional Plan for the Hill Country*. Austin: Program in Community and Regional Planning, University of Texas at Austin.

Borsch-Supan, A. 1990. "Education and Its Double-Edged Impact on Mobility." *Economics of Education Review* 9(1): 39–53.

Bowman, M., H. Bowman, Z. DiGeronimo, B. Golden, J. Goldstick, D. Gutman, K. Roberts, C. Sellers, P. Willen, and R. Yaro. 2021. "Storm Surges and Rising Seas: A Plan for Survival for the next 100 Years." New York: Metropolitan NY-NJ Storm Surge Working Group National Institute of Coastal Harbor Infrastructure.

Bowman, M. J., W. B. Golden, C. M. Hughes, C. Sellers, and R. D. Yaro. 2018. "The Social Justice Case for a Metropolitan New York–New Jersey Regional Storm Surge Barrier System." *Environmental Law in New York Newsletter* 29(4): 69–93.

Bray, T., and V. Rhodes. 1997. "In Search of Cheap and Skinny Streets." *Places Journal* 11(2). https://placesjournal.org/assets/legacy/pdfs/in-search-of-cheap-and-skinny-streets.pdf.

Brightline. 2021. "Brightline Florida." https://www.gobrightline.com/florida-expansion.

Brogan, H. 2001. *The Penguin History of the United States*. London: Penguin Books.

Bunker, B. B., J. M. Zubek, V. J. Vanderslice, and R. W. Rice. 1992. "Quality of Life in Dual-Career Families: Commuting Versus Single-Residence Couples." *Journal of Marriage and Family* 54(2): 399–407.

Burnham, D. 1910. "Stirred by Burnham, Democracy Champion." *Chicago Record-Herald*, October 15.
Burnson, P. 2019. "Top 30 U.S. Ports 2019: Trade Tensions Determine Where Cargo Goes Next." *Logistics Management*. https://www.logisticsmgmt.com/article/top_30_u.s._ports_trade_tensions_determine_where_cargo_goes_next.
California Association for Local Economic Development. 2021. "How to Create an Enhanced Infrastructure Financing District (EIFD)." https://caled.org/how-to-create-an-eifd/.
Callenbach, E. 1975. *Ecotopia: The Notebooks and Reports of William Weston*. Berkeley, CA: Banyan Tree Books.
Caltrans. 2015. "Interregional Transportation Strategic Plan 2015." https://dot.ca.gov/-/media/dot-media/programs/transportation-planning/documents/f0009438-final-2015-itsp-a11y.pdf.
Campos, J., and G. D. Rus. 2009. "Some Stylized Facts About High-Speed Rail: A Review of HSR Experiences Around the World." *Transport Policy* 16: 19–28.
Cao, X. 2009. "E-Shopping, Spatial Attributes, and Personal Travel: A Review of Empirical Studies." *Transportation Research Record* 2135(1): 160–169.
Carbonell, A., and R. D. Yaro. 2005. "American Spatial Development and the New Megalopolis." *Land Lines* 17(2): 1–4.
Caro, R. 1974. *The Power Broker: Robert Moses and the Fall of New York*. New York: Knopf.
———. 1982. *The Path to Power,* vol. 1, *The Years of Lyndon Johnson*. New York: Knopf.
Chair of the Council of Economic Advisors. 2014. *The Economic Report of the President 2014 Together with the Annual Report of the Council of Economic Advisors*. Washington, DC: U.S. Government Printing Office.
Chatterjee, K., P. Goodwin, T. Schwanen, B. Clark, J. Jain, S. Melia, J. Middleton, A. Plyushteva, M. Ricci, G. Santos, and G. Stokes. 2018. "Young People's Travel: What's Changed and Why? Review and Analysis." Bristol, UK: Department for Transport, University of the West of England. www.gov.uk/government/publications/young-peoples-travel-whats-changed-and-why.
Chaudry, A., and C. Wimer. 2016. "Poverty Is Not Just an Indicator: The Relationship Between Income, Poverty, and Child Well-Being." *Academic Pediatrics* 16(3 suppl.): S23–29. https://doi.org/10.1016/j.acap.2015.12.010.
Chen, C.-L., and P. Hall. 2009. *The Impacts of High-Speed Trains on British Economic Geography: A Study of the UK's IC125/225 and Its Effects*. London: University College London.
China Ministry of Transport. 2021. "2020 Statistical Report on Transport Industry." [In Chinese.] https://xxgk.mot.gov.cn/2020/jigou/zhghs/202105/t20210517_3593412.html.
China State Council. 2021. "National Comprehensive Transport Network Plan." [In Chinese.] www.gov.cn/gongbao/content/2021/content_5593440.htm.
Choi, K., J. Jiao, and M. Zhang. 2017. "Reducing Vehicle Travel for the Next Generation: Lessons from the 2001 and 2009 National Household Travel Surveys." *Journal of Urban Planning and Development* 143(4). https://doi.org/10.1061/(ASCE)UP.1943-5444.0000405.
Circella, G., F. Alemi, K. Tiedeman, S. Handy, and P. Mokhtarian. 2018. "The Adoption of Shared Mobility in California and Its Relationship with Other Components of Travel Behavior." Davis: National Center for Sustainable Transportation, University of California at Davis. https://escholarship.org/uc/item/1kq5d07p.
Clark, W.A.V., Y. Huang, and S. Withers. 2003. "Does Commuting Distance Matter? Commuting Tolerance and Residential Change." *Regional Science and Urban Economics* 33(2): 199–221.
COD (City of Denver). 2014. "Transit-Oriented Denver." https://www.denvergov.org/content/dam/denvergov/Portals/193/documents/TOD_Plan/TOD_Strategic_Plan_FINAL.pdf.

Cohen, D. T. 2018. "60 Million Live in the Path of Hurricanes." U.S. Census Bureau, August 6. https://www.census.gov/library/stories/2018/08/coastal-county-population-rises.html.

CPGPRC (Central People's Government of the People's Republic of China). 2005. "Introduction to National Mid-/Long-Range Railway Network Plan." [In Chinese.] www.gov.cn/ztzl/2005-09/16/content_64413.htm.

Darbee, H., ed. 1959. "Mark Twain in Hartford: The Happy Years." *American Heritage* 11(1). https://www.americanheritage.com/mark-twain-hartford-happy-years.

Da Silva, D. C., S. Astroza, I. Batur, S. Khoeini, T. B. Magassy, R. M. Pendyala, and C. R. Bhat. 2019. "Are Millennials Really All That Different than Generation X? An Analysis of Factors Contributing to Differences in Vehicle Miles of Travel." www.caee.utexas.edu/prof/bhat/ABSTRACTS/MillennialsDifferent.pdf.

Davie, E. 2019. "Tidal Energy Companies Join Forces for Bay of Fundy Project." *CBC News*, October 2. https://www.cbc.ca/news/canada/nova-scotia/sustainable-marine-energy-minas-tidal-lp-bay-of-fundy-tidal-power-1.5304276.

Davis, B., T. Dutzik, and P. Baxandall. 2012. "Transportation and the New Generation: Why Young People Are Driving Less and What It Means for Transportation Policy." Washington, DC: U.S. PIRG Education Fund and Frontier Group.

De la Torre, V. 2017. "Left Behind: 20 Years After Sheff v. O'Neill, Students Struggle in Hartford's Segregated Neighborhood Schools." *Hartford (CT) Courant*, March 12. https://www.courant.com/education/hc-sheff-left-behind-day-1-20170319-story.html.

Dimock, M. 2019. "Defining Generations: Where Millennials End and Generation Z Begins." (January). https://www.pewresearch.org/fact-tank/2019/01/17/where-millennials-end-and-generation-z-begins/.

Doherty, S., E. Miller, K. Axhausen, and T. Garling. 2002. "A Conceptual Model of the Weekly Household Activity/Travel Scheduling Process." In *Travel Behaviour: Spatial Patterns, Congestion and Modeling*, ed. E. Stern, I. Salomon, and P. Bovy. Cheltenham, UK: Edward Elgar.

Drake, S. 2016. "WPA 2.0: Beauty, Economics, Politics, and the Creation of New Public Infrastructure." In *Nature and Cities: The Ecological Imperative in Urban Design and Planning*, ed. F. R. Steiner, G. F. Thompson, and A. Carbonell, 238–263. Cambridge, MA: Lincoln Institute of Land Policy.

Dubos, R. 1971. "Trend Is Not Destiny." *Engineering and Science* 34(3): 5–10.

Economist. 2020. "Innovation Is an Essential Part of Dealing with Climate Change." October 29. https://www.economist.com/leaders/2020/10/31/innovation-is-an-essential-part-of-dealing-with-climate-change.

Eisenhower, D. D. 1984. *The Papers of Dwight David Eisenhower*, vol. 11, ed. L. Galambos and D. Van Ee. Baltimore: Johns Hopkins University Press.

Eliasson, K., U. Lindgren, and O. Westerlund. 2003. "Geographical Labour Mobility: Migration or Commuting?" *Regional Studies* 37(8): 827–837.

Envision Central Texas. 2004. "A Vision for Central Texas." (May). https://web.archive.org/web/20090114185647/http://envisioncentraltexas.org/resources/ECT_visiondoc.pdf.

Envision Utah. 2000. "Envision Utah: Quality Growth Strategy and Technical Review." (January). https://static1.squarespace.com/static/5c059ead36099b1445c1d246/t/5d4d9ddde601f40001d551e1/1565367774598/Quality%2BGrowth%2BStrategy.pdf.

EPA (Environmental Protection Agency). 2007. "Environmental Dataset Gateway." https://edg.epa.gov/data/Public/ORD/NCEA/county_pop.zip.

———. 2017. "Updates to the Demographic and Spatial Allocation Models to Produce Integrated Climate and Land Use Scenarios (ICLUS) (Final Report, Version 2)." EPA/600/R-16/366F. Washington, DC: EPA. https://cfpub.epa.gov/ncea/iclus/recordisplay.cfm?deid=322479.

———. 2020. "Level III and IV Ecoregions of the Continental United States." https://www.epa.gov/eco-research/level-iii-and-iv-ecoregions-continental-united-states.

European Commission. 1999. *ESDP: European Spatial Development Perspective*. Potsdam, Germany: European Commission.

Evans, G. R. 2020. "An MIT of the North? We've Heard This Before." *Times Higher Education*, January 10. https://www.timeshighereducation.com/blog/mit-north-weve-heard-this-before.

Faludi, A., ed. 2002. *European Spatial Planning*. Cambridge, MA: Lincoln Institute of Land Policy.

———. 2007. *Territorial Cohesion and the European Model of Society*. Cambridge, MA: Lincoln Institute of Land Policy.

———. 2008. *European Spatial Research and Planning*. Cambridge, MA: Lincoln Institute of Land Policy.

———. 2015. "The 'Blue Banana' Revisited." *European Journal of Spatial Development* 56: 1–26.

Federal Communications Commission. 2019. "Office of Engineering and Technology Announces First Innovation Zones for Program Experimental Licenses. Public Notice DA19-923." https://docs.fcc.gov/public/attachments/DA-19-923A1.pdf.

Federal Works Administration. 1946. *Final Report on the WPA Program, 1935–1943*. Washington, DC: U.S. Government Printing Office.

Federal Railroad Administration. 2017. "NEC Future." Washington, DC: Federal Railroad Administration.

FHWA (Federal Highway Administration). 2014. "Regional Operations in the 21st Century: A Vital Role for MPOs." Washington, DC: Strategic Highway Research Program. https://ops.fhwa.dot.gov/program_areas/creating_foundation/presentations/ceo_presentation_mpo/index.htm.

———. 2018. "Megaregions and National Economic Partnerships." Washington, DC: U.S. Department of Transportation. https://www.fhwa.dot.gov/planning/megaregions/.

Fishman, R., ed. 1999. *The American Planning Tradition: Culture and Policy*. Baltimore: Johns Hopkins University Press.

Florida, R. 2002. *The Rise of the Creative Class*. New York: Basic Books.

Florida, R., T. Gulden, and C. Mellander. 2008. "The Rise of the Mega-Region." *Cambridge Journal of Regions, Economy and Society* 1(3): 459–476.

Foster, K. 2001. *Regionalism on Purpose*. Policy Focus Report. Cambridge, MA: Lincoln Institute of Land Policy.

Fountain, H. 2020. "Climate Change Is Making Hurricanes Stronger, Researchers Find." *New York Times*, May 18. https://www.nytimes.com/2020/05/18/climate/climate-changes-hurricane-intensity.html.

Francis (pope). 2015. *Laudato si': On Care for Our Common Home*. Vatican City: Libreria Editrice Vaticana.

Francis, P. 2017. "Conference Marks 10th Anniversary of HS1 Javelin High Speed Trains in Kent." *Kent Online*, November 10. https://www.kentonline.co.uk/ashford/news/high-speed-trains-transformed-kents-135071/.

Fry, R., R. Igielnik, and E. Patten. 2018. "How Millennials Today Compare with Their Grandparents 50 Years Ago." Washington, DC: Pew Research Center. http://pewrsr.ch/2Dys8lr.

Garikapati, V. M., R. M. Pendyala, E. A. Morris, P. L. Mokhtarian, and N. McDonald. 2016. "Activity Patterns, Time Use, and Travel of Millennials: A Generation in Transition?" *Transport Reviews* 36(5): 558–584.

Geddes, P. 1915. *Cities in Evolution*. London: Williams and Norgate.

Gerstel, N., and H. Gross. 1984. *Commuter Marriage: A Study of Work and Family*. New York: Guilford Press.

Glaser, E. 2007. "Do Regional Economies Need Regional Coordination?" In *The Economic Geography of Megaregions*, ed. K. S. Goldfeld. Princeton, NJ: Policy Research Institute for the Region, Princeton University.

Global Construction Review. 2020. "China Plans to Double High-Speed Rail Network by 2035." *Global Construction Review*, August 14. https://www.globalconstructionreview.com/news/china-plans-double-high-speed-rail-network-2035/.

Goh, K. 2020. "Planning the Green New Deal: Climate Justice and the Politics of Sites and Scales." *Journal of the American Planning Association* 86(2): 188–195.

Gold, E. M. 1979. "Attitudes to Intercity Travel Substitution." *Telecommunications Policy* 4: 88–104.

Gopal, P., and N. Buhayar. 2019. "California's Housing Crunch Is Pushing Developers Deeper into Dangerous Fire Zones." *Bloomberg Green*. https://www.bloomberg.com/news/features/2019-11-23/california-housing-crisis-centennial-built-as-wildfire-fortress.

Gottmann, Jean. 1961. *Megalopolis: The Urbanized Seaboard of the United States*. New York: Twentieth-Century Funds.

Green, A. E. 1997. "A Question of Compromise? Case Study Evidence on the Location and Mobility Strategies of Dual Career Households." *Regional Studies* 31(7): 641–657.

Green, A. E., T. Hogarth, and R. Shackleton. 1999a. "Longer Distance Commuting as a Substitute for Migration in Britain: A Review of Trends, Issues and Implications." *International Journal of Population Geography* 5: 49–67.

Green, A. E., T. Hogarth, and R. Shackleton. 1999b. *Long Distance Living: Dual Location Households*. Bristol, UK: Policy Press.

Green New Deal Superstudio. 2021. "Participation and Collaboration." https://sites.google.com/view/superstudiosite/participants.

Groff, S., and S. Rau. 2019. "China's City Clusters: Pioneering Future Mega-Urban Governance." *American Affairs* 3(2): 134–150.

Gross, H. E. 1980. "Dual-Career Couples Who Live Apart: Two Types." *Journal of Marriage and Family* 42(3): 567–576.

Hagler, Y. 2009. "Defining U.S. Megaregions." America 2050. Regional Plan Association. (November). https://s3.us-east-1.amazonaws.com/rpa-org/pdfs/2050-Paper-Defining-US-Megaregions.pdf.

Hagler, Y., and P. Todorovich. 2009. "Where High-Speed Rail Works Best." America 2050. Regional Planning Association. (September). https://rpa.org/work/reports/where-high-speed-rail-works-best.

Hall, P. 2011. "Comment: High-Speed Rail. Will It Play in Peoria?" *Town Planning Review* 82(3): 352–353.

Hall, P., and K. Pain, eds. 2006. *The Polycentric Metropolis: Learning from Mega-City Regions in Europe*. London: Earthscan.

Hanson, S., and O. J. Huff. 1988. "Systematic Variability in Repetitious Travel." *Transportation* 15(1): 111–135.

Hardill, I. 2002. *Gender, Migration and the Dual Career Household*. London: Routledge.

Hardill, I., and A. Green. 2003. "Remote Working: Altering the Spatial Contours of Work and Home in the New Economy." *New Technology, Work and Employment* 18(3): 212–222.

Hauer, M. E. 2019. "Population Projections for U.S. Counties by Age, Sex and Race Controlled to Shared Socioeconomic Pathway." *Scientific Data* 6: 190005. https://doi.org/10.1038/sdata.2019.5.

Hayashi, Y., A. Mimuro, J. Han, and H. Kato. 2017. "The Shinkansen and Its Impacts." In *High-Speed Rail and Sustainability: Decision-Making and the Political Economy of Investment*, ed. E. Deakin and B.L.P. Henríquez, 34–49. New York: Routledge.

Helminen, V., and M. Ristimaki. 2007. "Relationships Between Commuting Distance, Frequency and Telework in Finland." *Journal of Transport Geography* 15(5): 331–342.

High Speed Rail Alliance. 2021. "CrossRail Chicago." https://www.hsrail.org/midwest/crossrail-chicago.

Hirsh, M., J. N. Prashkea, and M. Ben-Akiva. 1986. "Dynamic Model of Weekly Activity Pattern." *Transportation Science* 20(1): 24.

Hiss, T. 1989. "II: Encountering the Countryside." *New Yorker*, August 20, 37. https://www.newyorker.com/magazine/1989/08/28/ii-encountering-the-countryside.

———. 2021. *Rescuing the Planet: Protecting Half the Land to Heal the Earth*. New York: Knopf.

Hjorthol, R. J. 2000. "Same City, Different Options: An Analysis of the Work Trips of Married Couples in the Metropolitan Area of Oslo." *Journal of Transport Geography* 8(3): 213–220.

Hogarth, T. 1987. "Long Distance Weekly Commuting." *Policy Studies* 8(1): 27–43.

Hogarth, T., and W. W. Daniel. 1988. *Britain's New Industrial Gypsies: A Survey of Long Distance Weekly Commuting*. London: Policy Studies Institute.

Holmes, M. 2004. "An Equal Distance? Individualisation, Gender and Intimacy in Distance Relationships." *Sociological Review* 52(2): 180–200.

———. 2006. "Love Lives at a Distance: Distance Relationships over the Lifecourse." *Sociological Research Online* 11(3): 70–80. https://doi.org/10.5153/sro.1423.

———. 2009. "Commuter Couples and Distance Relationships: Living Apart Together." *Work and Family Encyclopedia*. https://wfrn.org/encyclopedia/commuter-couples-and-distance-relationships-living-apart-together/.

Holmes, R. 2012. "The Commonwealth Approach." *Mammoth*. http://m.ammoth.us/blog/2012/07/the-commonwealth-approach/.

Horner, M. W. 2002. "Extensions to the Concept of Excess Commuting." *Environment and Planning A* 34(3): 543–566.

Horowitz, J., R. Igielnik, and R. Kochhar. 2020. "Most Americans Say There Is Too Much Economic Inequality in the U.S., but Fewer than Half Call It a Top Priority." Washington, DC: Pew Research Center. https://www.pewsocialtrends.org/wp-content/uploads/sites/3/2020/01/PSDT_01.09.20_economic-inequailty_FULL.pdf.

House Committee on Oversight and Reform. 2019. "Government Operations Subcommittee Examined DC Metro Funding, Oversight, and Reform Efforts." Press Release. October 23. https://oversight.house.gov/news/press-releases/government-operations-subcommittee-examined-dc-metro-funding-oversight-and.

Huang, Y. 2020. "The Effects of AV and SAV Availability on Long Distance Travel Within the Texas Triangle Megaregion." Unpublished report. Austin, TX: USDOT UTC Cooperative Mobility for Competitive Megaregions (CM2).

Hung, R. 1996. "Using Compressed Workweeks to Reduce Work Commuting." *Transport Research Part A* 30(1): 11–19.

Hydro-Québec. 2021. "Exports to New England." https://www.hydroquebec.com/international/en/exports/markets/new-england.html.

ITF (International Transport Forum). 2014. *The Economics of Investment in High-Speed Rail*. ITF Round Tables No. 155. Paris: OECD. https://doi.org/10.1787/9789282107751-en.

Jacobs, J. 1961. *The Death and Life of Great American Cities*. New York: Random House.

Jones, B. 2021. "Past, Present and Future: The Evolution of China's Incredible High-Speed Rail Network." *CNN*, May 26. https://www.cnn.com/travel/article/china-high-speed-rail-cmd/index.html.

Jones, P., and M. Clarke. 1988. "The Significance and Measurement of Variability in Travel Behaviour." *Transportation* 15(1): 65–87.

Kahn, H., and A. Wiener. 1967. "The Next Thirty-Three Years: A Framework for Speculation." *Daedalus* 96(3): 705–732.

Kelbaugh, D. 1997. *Common Place: Toward Neighborhood and Regional Design.* Seattle: University of Washington Press.

Knittel, C. R., and E. Murphy. 2019. "Generational Trends in Vehicle Ownership and Use: Are Millennials Any Different?" Working Paper 25674. Washington, DC: National Bureau of Economic Research.

Koh, K., and H. Yang. 2018. "The Effects of High Speed Trains on Local Economies: Evidence from the Korea Train Express." (September). Preprint available at SSRN. https://papers.ssrn.com/sol3/papers.cfm?abstract_id=3162633.

Krueger, R., T. H. Rashidi, and A. Vij. 2019. "X vs. Y: An Analysis of Intergenerational Differences in Transport Mode Use Among Young Adults." *Transportation* 47: 2203–2231. https://doi.org/10.1007/s11116-019-10009-7.

Kuznets, S. 1955. "Economic Growth and Income Inequality." *American Economic Review* 45: 1–28.

Lang, R. E., and D. Dhavale. 2005. *Beyond Megalopolis: Exploring America's New "Megapolitan" Geography.* Alexandra: Metropolitan Institute at Virginia Tech.

Lawrence, M., R. Bullock, and Z. Liu. 2019. *China's High-Speed Rail Development.* Washington, DC: World Bank.

Lee, R. 1995. "Travel Demand and Transportation Policy Beyond the Edge: An Inquiry into the Nature of Long Distance Interregional Commuting from the Northern San Joaquin Valley to the San Francisco Bay Area and Its Implications for Transportation Planning." Ph.D. diss., University of California, Berkeley.

———. 1996. "Exploration of Long-Distance Interregional Commuting Issues: Analysis of Northern California Interregional Commuters Using Census Data and Focus Group Interviews." *Transportation Research Record* 1521: 29–36.

Leinbach, T. 2004. "City Interactions." In *The Geography of Urban Transportation*, 3rd ed., ed. S. Hanson and G. Giuliano. New York: Guilford Press.

Levin, I. 2004. "Living Apart Together: A New Family Form." *Current Sociology* 52: 223.

Levinson, D., and Y. Wu. 2005. "The Rational Locator Reexamined: Are Travel Times Still Stable?" *Transportation* 32: 187–202.

Lincoln Institute of Land Policy and RPA. 2004. "Toward an American Spatial Development Perspective." Policy Roundtable Report, September. https://s3.us-east-1.amazonaws.com/rpa-org/pdfs/Toward-an-American-Spatial-Development-Perspective.pdf.

Liu, L., and M. Zhang. 2018. "High-Speed Rail Impacts on Travel Times, Accessibility, and Economic Productivity: A Benchmarking Analysis in City-Cluster Regions of China." *Journal of Transport Geography* 73: 25–40.

Luce, H. R. 1941. "The American Century." *Life Magazine*, February 17.

Lyon, P. 1968. "Is This Any Way to Ruin a Railroad?" *American Heritage* 19(2): 52–73.

Lyons, G., and K. Chatterjee. 2008. "A Human Perspective on the Daily Commute: Costs, Benefits and Trade-Offs." *Transport Reviews* 28(2): 181–198.

Lyons, G., and J. Urry. 2005. "Travel Time Use in the Information Age." *Transportation Research Part A: Policy and Practice* 39(2–3): 257–276.

Ma, K.-R., and D. Banister. 2006. "Excess Commuting: A Critical Review." *Transport Reviews* 26(6): 749–767.

MacKaye, B. 1928. *The New Exploration: A Philosophy of Regional Planning.* New York: Harcourt, Brace.
———. 1940. "Regional Planning and Ecology." *Ecological Monographs* 10(3): 349–353.

Madowitz, M., and D. Boesch. 2020. "The Shambolic Response to the Public Health and Economic Crisis Has Women on the Brink as the Job Recovery Stalls." Washington, DC: Center for American Progress. https://www.americanprogress.org/issues/economy/reports/2020/10/22/492179/shambolic-response-public-health-economic-crisis-women-brink-job-recovery-stalls/.

Malone, L. 2008. "Rural Electrification Administration." In *EH.Net Encyclopedia*, ed. R. Whaples. http://eh.net/encyclopedia/rural-electrification-administration/.

Malpai Borderlands Habitat Conservation Plan Technical Working Group and W. Lehman. 2008. "Malpai Borderlands Habitat Conservation Plan." Douglas, AZ: Malpai Borderlands Group.

Manjoo, F. 2020. "I've Seen a Future Without Cars, and It's Amazing." *New York Times*, July 9. https://www.nytimes.com/2020/07/09/opinion/sunday/ban-cars-manhattan-cities.html.

Marshall, A. 2010. "Back Up on the Interstate." *Governing: The Future of States and Localities*, August 16. https://www.governing.com/archive/back-up-on-the-interstate.html.

Martin, R. 2020. "Abolish Oil: From Green New Deal to Green Reconstruction." *Places Journal*, June. https://placesjournal.org/article/abolish-oil/?cn-reloaded=1.

Mather, M., L. A. Jacobsen, and K. M. Pollard. 2015. "Aging in the United States." *Population Bulletin* 70(2). https://www.prb.org/wp-content/uploads/2016/01/aging-us-population-bulletin-1.pdf.

McDonald, J. 2019. "The Facts on the 'Green New Deal.'" (February). https://www.factcheck.org/2019/02/the-facts-on-the-green-new-deal/.

McDonald, N. C. 2015. "Are Millennials Really the 'Go-Nowhere' Generation?" *Journal of the American Planning Association* 81(2): 90–103.

McHarg, I. L. 1969. *Design with Nature*. Garden City, NY: Natural History Press.

———. 1996. *A Quest for Life: An Autobiography*. New York: John Wiley and Sons.

McKinney, M., and S. Johnson. 2009. *Working Across Boundaries: People, Nature, and Regions*. Cambridge, MA: Lincoln Institute of Land Policy.

McKinney, M., L. Scarlett, and D. Kemmis. 2010. *Large Landscape Conservation*. Policy Focus Report. Cambridge, MA: Lincoln Institute of Land Policy.

Mena, B. 2021. "New York and Other Northeast States See Large Drop in Unemployment." *Wall Street Journal*, June 26. https://www.wsj.com/articles/new-york-and-other-northeast-states-see-large-drop-in-unemployment-11624699800.

Mills, E. 1972. *Studies in the Structure of the Urban Economy*. Baltimore: Johns Hopkins University Press.

Mokhtarian, P. L. 1990. "A Typology of Relationships Between Telecommunications and Transportation." *Transportation Research Part A* 24(3): 231–242.

———. 2002. "Telecommunications and Travel: The Case for Complementarity." *Journal of Industrial Ecology* 6(2): 43–57.

Mokhtarian, P. L., and I. Salomon. 2001. "How Derived Is the Demand for Travel? Some Conceptual and Measurement Considerations." *Transportation Research Part A: Policy and Practice* 35(8): 695–719.

Moller, S., A. Alderson, and F. Nielsen, F. 2009. "Changing Patterns of Income Inequality in U.S. Counties, 1970–2000." *American Journal of Sociology* 114(4): 1037–1101.

Muth, R. 1969. *Cities and Housing: The Spatial Pattern of Urban Residential Land Use*. Chicago: University of Chicago Press.

NACTO (National Association of City Transportation Officials). 2020. "Shared Micromobility in the US: 2019." https://nacto.org/wp-content/uploads/2020/08/2020bikesharesnapshot.pdf.

Nakicenovic, N., J. Alcamo, G. Davis, B. de Vries, J. Fenhann, S. Gaffin, K. Gregory, A. Grubler, T. Y. Jung, T. Kram, E. L. La Rovere, L. Michaelis, S. Mori, T. Morita, W. Pepper, H. Pitcher, L. Price, K. Riahi, A. Roehrl, H.-H. Rogner, A. Sankovski, M. Schlesinger, P. Shukla, S. Smith, R. Swart, S. van Rooijen, N. Victor, and Z. Dadi. 2000. *Special Report on Emissions Scenarios*. Cambridge: Cambridge University Press. www.grida.no/climate/ipcc/emission/index.htm.

NARC (National Association of Regional Councils). 2019. "What Is a Regional Council, COG, or MPO?" https://narc.org/about/what-is-a-cog-or-mpo/.

———. 2020. "Federalism and the Role of Regions: A Major Opportunity for the New Administration and Congress." https://narc.org/wp-content/uploads/2020/12/NARC-Transition-Memo-Federalism.pdf.

NASA Earth Observatory/NOAA NGDC. 2020. "Earth at Night." https://earthobservatory.nasa.gov/features/NightLights.

Nash, A. 2003. *Best Practices in Shared-Use High-Speed Rail Systems*. San Jose, CA: Mineta Transportation Institute, San Jose State University.

National Surface Transportation Policy and Revenue Study Commission. 2007. "Report of the National Surface Transportation Policy and Revenue Study Commission: Transportation for Tomorrow." https://rosap.ntl.bts.gov/view/dot/18125.

Nelson, A., and R. E. Lang. 2011. *Megapolitan America: A New Vision for Understanding American's Metropolitan Geography*. New York: Routledge.

Nelson, G. D., and A. Rae. 2016. "An Economic Geography of the United States: From Commutes to Megaregions." *PLoS ONE* 11(11): e0166083. https://doi.org/10.1371/journal.pone.0166083.

Newbold, K. B., D. M. Scott, J. E. Spinney, P. Kanaroglou, and A. Páez. 2005. "Travel Behavior Within Canada's Older Population: A Cohort Analysis." *Journal of Transport Geography* 13(4): 340–351.

New York State Department of Transportation. 2021. "I-81 Viaduct: About the Project." https://www.dot.ny.gov/i81opportunities/about.

New York State Thruway Authority. 2021. "Governor Mario M. Cuomo Bridge." https://mariomcuomobridge.ny.gov/history-timeline.

NPS (National Park Service). 2020. "FDR's Conservation Legacy." https://www.nps.gov/articles/fdr-s-conservation-legacy.htm.

NDRC (National Development and Reform Commission). 2009. "China Mid/Long-Range Rail Network Plan 2008." [In Chinese.] https://www.ndrc.gov.cn/fggz/zcssfz/zcgh/200906/W020190910670447076716.pdf.

———. 2016. "China Mid/Long-Range Rail Network Plan 2016." [In Chinese.] https://www.ndrc.gov.cn/fggz/zcssfz/zcgh/201607/W020190910670620449319.pdf.

Nordenson, G., C. Seavitt, and A. Yarinsky. 2010. *On the Water: Palisade Bay*. Stuttgart, Germany: Hatje Cantz Verlag.

Nunno, R. 2018. "Fact Sheet: High Speed Rail Development Worldwide." (July). https://www.eesi.org/papers/view/fact-sheet-high-speed-rail-development-worldwide.

Oden, M., and G. C. Sciara. 2020. "The Salience of Megaregional Geographies for Inter-Metropolitan Transportation Planning and Policy Making." *Transportation Research Part D* 80. https://doi.org/10.1016/j.trd.2020.102262.

Oeberg, S. 1995. "Theories on Interregional Migration: An Overview." IIASA Working paper WP-95-047. Laxenburg, Austria: International Institute for Applied Systems Analysis.

Ohlhaver, P., and W. Wilkinson. 2020. "We Know How to Beat the Virus. This Is How Republicans Can Do It." *New York Times*, June 29. https://www.nytimes.com/2020/06/29/opinion/republicans-coronavirus.html.

Öhman, M., and U. Lindgren. 2003. "Who Is the Long-Distance Commuter? Patterns and Driving Forces in Sweden." *Cybergeo: European Journal of Geography* 243: 2–24. http://cybergeo.revues.org/index4118.html.

Ohmori, N., and N. Harata. 2008. "How Different Are Activities While Commuting by Train? A Case in Tokyo." *Tijdschrift voor economische en sociale geografie* 99(5): 547–561.

OMB (Office of Management and Budget). 2000. "Standards for Defining Metropolitan and Micropolitan Statistical Areas: Notice." *Federal Register* 65 (249). https://www.govinfo.gov/content/pkg/FR-2000-12-27/pdf/00-32997.pdf.

O'Neill, B. C., E. Kriegler, K. L. Ebi, E. Kemp-Benedict, K. Riahi, D. S. Rothman, B. J. van Ruijven, D. P. van Vuuren, J. Birkmann, K. Kok, M. Levy, and W. Solecki. 2017. "The Roads Ahead: Narratives for Shared Socioeconomic Pathways Describing World Futures in the 21st Century." *Global Environmental Change* 42: 169–180.

Oak Ridge National Laboratory. 2020. "National Household Travel Survey 1983, 1990, 1995, 2001, 2009, and 2017." https://nhts.ornl.gov/.

Ørsted. 2021. "Our Offshore Wind Farms: Where We Operate." https://orsted.com/en/our-business/offshore-wind/our-offshore-wind-farms.

Parker, K., Minkin, R. and Bennett, J. 2020. "Economic Fallout from COVID-19 Continues to Hit Lower-Income Americans the Hardest." https://www.pewresearch.org/social-trends/2020/09/24/economic-fallout-from-covid-19-continues-to-hit-lower-income-americans-the-hardest/.

Pell, C. 1966. *Megalopolis Unbound: The Supercity and the Transportation of Tomorrow.* New York: Praeger.

Peterson, T. 2016. "Watching the Swiss: A Network Approach to Rural and Exurban Transport Policy." *Transport Policy* 52:175–185.

Pisarski, A. E. 2006. "Commuting in America III: The Third National Report on Commuting Patterns and Trends." Washington, DC: Transportation Research Board. https://onlinepubs.trb.org/onlinepubs/nchrp/ciaiii.pdf.

Plaut, P. O. 2006. "The Intra-Household Choices Regarding Commuting and Housing." *Transportation Research Part A: Policy and Practice* 40(7): 561–571.

Popik, B. 2007. "Texas Triangle (Dallas, Houston, San Antonio)." *The Lone Star State*, February 27. https://www.barrypopik.com/index.php/texas/entry/texas_triangle_dallas_houston_san_antonio/.

Popken, B. 2020. "Millions of Americans Moved During the Pandemic and Most Aren't Looking Back." *NBC News*, December 31. https://www.nbcnews.com/business/business-news/millions-americans-moved-during-pandemic-most-aren-t-looking-back-n1252633.

Porter, D., and A. Wallis. 2002. *Exploring Ad Hoc Regionalism.* Policy Focus Report. Cambridge, MA: Lincoln Institute of Land Policy.

Porter, E. 2019. "Ross Perot's Warning of a 'Giant Sucking Sound' on NAFTA Echoes Today." *New York Times*, July 9. https://www.nytimes.com/2019/07/09/business/economy/ross-perot-nafta-trade.html.

Powell, J. W., G. K. Gilbert, C. E. Dutton, A. H. Thompson, and W. Drummond. 1879. *Report on the Lands of the Arid Region of the United States, with a More Detailed Account of the Lands of Utah. With Maps*, 2nd ed. Washington, DC: U.S. Government Printing Office.

PSU (Portland State University). 2010. "Ecolopolis 4.0: Livability in Cascadia." https://pdxscholar.library.pdx.edu/cgi/viewcontent.cgi?article=1003&context=usp_planning.

Reagan, R. 1981. "Inaugural Address." https://www.reaganfoundation.org/media/128614/inaguration.pdf.

Recognizing the Duty of the Federal Government to Create a Green New Deal. 2019. H. Res. 109. 116th Congress, 1st session. Introduced in the House of Representatives February 7. https://www.congress.gov/bill/116th-congress/house-resolution/109/text.

Reidmiller, D. R., C. W. Avery, D. R. Easterling, K. E. Kunkel, K.L.M. Lewis, T. K. Maycock, and B. C. Stewart, eds. 2018. *Impacts, Risks, and Adaptation in the United States: Fourth National Climate Assessment*, vol. 2. Washington, DC: U.S. Global Change Research Program. https://doi.org/10.7930/NCA4.2018.

Reschovsky, A. 2017. *The Future of U.S. Public School Revenue from the Property Tax.* Cambridge, MA: Lincoln Institute of Land Policy.

Ronen, S., and S. B. Primps. 1981. "The Compressed Work Week as Organizational Change: Behavioral and Attitudinal Outcomes." *Academy of Management Review* 6(1): 61–74.

Roosevelt, F. D. 1932. "The Forgotten Man." In *The Public Papers and Addresses of Franklin D. Roosevelt*, vol. 1, *1928–1932*. New York: Random House.

———. 1933. "First Inaugural Address of Franklin D. Roosevelt." *Avalon Project.* https://avalon.law.yale.edu/20th_century/froos1.asp.

Rose, H. 2009. "Extreme Commuting: How Far Would You Go?" *Times*, November 14. https://www.thetimes.co.uk/article/extreme-commuting-how-far-would-you-go-6r6rvqhz5b6.

Ross, C. L., and M. Woo. 2009. "Identifying Megaregions in the United States." In *Megaregions: Planning for Global Competitiveness*, ed. C. L. Ross. Washington, DC: Island Press.

RPA (Regional Plan Association). 1968. "Second Regional Plan." New York: Regional Plan Association.

———. 2006. "American 2050: A Prospectus." New York: Regional Plan Association. https://s3.us-east-1.amazonaws.com/rpa-org/pdfs/2050-Prospectus.pdf.

———. 2019. *The Fourth Regional Plan.* New York: Regional Plan Association.

RPA and America 2050. 2012. *Landscapes: Improving Conservation Practice in the Northeast Megaregion.* New York: RPA and America 2050. https://s3.us-east-1.amazonaws.com/rpa-org/pdfs/RPA-Northeast-Landscapes.pdf.

RPA, Lincoln Institute of Land Policy, and America 2050. 2009. "New Strategies for Regional Economic Development." America 2050 Research Seminar, Healdsburg, California (March 29–31). https://s3.us-east-1.amazonaws.com/rpa-org/pdfs/2050-New-Strategies-for-Regional-Economic-Development.pdf.

Ryder, N. B. 1965. "The Cohort as a Concept in the Study of Social Change." *American Sociological Review* 30(6): 843–861.

Safire, W., and L. Safir. 1982. "Idealism." In *Good Advice*, ed. W. Safire and L. Safir. New York: Times Books.

Salomon, I. 1985. "Telecommunications and Travel: Substitution or Modified Mobility?" *Transport Economics and Policy* 19(3): 219–235.

———. 1986. "Telecommunications and Travel Relationships: A Review." *Transport Research Part A* 20(3): 223–238.

Sandow, E., and K. Westin. 2008. "Preferences for Commuting in Sparsely Populated Areas: The Case of Sweden." *Journal of Transportation and Land Use* 2(3): 87–107.

———. 2010. "The Persevering Commuting: Duration of Long-Distance Commuting." *Transport Research Part A* 44: 433–445.

Sassen, S. 1991. *The Global City.* Princeton, NJ: Princeton University Press.

———. 2012. "Novel Spatial Formats for Urban Inclusion: Megaregions and Global Cities." *Books and Ideas.* https://booksandideas.net/IMG/pdf/20120502_sassen.pdf.

SB 628. "Enhanced Infrastructure Financing Districts." 2014. https://leginfo.legislature.ca.gov/faces/billTextClient.xhtml?bill_id=201320140SB628.

Schade, W., J. Hartwig, S. Welter, S. Maffii, C. de Stasio, F. Fermi, L. Zani, and A. Martino. 2018. "The Impact of TEN-T Completion on Growth, Jobs and the Environment." European Commission. https://ec.europa.eu/transport/sites/transport/files/studies/ten-t-growth-and-jobs-synthesis.pdf.

Schmidt, E. 2019. "Study: I-10 in Arizona Is One of the Most Deadly Stretches of U.S. Highway in Summer." *Republic* (AZ). September 6. https://www.azcentral.com/story/news/local/phoenix-traffic/2019/09/06/study-10-arizona-one-most-deadly-stretches-u-s-highway-summer/2099941001/.

Schrank, D., B. Eisele, and T. Lomax. 2019. "2019 Urban Mobility Report." College Station: Texas A&M Transportation Institute.

Schwartz, S. A. 2019. "5 States Dominating Tech Employment." *CIO Dive*, March 26. https://www.ciodive.com/news/5-states-dominating-tech-employment/551315/.

Sciara, G. C. 2017. "Metropolitan Transportation Planning: Lessons from the Past, Institutions for the Future." *Journal of the American Planning Association* 83(3): 262–276.

Scott, A. J. 2001. *Global City-Regions: Trends, Theory, Policy.* New York: Oxford University Press.

Segbers, Klaus, ed., with Simon Raiser and Krister Volkmann. 2007. *The Making of Global City Regions: Johannesburg, Mumbai/Bombay, São Paulo, and Shanghai.* Baltimore: Johns Hopkins University Press.

Seltzer, E., and A. Carbonell, eds. 2011. *Regional Planning in America: Practice and Prospect.* Cambridge, MA: Lincoln Institute of Land Policy.

Semega, J., M. Kollar, J. Creamer, and A. Mohanty. 2020. "Income and Poverty in the United States: 2018." https://www.census.gov/content/dam/Census/library/publications/2019/demo/p60-266.pdf.

Shaban, H. 2020. "Not Even a Pandemic Can Break Rich Cities' Grip on the U.S. Economy." *Washington Post*, October 15. https://www.washingtonpost.com/road-to-recovery/2020/10/15/wealthy-cities-bounce-back-from-coronavirus/.

Shaw, A., A. Lustgarten, and J. W. Goldsmith. 2020. "New Climate Maps Show a Transformed United States." *ProPublica*, September 15. https://projects.propublica.org/climate-migration/.

Shore, W. B. 1967. *The Region's Growth: A Report of the Second Regional Plan.* New York: Regional Plan Association.

Sisson, P. 2018. "U.S. Public Transit's Precarious State Could Cost Country Billions." *Curbed*, May 17. https://www.curbed.com/2018/5/17/17366688/subway-infrastructure-mass-transit-bus.

Smith, T. 2018. "Bullet Train Developer Locks in up to $300M Investment from Japanese Backers." *Bisnow*, September 24. https://www.bisnow.com/houston/news/technology/bullet-train-developer-locks-in-300m-investment-from-japanese-backers-93176.

Snibbe, K. 2019. "Here's How Much Traffic Crosses the U.S.-Mexico Border." https://www.ocregister.com/2019/04/05/heres-how-much-traffic-crosses-the-u-s-mexico-border/.

Solar Energy Industries Association. 2021. "Solar State by State." https://www.seia.org/states-map.

Sorensen, A. 2018. "Tokaido Megalopolis: Developmental State Urbanism from Growth to Shrinkage." Foundation France-Japan Research Statement, August 21. http://ffj.ehess.fr/index/article/364/tokaido-megalopolis.html.

Starner, R. 2018. "Utah: The Best State for Business." Utah Governor's Office of Economic Development. https://siteselection.com/cc/utah/2018/business-climate-overview-utah-the-best-state-for-business.cfm.

Statista. 2019. "Total Length of the High-Speed Railway Lines in Use in Selected European Countries in 2019." https://www.statista.com/statistics/451818/length-of-high-speed-railway-lines-in-use-in-europe-by-country/.

Steiner, F. 2008. *The Living Landscape: An Ecological Approach to Landscape Planning.* Washington, DC: Island Press.

———. 2020. "Landscape Governance: The Prospects for the SITES Rating System." *Socio-Ecological Practice Research* 2: 301–310.

Steiner, F., G. Thompson, and A. Carbonell, eds. 2016. *Nature and Cities: The Ecological Imperative in Urban Design and Planning.* Cambridge, MA: Lincoln Institute of Land Policy.

Steiner, F., R. Weller, K. M'Closkey, and B. Fleming, eds. 2019. *Design with Nature Now.* Cambridge, MA: Lincoln Institute of Land Policy.

Steiner, F. R., and R. D. Yaro. 2009. "A New National Landscape Agenda." *Landscape Architecture Magazine* 99(6): 70–77.

Stolberg, S. G., and R. Pear. 2010. "Obama Signs Health Care Overhaul Bill, with a Flourish." *New York Times*, March 23. www.nytimes.com/2010/03/24/health/policy/24health.html/.

Striessnig, E., J. Gao, B. O'Neill, and L. Jiang. 2019. "Empirically Based Spatial Projections of US Population Age Structure Consistent with the Shared Socioeconomic Pathways." *Environmental Research Letters* 14: 114038. https://doi.org/10.1088/1748-9326/ab4a3a.

Sultana, S. 2006. "What About Dual-Earner Households in Jobs-Housing Balance Research? An Essential Issue in Transport Geography." *Journal of Transport Geography* 14(5): 393–395.

Tax Exempt Bonds for High Speed Rail Projects: Hearing Before the Committee on Finance, United States Senate. 1988. 100th Congress, 2nd session, S. 1245. Washington, DC: U.S. Government Printing Office. https://www.finance.senate.gov/imo/media/doc/hrg100-674.pdf.

Titheridge, H., and P. Hall. 2006. "Changing Travel to Work Patterns in South East England." *Journal of Transport Geography* 14(1): 60–75.

Todorovich, P., and Y. Hagler 2011. *High Speed Rail in America.* New York: RPA and America 2050. https://s3.us-east-1.amazonaws.com/rpa-org/pdfs/2050-High-Speed-Rail-in-America.pdf.

Toossi, M., and T. L. Morisi. 2017. "Women in the Workforce Before, During, and After the Great Recession." *Spotlight on Statistics.* https://www.bls.gov/spotlight/2017/women-in-the-workforce-before-during-and-after-the-great-recession/pdf/women-in-the-workforce-before-during-and-after-the-great-recession.pdf.

TransitMatters. 2018. "Regional Rail for Metropolitan Boston." http://transitmatters.org/regional-rail-doc.

Transportation and Climate Initiative. 2021. "About Us." https://www.transportationandclimate.org/content/about-us.

Turner, T., and D. Niemeier. 1997. "Travel to Work and Household Responsibility: New Evidence." *Transportation* 24(4): 397–419.

TxDOT (Texas Department of Transportation). 2019. "Capital-Alamo Connections Study: Transportation Planning & Programming Division, TxDOT." (February). https://ftp.txdot.gov/pub/txdot/get-involved/aus/capital-alamo-connections/022019-study-report.pdf.

UK2070 Commission. 2020. "Making No Litter Plans: Acting at Scale for a Fairer and Stronger Future." (February). http://uk2070.org.uk/wp-content/uploads/2020/02/UK2070-FINAL-REPORT.pdf.

University of Pennsylvania School of Design. 2004. *Planning for America in a Global Economy: 2004–2005.* Philadelphia: City Planning Studio Report.

U.S. Army Corps of Engineers. 2017. "Charles River Natural Valley Storage Area." March 20. https://www.nae.usace.army.mil/Missions/Civil-Works/Flood-Risk-Management/Massachusetts/Charles-River-NVS/.

U.S. Bureau of Economic Analysis. 2019. "Gross Domestic Product by County, 2018." November 1, 2020. https://www.bea.gov/data/gdp/gdp-county-metro-and-other-areas.

U.S. Bureau of Labor Statistics. 2009. "Women in the Labor Force: A Databook." www.bls.gov/cps/wlf-databook2009.htm.

U.S. Census Bureau. 1989–2019. "SAIPE Datasets." https://www.census.gov/programs-surveys/saipe/data/datasets.All.List_1743592724.html.

———. 1990. "Decennial Census of Population and Housing 1990." https://www.census.gov/programs-surveys/decennial-census/decade.1990.html.

———. 1991. "1990 Census of Population and Housing Summary Tape File 3 Dataset." November 30, 2020. https://www.census.gov/data/datasets/1990/dec/summary-file-3.html.

———. 2000. "Decennial Census of Population and Housing 2000." https://www.census.gov/programs-surveys/decennial-census/decade.2000.html.

———. 2010. "Decennial Census of Population and Housing 2010." https://www.census.gov/programs-surveys/decennial-census/decade.2010.html.

———. 2016a. "American Community Survey: Data Profiles." https://www.census.gov/acs/www/data/data-tables-and-tools/data-profiles/2016/.

———. 2016b. "State and County Intercensal Tables: 1990–2000." https://www.census.gov/data/tables/time-series/demo/popest/intercensal-1990-2000-state-and-county-totals.html.

———. 2017. "County Intercensal Tables: 2000–2010." https://www.census.gov/data/tables/time-series/demo/popest/intercensal-2000-2010-counties.html.

———. 2019a. "2011–2015 5-Year ACS Commuting Flows." https://www.census.gov/data/tables/2015/demo/metro-micro/commuting-flows-2015.html.

———. 2019b. "America Community Survey 2019." https://www.census.gov/acs/www/data/data-tables-and-tools/data-profiles/2019/.

———. 2019c. *Coastline America*. Washington, DC: Economics and Statistics Administration (June). https://www.census.gov/content/dam/Census/library/visualizations/2019/demo/coastline-america.pdf.

———. 2020a. "County Population by Characteristics: 2010–2019." November 30, 2020. https://www.census.gov/data/tables/time-series/demo/popest/2010s-counties-detail.html.

———. 2020b. "Terms and Definitions." https://www.census.gov/programs-surveys/popest/guidance-geographies/terms-and-definitions.html.

———. 2021. "Texas Added Almost 4 Million People in Last Decade." https://www.census.gov/library/stories/state-by-state/texas-population-change-between-census-decade.html.

Van der Klis, M., and L. Karsten. 2009a. "The Commuter Family as a Geographical Adaptive Strategy for the Work-Family Balance." *Community, Work and Family* 12(3): 339–354.

———. 2009b. "Commuting Partners, Dual Residences and the Meaning of Home." *Journal of Environmental Psychology* 29(2): 235–245.

Van der Klis, M., and C. Mulder. 2008. "Beyond the Trailing Spouse: The Commuter Partnership as an Alternative to Family Migration." *Journal of Housing and the Built Environment* 23(1): 1–19.

Van Ham, M., and P. Hooimeijer. 2009. "Regional Differences in Spatial Flexibility: Long Commutes and Job Related Migration Intentions in the Netherlands." *Applied Spatial Analysis and Policy* 2(2): 129–146.

Van Ommeren, J. 1998. "On-the-Job Search Behavior: The Importance of Commuting Time." *Land Economics* 74(4): 526–540.

Van Ommeren, J., and P. Rietveld. 2007. "Compensation for Commuting in Imperfect Urban Markets." *Papers in Regional Science* 86(2): 241–259.

Van Ommeren, J., P. Rietveld, and P. Nijkamp. 1997. "Commuting: In Search of Jobs and Residences." *Journal of Urban Economics* 42(3): 402–421.

———. 1998. "Spatial Moving Behavior of Two-Earner Households." *Journal of Regional Science* 38(1): 23–41.

———. 2000. "Job Mobility, Residential Mobility and Commuting: A Theoretical Analysis Using Search Theory." *Annals of Regional Science* 34(2): 213–232.

Vartabedian, R. 2020. "Las Vegas High-Speed Train Project, Once Stuck in Low Gear, Is Now Moving Forward." *Los Angeles Times*, March 25. https://www.latimes.com/california/story/2020-03-25/las-vegas-high-speed-train-project-moving-after-delays.

Verdant Power. 2021. "The RITE (Roosevelt Island Tidal Energy) Project." https://www.verdantpower.com/projects.

Vincent, G., and V. Velkoff. 2010. "The Next Four Decades: The Older Population in the United States, 2010 to 2050, *Current Population Reports*. P25-1138. Washington, DC: U.S. Census Bureau. https://www.census.gov/prod/2010pubs/p25-1138.pdf.

Vlassis, A. 2007. "Council of Governments." In *Encyclopedia of Governance*, ed. M. Bevir. Thousand Oaks, CA: SAGE.

Wagner, M., J. Mersin, and E. A. Wentz. 2016. "Design with Nature: Key Lessons from McHarg's Intrinsic Suitability in Wake of Hurricane Sandy." *Landscape and Urban Planning* 155: 33–46.

Wallace, N. 2020. "Where Are Retirees Moving? 2016 Edition." *Smart Asset*, February 20. https://smartasset.com/retirement/where-are-retirees-moving.

Walls, M., E. Safirova, and Y. Jiang. 2007. "What Drives Telecommuting? Relative Impact of Worker Demographics, Employer Characteristics, and Job Types." *Transportation Research Record: Journal of the Transportation Research Board* 2010(1): 111–120. https://doi.org/10.3141/2010-13.

Wayne, G. 2013. "The Beginner's Guide to Representative Concentration Pathways." *Skeptical Science*. https://www.skepticalscience.com/docs/RCP_Guide.pdf.

Weller, R. 2020. "Constructing an Ecological Civilization." In *Beautiful China: Reflections on Landscape Architecture in Contemporary China*, ed. R. Weller and T. Hands, 82–89. Los Angeles: ORO Editions.

Wetwitoo, J., and H. Kato. 2017. "High-Speed Rail and Regional Economic Productivity Through Agglomeration and Network Externality: A Case Study of Inter-Regional Transportation in Japan." *Case Studies on Transport Policy* 5(4). https://doi.org/10.1016/j.cstp.2017.10.008.

Wheeler, T. B. 2020. "EPA Hit with Lawsuits over Chesapeake Bay Cleanup." *Bay Journal*, September 11. https://www.bayjournal.com/news/policy/epa-hit-with-lawsuits-over-chesapeake-bay-cleanup/article_db7ad7e0-f429-11ea-833a-87109c15a521.html.

White House. 2021. "Fact Sheet: Historic Bipartisan Infrastructure Deal." July 28. https://www.whitehouse.gov/briefing-room/statements-releases/2021/07/28/fact-sheet-historic-bipartisan-infrastructure-deal/.

Wikipedia, *The Free Encyclopedia*. 2021. s.v. "List of United States Commuter Rail Systems by Ridership." Last modified July 10, 2021. https://en.wikipedia.org/wiki/List_of_United_States_commuter_rail_systems_by_ridership.

Wilson, E. O. 2016. *Half-Earth: Our Planet's Search for Life*. New York: Liveright.

Witt, U., and C. Gross. 2020. "The Rise of the 'Service Economy' in the Second Half of the Twentieth Century and Its Energetic Contingencies." *Journal of Evolutionary Economics* 30: 231–246. https://doi.org/10.1007/s00191-019-00649-4.

World Bank. 2020. "Poverty and Shared Prosperity 2020: Reversals of Fortune." Washington, DC: World Bank.

Worldometer. 2021. "United States: Coronavirus Cases." https://www.worldometers.info/coronavirus/country/us/.

World Population Review. 2021. "Poorest Cities in America 2021." https://worldpopulationreview.com/us-city-rankings/poorest-cities-in-america.

WWF (World Wildlife Fund). 2020. *Living Planet Report 2020: Bending the Curve of Biodiversity Loss*, ed. R.E.A. Almond, M. Grooten, and T. Petersen. Gland, Switzerland: WWF.

Xu, J., and A.G.O. Yeh. 2011. *Governance and Planning of Mega-City Regions: An International Comparative Perspective*. New York: Routledge.

Xu, J., M. Zhang, X. Zhang, D. Wang, and Y. Zhang. 2019. "How Does City-Cluster High-Speed Rail Facilitate Regional Integration? Evidence from the Shanghai-Nanjing Corridor." *Cities* 85: 83–97.

Yaro, R. D., R. G. Arendt, H. Dodson, and E. A Brabec. 1988. *Dealing with Change in the Connecticut River Valley: A Design Manual for Conservation and Development*, vol. 2. Amherst: Center for Rural Massachusetts, University of Massachusetts at Amherst. https://works.bepress.com/elizabeth_brabec/33/.

Yaro, R., H. Dodson, R. Gearheart, and Daylor Consultants. 1987. "Sapphire Necklace Plan." Boston, MA, submitted to the Boston Society's 1988 Boston Visions International Design Competition.

Yaro, R. D., and K. Gradinger. 2004. *Toward an American Spatial Development Perspective*. New York: Regional Plan Association.

Yaro, R. D., and T. Hiss. 1996. *A Region at Risk. The Third Regional Plan for the New York–New Jersey–Connecticut Metropolitan Area*. Washington, DC: Island Press.

Zaidi, K. 2007. "High Speed Rail Transit: Developing the Case for Alternative Transportation Schemes in the Context of Innovative and Sustainable Global Transportation Law and Policy." *Temple Journal of Science, Technology and Environmental Law* 26(2): 302–340.

Zelinsky, W. 1971. "The Hypothesis of the Mobility Transition." *Geographical Review* 61(2): 219–249.

Zhang, M., F. Steiner, and K. Butler. 2007. "Connecting the Texas Triangle: Economic Integration and Transportation Coordination." In *The Healdsburg Research Seminar on Megaregions*, ed. P. Todorovich. New York and Cambridge, MA: Regional Plan Association and Lincoln Institute of Land Policy.

Zhou, L., and P. Winters. 2008. "Empirical Analysis of Compressed Workweek Choices." *Transportation Research Record: Journal of the Transportation Research Board* 2046(1): 61–67.

INDEX

Note: Page numbers in italics refer to illustrative items, followed by figure number (fig.) or table (t.) number.

Abbott, Gordon, Jr., 286, 288
adaptation to climate change, 173, 175, 178, 180, 183–184, 204, 304; investment in, 195, 199; large-scale initiatives, 226, 276; megaregion planning for, 202, 206, 231–241. *See also* climate change
Adirondacks, 142, 143–144
affordability: declining, 67–102; housing, 92, 194, 198, 203; Northern California, 42
Affordable Care Act, 186
African Americans, 98, 161, 171, 186, 194, 208. *See also* Black communities; Black Lives Matter movement; minority communities
age structure, 67, 68, 74, 78, 79 t. 3.3, *80* t 3.4, 98
agglomeration, 53, 59, 60, 125, 164, 180, 244
agriculture, 6, 139, 157, 173; California, 190; Central Plains, 47; Europe, 179; farmland preservation, 178, 300; irrigation, 10, 188, 190, 192; Northeast, 235, 236, 288
airports, 38, 189, 199, 216, 217, 261, 262; America 2050 and, 13; Florida, 51; Great Lakes, 56; investment in, 199, 304; low-lying, 130; Northeast, 5, 134, 135, 213; overcrowded, 244, 260; Piedmont Atlantic, 59; Southern California, 42, 44. *See also* air transportation

air quality: automobile emissions, 198, 210, 221; clean, 6, 172; mitigation, 214, 236; pollution, 59, 92, 168
air transportation, 31, 112, 166; COVID-19 pandemic and, 162, 163; HSR vs., 149, 260
Alaska, 22, 44, 270
algorithms, 164–165, 168; of ride sharing companies, 213, 262
Amazon, 107, 123
America 2050, 9, 13–14, *259* fig. 9.3, 298
American Association of State Highway and Transportation Officials, 200
"American Century, The," 200, 303
American Jobs Plan, 197, 241
American Planning Association, 200
American Planning Tradition, The (Fishman), 9–10
American Public Transit Association, 200, 210
American Recovery and Reinvestment Act (2009), 13, 258
American Rescue Plan (2021), 101
American Society of Landscape Architects, 177, 200
Amtrak, 15, 207, 212, 220, 259, 265; Acela, 218, 258; Downeaster service, 218, 219, 220; Infrastructure Investment and Jobs Act, 263; Northeast Corridor, 219, 242, 257, *260* fig. 9.4, 275; Valley Flyer, 218, 219

amusement parks, 51, 112
Appalachian Highlands, 6, 58, 140
Appalachian Regional Commission, 272, 276
Appalachian Trail, 140, 142, 285
APS (advanced producer services), 107, 114, 119 t. 4.9, 120 t. 4.10, 121 t. 4.11, 125, 126; Arizona, 111, 118; Cascadia and Northern California, 107
architecture, architects, 149, 200, 237, 292, 293, 296, 301, 302. *See also* landscape architecture, landscape architects
Arizona Sun Corridor megaregion, 11, 35–36, 86, 114, 175, 190, 268, 274; aging population in, 75, 78; APS industries in, 111, 118; binational, 26; development, 13; drought and climate change, 128, 137, 208; Maricopa County, Az., 108, 110; Phoenix, 35, 108, 111 fig. 4.3, 301; population growth, 68; profile of, 35–38, 37 fig. 2.8; strengthening specialized services, 107, 108, 110
Asia: HSR, 15, 18, 149, 245, 255, 260, 263, 305; megaregions, 3, 4, 103. *See also* Southeast Asia; *and names of specific countries*
asthma and pulmonary disease, 210, 221
Atlanta BeltLine, 137, 178
Atlantic coast, 58, 60; megaregions, 129, 174
Austin, Tex., 28, 60, 62, 81 fig. 3.4, 114, 137, 188, 297; Edwards Aquifer, 140–141; Houston and, 146; innovation, 203; studies and plans, 31, 167, 278, 296, 301
Australia, 128, 209; HSR, 18, 245
automobility, automobiles, 31, 83, 86, 196, 198, 232, 260, 294. *See also* commuting; highways, parkways, and expressways; Interstate Highway System; mobility; traffic congestion
autonomous vehicles and autonomous technology, 16, 74, 149, 165–168
average daily trips, 86, 87 t. 3.5, 88 fig. 3.8, 89, 89 t. 3.6

Babbitt, Bruce, 110
baby boomers, 68, 74, 75, 76–77 t. 3.2; mobility of, 86, 87 t. 3.5, 88 fig. 3.8, 89 t. 3.6, 90 fig. 3.9

Baltimore, Md., 60, 207, 237; flood prevention, 134, 136, 240
Basin and Range megaregion, 11, 78, 97, 116, 123, 208; generations in, 75, 86; profile of, 38–40; strengthening specialized services, 107, 110–111
Bay Circuit, 142, 143
Bay of Fundy, 233, 234
Beatley, Timothy, 141, 176–177
BellSouth Corporation, 104
Belt and Road project (China), 18, 183
Bergstrom, Kip, 229
berms, 132–135, 193
Better Deal, 185
"Beyond Traffic 2045: Trends and Choices" (U.S. Department of Transportation), 298
Biden, Joe, 186, 191, 225, 239; American Jobs Plan, 197, 241; American Rescue Plan, 101; Build Back Better, 267; executive orders, 188; fossil fuels transition, 176; Green New Deal and, 172, 185; HSR, 242–243; leadership, 200; national rail network investment, 258; New Deal, 187, 272; president, 17, 140; renewable energy research, 175–176; vice president, 15
biking, bikes, 86, 89, 163
binational megaregions, 26
biodiversity, 38, 140, 145, 180
biology, biologists, 34, 140
biomass, 234
biosphere reserves, 140
biotechnology and biomedicine, 183, 206, 211
birds, 176–177, 236
Black communities, 101, 194, 224, 257, 277, 280, 304; COVID-19 pandemic and, 161, 207, 208. *See also* African Americans; Black Lives Matter movement; minority communities
Black Lives Matter movement, 96, 102, 123, 184, 186, 197, 208
Block Island Wind Farm, 233
Blue Acres Buyout Program, 131
Blue Banana (Dorsale européenne) megaregion (Europe), 7, 8–9, 9 fig. 1.1, 22
blue line preservation, 142, 144

Blunt, Terry, 287, 288
Boeing Company, 107, 123, 191
Bonneville Power Administration, 10, 190–191, 272
Boston, 7, 60, 89, 162, 207, 219, 232, 237; Back Bay, 138, 217, 218, 237; Big Dig, 221–222; Charles River, 137–138; commuter and regional rail, 199, 222 fig. 8.3; downtown, 130, 221; Emerald Necklace, 142, 178; flood prevention, 134, 136–138, 240; HPR, 92, 219; HSR, 7, 16, 213, 219, 220, 225, 243, 257; innovation center, 124, 203; Logan airport, 213; MBTA, 210, 221; metro region, 142, 217, 269, 270; Seaport, 162, 218, 221, 237, 240; train stations, 217, 219; Yaro and, 285
Boston Harbor, 136, 138, 240, 285
BosWash, 60
boundaries of megaregions, 24
Bradley International Airport, 216
Brattleboro, Vt., 208, 219
bridges and tunnels, 182, 216, 220, 225, 238, 241, 262, 295; Big Dig, 221–222; New York metro region, 134, 135, 189, 195. *See also names of particular structures*
Brightline intercity rail system, 51, 264
broadband, universal, 161, 184, 192, 203, 208, 265
Bronx, 197, 216, 221
Brookings Institution, 124, 203
Brooks, Ken, 300
Buell, Carmen, 289
Build Back Better, 267
buildings and built environment, 176, 177, 188, 189, 301
Burnham, Daniel, 302
Bush, George W., 14, 258
Bush, Jeb, 258
bus service and buses, 158, 165, 216, 221, 243, 259, 292; long distance, 38, 196
Butler, Kent, 13, 142, 296

California, 11–12, 40–44, 144, 178, 203, 233, 258; climate change, 128–129; Enhanced Infrastructure Financing Districts, 191, 201, 281; HSR, 258, 260 fig. 9.4; wildfires, 174, 209. *See also* Northern California megaregion; Southern California megaregion
California High-Speed Rail authority, 228, 264
Canada, 83, 233, 234, 245, 268; border, 22, 44, 56, 199, 272; British Columbia, 22, 44, 139, 256; Yellowstone to Yukon Conservation Initiative, 178, 183
canals, 10, 181, 190
cap and trade programs, 211, 232, 272
Cape Cod, 129, 289–290
carbon capture and sequestration, 6, 235; reserves, 6, 177, 178, 193, 205, 234–235; sinks, 177, 193, 236
Carbonell, Armando, 11, 289, 296
carbon emissions: HSR and electric transit, 149, 214, 244, 247; Northeast, 230, 231; power plants, 211, 232; reduction, 3, 230, 233, 272; transportation, 31, 173, 232, 250, 275. *See also* cap and trade programs; fossil fuels; greenhouse gases; net-zero emissions goal; *and other "carbon" entries*
carbon neutrality, 161, 304; decarbonization, 177, 185, 192, 195. *See also* net-zero emissions goal
carbon tax, 185, 201
CARES (Coronavirus Aid, Relief, and Economic Security) Act (2020), 101
Caro, Robert, 302
Carter, Jimmy, 144
Cascadia megaregion, 4, 13, 33, 46 fig. 2.15, 125, 268; age groups, 75, 82; Canada, 22, 26; drought and climate change, 174, 208; GDP, 116, 117, 122; innovation technology, 122–123, 202–203; profile, 44–47; as successfully transformed, 106–107, 125; wildfires, 128, 183, 207, 209
CBSAs (core-based statistical areas), 27, 29, 30 fig. 2.3
CCC (Civilian Conservation Corps), 189, 193, 236
Center for Rural Massachusetts, 288, 289
Central Plains megaregion, 11, 24, 33, 82, 96, 116; profile, 47–48, 48 fig. 2.16, 49; resource dependent but gradually transforming, 112, 114, 125
Charles River, 137–38

Chesapeake Bay, 275, 276
Chicago, 54, 55 fig. 2.21, 92, 137, 256, 269; prosperity, 256
children, 101, 208; childcare, 148, 160, 164
China, 15, 18, 198; Beijing, 15, 18, 292, 293, 298; Guangzhou (Hong Kong), 18, 293, 295; HSR, 243, 245, 251–253, 255, 263, 293, 297–298; megaregions, 3, 4, 18; Shanghai, 18, 297; U.S. competition with, 15, 303, 304; vehicle ownership, 297–298; Wuhan, 293, 294, 298; Zhang in, 292–294
Church of Jesus Christ of Latter-day Saints (Mormons), 38
Cincinnati, Ohio, 105, 269, 293, 294
Cities in Evolution (Geddes), 7
city, cities, 15, 153, 154, 158, 173, 292, 294; center-, 91, 92, 161–163, 168, 263, 265, 280, 285; -clusters, 251, 253, 297, 298; coastal, 231, 232, 261; counties and, 53, 279–280; governance, 4, 28, 112, 294; industrial, 16, 105, 213, 227; inner-, 18, 161, 210; Northeast, 211, 220–222, 227, 229, 232, 236. *See also* midsize cities; supercities; *names of particular cities; and "metropolitan" and "urban" entries*
Civilian Conservation Corps. *See* CCC
Clay, Lucius, 196
Clay Committee, 196, 198, 199, 303
Clean Water Act, 290
climate change, 14, 58, 71, 114, 198, 200; agriculture and, 128–129; effects of, 19, 20, 127, 172, 207–208, 236; existential threat, 5, 144, 171, 184; megaregions, 3, 6; migration and, 6, 102; Northeast, 209, 232–234; rising temperatures, 110, 128, 208. *See also* adaptation to climate change; climate change mitigation; drought; resilience, climate
climate change mitigation, 143, 173, 175, 177–178, 184, 193, 199; Northeast megaregion, 206, 231–241; strategies, 143, 175, 199, 235, 276. *See also* carbon capture and sequestration
climate justice, 229–231
Clinton, Bill, 144
CM² (Cooperative Mobility for Competitive Megaregions), 16, 298

coastal flood zones, 127, 129, 132, 134, 139, 172, 178
COGs (councils of government), 27, 28
Cold War, 198, 303
collaboration, 27, 28, 31, 204, 207, 241
Colorado River, 10, 190, 272
Columbia River, 10, 272
Columbia University, 177, 207
communications technology, 3, 74; COVID-19 pandemic and, 161–162; telephone, 104–105
commuter rail: networks, 210, 218, 222 fig. 8.3, 259; service, 210, 216, 220–221
commuting, commuters, 31, 146–152, 214; COVID-19 pandemic and, 162; flows, 5, 32 t. 2.1, fig. 2.4; long-distance, 148, 150, 152–161; women and couples, 148, 159–161
compressed workweeks, 150–151
Concord, N.H., 219, 220
Connecticut, 6, 16, 139, 151, 208, 212, 233, 285; Bridgeport, 217, 219; local governance and schools in, 270, 280–281; NAR phase 1, 216–217; New Britain, 208, 285; New Haven, 216, 219; Stamford, 132, 217; Waterbury, 208, 217, 219, 256. *See also* Hartford, Conn.
Connecticut River Valley, 224–226, 276, 287, 288
CONRAIL, 212
conservation, 38, 177, 189, 193, 236; easements for, 285–286, 300–301; landscape, 6, 7, 48, 140; Yaro, 285–292
construction sector, 108, 111–112
consumer service sector, 110–111
conurbations, 7, 60, 179
cooperatives, 192, 300
coral reef decline, 172
core-based statistical areas. *See* CBSAs
core-periphery model, 23
cost of living, 42, 59, 266
counties, 23, 27, 116–117, 118, 279–280, 300; Northeast, 60, 279; rural, 98–99; suburban, 82–83; Texas, 63, 112, 117
COVID-19 pandemic, 51, 59, 74–75, 147–148, 161–164, 186–187, 213, 220, 226, 241; as catalyst, 195, 210, 230, 305; deaths, 20, 208; impacts of, 101, 184, 185,

207; megaregions and, 3–4; minorities, 208, 224; mobility and, 91, 265
creative industry, 75, 107
criteria for megaregions, 22
cultural heritage and history, 33, 38, 41, 47, 62, 127, 144, 182, 286; Great Lakes, 53, 54; historic resource development, 16, 193; Northeast, 206, 236, 237. *See also* culture
culture, 33, 38, 42, 189, 193, 212; of innovation, 191–192. *See also* cultural heritage and history
Cuomo, Andrew, 231
Cuomo, Mario, 231

Dallas, Tex., 114, 297; HSR to Houston, 227, 264, 298
Dallas–Fort Worth, Tex., 28, 60, 62, 63, 112, 167, 173, 278
dams and dikes, 179, 180, 190, 193, 239; New Deal, 188, 190–191, 192
Davis, Hugh, 286
Dealing with Change in the Connecticut Valley (1988), 288
deed restrictions, 287
deindustrialization, 54, 172, 227
Delano, Frederic, 189
Delaware Basin, 272, 276
Delaware River, 129, 272
Democrats, 185, 197, 263
Denver, Col., 53, 59, *81* fig. 3.3, 301, 304
deserts, 36, 110, 190
Design with Nature (McHarg, 1969), 129–130, 299, 301
Design with Nature Now (Steiner et al., 2019), 178, 301
Detroit, Mich., 54, 56
development: economic, 96, 212, 213; global, 74; land, 115, 117; regional, 192; strategies for, 13; transit-oriented, 53, 214, 294; urban, 7, 138
Dewar, Margaret, 12, 13
Dhavale, Dawn, 23, 24, *25* fig. 2.1
dikes. *See* dams and dikes
disabled people, 128, 172
disasters, 56, 102, 131, 232, 296. *See also* drought; flooding; hurricanes; wildfires
Disney, 112

Dodson, Harry, 286, 288
Doris Duke Foundation, 14
DOTs (departments of transportation), state, 29
drainage basins, 34, *34* fig. 2.6
drinking water, 54, 129. *See also* water resources and water supply
drought, 114, 127, 132, 137, 192, 208, 209, 231–232. *See also* extreme heat
Dubos, René, 102
Dukakis, Kitty, 288
Dukakis, Michael, 288
dunes, 134, 193; fortified, 238–239, 240; as protection from storm surges, 129, 132, 135–37
Dust Bowl, 127, 189

Earth Day, 285, 299
East River, 234, 238
ecology, 3, 8, 33, 172
economic equality and economic justice, 177, 186; NAR, 229–231
economic growth, 71, 96, 196
economic inequality and economic injustice, 5, 14, 96, 172, 199, 208, 304
economic integration, 295, 297
economic productivity, 103, 115–117, 125–126, 130
economy, economics: of California megaregions, 40–41, 42; of individual megaregions, 35, 44, 47, 49, 51, 56, 58, 63–64; megaregions and, 24; of Northeast megaregion, 60, 206
ecopolis, 46
ecoregions, 33, *33* fig. 2.5, 58
ecosystems, 48; estuarine, 6, 8, 133, 239; forest, 6; preservation and restoration, 173, 174, 234–236
ecosystem services, 127, *128* fig. 5.1, 129, 176, 178, 235; large landscapes and, 139–144
ecotopia, 46, 107
education, 146, 157, 193; higher, 105–106, 111, 147, 160, 176, 185, 186; school finance reform, 277, 279, 280–281; as socioeconomic factor, 71, 155, 156, 157, 159
Edwards Aquifer, 141–142

Eisenhower, Dwight D., 301; Interstate Highway System, 196, 303
elderly people, 128, 172, 232
electric vehicles, 16, 149, 165, 168, 233
electrification: of rail lines, 214, 217, 218, 264; rural, 188, 192
Eliot, Charles, 142
Eliot, Charles, II, 142
Emerald Necklace, Boston, 142, 178
emerging technologies, 164–168
eminent domain, 139
employment, 22, 124, 216, 257; patterns, 24, 124 fig 4.5. *See also* job creation; *and* "labor" *entries*
Emscher Landscape Park, 178, 180–183
endangered and extinct species, 128, 140, 141, 286
energy: alternative, 178, 192, 202, 232, 233, 304; Northeast, 232–234; production and distribution, 54, 192; renewable, 173, 175–176, 184, 185
England, 7, 16, 158, 191, 202, 254 fig. 9.2, 298. *See also* London; United Kingdom
Enhanced Infrastructure Financing Districts, 191, 201, 281
environment: built, 176, 177, 188, 301; conservation of, 40, 143; restoration of, 136–137; sustainable, 172
environmental groups and movement, 136, 179
environmental laws and management, 31, 107, 175, 178
Envision Central Texas initiative (2004), 64, 301
Envision Utah initiative (2000), 40
EPA (U.S. Environmental Protection Agency), 38, 68, 275; ecoregions, 33, 33 fig. 2.5, 38, 47, 58; ICLUS and, 68, 69 t. 3.1, 74
ESDP: European Spatial Development Perspective (1999), 7, 8–9, 12
estuaries, 6, 134, 137, 235, 275, 276; interstate, 275, 276. *See also* ecosystems: estuarine; rivers
EU (European Union), 7–9, 227; HSR, 243, 245, 247. *See also* Europe
Eugster, Glenn, 300

Europe, 8, 9, 18, 155, 163, 179, 209; HSR, 18, 19 fig. 1.3, 149, 245–247, 255, 260, 263, 305; megaregions, 3, 4, 7–8, 15, 22, 103, 118. *See also* EU; *and names of European countries*
Everglades National Park, 48
experimentalism, 302; Green Mega Deal, 191; New Deal, 189–192, 198, 305
export-oriented industry, 103, 104, 106–108, 125; largest, 105 t. 4.1, 109 t. 4.3, 110 t. 4.4, 113 t. 4.5
extreme heat, 127, 132, 172, 209. *See also* drought

FaceTime, 161
Fairmont Water Works, Philadelphia, 178, 211
fall lines, 236
Faludi, Andreas, 7, 8, 11, 129
family composition, 98, 159–161
Fannie Mae Foundation, 12, 13
Farmer, Lee, 11
Federal-Aid Highway Act (1962), 29
Federal Communications Commission, 123
federal emergency mitigation agency, 131
federal flood insurance, 131
federal funding, 28, 124–125, 204; disaster relief, 131, 139; research and technology, 124, 175; safety net programs, 100, 101; transportation, 10, 14, 29, 30, 173, 195–196, 226, 257, 262–263
federal government, 271; addresses inequality, 124–125; Green Mega Deal and, 186, 191. *See also* governance; New Deal; U.S. Congress; *and names of U.S. presidents*
Federal Railroad Administration, 14, 15, 258, 275
FHA (Federal Housing Administration), 189, 194, 197
FHWA (U.S. Federal Highway Association), 24, 25 fig. 2.1, 231
finance and banking, 98, 108, 118
financing: by deficits, 304; Green Mega Deal, 200–201; NAR, 226–227; national HSR network, 262–263; New Deal, 194–195; public, 304; reform of, 277, 279; by revenue bonds, 195; by U.S.

332 | INDEX

Treasury bonds, 200. *See also* Enhanced Infrastructure Financing Districts; federal funding
Finnegan, Mike, 290
firewood, 234
fishing, fisheries, 129, 136, 236, 238
Fishman, Robert, *The American Planning Tradition* (1999), 9–10
5G networks, 123
5R framework for climate change, 127, 129–139, 237
Fixing America's Surface Transportation Act (2015), 298
Fleming, Billy, 301
flexibility, 149, 150, 160, 302
flooding, 114, 127, 128, 179, 237, 277 fig. 10.2; control and prevention, 10, 131, 132–133, 173, 188, 192, 202; Northeast, 209, 232, 237, 238 fig. 8.6; urban, 137, 232; zones of, 130–131, 199, 237. *See also* hurricanes
flood insurance, 131, 138
Florida, Richard, 24, 122
Florida megaregion, 56, 68, 122, 128, 258, 268, 269, 280; age groups and generations, 75, 78, 82; Fort Lauderdale, 51, 264; HSR, 13, 258, 263, 264; hurricanes, 129, 208; Miami, 49 fig. 2.17, 51, 130, 264, 280, 300; Orlando, 51, 264; poverty rate, 100–101; profile, 48–51, 50 fig. 2.18; strengthening specialized services, 107, 112; Tampa, 51, 264; West Palm Beach, 51, 264
Florida Brightline, 264
Florio, Jim, 144
Floyd, George, 161, 208
food, 6, 47, 102, 127, 172, 173, 270; production, 230, 235; security, 72, 195, 235, 236
Ford Foundation, 11
forest ecosystems, 6, 232, 234, 235, 236
forgotten man, 195
fossil fuels, 73, 112, 175, 176, 192. *See also* "carbon" entries
Fourth National Climate Assessment (UN, 2018), 172
France, 168; HSR, *19* fig. 1.3, 243, 244, *260* fig. 9.4; Paris, 8–9, 245–247

Front Range megaregion, 4, 22, 33, 107, 208, 301; age groups and generations, 75, 78, 82, 86; design consultancy, 118, 122; GDP, 115, 117; profile, 51–53, *52* fig. 2.19
fuel efficiency, 149
Fundación Metrópoli, Madrid, 4, 11, 15

Gakenheimer, Ralph, 295
Gallatin, Albert, 1808 plan of, 10
GDP (gross domestic product), 115–117, 123, 125–126; declining, 303
Geddes, Patrick, 299; *Cities in Evolution* (1915), 7
gender, 74, 147–148, 175
generational analysis, 67, 68; population growth, 74–92; travel characteristics, 83–92
Generation X, 68, 74–75, 76–77 t. 3.2, 83, 91; mobility, 86, 87 t. 3.5, 88 fig. 3.8, 89 t. 3.6, *90* fig. 3.9
Generation Y (millenials), 68, 74, 75, 76–77 t. 3.2, 83, 91; mobility, 86, 87 t. 3.5, 88 fig. 3.8, 89 t. 3.6, *90* fig. 3.9
Generation Z, 68, 74, 75, 76–77 t. 3.2, 91, 164
genetic diversity, 173
geneways, 6
gentrification, 203, 212
geo-engineering, 73
geography, geographers, 7, 12, 33, 96, 146, 157, 206
geology, 51, 235, 302
Georgia, 12, 137; Atlanta, 59, 190, 222
geothermal power, 192
Germany, 8, 54, 83, 245, 303; Emscher Landscape Park, 178, 180–183; HSR, 245, 246
Gerstel, Naomi, 159, 160
GI Bill of Rights, 189, 193
Gillibrand, Kirsten, 263
GIS (geographic information systems), 294–295
global gateways, 13, 199, 262
globalism and globalization, 71, 103, 107, 118, 125, 146, 184, 195
global warming, 58, 177. *See also* climate change
Golden, Bill, 240

Golden Gate National Park, 140
Goodstadt, Vincent, 11
Google Meet, 148, 161
Gottmann, Jean, 11, 60, 299; *Megalopolis* (1961), 7, 29, 296
Gould, Ernie, 286
governance, 28, 191, 203; COVID-19 pandemic, 3–4; megaregions, 6, 20, 173, 267–282; Northeast, 206, 209, 279; reinventing, 267–270, 304
Governor Mario Cuomo Bridge, 231, 241
governors, state, 3–4, 13, 29
GPS and routing systems, 165
Gradinger, Kyle, *Toward an American Spatial Development Perspective* (2004), 11–12
Grand Canyon, 36
Great American Outdoors Act (2020), 177
Great Crash and Great Depression, 142, 171, 184, 187, 195, 207, 236. *See also* New Deal; Roosevelt, Franklin D.
Great Lakes megaregion, 4, 13, 26, 33, 47, 59, 173, 192, 272; age groups, 75, 82; Canada and, 22, 26; climate change, 127–128; income inequality, 96, 97; left-behind in, 256–257; manufacturing, 104–106, 125; profile, 53–56, 54 fig. 2.20
Great Recession (2008), 100, 124, 147
great U-turn, 96
greenbelts and greenway systems, 6, 8, 138, 140, 142, 186, 294
green design, 138–139, 178
green economy, 137, 229
green hearts, 48
greenhouse gases, 71, 172; reduction, 40, 172, 173, 178, 232; transportation sources, 163, 176, 298. *See also* carbon emissions
Green Mega Deal, 186, 193, 194, 196–200, 201, 205; governance, 204, 267
Green New Deal, 14, 171–178, 185, 198
Green Party, 185
greenprint for megaregions, 184–185
green reconstruction, 178–184
Gross, Harriet, 159, 160
groundwater, 138, 140–141; protection, 38, 142, 288. *See also* water resources
Groundwater Management Act (1980), 110

Growing Smart, 288
Gulf Coast megaregion, 24, 26, 63; economy, 89, 101, 115, 116, 123; hurricanes and storm surges, 129, 174, 208, 296, 297; income inequality, 96, 97; profile, 56–58, 57 fig. 2.23; resource dependent but gradually transforming, 112, 114, 125; Zhang's study, 296–297
Gulf of Mexico, 56, 58

habitat management and preservation, 20, 129, 138, 141, 176, *178* fig. 7.4, 179
Hagler, Yoav, 24, 92
Hall, Peter, 11, 107, 118, 155, 255, 256
Harris, Walter, 285
Hartford, Conn., 216, 219, 220, 281; fixing urban highways, 222–226
Hartford400, 222, 223 fig. 8.5, 224–226
Harvard University, 11, 140, 285
Harvard University Forest, 142, 236, 286
Hatley, Norm, 300
Hawaii, 22, 270, 271
health care and hospitals, 5, 78, 106, 112, 185, 206, 304
high-performance rail. *See* HPR
High Speed 1 (United Kingdom), 245, 254 fig. 9.1, 255, 261, 262–263, 265
High-Speed Ground Transportation Act (1965), 257
high-speed rail. *See* HSR; HSR networks
High Speed Rail in the US (2011), 13
Highstead Foundation, 142, 236
high-tech industry, 52, 54, 75, 106, 116
highways, parkways, and expressways, 38, 142, 189, 193, 197, 221, 249, 262; congestion, 5, 59, 244, 295–296; funding, 30, 258; interstate, 51, 106, *107* fig. 4.2, 179, 188–189, 193, 196, 202; limited access, 209, 262; in South, 62, 86 fig. 3.7. *See also* Interstate Highway System
Hilberseimer, Ludwig, 293
Hill Country Conservancy, 141, 301
Hispanics and Latinx people, 161, 208, 224, 280, 304; economic inequality, 98, 101, 277; left-behind, 208, 257
Hiss, Tony, 140, 141, 289
Holmes, Robert, 34, 34 fig. 2.6

homelessness, 172, 194, 199, 203, 210
home ownership, homeowners, 153, 156, 189, 194, 233. See also "housing" entries
Hong Kong. See China: Guangzhou
household income, 92, 99 fig. 3.12, 156; dual-earners, 147–148, 153, 158; Gini indexes of, 96, 97 fig. 3.11, 98 t. 3.8
housing, 147, 152, 157, 186, 193, 194, 208, 236, 281; access, 211–212; affordable, 187, 287; mortgages, 189, 194; policies, 198–199, 209; public, 189, 194
housing prices, 152, 154, 199; Northeast, 162, 209–210; rising, 5, 203, 214
Houston, Tex., 56, 60, 62–63, 112, 114, 138, 146, 167, 173, 297; flooding, 136, *174* fig. 7.1; HSR to Dallas, 227, 264, 298
HPR (high-performance rail), 219, 242–266, 275; intercity, 185, 187, 199, 202, 204, 213, 227; networks, 212, 260–265. See also NAR
HSR (high-speed rail), 5, 92, 147, 161, 199, 201, 248–266, 275; advantages, 149–150, 245, 254–256; around world, 245, *260* fig. 9.4, 305; Asia, 15–16, 149, 257, 293, 297–298; Cascadia, 46; Europe, *19* fig. 1.3, 149, 227, 246–247, 257; Florida, 51; Great Lakes, 54; investment, 4, 16; Northeast, 7, 212, 243; planning and funding, 13, 173, 198; spines, 212, 219, 258, 261; Texas, 227, 296; timing, 242–243. See also HSR (high-speed rail) networks
HSR (high-speed rail) networks, 13, 15, 20, 185, 197; designing, 260–265; Europe and Asia, 9, 18; NAR phase 2, 219–220; national, 207, 263; obstacles, 257–260
Huazhong University of Science and Technology, 293, 294
Huber, Don, 299
Hudson River, 15, 220, 238, 276
hurricanes, 56, 58, 114, 173, 232; of 1938, 132, 240; Atlantic, 208; Carol, 132; flooding, 138, *174* fig. 7.1, *238* fig. 8.6; Harvey, 131, 138, *174* fig. 7.1; Hazel, 132; Katrina, 58, 116, 131, 132, 136, 276, 297; New England, 132, 240; Rita, 297; Sandy, 129–130, *130* fig. 5.2, 131, 232, 237, *238* fig. 8.6. See also storm surges

hybrid passenger rail systems, 243
hydrology, 34
hydropower systems, 10, 188, 190, 192, 233
hyperlocalism, 269–270, 277, 279, 280
hyperloop, 296

IBA Emscher Park, 181–183
ICLUS (Integrated Climate and Land Use Scenarios) project, 68, 74
ICTs (information and communications technologies), 157, 159; commuting and, 91, 146–147, 151, 153; new, 148–150
Idaho, 38, 300
immigration, immigrants, 19, 304; left-behind, 208, 257
incentivization, incentives, 125, 131, 165, 201, 204; economic, 156, 280, 282, 305; federal, 204, 275, 305; green streets design, 138–139; TCI, 232–233
India, 4, 245
Indiana, 54, 105, 256, 280
Indigenous peoples and First Nations, 34, 172, 183, 207, 236, 272
Indonesia, 18, 245
Industrial Revolution, 236
inequality, 73, 92, 164, 174, 277; economic, 123–125, 126, 161; income, 96–102, 230; racial, 67, 96, 123; socioeconomic, 5, 19, 20, 67–102
information technology industries and services, 106, 122, 203
infrastructure, 14, 198, 241, 258; decaying, 184, 206, 210; development, 10, 211; green, 178, 186, 196; investment, 5, 8, 13, 172, 184, 186, 195, 226–227, 303; New Deal rebuilds, 188–189; state and regional, 190, 271; systems, 130, 198–199; transportation, 8, 23, 29, 59, 134–136, 167, 173, 184, 186
Infrastructure Investment and Jobs Act (2021), 197–198, 204, 226, 263, 305
inland navigation, 190, 199, 262, 276
innovation, 107, 175; megaregions and, 24, 202–203; promoting culture of, 191–192. See also research and development; research universities
innovation economy, 266, 304; Northeast, 206–207, 209, 213

insurance, 98, 108, 118, 131, 138
intercity passenger rail, 197, 202, 259, 263
Intermodal Surface Transportation Efficiency Act (1991). *See* ISTEA
intermodal transportation hubs, 165, 216, 225
international borders, 13, 199; Arizona, 38; megaregions cross, 22, 38, 56. *See also* Canada; Mexico
interstate compacts, 207
Interstate Highway System, 189, 193, 196; approaching capacity, 5, 221, 260; Cold War, 303; funding, 226–227, 274; I-10, 273–275; I-35, 278; I-81, 221; I-84, 216, 220, 222, 224–225; I-91, 222, 223 fig. 8.5, 224–225; I-93, 221–222; I-95, 142; I-287, 216; unforeseen consequences, 196–197; urban segments, 197, 199, 210
Invest Act (2021), 263
Iraq war, 255
ISTEA (Intermodal Surface Transportation Efficiency Act) (1991), 29
Italy, 7, 9, 301; HSR, 245, 246; Milan, 7, 15, 245

Jackson, Kenneth, 207
Jacobs, Jane, 302
Japan, 3, 151, 152, 190, 227, 244, 264; HSR, 243, 245, 248, 250, 255–256, 260 fig. 9.4, 265, 297
Jefferson, Thomas, 10, 34, 53
Jiangxi Normal University, 297
Jing-Jin-Ji megaregion (China), 15, 18
job creation, 8, 92, 172, 174–175, 199, 226, 236
job location, 152–153
Johns Hopkins University, 175
Johnson, Boris, 255
Johnson, Lyndon B., 100, 102, 188, 269, 294
Jorgensen, Neil, 286
JR Kyushu Rail company, 255

Kahn, Herman, 60
Kansas, 24, *114* fig. 4.4
Kansas City, Mo., *114* fig. 4.4, 269
Kartez, Jack, 300
Kazakhstan, 245

Kihn, Cecily Corcoran, 300
Kirkwood-Cohansey Aquifer System, 234
Klein, Bill, 287
knowledge economy, 126, 244
knowledge-intensive business services, 118–123
Kuala Lumpur, 16
Kuznets, Simon, hypothesis of, 96

labor, 13, 74, 125, 157, 185; practices, 204, 228, 231, 241
LaGuardia, Fiorello, 189
Lake Charles, La., 56, 63
Lake Michigan, 55 fig. 2.21
Lake Tahoe, 144, 275
Lamont, Ned, 225
Land and Water Conservation Fund (1964), 177
land banks, 287
land development, 53, 108
land grants, 10, 199
land ports, 42, 44, 56
land preservation, 131, 300
landscape, landscapes, 140, 176, 180; preservation and conservation, 4, 14, 46, 47, 143, 200, 286, 300. *See also* large landscapes
landscape architecture, landscape architects, 142, 177, 200, 288, 299
land trusts, 142, 288
land use: patterns, 92, 153; policies and regulations, 198–199, 212, 270, 288
land values, 130, 134, 286
Lang, Robert, 11, 12, 13, 23, 24, 25 fig. 2.1
large landscapes, 209; ecosystem services and, 139–144; protection, 178, 289, 291–292
Last Green Valley National Heritage Corridor, 16
Las Vegas, Nev., 190, 264
Latin America and Caribbean nations, 51, 112, 163, 269
Latinx people. *See* Hispanics and Latinx people
Laudato Si' (Pope Francis, 2015), 172
leadership, 196, 200, 292; federal, 262–263, 290, 305
Lee, Tunney, 295

left-behind communities, 14, 16, 124, 186, 191, 202, 272, 304; economic development in, 96, 125, 187, 198, 276; HSR and, 211, 256–257
LESA (land evaluation and site assessment), 301
levees, 132–133, 135, 179, 225; onshore, 237, 240
life stages, 67
Lincoln Institute of Land Policy, 4, 11, 13, 21–22, 60, 140
Lindell, Michael, 296
Liu, Liwen, 297
Living Landscape, The (Steiner), 301
Lomax, Tim, 295
London, 11, 15, 132, 158, 202, 262; HSR, 245, 255
Long Island, 8, 238, 290, 291
Long Island City, N.Y., 8, 219
Long Island Rail Road, 219, 220
Long Island Sound, 134–135, 238
Los Angeles, Calif., 42, 44, 92, 190, 203, 256, 266
Louisiana, 24, 137, 297
Louisiana Purchase, 10
Louisiana State University, 16, 298
low-income communities and households, 163, 194, 197, 209
low-lying areas, 130–131, 180
LQs (location quotients), 103–104, 118, *121* t. 4.11
Luce, Henry, 303
lunar power, 233, 234
Lyft, 16, 161, 164, 213, 262

MacKaye, Benton, 140, 142, 286; *The New Exploration*, 141
Maine, 207, 208, 219, 220, 233, 287; Portland, 60, 231; tidal power, 233–234
Malaysia, 16, 245
Manhattan Project, 190
manufacturing, 54, 106, 111, 116, 209, 236; megaregions of, 104–107, 125
Mao Tse-tung, 300
Maraziti, Joe, 290
Markey, Ed, 172, 185
Marshall, Alex, 197
Maryland, 233, 269, 275

Massachusetts, 53, 139, 142, 172, 212, 224, 233, 256, 288; cities, 132, 208, 218, 219, 270; heritage resources, 286, 300; pine barrens, 207–208; Springfield, 208, 216, 219, 256; Worcester, 218, 219; Yaro and, 285–287. *See also* Boston; Cape Cod
MBTA (Massachusetts Bay Transportation Authority), 210, 218, 219, 221
McHarg, Ian, 300; *Design with Nature*, 129–130, *130* fig. 5.2, 299
McHarg Center, University of Pennsylvania, 177
M'Closkey, Karen, 301
McSherry, Laurel, 34, *34* fig. 2.6, 301
Mediterranean Diamond megaregion, 15
megalopolis, 7, 8–9, 23, 295, 299
Megalopolis (Gottmann, 1961), 7, 296
Megalopolis Unbound (Pell), 7
megaregion, megaregions: aging populations, 75–83; authorities, 271–275; climate change, 127–129; competitiveness, 103–126; concept, 3–6; defined and delineated, 4, 21–25, 64; governance, 267–282; HSR, 256–257; knowledge-intensive business services, 118–123; manufacturing, 104–107, 125; maps, 11, *12* fig.1.2, *35* fig. 2.7, *70* fig. 3.1; profiles, 35–64; resource dependent but gradually transforming, 104, 112–114; strengthening specialized services, 104, 107–112; successfully transformed, 104, 106–107, *108* t. 4.2; summary statistics, *36* t. 2.2; world, 15, 24. *See also names of specific megaregions*
Menendez, Bob, 234
Metcalf, Gabriel, 13
methodology of book, 26–34
Metro-North Railroad, 151, 220
metropolitan areas, 23, 27, 29, 203, 303; Arizona, *37* t. 2.3; Basin and Range, 38, *39* t. 2.4; Cascadia, *47* t. 2.7; Central Plains, *49* t. 2.8; Florida, *51* t. 2.9; Front Range, *53* t. 2.10; Great Lakes, 55 t. 2.11; Gulf Coast, *57* t. 2.12; Northeast, 60, *62* t. 2.14; Northern California, 42; Piedmont Atlantic, *59* t. 2.13; Southern California, *44* t. 2.6; Texas Triangle, 63, *64* t. 2.15. *See also* MPOs; MSAs

INDEX | 337

metropolitan planning organizations. *See* MPOs
metropolitan statistical areas. *See* MSAs
Mexico, 301; Baja peninsula, 22, 268; borders megaregions, 22, 38, 44, 199, 268, 269
micropolitan areas, 23, 27, 29
Microsoft Corporation, 106–107
Mid-Atlantic megaregion, 4
Mid-Atlantic Rail, 212
middle class, 123, 163, 189, 195, 208
midsize cities, 212, 220, 227, 244, 245, 255, 256, 258, 261, 297; HSR, 212, 244; New England–downstate New York, 213, 220, 229–230; Northeast, 208–209, 210, 212, 227
migration, migrants, 68, 102, 157, 172, 189, 196; long-distance commuting vs., 157–159; species, 127, 144, 177, 183, 193, 209, 238
millennials. *See* Generation Y
minimum wage, 98, 185
mining, 112, 114, 181
Minneapolis–Saint Paul, Minn., 222, 271, 280
minority communities, 172, 221, 232, 270, 280. *See also under specific nonwhite groups*
Mississippi River, 62, 199, 272, 276; delta, *178* fig. 7.4, 272, 276
Missouri Pacific Railroad, 62
Missouri River, 199, 276
MIT (Massachusetts Institute of Technology), 175, 237, 295
mobility, 5, 8, 20, 59, 149, 156, 159, 212, 229; generational, 86, *87* t. 3.5, *88* fig. 3.8, 89, *89* t. 3.6; new, 16, 92, 157, 161–168, 185, 293; shared, 74, 261–262; sustainable, 196, 226. *See also* automobility, automobiles
Model Cities program, 294, 299
Montana, 22, 270
Morgan, Arthur, 299–300
Mormons (Church of Jesus Christ of Latter-day Saints), 34, 38
Morocco, 15, 245
Moses, Robert, 189, 195, 197
Moulton, Seth, 263

Moynihan, Daniel Patrick, 212
MPOs (metropolitan planning organizations), 26–31, *30* fig. 2.3, *32* t. 2.1
MSAs (metropolitan statistical areas), 86; Arizona, 35, *37* t. 2.3; Cascadia, 44; Central Plains, 47; Florida, 49; Front Range, 51; Great Lakes, 53; Gulf Coast, 56; megaregion building block, 27, 31; Northeast, 60; Northern California, 40; Piedmont Atlantic, 58; Southern California, 42
multistate commissions and authorities, 272
Mumford, Lewis, 197
municipal bonds, 194, 195
municipal finance reform, 277, 279

NAICS (North American Industry Classification System), 104, 118
Nantucket, 287–288
NAR (North Atlantic Rail), 16, 219, 243, 271, 305; components, 212–213; economic and climate justice, 229–231; financing, 226–227; governance, 227–228; phase 1, 216–219; phase 2, 219–220; phase 3, 220–226; phased development, 214–226; project delivery, 228, 231; project maps, *215* figs. 8.1, 8.2, *222* fig. 8.3, *223* fig. 8.4; right-of-way acquisition, 219
National Academy of Sciences, 237
National Association of Regional Councils, 28
National Basketball Association, 62
national climate reserve system, 235, 236
national debt, 194
national defense, 196
National Defense and Interstate Highway System. *See* Interstate Highway System
National Interstate and Defense Highways Act (1956), 196, 209, 303
national landscape strategy, 14
national map, 199
National Park Service, 193, 300
national reserves, 144
National Resources Planning Board, 189, 196, 201
National Science Foundation, 296
national transportation systems, 10, 13

natural resources, 41, 140; development of, 10, 16; protection of, 13, 38; systems of, 6, 139, 271, 272, 275
nature, 172, 179
Nature Conservancy, 143–144, 286, 291
Nebraska, 22, 270
Nelson, G. D., 5, 23
Netherlands, 8, 129, 132, 134, 246; Amsterdam, 179, 245; commuting in, 156, 160; Randstad, 179, 299; Room for the River, 178, 179–180, 299; Rotterdam, 132, 179, 237; Steiner in, 300
network-galaxy agglomerations, 54, 59
net-zero emissions goal, 172, 173
Nevada, 117, 263, 268, 275; Reno, 40, 41. *See also* Las Vegas, Nev.
New Deal, 10, 171–177, 186, 194; experimentalism, 198, 267, 305; funding and governance, 194–196, 304; Greenbelt Towns program, 294, 299; as precedent and inspiration, 184–185, 187–194, 272, 305. *See also* Roosevelt, Franklin D.; *and names of specific New Deal programs*
New England, 4, 16, 219, 232; hyperlocal governance, 277, 279; town meetings, 277, 279
New England–downstate New York area, 4, 210, 216; described, 212, 214, 216, 226, 229, 231, 243; NAR, 212, 214, 216, 226, 229, 231, 243
New England Wildlands and Woodlands project, 142
New Exploration, The (MacKaye), 141
New Hampshire, 141, 219, 233; Manchester, 208, 219, 220; Nashua, 219, 220
New Jersey, 6, 129–132, 139, 208, 233, 290; flood prevention, 134, 136, 237–240; highlands, 8, 290; pine barrens, 144, 207–208; transit, 220, 221
New Jersey Pinelands National Reserve, 234–235, 290
New Orleans, 24, 132, 222, 297; flood prevention system, 136, 239, 276
New York, 4, 6, 142, 144, 191, 212, 233, 290; cities, 56, 208, 216–217, 219, 221; pine barrens, 207–208
New York City, 6, 60, 89, 123, 132, 142, 197, 237, 256, 266, 289–290; Central Park, 178, 189; flooding in, 130–131, 134; HPR, 92, 219; HSR to Boston, 16, 213, 225; Manhattan, 8, 10, 130, 151, 162, 216–219; Northeast, 4, 207. *See also* New York metropolitan region
New Yorker magazine, 289
New York Harbor, 137, 138, 232
New York metropolitan region, 139, 162, 199, 213, 220, 269; flood prevention and mitigation in, 134–136, 237–240; New Deal, 188–189; plan for, 8, 203; Regional Express Service, 223 fig. 8.4; RPA's Third Regional Plan, 289–290
New York Metropolitan Transportation Authority, 210, 221
New York State Department of Transportation, 221
New York State Thruway Authority, 231
Next "American Century," 303–305
nighttime light data, 24, 26 fig. 2.2
North Atlantic megaregion, 4
North Atlantic Partnership, 214, 227
North Atlantic Rail Alliance, 214, 227
North Atlantic Rail Corporation, 228
North Carolina, 233, 280
North Dakota, 22, 270
Northeast Corridor, 16, 197, 207, 212, 217, 228, 255, 272, 275; Amtrak, 219, 242, 257–258, 263
Northeast megaregion, 3–5, 7, 11, 46, 178, 208–209, 229; age groups and generations, 75, 86, 89; Appalachian Highlands, 6, 140; challenges, 207–211; climate change, 209, 232–234; defined, 206–207; economy, 100, 115–118, 123–126, 176, 211, 256; ecosystems preservation, 232, 234–236; governance and taxes, 206, 209, 269–270, 280; higher education, 111, 175; income inequality, 96, 97; infrastructure, 192, 210; innovation technology, 202–203; landscape conservation, 14, 142–146; midsize urban centers, 208–209; planning and development, 13, 211–212; population, 6, 206, 237; profile, 60, 61 fig. 2.25; rail and transit, 29, 47, 173, 209; socioeconomic divisions, 208–209; strengthening specialized services, 107, 111

INDEX | 339

Northern Border Commission, 272, 276
Northern California megaregion, 4, 13, 41, 140, 154, 173, 268, 271; Cascadia and, 44, 268; drought, 137, 208; economy, 96, 100, 115–117, 122–123, 125–126; innovation, 176, 202–203, 207; Oakland, 41, *106*, 271; fig. 4.1; profile, 40–42, *41* fig. 2.11; San Jose, 41, 124, 271; as successfully transformed, 106, 125; wildfires in, 128, 207. *See also* San Francisco, Calif.
Northern Powerhouse Partnership (U.K.), 191, 202, 227, 276, 298
North River, 220, 287
North Sea, 129, 133, 179
Northwest Ordinances (1780s), 53
Northwest United States, 190, 300
nuclear family, 159, 160
nuclear power, 190, 244

Obama, Barack, 13, 14, 231, 258
Ocasio-Cortez, Alexandria, 172, 185
ocean temperatures, 129
Ohio, 13, 256, 258; cities, 54, 105–106, 256
Ohio River, 199
Oklahoma, 24, 268
Olin, Laurie, 301
Olmsted, Frederick Law, 142, 285, 286, 291
OMB (U.S. Office of Management and Budget), 23, 27, 29, 31
online shopping, 91, 210
Oregon, 44, 271. *See also* Cascadia megaregion; Portland, Ore.
Organization for Economic Co-operation and Development, 8, 96, 123
oyster beds, 136, 137, 193, 239

Pacific Northwest, 178
Pain, Kathy, 107, 118
Passenger Rail Investment and Improvement Act (2008), 207
Pataki, George, 290
patents, 122–123, *122* t. 4.12
Pearl River Delta megaregion (China), 3, 18, 295
Pell, Claiborne, 15, 257; *Megalopolis Unbound* (1969), 7, 29

Penn (University of Pennsylvania), 4, 5, 140, 296, 298; 2004 Pocantico roundtable discussion and, 12–13; Ian L. McHarg Center for Urbanism and Ecology, 177, 301; megaregion and supercity research, 14–16, 21–22; NAR, 214, 228; Steiner, 300; Yaro, 11. *See also* Stuart Weitzman School of Design, University of Pennsylvania
Penn Station, 217, 220
Pennsylvania, 208, 233, 256, 275, 280. *See also* Philadelphia
Pentagon megaregion (Europe), 3, 8, 9, 22
permitting, 204, 228, 241; expedited, 231, 264
Pew Research Center, 68, 96, 123, 164
Philadelphia, 60, 129–130, 178, 207, 210–211, 232, 237, 269, 300; flood prevention, 134, 136, 240
physiography, 34
Piedmont Atlantic megaregion, 13, 33, 68, 97, 128, 178, 208; age groups and generations, 86, 89; manufacturing, 104–105, 125, 173; profile, 58–59, *58* fig. 2.24
Pinchot, Gifford, plan of (1908), 10
pine barrens, 207–208, 234, 290
Pinelands Commission, 234–235
Pinelands Protection Act (New Jersey, 1979), 234
Pisano, Mark, 11, 13
Plan for America studio 2004, 11–16, *14*
planning, 107, 138, 173, 189, 288, 295, 301; environmental and landscape, 6, 127, 178, 300; megaregional, 6, 20, 202–203, 211–212; metropolitan, 8, 26, 31, 203, 278; national, 9–11, 12, 201–204; planners, 11, 12, 300, 302; statewide, 178, 203; strategic, 211–212; transportation, 146, 167, 173; urban development and, 7, 197, 285. *See also* regional planning
Pocantico Conference Center RPA and Penn roundtable, 12–13
political dysfunction, 184, 185, 305
poor people and poverty, 123, 164, 175, 224, 232; climate change, 128, 172; poverty rates and trends, 96–102, *100* t. 3.9

Pope Francis, *Laudato Si'*, 172
Popik, Barry, 62
population, 23, 71, 129; aging, 75–83; densities, 22, 24, 68, 70 fig. 3.1, 130; projections, 68, 70 fig. 3.1B. *See also* population growth
population growth, 22, 59, 62, 92; in 21st-century United States, 9, 10, 19; Front Range, 51, 53; generational trends, 74–92; in megaregions, 68–74, 69 t. 1, 70 fig. 3.1
Portland, Ore., 44, 82 fig. 3.5, 107, 139, 190, 256; metro region, 269, 271, 280
Portland State University, 12, 13, 15
Portugal, 15, 209
postcarbon economy, 176, 184, 233
Potomac River, 237
poverty. *See* poor people and poverty
Powell, John Wesley, 34
Preston, Katharine, 286
procurement, 204, 241, 264; innovative, 228, 231
progressives, 185, 263
Progressives, 195
public health and safety, 4, 198, 291
Public Housing Administration, 189
public-private partnerships, 264–265
public works employment programs, 187, 188, 193
pulmonary and cardiovascular disease, 210, 221
PWA (Public Works Administration), 188

quality of life, 5, 6, 59, 160–161, 304

race and racial divisions, 96, 98, 208–209; de facto segregation, 280, 281
racial equality and justice, 175, 177, 186, 198, 208, 226
racial inequality and injustice, 67, 194, 280; redlining, 171, 194, 197, 270; systematic racism, 102, 184, 270
Rae, Karen, 14
railroads and rail networks, 8, 38, 47, 54, 56 fig. 2.22, 179, 199, 212, 262, 293; declining, 196, 257; freight, 13, 62; Northeast, 7, 16; rail service, 5, 7, 29, 209; Texas Triangle, 62, 173. *See also* Amtrak; HPR; HSR
rainfall, 127, 132, 137, 138, 192; Northeast megaregion, 209, 231. *See also* hurricanes
rainforests, 173
rapid transit, 165, 198, 199, 210, 213, 217, 294; bus, 213, 216, 218, 225, 261
Reagan, Ronald, 28, 144, 194, 241, 304
real estate, 98, 112
Rebooting New England plan, 16, 214
reconciliation package, 198, 204
recreation and recreational resources, 6, 14, 53–54, 107, 142, 179–180, 188–189; amusement parks, 51, 112; Florida megaregion, 51, 112
Red River Basin Commission, 272
refrigerants, 173
region, regions, 7, 26, 71, 72, 103; governance, 28, 269, 270–271, 291
Regional Greenhouse Gas Initiative (2005), 211, 272, 276
Regional Plan Association. *See* RPA
regional planning, 22, 27–29, 142, 197, 295, 300; land conservation and, 285–292. *See also* RPA
regional rail networks, 225, 261; NAR, 213, 220–221
regional tech centers, 124–125
Region at Risk, A (Yaro and Hiss, 1996), 289
relocalization, 230, 240
remote work and remote learning, 208, 210; COVID-19 pandemic, 161, 162
renters, 153, 156, 194, 209
Republican Party, Republicans, 13, 197, 255, 258, 290, 303, 304
research and development, 106, 303; federally funded, 125, 175; investment, 176, 186
research universities, 5, 122, 203; in megaregions, 175–176, 304; Northeast, 206, 213
Resettlement Administration, 189
residential location theory, 152
resilience, climate, 6, 144, 172, 195, 204, 212, 297; in 5R framework for climate change, 127, 131–132
resilience, environmental, 127–145

INDEX | 341

resistance, in 5R framework for climate change, 127, 132–136
resource dependent but gradually transforming megaregions, 104, 112–114, 125
restoration, in 5R framework for climate change, 127, 136–137
retention, in 5R framework for climate change, 127, 137–139
retirement, retirees, 51, 74, 78
retreat, in 5R framework for climate change, 127, 139
revenue bonds, 194, 195
RGGI (Regional Greenhouse Gas Initiative), 232–233
Rhine River, 179, 181
Rhine-Ruhr urban agglomeration, 180, 299
Rhode Island, 16, 207, 224, 233, 300; Providence, 132, 208, 217, 220
Rhodes, Victor, 139
rights of way, 15, 139, 197, 214, 219, 220, 257, 265
rivers, 139, 231, 236, 262; scenic, 286, 287. *See also* estuaries
road networks, 189, 193
Rockaway Peninsula, 238
Rockefeller, Nelson, 144
Rockefeller Brothers Fund, 12
Rockefeller Foundation, 9
Rockefeller Institute of Government, 295
Rocky Mountains, 51, *81* fig. 3.3
Rohrbach, Gerwin, 299
Room for the River (Netherlands), 178, 179–180, 299
Roosevelt, Franklin D., 171, 174, 233; inspirational, 200, 305; New Deal, 184–187, 189–190, 193, 195, 198, 201, 294
Roosevelt, Theodore, 10, 195
Roosevelt Island Tidal Energy, 234
Ross, Catherine L., 12, 13, *25* fig. 2.1; core-periphery model of, 23–24
RPA (Regional Plan Association), 10, 22, 60, 199, 207, 298; America 2050, 13; Second Regional Plan, 7; Third Regional Plan, 8, 289–290; Fourth Regional Plan, 203, 221; New York, 6, 189; supercities, 21–22; 2004 Pocantico roundtable discussion and, 12–13; 2006 identification of megaregions, 24, 268

Ruhr River, 180
rural areas, 172, 187, 270; income inequality, 98–99; landscapes, 6, *143* fig. 5.6; as megaregions' hinterlands, 22, 29
Rural Electrification Administration, 188, 192
Russia, 132, 237, 245
Rust Belt, 102

safety net programs, 100
Salt Lake City, Utah, 38, 40, *40* fig. 2.10, 123
Sandy Hook, N.J., 237, 238
Sandy Sea Gate System, 237–240, *239* fig. 8.7, *240* fig. 8.8
San Francisco, Calf., 13, 41, *106*, 271, fig. 4.1; Bay area, 140, 151, 154, 203; as high-tech hub, 106, 124, 266
Sassen, Saskia, 107, 118, 125
satellite imagery, 24, *268* fig. 10.1
sea gates and sea walls, 132, 133, 136, 193, 238. *See also* Sandy Sea Gate System
sea level rise, 114, 129, 178, 193, 199, 214, 276; Atlantic, 209, 231, 237–241; Boston, 240–241; New York metro region, 5.5, *135* figs. 5.4; resilience and, 131–132
seaports, 13, 42, 44, 130, 134, 199, 262
search theory, home location and, 152–153
seashores, 139
Seattle, Wash., 44, *107* fig. 4.2, 139, 190; as top innovation metropolitan area, 124, 203, 266
Seidel, Peter, 293–294
self-interest, enlightened, 291
Seltzer, Ethan, 12, 13
September 11, 2001, terrorist attacks, 10
service sector, 5, 54, 106, 107, 112, 114
settlement patterns, 197
sewage treatment plants, 135–136, 182, 192
sewers, 138, 192
shale drilling, 117
shared mobility systems, 16, 74
shared socioeconomic pathways. *See* SSPs
sharing economy, 74
Sheridan Expressway, 221
Shinkansen high-speed trains, 227, 244, 248, 264, 265

SIC (Standard Industrial Classification), 104, 118
Silicon Valley, 106, 122, 203, 224
Singapore, 15–16, 132, 165, 245
SITES rating system, 137, 138
skilled labor, 78, 97–98
small businesses, 164
smart growth, 288–289
smartphones, 165
smart truck parking, 275
snowstorms, 232
social equality and social inequality, 5, 172, 198, 199
social justice, 176, 226
Social Security, 78, 185
sociologists, 157
soil conservation, 6, 34, 54, 193, 300
solar power, 192, 233, 277 fig. 10.2
South Dakota, 22, 270
Southeast Asia, 4, 15, 18
Southeast United States, 190
Southern California megaregion, 4, 11, 13, 35, 40, 44, 86, 92, 149, 268; climate change and drought, 128, 137, 208; economy, 92, 96, 100, 117, 126, 256, 257; Mexico and, 22, 26; profile, 42–44, 43 fig. 2.12; Riverside and San Bernardino counties, 92, 257; San Diego city and county, 92, 114, 124, 190, 271, 273; strengthening specialized services, 107, 111–112; wildfires, 128, 175 fig. 7.2, 207
Southern United States, 10, 196
South Korea, 245, 249–250, 255
Southwest United States, 62, 137, 190, 273
Soviet Union, 198
Spain, 15; HSR, 245, 246, 260 fig. 9.4; Madrid, 4, 11, 15, 245, 296; planning studios and charrettes, 4, 14–15
spatial characteristics, of aging population, 82–83, 84–85 fig. 3.6
spatial cluster analysis, 23, 30–32
spatial inequality, 67, 199
specialization, industrial, 103, 125
sprawl, 138, 164, 196, 209, 287, 289
Square Deal, 195
SSPs (shared socioeconomic pathways), 69 t. 3.1, 71–73, 74

SSWG (New York–New Jersey–Long Island Storm Surge Working Group), 237–240
standard of living, 78, 198, 303, 304
Stanford University, 122
Staten Island, 129–130, 130 fig. 5.2, 139
states, 203, 207, 268, 269; governance, 207, 273
statistical analysis, 23
Steer, Jim, 261
Steiner, Frederick "Fritz," 12–14, 16, 296, 299–302; *Design with Nature Now*, 178
St. Louis, Mo., 62, 269
storm surges, 129, 133, 193, 199, 214, 232, 238, 276; Boston, 240–241; New York City, 134; Northeast, 209, 237–241; resilience and, 131–132
stormwater management, 139, 192, 202
strengthening specialized services megaregions, 104, 107–112
Striessnig, Erich, 74
Strong, Ann Louise, 300
Stuart Weitzman School of Design, University of Pennsylvania, 60, 261, 301; megaregion research at, 4, 14–16; NAR, 214, 228, 243
subsidiarity, 204, 270–271
suburbs, 11, 82, 138, 196, 294; whites, 280, 281
successfully transformed megaregions, 104, 106–107, 108 t. 4.2
Sunbelt, 102, 190, 274
SUNY (State University of New York), 237, 294–295
supercities, 11, 12, 21–22
Superstorm Sandy. *See* hurricanes: Sandy
supporting services, 127
surge barriers, 132, 136, 139
sustainability, 67, 71–72, 172, 180, 195, 301; commuting and, 154, 161
sustainable development, 10, 53
Sweden, 155, 156
Switzerland, HSR in, 246, 259
Syracuse, N.Y., 221

Taiwan, HSR in, 245, 255
Talmadge, Phil, 300
Tangier-Casablanca megaregion, 15
Tappan Zee Bridge, 133, 231

tax policy, taxes, 209, 241, 279, 287, 304; fuel, 195, 196; municipal, 277, 279; property, 277, 280; reform of, 280–281
Taylor, Breonna, 161, 208
Taylor, Marilyn, 15
TCI (Transportation and Climate Initiative), 232–233
technology: advanced, 5, 52; communications, 3, 106; hubs of, 199, 202; innovative, 71, 97–98, 122, 124, 149
telecommuting, 91, 146, 148, 164, 210, 296
teleconferencing and video conferencing, 148, 149; COVID-19 pandemic and, 161, 162
Tennessee, 24, 190; Memphis, 24, 62, 280
Tennessee River, 10, 199
Tennessee Valley Authority, 10, 34, 175, 190, 192, 272, 299
TEN-T (Trans-European Transport Network), 247
Texas, 31, 68, 117, 128, 188, 273, 297; annexation laws, 112, 280; collapse of power grid, 19, 132; El Paso, 114, 273, 274; HSR, 150, 258, 263; Interstate 10, 273, 274; Port Arthur, 56, 63. *See also* Texas Triangle megaregion; *and names of particular Texas cities*
Texas A&M University, 59, 295
Texas Central Rail, 227, 264, 298
Texas Hill Country, 6; electrification, 188; protection of, 140–141
Texas Southern University, 16, 298
Texas Triangle megaregion, 4, 22, 24, 56, 118, 146, 173, 268, 268 fig. 10.1, 296, 301; age groups and generations, 75, 78; autonomous vehicle adoption, 166–168; climate change and hurricanes, 128, 208; economy, 96, 117; HSR, 150, 258, 263; innovation technology, 202–203; planning and development, 13, 278; population, 4, 68, 75, 78; profile, 60, 62–64, 63 fig. 2.26; resource dependent but gradually transforming, 112, 114, 125; San Antonio, 31, 60, 62, 140–141, 167, 173, 188, 278. *See also* Texas
T. F. Green Airport, 217
Thames Barrier, London, 132, 133, *133* fig. 3.5, 134, 136

Throgs Neck Bridge, 238
tidal power, 192, 233
tolls and toll roads, 165, 189, 194, 241, 304
tornadoes, 232
tourism, 14, 36, 51, 53, 247, 251
Toward an American Spatial Development Perspective (Yaro and Gradinger), 11–12
town meetings, 277, 279, 287
toxic land restoration, 178
traffic congestion, 20, 161, 187, 199; easing, 5, 8, 198, 214, 221, 261–262; Florida, 49 fig. 2.17; high-traffic corridors, 93 fig. 3.10; impact, 5, 154, 295–296; management, 165, 168; New York City, 162, 163; Northeast, 209–210; Piedmont Atlantic, 59; Southern California, 86 fig. 3.7
TransitMatters, 199, 221
transit systems, 91; COVID-19 pandemic and, 162, 163; high-performance, 92–96, *94–95* t. 3.7, 173; mass, 210, 261; regional, 8
transportation, 30, 53, 125, 152, 156, 173, 297; greenhouse gas production, 31, 176; networks and systems, 92, 164–165, 262, 275; new ICTs, 148–149
Transportation and Climate Initiative, 272
transportation infrastructure. *See* infrastructure: transportation
transportation sector, 42, 112
Transport for the North (U.K.), 191, 202, 227, 228
travel, 148; attitudes to, 151–152; generational characteristics, 83–92; patterns of, 146–168, 186
traveler accommodation industry, 112
T-REX (Trans-Regional Express), 199, 221
Trillion Tree Initiative, 236
Trottenberg, Polly, 14
Trump, Donald J., 14, 38
Trustees of Reservations, 286, 288
Tsinghua University, 292, 293, 298, 301
Tsongas, Paul, 289
tunnels. *See* bridges and tunnels
Twain, Mark, 224

Uber, 16, 161, 164, 213, 262
UMass Boston, 240
unemployment, 157, 164, 189, 207, 209; benefits for, 101, 185
United Kingdom, 83, 155, 191, 202, 209, 298; GDP, 213, 303; governance, 271, 280; HSR, 9.2, 245, 247, 254 figs. 9.1, 255; Northern Powerhouse Partnership, 16, 191, 202, 227, 276, 298. *See also* England; London
United Nations Intergovernmental Panel on Climate Change, 71, 172
universal job guarantee, 185
University College London, 11, 255
University of Cincinnati, 294, 299–302
University of Massachusetts, Amherst, 288
University of Michigan, 4, 12, 15, 296
University of Pennsylvania. *See* Penn; Stuart Weitzman School of Design, University of Pennsylvania
University of Texas at Austin. *See* UT Austin
urban belts, 294
urban design and development, 10, 11, 178, 197, 299; Boston, 137–138
urban forests, 6, 209, 236
urban growth management, 178
urban heat islands, 128, 209, 232, 236
urban highways, 221–226
urbanization, 5, 35, 71, 98, 117, 180
Urban Mobility Report (Texas A&M Transportation Institute, 2019), 59, 295
urban renewal, 194, 224
U.S. Army Corps of Engineers, 136, 137, 138, 239, 276
U.S. Bicentennial, 285
U.S. Bureau of Labor Statistics, 147, 164
U.S. Bureau of Transportation Statistics, 92
U.S. Census Bureau, 22, 23, 27, 31, 74, 118, 154, 276; CBSAs and, 29, 30 fig. 2.3; forecasts of 21st century by, 9, 19, 22, 68; 2020 census, 112, 123
U.S. Chamber of Commerce, 13, 200
U.S. Congress, 177, 184–187, 195, 204, 225, 264, 290; Democrats, 258, 263; Green New Deal, 14, 172, 185; Interstate Highway System, 196, 197; members, 13, 144; North Atlantic Rail Corporation, 227–228; Northeast Corridor Commission, 272, 275; reconciliation package, 198; Republicans, 13, 303; state collaboration, 207, 276. *See* U.S. House of Representatives; U.S. Senate
U.S. Constitution: Bill of Rights, 207; interstate compacts, 207, 271–272
U.S. Department of Agriculture, 193, 300–301
U.S. Department of Transportation, 4, 16, 298; America 2050 and, 13–14
U.S. Environmental Protection Agency. *See* EPA
user fees, 194, 200, 241, 281, 304
U.S. Federal Highway Association. *See* FHWA
U.S. Fish and Wildlife Service, 38, 141
U.S. Forest Service, 10, 33
U.S. General Services Administration, 137
U.S. House of Representatives, 172, 255, 263, 269
U.S. Interstate Passenger Rail Development Corporation, 263–264
U.S. National Geophysical Data Center, 24
U.S. National Oceanic and Atmospheric Administration, nighttime light data, 24, 26 fig. 2.2
U.S. Office of Management and Budget. *See* OMB
U.S. Senate, 172, 185, 207; Infrastructure Investment and Jobs Act, 197, 226, 241, 263, 305; members of, 212, 234, 289
U.S. Supreme Court, 272
U.S. Treasury bonds and debt, 194, 195, 200, 226, 264
UT Austin, 4, 12, 13, 15, 16, 140, 141, 188, 298, 299; Steiner at, 301; Zhang at, 296

value capture systems, 281
value creation, 200
van der Rohe, Ludwig Mies, 293
Vegara, Alfonso, 11
venture capital firms, 176
Vermont, 219, 233, 280
Veterans Administration, 194

Vietnam, 245
Vietnam War, 299
Virginia, 53, 207, 232, 233, 275; Norfolk, 60, 134, 231; northern, 4, 269
visionary thinking, 291, 299, 302
VMT (vehicle miles traveled), 89, 89 t. 3.6, 90 fig. 3.9, 166–167

Wagner, Bill, 300
walking, 86, 89, 163
War on Poverty, 100, 102
Washington, 44, 300. *See also* Seattle, Wash.
Washington, DC, 60, 123, 130, 193, 207, 237, 266, 275; Boston HSR, 7, 243, 257; flood prevention, 134, 136, 240; mass transit, 89, 210, 269; TCI, 232–233
Washington State University, 300, 301
waste management systems, 192
wastewater treatment, 202, 290
waterfront: Boston, 221; flooding, 133, 235, 238; Hartford, 223 fig. 8.5, 224, 225; parks, 85
water management, 192–193, 199
water ports, 56
water quality, 172
water resources and water supply, 36, 110, 188, 190, 192, 209, 291; aquifers, 234, 289, 290; drought, 231–232; in Great Lakes megaregion, 53, 54, 127–128; North Jersey, 290–291; public, 6, 8, 140. *See also* watersheds
watersheds, 34, 138, 139, 289; protection of, 6, 8
wave power, 192
Weitzman School of Design. *See* Stuart Weitzman School of Design, University of Pennsylvania
Weller, Richard, 15, 140, 301
Western United States, 10, 34, 51, 97
Westin, Kerstin, 155, 156
wetlands, 129, 136, 193; restoration, 137, 238
Whitaker, Bill, 301
White House, 15, 184; Biden's, 197, 200, 243

White Mountain National Forest, 141
whites, 98, 101, 123
Wi-Fi, 151
Wilderness Society, 142
wildfires, 106, 114, 127, 132, 172, 173, 175 fig. 7.2; California, 174, 183; climate change, 128, 207–208; Northeast, 209, 236
Wildlands and Woodlands Projects, 236
wildlife, 180
Wildlife Conservation Society, 236
wildlife corridors, 183
wildlife crossings, 177 fig. 7.3
wildlife sanctuaries, 6
Wilson, E. O., 140
wind power, 192, 233
Winship, Tom, 289
Wisconsin, 13, 258
women: changing family role of, 160; COVID-19 pandemic and, 164; as heads of household, 98; in higher education, 147; in labor market, 147–148, 158; as trailing spouses, 159
Woo, Myungje, 23–24, 25 fig. 2.1
workers, 5, 116–117, 161; flows of, 93 fig. 3.10
work-family balance, 160
work patterns, 146–168, 185
Work Projects Administration. *See* WPA
work scheduling, 150–151
Works Progress Administration (WPA), 175, 188
World Bank, 164, 201
World Trade Center attacks (September 11, 2001), 10
World War II, 142, 188, 193, 303; defense production, 188, 190, 191; Maine tidal power project, 233–234
World Wildlife Fund, 236
WPA (Works Progress Administration; Work Projects Administration), 175, 188, 189
WPA 2.0, 204
Wright, Lloyd, 301
Wu, Liangyong, 292, 298

Xu, Jie, 297

Yangtze River, 18, 293, 297
Yaro, Bob, 9, 15, 139, 197, 201, 234, 240–241, 285–292, 296, 298; background, 285; national planning and, 10–11, 14, 258; New England railroads and, 16, 255; RPA, 8, 207; Steiner and, 300; *Toward an American Spatial Development Perspective* (2004), 11–12
Yellowstone to Yukon Conservation Initiative, 178, 183, 270

younger generation, 19
youth, 172
youth dependency ratios, 82

Zelinsky, Wilbur, 157
zero-emission vehicles, 173. *See also* electric vehicles
Zhang, Ming, 13, 91, 292–299
zoning, 130, 138, 212, 288; exclusionary, 197, 270
Zoom, 148, 161

ABOUT THE AUTHORS

Robert Yaro is Professor of Practice Emeritus in the Stuart Weitzman School of Design at the University of Pennsylvania, where he taught from 2002 to 2020. Yaro is also a president emeritus of the Regional Plan Association, which he led from 1990 to 2014. He now serves as the president of the North Atlantic Rail Alliance, which is planning for a high-speed and high-performance rail network serving the New England–downstate New York region.

Ming Zhang is the program director and Professor of Community and Regional Planning at the University of Texas at Austin and the director of the USDOT University Transportation Center: Cooperative Mobility and Competitive Megaregions (CM^2). Before joining UT Austin, Zhang was an assistant professor in the Department of Landscape Architecture and Urban Planning at Texas A&M University, worked as a research scientist at the Rockefeller Institute of Government in Albany, New York, and was a lecturer and licensed planner and architect at the Huazhong (central China) University of Science and Technology, Wuhan.

Frederick R. Steiner is the dean and Paley Professor at the Stuart Weitzman School of Design at the University of Pennsylvania. Before returning to Penn in 2016, he was the dean and Henry M. Rockwell Chair at the School of Architecture at the University of Texas at Austin for 15 years. He is a fellow of the American Academy in Rome and of the American Society of Landscape Architects.

ABOUT THE LINCOLN INSTITUTE OF LAND POLICY

The Lincoln Institute of Land Policy seeks to improve quality of life through the effective use, taxation, and stewardship of land. A nonprofit private operating foundation, the Lincoln Institute researches and recommends creative approaches to land as a solution to economic, social, and environmental challenges. Through education, training, publications, and events, we integrate theory and practice to inform public policy decisions worldwide. With locations in Cambridge, Massachusetts; Washington, DC; Phoenix; and Beijing, we organize our work around the achievement of six goals: low-carbon, climate-resilient communities and regions; efficient and equitable tax systems; reduced poverty and spatial inequality; fiscally healthy communities and regions; sustainably managed land and water resources; and functional land markets and reduced informality.

75 YEARS
LINCOLN INSTITUTE
OF LAND POLICY